Public Personnel Management— A Contingency Approach

Public Personnel Management— A Contingency Approach

Perry Moore
Wright State University

Lexington Books
D.C. Heath and Company/Lexington, Massachusetts/Toronto

Library of Congress Cataloging in Publication Data

Moore, Perry.
  Public personnel management—a contingency approach.

  Includes index.
  1. Civil service—United States—Personnel management. I. Title.
JK765.M575   1985   353.001   83-49502
ISBN 0-669-08202-3 (alk. paper)

Published simultaneously in Canada
Printed in the United States of America on acid-free paper
International Standard Book Number: 0-669-08202-3
Library of Congress Catalog Card Number: 83-49502

To Mother

Contents

Tables and Figures   xiii

Preface and Acknowledgments   xv

1. **The Context of Public Personnel Management   1**

    The Importance of Public Personnel Management   1

    Public versus Private Personnel Management   2

    The Environment of Public Personnel Management:
    An Open-Systems View   5

    The Environment of Public Organizations   7

    The Contingency Approach to Organizational Design and
    Management   16

    The Contingency Approach to Public Personnel Management   19

    **Appendix 1A: Applications of the Contingency Approach,
    by Chapter   23**

2. **Development of the Merit System   27**

    Introduction   27

    Government by Gentlemen (1789–1829)   29

    Patronage and the Spoils (1829–1883)   31

    Civil Service Reform (1883–1906)   34

    Scientific Management and Efficiency (1906–1937)   37

    The Integration of Personnel Administration and Management
    (1937–1955)   38

    Professionals, Unions, and Minorities in Public Personnel
    Management (1955–1978)   40

The Expansion of Merit Systems   43

The Problems of Merit Systems   43

The Civil Service Reform Act of 1978   46

State and Local Civil Service Reform   49

Organization for Personnel Management   50

Conclusion   51

3. **Job Evaluation   55**

Introduction   55

Job Evaluation and Public Personnel Management   56

The Location of Job Evaluation Authority   59

Fact Finding in Job Evaluation: Job Analysis   60

Position Descriptions   61

The Evaluation System and External Pay Alignment   63

Classification Appeals   63

Methods of Job Evaluation   63

The Impact of Unions on Job Evaluation   70

Comparisons of Position Classification and Factor Ranking   71

Mechanistic versus Organic Organizations and Job Evaluation   72

Conclusion   74

4. **Recruitment and Selection   79**

Introduction   80

Human Resource Planning   81

Recruitment   83

Discrimination in Selection   86

Biographical Data, Minimum Qualifications, and the
Application Form   88

References and Background Investigation   90

Tests   90

Interviews   92

Assessment Centers   93

Test Administration and Eligibility Lists   95

Orientation and Probation   97

Promotions   98

Selection and Promotion in Organic and Mechanistic Organizations   101

Conclusion   103

5. **Motivation and Performance**   **107**

Introduction   107

Definition of Motivation   108

Content Theories of Motivation   109

Process Theories of Motivation   112

Reinforcement Theory   115

A Model of the Motivation Process   118

Satisfaction and Performance   120

Styles of Leadership and Motivation   121

The Situational Nature of Leadership   122

The Motivation Process and the Management of Other
Personnel Functions   124

The Contingency Approach, Motivation, and Rewards   125

Conclusion   126

6. **Performance Appraisal**   **131**

Introduction   131

The Purposes of Appraisal   132

The Performance Appraisal Process   134

The Performance Appraisal Interview   146

The 1978 Civil Service Reform Act and Performance Appraisal   148

Performance Appraisal and the Law   149

The Contingency Approach and Performance Appraisal   150

Conclusion   151

7. **Compensation: Pay and Benefits   155**

Introduction   156

Compensation and Organizational Effectiveness   156

The Importance of Pay   157

Pay and Equity   157

Government Salaries and Salary Surveys   158

Internal Equity: Establishing a Pay Plan   162

Pay and Performance   163

Pay for Performance and the 1978 Civil Service Reform Act   164

Obstacles to Implementation of the Pay-for-Performance System   166

Equal Pay for Comparable Worth   168

Benefits in the Public Sector   170

The Contingency Approach and Compensation in Organic and Mechanistic Organizations   177

Conclusion   177

8. **Training and Development   181**

Introduction   182

Factors That Affect Learning in Training and Development Programs   184

Assessment of Training and Development Needs   185

Training and Development Methods   187

Organization Development   191

Evaluation of Training and Development   195

Effectiveness of Training and Development Methods   196

Training and Development in Mechanistic and Organic Organizations   197

9. **Retrenchment and Productivity   201**

Introduction   201

Retrenchment and Personnel Planning   202

Problems of Retrenchment   202

Productivity   206

Conclusion   218

Appendix 9A: *Firefighters Local 1784 v. Stotts*   223

10.   **Public-Sector Labor Relations   227**

Introduction   228

The Development of Unions in the Public Sector   228

The Growth of Public-Sector Unions   229

Public-Sector Unions   231

The Political Environment of Public-Sector Collective Bargaining   231

The Legal Environment of Public-Sector Collective Bargaining   234

Determining the Bargaining Unit   236

The Certification Election   239

The Negotiating Process   239

Impasse Resolution   243

Strikes   246

The Union Impact on Public Personnel Management   248

Conclusion: Public Unions, Democracy, and the Public Interest   250

11.   **Representative Bureaucracy and Affirmative Action   257**

Introduction   257

The Theory of Representative Bureaucracy   258

Minorities and Women in the Public Sector   264

Equal Employment Opportunity   266

Equal Employment Opportunity and the Elements of Personnel Management   268

The Number of Minorities and Women in the Public Service   271

Affirmative Action: More Than Nondiscrimination   275

Conclusion   279

Appendix 11A: Audit Requirements   283

12. Rights and Duties of Public Employees 289

Introduction 290

Rights of Public Employees 290

Personal Liability of Public Employees 299

Codes of Ethics for Public Employees 302

Discipline 303

Appeals Procedures 307

Conclusion: Control of Public Employee Behavior in Organic and Mechanistic Organizations 309

13. Conclusion 313

Index 317

About the Author 331

Tables and Figures

Tables

1–1. A Comparison of Some of the Key Dimensions of Mechanistic and Organic Organization Structures   17

3–1. Utilization of Job Evaluation Methods   65

6–1. Types of Appraisal Formats Used in State Governments   143

7–1. Sample Pay Schedule   162

8–1. Effectiveness and Utilization of Training Techniques   197

11–1. The Legal Framework for Equal Employment Opportunity   267

11–2. Number and Percentage of Full-Time Federal Employees, by Pay System, General Schedule and Equivalent Grade Grouping, Sex, and Minority/Nonminority, November 1980   273

11–3. Composition of State and Local Employment, by Function, 1973 and 1980   274

Figures

1–1. The Public Organization and Its Environment   8

1–2. Personnel Management Activities in the Public Organization   20

5–1. Maslow's Need Hierarchy   109

5–2. Expectancy Model for a Social Worker   114

5–3. Model of the Motivation Process   119

6–1. The Performance Appraisal Process   135

6–2. A Conventional Rating Scale Form That Uses Five Discrete Steps for Each Factor Being Rated   141

7–1. Model of the Determinants of Pay Satisfaction   159

7–2. Model of the Consequences of Pay Dissatisfaction 160

11–1. Model of the Linkages in the Theory of Representative Bureaucracy 261

Preface and Acknowledgments

Public personnel management is a complex, interesting, and crucial subject that is concerned with the recruitment, selection, motivation, and compensation of the more than 16 million Americans who work at all levels of government. These workers, who represent one out of six employees in the United States, determine whether public laws and policies are implemented as intended and with vigor and integrity. Their salaries constitute nearly two-thirds of all state and local budgets. Public personnel management should assure that this vast expenditure of public funds produces efficient, productive, and compassionate public employees. All public managers, students of public administration, and those truly concerned about effective government must understand the basic elements and the context of public personnel management.

One persistent criticism of public personnel management texts is that they lack a unifying theory that integrates topics in various chapters. This text avoids this pitfall by using the contingency theory of management as a unifying systems model for discussion of different topics. As a result, the student can better see how a personnel function—job evaluation, for example—is related to other personnel activities such as compensation, recruitment, motivation, and job design. The contingency approach stresses that public personnel management must change in response to various environmental influences, and suggests that there is no one best way to manage personnel activities. Rather, the appropriate way is contingent; that is, it depends upon the stability of the organization's environment, the complexity of its tasks, and the education and expectations of its employees.

Too often public personnel texts discuss technical nuts-and-bolts issues without first providing a theoretical base for those discussions. Public personnel management, however, is much too crucial to be treated simply as a collection of activities performed by technical specialists. Therefore, this text examines public personnel management activities within the broad context of public organizations' needs and the demands of their environments. In addition, theoretical models or frameworks, which help integrate theory and practice, are included in many chapters.

Because most students find their first jobs in state and local governments, this book covers personnel management at the local level as well as at the federal level. By concentrating on generic principles, problems, and applications, this text helps students understand the basic personnel management approaches and problems that are found in a variety of organizations. In addition, the use of contingency theory helps students recognize the best approach for a particular organization.

Public personnel management can be viewed from three primary perspectives—political, behavioral, and legal. Some texts emphasize one and give little attention to the other approaches, but this book gives balanced attention to all three views. The history of the U.S. merit system presented in chapter 2 reveals how different political movements have affected public personnel management. The influence of politics is evident in nearly every personnel activity from job evaluation to collective bargaining. Indeed, the primary difference between public-sector and private-sector personnel management is politics.

The behavioral approach to public personnel management is most apparent in chapter 5, "Motivation and Performance." This model of the motivation process provides a basic behavioral analysis for the discussions of performance appraisal, compensation, training, development, and productivity improvement found in chapters 6, 7, 8, and 9. The contingency theory of management is also useful for integrating these discussions.

The legal approach to public personnel management emphasizes the role of judicial decisions in the continuing development of the public service. Courts have a dramatic impact on all personnel functions from job evaluation (chapter 3) and recruitment (chapter 4) to performance appraisal (chapter 6) and retrenchment (chapter 9). Moreover, courts have great influence in assuring equal employment opportunity and affirmative action in the public service (chapter 11) and in defining the rights and responsibilities of public employees (chapter 12).

Although this book emphasizes the theoretical context of public personnel management, it does not neglect the contemporary issues in the field, such as affirmative action, comparable worth, merit pay, and retrenchment. Similarly, this text reviews recent decisions, changes, and innovations that affect public personnel management, including the 1984 *Stotts* decision, the 1978 Civil Service Reform Act, quality circles, flexitime, productivity bargaining, and assessment centers. In addition, recent research on private-sector organizational and personnel behavior is included. This text's integration of theory and contemporary issues, its emphasis on public personnel management at all levels, and its multifaceted perspective should appeal to a wide and varied audience. It is particularly appropriate for graduate and undergraduate courses in public personnel management.

Acknowledgments

I am indebted to my efficient and congenial office staff, who assumed some of my duties while I was working on this project and who displayed considerable good humor during my occasional bouts with frustration. I am particularly grateful to Joanne Ballmann for her typing and editorial assistance. Finally, I owe a big debt to my close friend and secretary, Sue Sarner, whose hard work, patience, and support contributed much to the completion of this project.

1
The Context of Public Personnel Management

Key Words

Organizational environment

Open-system approach

Robert Fried's three performance criteria

Maintenance subsystem

Boundary-spanning subsystem

Production subsystem

Managerial subsystem

Contingency approach

Complexity and volatility of environments

Organic and mechanistic organizations

The Importance of Public Personnel Management

The management of public personnel is vitally important because of the number of people involved. More than 16 million individuals, or one out of six workers in the United States, are employed by government. Most of these (more than 13 million) are employed by state and local governments. Furthermore, more than a third of all professionals are employed by governments. The occupations represented in government employment are numerous and diverse, including physicians, attorneys, engineers, computer scientists, social workers, chemists, teachers, plumbers, welders, carpenters, typists, purchasing agents, auditors, and a host of others.

Public personnel management is also crucial because of the money involved. Generally, two-thirds of all state and local budgets are allocated to personnel costs. Such a large proportion of government budgets is spent on personnel because governments, particularly state and local governments, provide services and people, not machinery, are needed to provide much of what citizens expect of government. Citizens want their children better educated, their streets free from crime, their homes safe from fires, their mail delivered promptly, and their health protected. Fulfillment of these needs and others depends heavily on the skills, motivation, and dedication of public employees. Public personnel management is concerned with the recruitment, selection, training, motivation, evaluation and compensation of the millions of employees who must answer citizen demands on government.

This expansive view of public personnel management corresponds to the approach taken in this book which assumes that personnel management functions are performed by both personnel specialists and general line managers. According to this view, personnel management functions are intimately involved with the general management of organizations. This book, therefore, does more than stress the relationship of each personnel function to other personnel functions (for example, the relationshop of job classification to training and promotion); it also emphasizes the intimate involvement of personnel management with general management's efforts to meet the needs of the organization.

This chapter will explain how public personnel activities are vital to public organizations' adaptation to their environments. Before this can be done, however, we must describe the environment of public organizations. One method of describing this environment is to note the differences between public-sector and private-sector management, because the contrasts between the two sectors bring the public organization's environment into sharper focus. After discussing the differences between the two sectors, we will examine in greater detail the effect of the general and specific environments of public organizations on public personnel management.

After examining the environmental impacts on public organizations, one is better able to see that those organizations must adapt to their environments to survive. This necessary adaptation indicates that there is no one best way to design or manage all public agencies, which is the thesis of the contingency approach to organizational design and management. The usefulness of this approach as a framework for integrating public personnel management activities is described at the end of this chapter.

Public versus Private Personnel Management

Although the similarities between public and private personnel management are numerous, an examination of the differences provides a sharper focus of public personnel management's unique environment and special problems.

No Profit Motive in the Public Sector

The most significant difference between public and private personnel management results from the lack of the profit motive in public organizations. Because managers of private organizations must worry about their profit margins and the "bottom line," they actively avoid overstaffing. Furthermore, they have very real interests in attracting the most productive employees, rewarding outstanding performance, and dismissing unproductive personnel.

Conversely, public organizations are judged by how well they provide a service or correct a problem. The public generally knows little about the cost of a government service, but they do recognize and complain about the quality, quantity, and timeliness of public services. As public organizations acquire more employees to perform the same number and type of services, they generally are able to provide better and more timely services. The astute public manager, therefore, may seek more than the minimal number of employees required to deliver a service. Moreover, because public organizations generally do not sell their services directly to citizens, they need not worry that excess personnel will increase the price of services and therefore reduce the demand for them. Indeed, the reverse could be true; as additional personnel improve services, demand for those services may increase.

These disincentives to control labor costs in public organizations can affect public personnel management in several ways:

1. There may be less concern about attracting and selecting the most productive employees. Other values, such as political loyalty, interest group representation, affirmative action, and veterans preference, may have a larger impact in selection than they would if profit and market concerns were primary in public organizations.

2. There may be less interest in defining and measuring employee performance and productivity. Moreover, the lack of profit motive deprives public organizations of a comprehensive, easy-to-measure indicator of performance. Therefore, measurement of performance and productivity in public organizations is much more difficult.

3. Because performance measurement is difficult, public organizations may rely more on seniority and step increases for determining rewards and employee compensation. Merit pay or pay-for-performance is generally difficult to administer in public organizations.

4. Public managers have less incentive to correct substandard performance or to dismiss nonproductive or problem employees. Moreover, the extensive procedural and due-process rights bestowed on public employees by legislatures and courts to protect them from partisan or arbitrary supervisors act as an additional disincentive to correct substandard preformance. A public manager may find that it is frustrating, time-consuming, and risky to discipline or dismiss an em-

ployee. Rather than dismissing unproductive employees, the public manager may attempt to obtain more employees to compensate for the unproductive ones—or may attempt to transfer unproductive employees to other units.

5. Public managers have fewer incentives to oppose grade inflation in the public sector. Since employees are usually paid according to their level, they often seek to have their positions upgraded to obtain higher salaries. An employee and a manager may agree to rewrite the specifications for the employee's position, even though the job has not really changed. If the manager were evaluated on the basis of his unit's total labor costs, he would have much less incentive to participate in such subterfuge.

In recent years, declines in tax revenues during recessions, citizen opposition to tax increases, and successful citizen movements to reduce taxes have imposed severe fiscal constraints on governments. Because state and local governments spend more than two-thirds of their budgets on personnel, an obvious result of these fiscal constraints is pressure to reduce the number of employees in government. Therefore, many of the discentives to control labor costs in public organizations have been reduced in recent years. Public managers have been forced by inadequate appropriations to become more concerned about employee performance and productivity. In addition, Congress passed the 1978 Civil Service Reform Act, which stresses performance and merit pay. Many states also have passed civil service reforms that attempt to improve performance and productivity. As a result of these changes, public managers at all levels have given more attention to improving employee productivity. (Retrenchment and productivity improvement are discussed in chapter 9.)

Diffusion of Authority in the Public Sector

Another major difference between the public and private sectors is the diffusion of authority in the public sector. In private organizations, authority tends to be concentrated in the formal line or chain of command. Private employees generally perceive that they have only one boss. In contrast, there are multiple bosses in public organizations. Public employees must respond to both executive and legislative political superiors. Moreover, the courts have become very involved in public personnel management. In some jurisdictions, independent civil service commissions further diffuse authority.

This diffusion of authority can cause considerable problems for public managers. They have weaker, more fragmented authority over subordinates. In addition, public employees may have to implement law that has strong legislative support but is opposed by elected political leaders in the executive branch. Thus, diffusion of authority forces public employees to be concerned not only about accomplishing the goals of the agency but also about how they can please all of their powerful superiors.

Multiple Purposes of Public Personnel Management

One consequence of the existence of multiple bosses in the public sector is that public personnel systems must serve multiple and sometimes conflicting purposes. Government is expected not only to produce services and goods but also to provide jobs as rewards for political support and for service in the armed forces (veterans preference). In addition, public jobs are often distributed according to regional or state quotas. Moreover, government employment is used to reduce unemployment and to stimulate the economy. These multiple purposes indicate that effectiveness may be only one concern of public agencies. The agencies are also expected to be responsive to political superiors and to be representative of the major racial, regional, and economic groups within the nation.

Citizens' Higher Expectations of Public Employees

Another major difference between public-sector and private-sector management is that citizens tend to have higher expectations concerning public employees' behavior. The public is much more likely to accept questionable behavior by private employees, but they expect public employees to be above reproach. Most jurisdictions have conflict-of-interest laws and ethical codes that circumscribe public employees' behavior. Some codes even attempt to control length of hair, sexual conduct, and other off-the-job behavior.

The Environment of Public Personnel Management: An Open-Systems View

Differences between public-sector and private-sector management highlight the impact of the environment on public organizations and on public personnel management. An open-systems view allows one to see how organizations respond to their environments, and it reveals how public personnel management functions allow organizations to adapt to their environments and accomplish their goals. Therefore, the remainder of this chapter uses the open-systems approach to explain the crucial role of personnel management in the effective operation of public organizations.

The open systems approach views the entire organization as a system of interrelated components surrounded by a boundary that absorbs inputs from the environment and transforms them into outputs that serve as inputs for other systems.[1] The internal components include production, boundary-spanning, maintenance, and managerial subsystems, which will be defined and discussed here. Inputs—the resources needed by the organization—include labor, capital, and political support. Outputs—the products of the organization—include goods and services. Most public personnel functions are in the maintenance and boundary-spanning subsystems.

The Production Subsystem

The organization uses the production subsystem to transform inputs, or resources, into outputs, or goods and services.[2] The production subsystem of a sanitation department, for example, includes the personnel, equipment, and facilities needed to collect and dispose of garbage and sewage. A fire department's production subsystem contains the personnel, facilities, and equipment needed to prevent and extinguish fires. A hospital's production subsystem includes the facilities (emergency rooms, surgical suites, and general rooms) and personnel (doctors, nurses, technicians) needed for the direct care and healing of the patients. A university's production subsystem includes the faculty, classrooms, labs, and equipment needed to teach students.

Job design—the nature and scope of responsibilities and skills required of a position—is one element of public personnel management that is directly involved in the production subsystem. Personnel management seeks to design positions that complement the needs and abilities of the occupants and the requirements for efficient production of goods and services. (See chapters 3 and 9 for discussions of job design.)

Since the production subsystem is the main technical core of the organization, it generally consumes most of the organization's resources. Since it is the most expensive subsystem, the organization attempts to reduce the impact of wide fluctuations in the environment on this subsystem. The other subsystems of the organizations are often concerned with buffering, or smoothing, activities to eliminate or moderate the impact of environmental fluctuations on the production subsystem.[3] The subsystem that is most extensively involved in this buffering for the technical core is the boundary-spanning subsystem.

The Boundary-Spanning Subsystem

The boundary-spanning subsystems of public organizations buffer, or protect, the central production subsystems by assuring a steady, predictable flow of resources from the environment into the production subsystem and by distributing the goods and services of the production subsystem to the environment. The admissions office in a university, for example, seeks to protect the production subsystem (teaching) by assuring a steady and predictable flow of students into the classroom. Similarly, the marketing and public relations departments in public hospitals seek to assure a steady flow of patients into the hospitals.

Many public personnel management activities are located in the boundary-spanning subsystem; for example, recruiting and selecting employees to work in the production subsystem is a boundary-spanning activity. Recruiting includes planning for the organization's manpower needs and developing strategies to provide a sufficient quantity of qualified applicants. Recruiting also entails testing, interviewing, and selecting employees. (These activities are discussed in chapter 4.)

The Maintenance Subsystem

The maintenance subsystem seeks to ease the operating problems of the other subsystems and to monitor their internal operations.[4] Many public personnel management activities can be found within the maintenance subsystem. Activities in the production subsystem go more smoothly when employees are highly motivated and have "proper," or organizationally desirable, values and attitudes. Thus, the maintenance subsystem and personnel management provide orientation sessions for new employees and attempt to indoctrinate them in these proper values and attitudes. (These activities are discussed in chapters 4 and 8.) Maintenance activities also include the establishment, measurement, and supervision of performance standards. (These activities are discussed in chapter 6.) The maintenance subsystem also trains and educates employees so that they can better perform their tasks. (Training is discussed in chapter 8.) Finally, the maintenance subsystem rewards or punishes employees who adhere to or violate standards, norms, and expectations. (Chapters 5 and 7 discuss motivation, rewards, and compensation.)

The Managerial Subsystem

The managerial subsystem is concerned with general policy questions. This subsystem determines the most appropriate strategy for interacting with the environment, and it also uses its authority to resolve internal conflicts among the other subsystems.

The Environment of Public Organizations

Organizations' environments influence their internal structure and operation.[5] Environmental conditions can be divided into two categories, as noted in figure 1–1. The first category includes the variables that affect all organizations, including technological, political, economic, cultural, and demographic conditions. The second category—the specific environment—includes the direct interactions that an organization has with its suppliers, such as legislatures, political executives, and labor unions, with its clients or the recipients of the organization's goods and services, and with competing organizations.[6]

The General Environment

Demographic Conditions. Demographic conditions, such as population shifts and distributions, may affect public organizations and public personnel management.[7] The shift of middle-class populations out of the core of large metropolitan areas has seriously altered the clienteles of schools, police departments, and other urban public organizations. These changes have affected, in turn, the recruiting

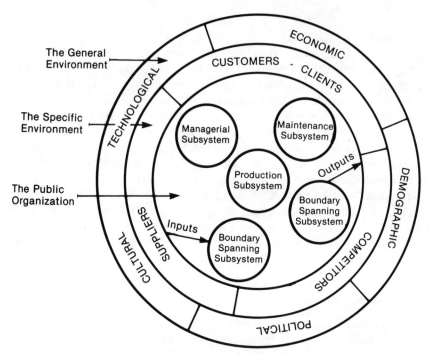

Figure 1–1. The Public Organization and Its Environment

and management procedures of urban bureaucracies. As whites have moved to the suburbs, minorities have become a much larger proportion of center-city populations. As a result, city personnel departments are under much more pressure to recruit minorities for urban bureaucracies. (Problems involved in recruiting minorities are discussed in chapters 4 and 11.)

Similarly, as more women have entered the labor force, new issues concerning the recruitment of women, sexual harassment, and equal pay for women have arisen in the field of public personnel management. (See chapter 11 for a discussion of this problem.) Also, as the "baby boom" generation enters the labor market, finding competent employees becomes easier, but defending selection procedures becomes more important and more difficult, because additional qualified applicants must be rejected.

Cultural Conditions. Robert Fried notes that American bureaucracy is evaluated by three performance criteria.[8] These criteria, which are rooted in American cultural values, are liberalism, responsiveness, and effectiveness.

According to Fried, liberalism stresses the following conditions:

1. Universal and equal rights of people as individual human beings.
2. Governing relations among people, not by custom, tradition, or ancient prejudice, but by universal laws adopted for the benefit of the community.
3. The sharp distinction between public and private pursuits, interests, rights and obligations.
4. Limited and carefully defined jurisdictions and authority of governmental organs.
5. The duty of civic obedience to persons occupying legally created "offices" with specified and delimited powers.[9]

Liberalism's heritage is the concept of limited government and the fear that extensive government equals oppression. This is revealed in the emphasis on separation of governmental powers and in constitutions that restrict the power of national and state governments. Liberalism affects the management of public organizations in numerous ways. Primarily, it implies legality and the rule of law. Public organizations must observe due process, or fair procedures, in their rule making. In a bureaucracy, due process is designed to make decisions predictable, understandable, and equitable.

Liberalism also affects many areas of public personnel management. The merit system, for example, rests in part on liberalism's emphasis on equal rights for all people. Employee grievance procedures and employee rights also reflect liberalism. Even position classification, with its emphasis on accurate description and classification of positions and on objective performance evaluation and equal pay for equal work, partly reflects liberalism's emphasis on treating people similarly in similar circumstances.

The second performance criterion noted by Fried is responsiveness. In democratic societies, bureaucracies are expected to operate in broadly responsive ways; public agencies are supposed to carry out the people's will. The responsiveness criterion affects public personnel management in several ways. The concept of representative bureaucracy, for example (discussed in chapter 11), is a direct outgrowth of the responsiveness criterion. Affirmative action is an attempt to assure that all significant elements of the population have representation in the bureaucracy. Moreover, the responsiveness criterion has affected both leadership and motivation theory and practice within public organizations. This criterion leads to more democratic management and leadership within the bureaucracy, as employees are encouraged to seek more control and direction over the workplace.

The third performance criterion noted by Fried is effectiveness. Bureaucracies are judged on their ability to accomplish the goals for which they were established. The civil service reform movement and the development of the merit system emphasized both liberalism and effectiveness. The city manager movement, which attempted to remove politics from administration and establish professional managers for cities, was a reflection of the effectiveness criterion. Recent attempts to improve productivity and peg compensation to performance are also based on the effectiveness value. Such attempts include merit pay, management by objectives, objective performance evaluations, performance budgeting, and zero-base budgeting.

Economic Conditions. Economic conditions have a dramatic impact on government organizations. Most obviously, more tax revenues are available for public organization budgets when the general economy is robust. When budgets are ample, public programs can grow—and a growing organization is generally much easier to manage, because more promotions are possible and the employees' morale is usually high. Recessions, however, may demand reductions in government budgets and retrenchments in public organizations. Thus, public personnel management is much more difficult during retrenchment.[10]. Employee morale plummets during such times, and personnel officers are more concerned with hiring freezes, reductions in force, and legal problems. Seniority may determine who stays during retrenchment, so the personnel department's emphasis on merit and performance evaluation is subverted. Similarly, affirmative action is much more difficult during retrenchment, because few new positions are available for minorities and because seniority or "last hired, first fired" policies may result in a disproportionate reduction of minority employees. (Chapter 9 provides an extended discussion of retrenchment.)

The economy is important for public organizations and public personnel management in more ways than just its relationship to the gross size of the organization. Changing economic conditions do not affect all parts of an organization equally. When public organizations cut budgets, they try to reduce the elements of the organization that are considered least essential. An organization may attempt to protect its core production subsystem by cutting back in the other subsystems. For example, during cutbacks, a university might cut positions in the personnel or security departments (both in the maintenance subsystem) in attempt to avoid large cuts in faculty (the production subsystem). Of course, this situation contributes to considerable competition and distrust among departments in the organization.

Political Conditions. Political conditions that affect the public organization occur in both its general and specific environments. Two significant political conditions in the general environment are the level of public trust in government and the political party in control.

If citizens have great trust in their governments and bureaucrats, they are more likely to accept bureaucratic intrusion into their lives. Also, if citizens respect bureaucracy, public organizations find it much easier to obtain sufficent resources and recruit talented employees. A lack of citizen trust in bureaucracy however, can result in budget cutbacks during severe economic conditions and difficulties in finding good employees during periods of full employment.

Charles Goodsell has found that many Americans tend to be suspicious of government and have little respect for bureaucrats.[11] Goodsell notes that, in popular culture, bureaucracy is displayed as overstaffed, unresponsive, and power-hungry, all at once.[12] Such views are held by writers and groups of all kinds. The evidence used to support this stereotype, however, is generally anecdotal, and cases used to support such images are selected because they attract attention, not because they are representative.[13] A random selection of cases would yield routine, uninteresting subject matter.[14] Also, the media select bureaucratic horror stories to show that the press is independent of the government.

Politicians, like newsmen, also castigate bureaucrats. Goodsell has found that many politicians blame most of the ills of society on bureaucrats—their red tape and wasteful ways. Goodsell notes that many political candidates promise that they will control the wasteful bureaucrats. After these politicans are elected, however, neither the bureaucrats nor the perceived problems disappear. Voters conclude, therefore, that the "survival of the former has caused the perpetuation of the latter."[15]

Although the popular stereotype of the bungling and oppressive bureaucracy continues, surveys of clients' actual experiences with bureaucracies reveal that most client–bureaucracy contacts are positive. Goodsell's review of a number of client surveys found that most had positive evaluation rates of at least the two-thirds level, and many reached beyond the 75 percent level.[16] In most instances, bureaucratic personnel are described as helpful, efficient, fair, considerate, and courteous; yet the generally negative stereotype of the bureaucracy continues, because citizens do not generalize from their own experiences with bureaucracy. Although they may believe that they were treated fairly, they may doubt that others are so treated. They generalize from bad experiences but not from good ones, because positive experiences do not complement the negative stereotype.[17]

Politicians also have reasons for maintaining the negative stereotype of the bureaucracy. Goodsell states:

> Incumbent officeholders can point to an incompetent bureaucracy as the reason past policies did not achieve their touted ends. Candidates challenging incumbents can use bloated bureaucracy as an issue to address without saying anything substantive or risking rebuttal or opposition. Conservatives can employ the myth [the negative stereotype] as a rationale to reduce spending and taxes, cut back government regulation, decimate welfare programs, and push Proposition 13–type constitutional amendments. Liberals find it convenient as well; they can denounce bureaucracy as oppressing the poor, suppressing its employees, helping big business, and endangering civil liberties. With a little creativity even the extreme ends of the political spectrum are able to exploit the myth. The far right portrays public bureaucracy as the harbinger of communism, while the far left associates it with efficient management of Nazi concentration camps.[18]

This negative stereotype adversely affects public personnel management in several ways. First, the bad image may dissuade the best, most talented individuals from careers in the public service. Second, the stereotype often prevents proper compensation of executives in public agencies. Finally, the negative view often drives a wedge between public employees and elected political superiors, who must pay homage to the stereotype. This wedge contributes to distrust and frustration among public employees, which make innovation and change difficult.

A second general political condition is the political party in control. Although the two major parties agree on many fundamental issues, and although the same political party in different states and cities may take conflicting stands on policy issues, very basic differences remain between the two parties. Since the New Deal, the Democratic party has been the architect and main defender of policies for the poor and the middle class, civil rights, rehabilitation of cities, aid to education, mass transit, Medicare and Medicaid, and the rights of workers to engage in collective bargaining. Therefore, when Democrats control the political machinery in a particular jurisdiction, they are more likely to support public organizations that are concerned with these issues. Also, a Democratic governor and legislature are more likely to support affirmative action; thus, public organizations must be more concerned about recruiting minorities when Democrats are in power. Moreover, when Democrats control a statehouse or a city council, public employees may obtain more power and public employee unions may gain influence.

The Republican party has a business orientation and generally opposes business regulation and taxes. In addition, Republicans generally support a larger military budget and oppose attempts by government to correct social problems. Therefore, when Republicans hold power in a jurisdiction, most public organizations find it more difficult to obtain the funding they desire. Also, public employee unions tend to have less influence and affirmative action programs may slow down during periods of Republican control.

Technological Conditions. Technology is the basic process by which the production subsystem of the organization transforms inputs to outputs. Changes in technology can influence the internal operation of the public organization.[19] Innovations in garbage collection procedures, for example, may decrease the need for manpower and change the types of skills required of the typical garbage collector. Similarly, computer innovations may change the processing of cases and forms in numerous human service organizations; fewer clerical employees may be needed, and counselors may find it necessary to become more proficient in information retrieval using computers.

Technological changes also involve nonhardware changes. In personnel management, for example, such changes include management by objectives, job enrichment, flexitime, quality circles, labor—management commmittees, and productivity bargaining. (These innovations and others are discussed in chapter 9.)

The Specific Environment

The specific environment of a public organization is composed of other organizations and groups with which the public organization has direct contact. These groups and organizations in the specific environment provide immediate inputs into the public organization, exert significant pressure on decisions inside the organization, or make direct use of its outputs (see figure 1–1). Most of the groups and organizations in the specific environment can be subsumed in one of three categories: suppliers, customers and clients, and competitors.

Suppliers of Public Organizations. Since most public organizations are service-oriented and labor-intensive, maintaining an adequate supply of motivated and skilled labor is a crucial task. Public personnel management seeks to maintain a talented and committed labor force by planning for the organization's future labor needs. (Workforce planning is discussed in chapter 4.) Since employees are continually leaving public organizations as a result of resignations, retirement, disability, or death, public personnel management's first task is to predict such turnover and assure that adequate replacements will be available at the appropriate times. Effective workforce planning, however, demands more than finding replacements for employees lost through normal attrition. Predictions must also be made concerning future changes in the basic production subsystem of the organization. Some changes will occur as the result of shifts in technology that demand different types of training and skills. Other changes will occur when new statutory program responsibilities are added to the public organization's jurisdiction.

Before the organization can recruit employees for a position, it must know the skills and talents required. Therefore, personnel management specialists analyze and evaluate the position and determine the types of skills, experience, and education that are required to do the job. (See chapter 3 for a discussion of job evaluation, classification, and design.) Personnel specialists also develop testing procedures to determine whether applicants satisfy the requirements. (See chapter 4 for a discussion of testing and selection.)

Before an individual will supply his labor to a public organization, he must believe that the inducements provided by the organization are equal to or greater than his contributions.[20] Public personnel management seeks to assure that sufficient, but not excessive, inducements are available to attract needed labor. Therefore, public personnel specialists conduct salary surveys to determine what organizations in the same labor market are paying for labor. A potential employee's inducements–contributions calculation is governed, in part, by the salary he believes he could receive in a competing organization. (Salary surveys are discussed in chapter 7.)

Inducements include more than salary, however; fringe benefits are also inducements. Personnel specialists compare fringe benefits in their organization to those of competitors. They also consider current employees' attitudes concerning benefits: Which benefits do the employees value? Is employee satisfaction with a benefit sufficient to justify the costs of the benefit? Do particular types of employees value some benefits more than others? In seeking answers to these questions, personnel specialists collect information that is useful in presenting an appropriate inducement–contributions ratio to attract needed labor. (Benefits are discussed in chapter 7.)

The nature of the position—how it is structured, the responsibilities involved, and the discretion allowed the occupant—is another inducement. There are different ways to design a position, and some designs are more attractive to particular kinds of employees. The personnel specialist's involvement in designing jobs and classifying positions should help the organization attract the kinds of employees it desires. (Chapters 3 and 9 discuss job design and evaluation.)

Other inducements include the style of supervision, the method used to evaluate performance, grievance procedures for employees, and the general organizational climate. Personnel specialists are intimately involved in these areas.

Another potentially rich source of information concerning inducements–contributions ratios is the exit interview, which is often conducted by personnel specialists. Employees resigning from the organization may provide valuable insights into the inducements and contributions required for a particular position. Changes that result from this information may prevent the recurrence of unwanted resignations.

Public organizations also seek to assure an adequate supply of needed skills by producing them inside the organization. Hospitals, for example, have nursing schools to provide themselves with nurses. Police departments maintain police academies to train new recruits. Other organizations maintain extensive training programs to assure their supply of neccessary skills. Personnel specialists often provide such training or advise others concerning the most effective training methods. (Training and development activities are discussed in chapter 8.)

Organizations may provide needed skills for crucial positions by developing career plans that assure that talented people are moving up career ladders and will be available when required. Public personnel management is intimately involved in developing career ladders when it prepares job design and classification plans. Personnel specialists also may be involved in job design for other reasons. If considerable turnover has occurred in a position, for example, personnel specialists may suggest enlarging or redefining the responsibilities and skills of the position in the hope of reducing turnover.

Efforts by personnel specialists to advertise openings also assist in supplying labor to public organizations. At one time, advertising of positions in many public organizations involved little more than flyers on post office walls. Now, however, public personnel specialists engage in much more sophisticated recruitment. Recruiters may visit colleges and universities in search of talented people, and advertisements of positions may appear in various media. (These activities are discussed in chapter 4.)

Public employee unions have recently become much more significant suppliers of labor in public organizations. Because membership in public unions has increased dramatically in the last twenty years, these unions have considerable influence on the cost of labor and on working conditions. Also, strikes by unions can deny labor to public organizations. Public personnel specialists must be able to prepare for negotiations with the unions and must know successful strategies to use at the bargaining table. Furthermore, they must know how to prepare for and survive strikes.

Clients and Customers of Public Organizations. The second major group in the specific environment of public organizations includes the clients and customers of the organization. Although some public organizations sell their goods or services directly to consumers, comparatively few government agencies generate much of their operating revenue in direct sales. Some examples of such direct sales are charges for water, for garbage and sewage collection, and for the use of recreation and transportation facilities, toll bridges, and highways. Generally, the clients of a public organization are those who receive services from the organization or those who are regulated by it.

Clients of public organizations may also be suppliers of political support.[21] The clientele of a public organization can help it sell programs to elected politicians. Public agencies realize that they need a vocal and active clientele to demonstrate that their programs are desirable and that the agencies should receive proper funding. A symbiotic relationship often develops between a public organization and its major clientele; the organization offers goods and services to the clientele in return for the clientele's support and defense of the organization.

Public personnel management may find it necessary at times to act as a buffer between the clientele and the organization. Some clients may seek exceptions to merit procedures so that they can be employed in the organization. Individuals in the managerial subsystem of the organization may ask the personnel department to facilitate the employment of individuals supported by client groups. Personnel specialists may find that they are caught between political demands and the merit policies of the organization. Dedication to merit procedures, however, protects the organization against continual attempts by client groups to place unqualified members of their groups in the organization.

Competitors of Public Organizations. Public organizations have several types of competitors.[22] First, they compete with all other public organizations in the same jurisdiction for a bigger slice of the total budget. Police, for example, compete with sanitation workers for a larger share of any salary increase monies. Second, public organizations compete with other public organizations for control over new programs or projects. Hospitals in the same city, for example, compete for the right to add new technologies and units. Third, similar organizations compete for clients and personnel. Hospitals compete for patients, doctors, nurses, and other technicians. Universities compete for students and professors. Police departments attempt to lure officers away from other departments.

Public personnel management can be most helpful in the competition for employees. Specialists in public personnel can predict where labor shortages might occur and plan a recruitment strategy to fill the shortage. In addition, they can conduct salary surveys to identify what competitive salaries are for crucial positions. They can also analyze the workplace and suggest methods to improve additional nonmonetary inducements that would attract the desired personnel.

The Contingencey Approach to Organizational Design and Management

As we have seen, an organization's environment has a significant impact on its operation. Different environments produce different types of organizations. The contingency approach to management suggests that there is no one best way to design and manage organizations. The thesis of this approach is that organizational design and management must be contingent on or responsive to an organization's environment, technology, and employees.[23]

The Complexity and Volatility of the Environment

Environments of public organizations can be characterized according to their complexity and volatility. *Complexity* refers to the variety and number of interactions that an organization has with its environment. A sanitation department's environment, for example, is likely to be considerably less complex than that of the police department. *Volatility* refers to the amount and the predictability of change in the organization's environment. The degree of uncertainty in the environments of public organizations depends on the interaction of the volatility and complexity of their environments. The simplest environments contain only a small number of interactions with the organization, and these interactions are of the same variety and remain basically the same across time. The most complex environments contain a large number of interactions that are of different varieties and that change rapidly. Changes in complex environments are difficult to predict.

Tom Burns and G.M. Stalker investigated how changes in the technological and market environments of twenty industrial organizations in Britain affected management processes.[24] They were able to identify five different kinds of environment, ranging from "stable to least predictable." They also were able to identify the management processes and structures used in each type of environment. "For purposes of contingency organizational design the most important contribution of the Burns and Stalker study is the construct it provides for analyzing organizations."[25] Burns and Stalker describe mechanistic and organic organizations, which represent opposite ends of a continuum: *mechanistic organizations* are highly structured, bureaucratic, and rigid; *organic organizations* are more flexible, open, and adaptive. The contrasts between mechanistic and organic organizations are shown in table 1–1. These models are ideal constructs, however,

Table 1–1
A Comparison of Some of the Key Dimensions of Mechanistic and Organic Organization Structures

Systems and Their Key Dimensions	Characteristics of Organizational Systems	
	Closed, Stable, Mechanistic	Open, Adaptive, Organic
Overall environmental system		
General nature	Calm	Turbulent
Predictability	Certain	Uncertain
Degree of influence on the organization by the environment	Low	High
Technology	Stable	Dynamic
Overall organizational system		
Boundary	Basically closed	Basically open
Emphasis of the organization	On performance	On problem solving
Decision making processes	Programmable	Nonprogrammable
Goals and values		
Pervading values	Efficiency, predictability, security	Effectiveness, adaptability, risk taking
Involvement in goal setting	Hierarchical from the top down	Participatory involving, bottom up as well as top down
Technical system		
General nature of the task	Routine and repetitive	Nonroutine and varied
Task interdependency	Low	High
Time perspective	Short-term	Long-term
Psychosocial system		
Interpersonal relationships	Formal	Informal
Definition of roles	Fixed and specific	Flexible, based on the needs of the situation
Motivation processes	Emphasis on extrinsic rewards	Emphasis on intrinsic rewards
Managerial system		
Planning processes	Fixed and repetitive	Flexible and changing
Decision making processes	Programmed and autocratic	Nonprogrammed and participatory
Control processes	Impersonal, using means such as rules and regulations	Interpersonal, using contacts such as suggestions and persuasion

Source: Adapted from Fremont E. Kast and James E. Rosenzweig, *Contingency Views of Organization and Management* (Chicago: Science Research Associates, 1973), pp. 315–318. Taken from Richard M. Hodgetts and Steven Altman, *Organizational Behavior* (Philadelphia: W. B. Saunders, 1979), p. 237. Reprinted with permission.

and few organizations perfectly match either model. The particular situation will dictate the appropriate design for an organization. If public organizations experience more dynamic environments in which there is considerable uncertainty, they must move to organic designs. Similarly, as organic organizations find that their environments are becoming more routine, stable, and predictable, they may pursue more mechanistic designs.

The Technologies of Public Organizations

The nature of the technology performed by a public organization can also affect whether it tends to be more organic or more mechanistic. Richard Hall, who studied the impact of technology on management processes in five profit-making companies and five government agencies, found that departments dealing with routine administrative tasks required organizations similar to the mechanistic model. He also found that departments dealing with nonroutine tasks were similar to the organic model.[26]

Some technologies in public organizations are more complex than others. Any technology that is concerned with changing human behavior is more complex than most technologies that involve physical objects. For example, a human service organization that is attempting to change human behavior through counseling, training, and rehabilitation is engaged in a much more complex technology than is a sanitation department or a street and maintenance department. In contrast, a human service organization whose major task is to distribute money to clients has a comparatively simple technology.

Organization Size and the Design of the Organization

Size has long been recognized as an important variable in the design of organizations. When the number of employees at a given location increases, more formalization tends to occur in the organization. Employees find it increasingly difficult to interact casually, face-to-face, and still complete the work efficiently. More rules, policies, and procedures are introduced to assure coordination. In other words, the organization becomes more mechanistic.

Employee Characteristics and the Design of Organization

Employee characteristics also affect the design of organizations. Some employees may desire or need a highly structured environment, while others resist structure. The younger worker may desire a larger decision-making voice in the organization. The better educated, more professional employee will desire more involvement in decision-making and will offer more resistance to tight control by rules. If a large proportion of an organization's workforce is composed of highly educated professionals, the organization is more likely to have an organic design.

The higher the employees' intelligence, the more likely the organization is to be organic in design. "The best way to employ the talents of highly intelligent personnel is to develop a flexible structure within which they can operate with great degrees of freedom."[27]

Contingency Factors and Mechanistic versus Organic Designs

Hodgetts and Altman provide the following summation of the contingency factors that favor a mechanistic or an organic organization:[28]

Mechanistic	Organic
Many people in one locale	Few people in one locale
Not well trained	Highly trained
Older people	Younger people
Low intellect	High intellect
Low experience	High experience
Perceived simple static environment	Perceived dynamic, complex environment
Independent of external forces	Dependent on external forces
Stable environment	Volatile environment
Low technology	High technology
Routine work	Nonroutine work

The Contingency Approach to Public Personnel Management

Public personnel management's chief goal is to obtain and develop employees who will achieve the organization's goals in the context of the demands of the organization's environment and technology. Figure 1–2 illustrates the two major methods by which public personnel management can accomplish this goal. First, it obtains the most appropriate employees for the organization, given its goals, technology, and environment. Most of the activities under the boundary-spanning subsystem are directed toward this end. Second, public personnel management recommends changes in the organization's procedures and structure, which in turn produce changes in the employee's behavior. Most of these activities fall under the maintenance subsystem. The personnel management activities discussed in this book and noted in figure1–2 are concerned with these two primary tasks.

The contingency approach assumes that public personnel management activities must be appropriate to the demands of the organization's environment, technology, and employee characteristics. Some organizations may require me-

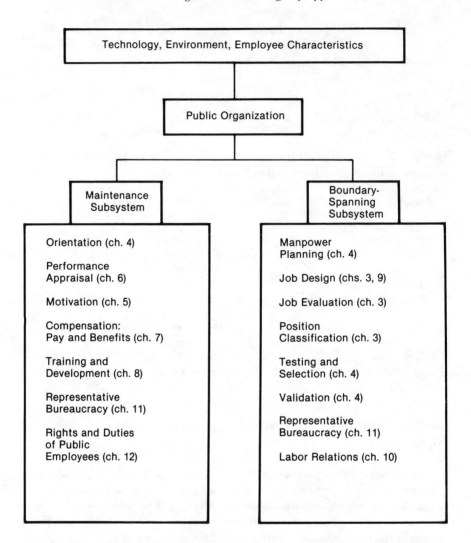

Figure 1–2. Personnel Management Activities in the Public Organization

chanistic management. Others demand organic management. There is no "right" approach for all organizations. It should be noted that although an entire organization may be mechanistic, it may contain levels, or departments, or field offices that are more organic. Conversely, some organic organizations may contain mechanistic departments and units. Such disparities between the nature of the total organization and the nature of its subunits create additional problems in selecting an appropriate management style. In most instances, the approach or style selected should be most appropriate for the subunit under consideration.

The contingency approach is useful in providing a theoretical framework for discussing public personnel management activities. It can better reveal, for example, how a job design and classification system that is appropriate for a particular group of positions is also related to the appropriate performance evaluation and compensation plans for those positions. Appendix 1A presents applications of the contingency approach as they are incorporated in the chapters of this book.

Notes

1. James Thompson, *Organizations in Action* (New York: McGraw-Hill, 1967), p. 6. The distinction between a closed and open-system approach to organizations has its modern roots in Alvin Gouldner, "Organizational Analysis," in R.K. Merton, L. Broom, and L.S. Cottrel, Jr., eds., *Sociology Today* (New York: Basic Books, 1959) An excellent exposition of the open-systems concept can be found in Daniel Katz and Robert Kahn, *The Social Psychology of Organizations* (New York: Wiley, 1967).

2. The concept of a production or technical subsystem in organizations was used by Talcott Parsons, *Structure and Process in Modern Societies* (New York: Free Press, 1960). For a discussion of organization subsystems, see Katz and Kahn, *Social Psychology of Organizations*, pp. 39–47. For a discussion of the production subsystem, see Thompson, *Organizations in Actions*.

3. For an explanation of buffering, see Thompson, *Organizations in Action*, pp.20,21.

4. Katz and Kahn, *Social Psychology of Organizations*, p.40.

5. A seminal work on the impact of the environment on an organization is Philip Selznick, *TVA and the Grass Roots* (Berkeley: University of California Press, 1949). For a description of the environment's impact on organizational goals, see James D. Thompson and William McEwen, "Organizational Goals and Environment: Goal Setting as an Interaction Process," *American Sociological Review* 23 (February 1958): 23–31.

6. The specific environment is described by William Evan, "The Organization-Set," in James D. Thompson, ed., *Approaches to Organizational Design* (Pittsburgh: University of Pittsburgh Press, 1966), pp. 79–91. Also see Eugene Litwak and Lydia F. Hylton, "Interorganizational Analysis," *Administrative Science Quarterly* 6 (March 1962): 395–420; and Roland L. Warren, "The Interorganizational Field as a Focus for Investigation." *Administrative Science Quarterly* 12 (December 1967): 369–419.

7. Arthur L. Stinchcombe, "Social Structure and Organizations," in James G. March, ed., *Handbook of Organizations* (Chicago: Rand McNally, 1965), pp.150,151.

8. Robert Fried, *Performance in American Bureaucracy* (Boston: Little, Brown, 1976). David Rosenbloom notes similar factors, which he calls the managerial, political, and legal approaches to public administration. See David Rosenbloom, "Public Administration Theory and the Separation of Powers," *Public Administration Review* 43 (May-June 1983): 219–227.

9. Fried, *Performance in American Bureaucracy*, p. 44.

10. For a discussion of how retrenchment affects public personnel management, see the symposium on retrenchment in *Public Administration Review* 40 (November-Decem-

ber 1980): 603–626. Also see Charles H. Levine, Irene S. Rubin, and George Wolohojian, "Managing Organizational Retrenchment," *Administration and Society* 42 (May 1982): 101–136; and Arthur Johnson, "Cutback Strategies and Public Personnel Management: An Analysis of Nine Maryland Counties," *Review of Public Personnel Administration* 3 (Fall 1982): 41–56.

11. Charles T. Goodsell, *The Case for Bureaucracy* (Chatham, N.J.: Chatham House, 1983), p. 2.

12. Ibid.

13. Ibid., p. 4.

14. Ibid.

15. Ibid., p. 5.

16. Ibid., p. 29.

17. Daniel Katz and Robert Kahn, *Bureaucratic Encounters* (Ann Arbor: University of Michigan, Institute for Social Research, 1975).

18. Goodsell, *Case for Bureaucracy*, p. 145.

19. For an excellent analysis of the impact of technology on organizations, see Thompson, *Organizations in Actions*, pp. 14–82. A classic study of the impact of technology on organizational processes is Joan Woodward, *Industrial Organization: Theory and Practice* (London: Oxford University Press, 1965).

20. The inducements–contributions theory was first propounded by Chester Barnard, *The Functions of the Executive* (Cambridge, Mass.: Harvard University Press, 1938). The theory was expanded by James March and Herbert Simon, *Organizations* (New York: Wiley, 1958).

21. For an excellent analysis of the impact of clients and customers on public administration, see Francis E. Rourke, *Bureaucracy, Politics and Public Policy*, 3d ed. (Boston: Little, Brown, 1978). Also see Randall Ripley and Grace Franklin, *Congress, the Bureaucracy and Public Policy* (Homewood, Ill.: Dorsey Press, 1980).

22. Rourke, *Bureaucracy, Politics and Public Policy.*

23. Paul R. Lawrence and Jay W. Lorsch, *Organization and Environment* (Homewood, Ill.: Richard D. Irwin, 1967).

24. Tom Burns and G.M. Stalker, *The Management of Innovation* (London: Tavistock, 1961).

25. Richard Hodgetts and Steven Altman, *Organizational Behavior* (Philadelphia: W.B. Saunders, 1979), p. 236.

26. Richard Hall, "Intraorganizational Structural Variation: Application of the Bureaucratic Model," *Administrative Science Quarterly* 7 (December 1962): 295–308.

27. Hodgetts and Altman, *Organizational Behavior*, p. 231.

28. Ibid., p. 247.

Appendix 1A: Applications of the Contingency Approach, by Chapter

Chapter	Stable, Rigid, Mechanistic Situations	Unpredictable, Flexible, Organic Situations
1. "The Context of Public Personnel Management"	The open-systems approach stresses that public organizations that have a routine technology and exist in a stable environment adopt more mechanistic designs.	The open-systems approach suggests that public organizations that have a complex technology and exist in a dynamic environment adopt an organic approach.
2. "Development of the Merit System"	At different times in history, public organizations have responded to different demands in the environment. When demands and technology have been relatively simple, public organizations have been organized according to classical bureaucratic, mechanistic procedures.	As the technologies required of public organizations have become more complex and the number of environmental demands have increased and become more dynamic, public organizations have adopted some organic methods.
3. "Job Evaluation"	When the organization's technology is simple and its environment is stable and predictable, most positions are highly specialized and structured.	When the organization's technology is complex and its environment is dynamic, many positions cannot be easily structured and demand occupants who can be given considerable latitude and responsibility.
4. "Recruitment and Selection"	Staffing is inherently situational. The goal is to find the right person for the right job. A mechanistic organization is likely to have highly structured routine positions that provide comparatively clear-cut job descriptions. Tests and selection procedures are more readily apparent and available for such positions.	In organic organizations, jobs are less well defined and may change from day to day; this demands different staffing methods and selection procedures. More emphasis must be placed on general abilities and potential of recruits.

Chapter	*Stable, Rigid, Mechanistic Situations*	*Unpredictable, Flexible, Organic Situations*
5. "Motivation and Performance"	Process theories of motivation state that employees will exert effort to perform a task if they believe that they have a reasonable probability of success in performing the task, and if successful performance will result in rewards that satisfy the individuals' needs. Individuals in highly mechanistic organizations may place greater emphasis on lower-order needs, such as money, job tenure, and fringe benefits, and may be less concerned about self-actualization on the job.	Employees in organic organizations may be better educated, more intelligent and more professional. They may demand higher-level incentives, such as more interesting jobs, more control over the workplace, and a greater sense of achievement or fulfillment on the job.
6. "Performance Appraisal"	Mechanistic organizations that have routine, structured jobs can have performance evaluations that include specific performance-based expectations and criteria.	Organic organizations have positions demanding highly independent employees who perform nonroutine tasks. These positions demand more goal-oriented evaluations, such as management by objectives.
7. "Compensation: Pay and Benefits"	Pay may be more important to employees of mechanistic organizations, because they are less interested in other higher-order incentives, such as interesting work and a sense of achievement on the job. Employees of mechanistic organizations may believe that pay should be based on longevity and within-grade increases. Pay ranges for routine jobs that require little time to master may be comparatively narrow.	Pay may be less important to employees in organic organizations, because they may obtain satisfaction from other elements of their positions. Employees are more likely to believe that their pay should be based on performance. Pay ranges for organic positions tend to be wider.
8. "Training and Development"	Some training measures, such as lectures and programmed instruction, may be appropriate for both mechanistic and organic organizations. Training and development goals may be more limited and specific in mechanistic organizations. The need for development may be less pressing in mechanistic organizations. Evaluation and measurement of training efforts may be more objective and easier in mechanistic organizations.	Organizational development techniques aimed at increasing sensitivity, openness, and supportiveness seem especially appropriate under the rapidly changing conditions in organic organizations. Goals of training and development efforts cannot be so clearly specified in organic organizations, nor can measurement or evaluation of their success be easily quantified.

Chapter	Stable, Rigid, Mechanistic Situations	Unpredictable, Flexible, Organic Situations
9. "Retrenchment and Productivity"	When productivity is defined as efficiency (that is, the ratio of inputs to outputs), mechanistic organizations can usually attain more significant improvements more rapidly than organic organizations can. Mechanistic organizations often involve functions that can be mechanized or automated. Productivity bargaining is more appropriate for mechanistic organizations, not only because unions are more visible and influential in mechanistic organizations but also because productiviity improvements are more easily measured in these organizations.	Productivity improvements in organic organizations generally involve effectiveness or the quality of service delivery in addition to the efficiency of service delivery. Most popular productivity improvement techniques (job enrichment, quality circles, flexitime, labor–management committees) imply a movement toward the more open, decentralized, less hierarchical managerial style that is typical of organic organizations.
10. "Public-Sector Labor Relations"	Mechanistic organizations in both the private and public sectors are more likely to be unionized, because employees view unions as useful tools to obtain the rewards they most desire—pay, job security, and good working conditions. Unions in mechanistic organizations are more likely to stress pay and to be more hierarchical.	Employees of organic organizations are less likely to join a union, because they view it as unprofessional or because they are fearful that unions will reduce their discretion and latitude. If employees of organic organizations are in unions, they are more interested in the leadership and governance of their unions. Therefore, these unions must be more democratic and open. As a result, volatility in the leadership of unions may be greater in organic organizations. Employees may ask their unions to make demands that are unrelated to pay. For example, employees may want their unions to decide how the work is to be done. Because of the more dynamic employee–union relationships in organic organizations, negotiations with unions may be more complex in such organizations.
11. "Representative Bureaucracy and Affirmative Action"	Obtaining an organization that is representative of all segments of the population is a goal in both mechanistic and organic organizations. This goal is easier to attain in mechanistic	A representative bureaucracy is more difficult to attain in an organic organization, because positions require more experience and education. Qualified minority applicants

Chapter	Stable, Rigid, Mechanistic Situations	Unpredictable, Flexible, Organic Situations
	organizations, because the job requirements demand fewer skills and less education and experience.	with appropriate skills and experience may be comparatively few.
12. "Rights and Duties of Public Employees"	Mechanistic organizations are more likely to have specified rules and regulations concerning appropriate employee behavior. Detailed grievance processes for employees may be more pronounced in mechanistic organizations.	Organic organizations may depend more on internal, professional codes of conduct and ethics to control the behavior of employees.

2
Development of the Merit System

Key Words

Patronage and the spoils system

Pendleton Act of 1883

Merit principle

Rank-in-person

Rank-in-position

Scientific management

Classification Act of 1923

Professionalism

Netherworld of public personnel management

Inflated job descriptions

Civil Service Reform Act of 1978

Office of Personnel Management

Merit Systems Protection Board

Senior Executive Service

Whistle-blowing

Pay cap

Introduction

The most prominent characteristic of public service in the United States is the merit system. The merit principle emphasizes that people are hired, promoted, rewarded, and dismissed on the basis of their performance, rather than because of their political ties, race, sex, or age. The merit system refers to all the laws and regulations designed to achieve the merit principle. More than 90 percent of all federal employees, most state employees, and a large percentage of city and county employees are included in merit systems.

Although the merit principle seems pervasive today, the concept of a merit-based career civil service is a relatively recent development in the broad sweep of history.[1] The industrial revolution in Europe generated the need for a dependable postal service, transportation network, and other government services based upon merit.[2] Moreover, the modern nation-state was beginning to appear in Europe at approximately the same time. These new nations required a large, more professional civil service. Also, much of the new entrepreneur class in these nations feared the growth, power, and influence of the growing bureaucracy of public officials. The new capitalists had little desire to see governmental power extended more than was absolutely necessary. According to Van Riper, "a politically neutral public service" was an effort to keep expanding governmental bureaucracies from gaining too much power.[3] Therefore, Western European nations, particularly Great Britain, adopted a nonpolitical, merit-based civil service during the first half of the nineteenth century.

The development of a nonpolitical, merit-based system came later in the United States. Van Riper notes several reasons for the late arrival of civil service reform. The availability of land, many economic rewards, and the physical isolation of the United States reduced the need for a centralized government with a large bureaucracy.[4] Moreover, a major theme of the U.S. Constitution is limited government. In a sense, the United States could afford a more politically oriented, less professional civil service because the U.S. government was not expected to do as much as its counterparts in Europe. As a result, the development of the civil service in the United States is unique. It is more political, more democratic, and less elite than most European civil service systems.

One cannot understand the present U.S. public personnel system without a knowledge of its history. Therefore, this chapter reviews the evolution and development of U.S. public personnel institutions and management. The discussion is divided into six major phases that generally parallel those used by Frederick Mosher:[5] government by gentlemen (1789–1829); patronage and the spoils (1829–1883); civil service reform (1883–1906); scientific management and efficiency (1906–1937); integration of personnel administration and management (1937–1955); and professions, unions, and minorities in the public service (1955–1978). The most significant recent development in the federal merit system is the 1978 Civil Service Reform Act, so the chapter also reviews the forces that contributed to the passage of this law, the major changes provided by it, and the impact of these changes. The chapter concludes with a discussion of civil service reform in the states and cities and a brief note on different organizational arrangements for personnel management.

Government by Gentlemen (1789–1829)

During the forty years between 1789 and 1829, precedents were established that continue to affect the public service in the United States. George Washington and the other five presidents during this period sought competence and honesty in the public service. As a result, they assured not only effectiveness within the public service but also the viability of the young republic. Of course, to these early presidents, competence generally meant educated white men of wealth. Thus, the early bureaucracy was competent and elite.

Washington's Precedents

The Constitution provides little direction concerning the appointed offices of the executive branch except that the president should appoint and the Senate must confirm. Therefore, when George Washington became president, there was little in the Constitution or the law to direct him and no precedents to determine his power of appointment and dismissal. Furthermore, Washington was able to appoint an entirely new administration; there were no incumbents to restrict his power. Similarly, the absence of political parties at the start of Washington's administration freed him from the constraints of party obligations when making appointments.

Washington was well aware that, as the first president, he could establish precedents that would be followed by his successors. He took his appointive power quite seriously and used the standard of "fitness of character" in making appointments. By Washington's definition, fitness suggested a good family background, educational attainment, honor, esteem, and loyalty to the new government.[6] In other words, Washington selected most of his appointees from the elite of his society. Throughout Washington's term and until 1829, most persons appointed to high positions were wealthy, owned considerable land, and were far better educated than the general populace.

Although Washington's appointments appear at first glance to be a capitulation to a powerful elite, they must be viewed in the context of the time. Fewer than one percent of the population had a formal education; during Washington's time, educated individuals generally were wealthy. Furthermore, wealth, education, and family background were not sufficient for appointment; Washington also required competence. As a result of the great care Washington took in making appointments, most historians agree that his selection criteria produced a highly effective and honest civil service.

Although Washington did place primary importance on competence and integrity, he did not completely ignore political realities in making appointments. He regularly conferred with senators before making appointments—seeking their suggestions to assure a geographical balance in representation in the federal service. Of course, his conferral with senators also helped assure subsequent Senate confirmation of his appointments.

An issue decided early in Washington's administration concerned the president's power to remove someone whose appointment had been approved by the Senate. In what is known as the "decision of 1789," Congress agreed that the president can remove someone even if the Senate confirmed the appointment.[7] As a result of this decision, the executive's power over appointment and removals has reigned supreme.

Another important precedent established during Washington's administration was the division of the public service into two broad groups: (1) the high-ranking officials who had considerable influence on public policy and (2) the workers in the offices and in the field. The two groups differed not only in terms of their social origins but also in terms of their tenure. The first group clearly came from the educated, wealthy, elite class, whereas employees in the second group came primarily from the middle and upper middle class. The first group served at the pleasure of the president and therefore could be released whenever the president wished. It was generally taken for granted, however, that employees in the second group had tenure for life. Removals of employees in the second category were limited in number and were generally justified by cause.[8]

The Tradition Continues

Although a new political party assumed power with the presidency of Thomas Jefferson, many of the precedents established by Washington continued. Jefferson, Madison, Monroe, and Adams continued to recruit competent, educated, and often wealthy individuals to public service. The tradition of Washington continued until the election of Andrew Jackson.

Jefferson was the first president to enter office and find that the bureaucracy was full of many people from the opposing political party—the Federalists. Jefferson knew that both practical politics and good administration demanded some continuity and consistency among public officeholders. Therefore, he was reluctant to engage in any large-scale removal of Federalists. He did, however, devise the concept of "equal division of the offices" among the Republican and Federalist parties. As a result of this concept, Jefferson replaced approximately 15 percent of the Federalist civil servants with Republicans. Jefferson also continued Washington's tradition of appointing only competent, educated, and generally wealthy individuals to public office.

Presidents James Madison, James Monroe, and John Quincy Adams made few personnel changes during their administrations. As a result, many public officeholders came to think of their positions as permanent. Some even thought that tenure extended beyond the grave, when sons were appointed to positions once held by their dead fathers. Moreover, some elderly and senile employees maintained their positions because it was considered inhumane to release them in their old age.

In summary, during the first forty years of the Republic, individuals of competence, education, and wealth were appointed to major offices, and the President's appointive and removal powers were well entrenched. Moreover, the tradition of a geographically and politically representative public service was established. The young nation was indeed fortunate to have a public service that was competent, honest, and loyal to the new Constitution. The public service generated respect for the new Republic and provided the stability that was so necessary to the development of the new nation.

Patronage and the Spoils (1829–1883)

Although the period of the spoils system is identified with Andrew Jackson's administration, its origins began much earlier. During the forty years of Federalist and Republican control of the federal government, democracy was expanding rapidly across the new nation. Restrictions on suffrage were reduced, and the electorate expanded dramatically. Moreover, eleven new states were added to the nation during the 1820s, most of them in the western frontier. The new voters from the west were less educated and less wealthy than the eastern Federalists and Republicans, and they were much more egalitarian. The development of mass voting required strong party organizations to deliver the votes and win elections. Many voters either did not know how to read at all or could not read English. Therefore, many party workers were needed to communicate the party's platform and promote its candidates to the voters. Patronage—or the promise of a government job—was the reward promised to attract these workers. For the next half-century, the patronage and spoils system reigned supreme.

Jackson: Rhetoric versus Actions

Andrew Jackson was swept into power on the crest of the new tide of voters from the west. He made a populist, perhaps demagogic appeal to the newly enfranchised voters. He was the very embodiment of the antiestablishment frontiersman, dedicated to giving the common man a voice in government, and his rhetoric was antiestablishment and egalitarian. In one of his most famous speeches, Jackson said:

> The duties of all public officers are, or at least admit of being made, so plain and simple that men of intelligence may readily qualify themselves for their performance; and I can not but believe that more is lost by the long continuance of men in office than is generally to be gained by their experience.[9]

Jackson was thus stating that all men, not only elite Federalists and Republicans, could exercise the duties of public offices. He also said: "In a country where offices are created solely for the benefit of the people, no one man has any more intrinsic right to official station than another."[10]

Although Jackson's rhetoric asserted a belief in rotation in office and in the right of "common men" to hold public office, his actions did not parallel his rhetoric. He dismissed only about one-tenth of the government's total personnel[11]—a dismissal rate approximately the same as that of Jefferson. Moreover, Jackson was as careful as his predecessors in appointing competent and qualified individuals.[12] Sidney Aronson's data on federal officeholders in the Adams, Jefferson, and Jackson administrations reveal that although Jackson appointed more middle-class individuals, the majority of his appointees continued to come from the elite class.[13]

Although Jackson's practice of spoils and partronage was limited, his rhetoric provided an intellectual defense of the practice. He defended it as an extension of democracy, and he carried it out openly and proudly, rather than "apologetically and quietly as had been the fashion earlier."[14] Therefore, by his rhetoric if not by his actions, Jackson launched a movement that dominated U.S. politics and public personnel policies for more than fifty years. It should be remembered, however, that Jackson achieved a bloodless revolution by democratizing the U.S. political process. He opened the door for a more representative sample of the U.S. population to participate in governing.

Spoils in Action

Jackson's successors were much more vigorous practitioners of spoils and patronage. Martin Van Buren, Jackson's hand-picked successor, continued with only moderate removals. The Whigs had been extremely critical of Jackson's removals, and they criticized Van Buren for the same reason. When the Whigs attained power in 1841, however, they ignored their earlier criticisms and implemented patronage with great vigor. In 1845, James K. Polk, a Democrat came to power and another wholesale replacement of civil servants occurred. The Whigs returned to power in 1849 under Zachary Taylor, and new dismissals followed. When President Taylor died in office, a new twist occurred in the spoils system. Millard Fillmore, who succeeded Taylor, removed members of his party and replaced them with members of his own faction of the Whig party. Thus, the precedent was established that rotation followed any change in the presidency, even when the same party remained in power. The Democrats returned to power in 1853 with Franklin Pierce. In 1857, however, James Buchanan, another Democrat, came to power and followed Fillmore's precedent by replacing Pierce appointees with his own kind of Democrats. Abraham Lincoln used spoils and patronage more than any of his predecessors; indeed, he used the spoils system to obtain the cooperation of Congress in waging the Civil War.[15] The spoils system reached its zenith, however, under Lincoln and then entered a period of slow decline.

Congressional dislike of President Andrew Johnson encouraged proposals for a merit system that would curb the president's appointive and removal power. Although the various congressional proposals and reports between 1865 and 1868 were not implemented, they did attract considerable attention in the budding civil service reform movement, and they served as a base for subsequent reform. In 1870, President Grant publicly called for civil service reform; as a result, the Civil Service Commission was created in 1871. Grant named George William Curtis, editor of *Harper's Weekly* and a leader of the reform movement, as chairman of the commission.[16] The commission appeared to take seriously its task of conducting examinations. Congress, however, was fearful that the new commission would infringe on its patronage power; therefore, it withdrew financial support for the commission in 1873.

Although President Rutherford B. Hayes was personally in favor of reform, Congress remained hostile to it. President Hayes did introduce competitive examinations in the New York City Customs House, and he forbade political activity by government employees and tried, without much success, to ban political assessments on public workers. His most significant contribution to the reform movement was his commissioning of Dorman Eaton to prepare a report on competitive examinations in the British Civil Service and on the improvements resulting from the introduction of competitive examinations in the New York Customs House.[17] This report provided considerable ammunition for the reform movement.

A Defense of Spoils and Patronage

The spoils system came to a close in 1881 with the assassination of President James A. Garfield. It had lasted for more than fifty years and had helped to spread democracy in the United States. Since extensive participation in politics takes considerable time and energy, one must either have sufficient leisure time to spend on politics or sufficient incentive to invest the time and energy. Before the spoils system, only the wealthy elite had both the time and the incentive to participate. The lower classes had to spend most of their time earning a living. After the arrival of the spoils system, however, the average individual had a much greater incentive (a job) to participate in politics.

When evaluating the spoils period, one should remember that many government jobs were relatively simple and that there was some truth in Jackson's assertion that most positions were so "plain and simple" that most men could do them. Moreover, other conditions ameliorated the effects of the inexperience of civil service personnel.[18] Many who were removed from office when their party lost an election returned to power when their party was again victorious. In addition, a large number of employees remained in office under both parties because their functions were often judged too technical to permit frequent replacements.

Finally, the spoils system must not be judged only by an efficiency standard. Historically, U.S. public personnel have responded to several values, only one of which is efficiency. For example, public personnel are expected to be representative of the public, and the spoils system produced a public bureaucracy that was more representative of the U.S. population. Furthermore, it assured a bureaucracy that was more responsive to the elected political leaders.

Civil Service Reform (1883–1906)

Although civil service reform is usually traced to the assasination of President Garfield in 1881 and the passing of the Pendleton Act in 1883, the origins of reform predate these events. An 1853 act, for example, required that major departments establish examining boards to conduct "pass" examinations for clerical posts in Washington.[19] The pass examinations were not competitive, in that they were given only to the person to be appointed to determine whether he had the minimum qualifications for the job. Although the exams were so easy as to be ridiculous, they did represent official recognition at this early date that the spoils system was not perfect.

The reform attempts noted in the preceding section during the administrations of Johnson, Grant, and Hayes also provided a background for the subsequent efforts of civil service reformers. In 1877, the New York Civil Service Reform Association was formed; by 1880, it claimed 583 members in thirty-three states and territories.[20] The National Civil Service Reform League was organized in 1881. Although membership in these organizations was not large, they did distribute numerous monographs and pamphlets that significantly assisted the reform movement.

Most of the leading advocates of civil service reform were upper-class individuals who had previously supported the abolition of slavery. They viewed spoils, like slavery, as immoral and considered the spoilsman a successor to the slave owner. The reformers believed that neither the slave owner nor the spoilsman had any right to his "superior position or his ill-gotten gains."[21] They preached reform and blamed all kinds of sins on the spoils system. It is clear from the literature and speeches of the reformers that the movement was based primarily on moral indignation and only secondarily on any concern for efficiency and economy in government.

Although the reform movement involved considerable moral indignation, other motives also may have guided the reformers.[22] These primarily white, Anglo-Saxon, protestant reformers had looked upon civil service reform as one way to wrench power away from ethnic political machines. Under the spoils system, political parties obtained workers and money via political patronage and assessments made on the wages of their members in public office. Many of these party loyalists had ethnic and lower-class backgrounds. When civil service reform blocked the use of assessments and patronage to obtain funds, however, the parties had to turn to businessmen and the wealthy for money. Political power was thus transferred from the party members to the businessmen and other members of the elite who contributed to the party. Viewed from this perspective, civil service reform "was just another effort to take a measure of power away from the dominant political forces represented by the ethnic machine and transfer it to those who were, in their own opinion, more deserving of it."[23]

Whatever the true motives of the reformers were, there were serious disadvantages in the spoils system.[24] First, it encouraged the creation of extra jobs, both to provide more political rewards or incentives and to lighten the workload so that partisan workers would have time for their assigned political tasks. Second, many individuals were employed who were not qualified for their jobs. Third, the system tempted government employees to use their official position for personal gain, since they had only four years to realize a profit for their long years of laboring for the party. Fourth, many resources were needed to provide training and orientation for new employees. Fifth, many jobs were performed by employees who lacked sufficient experience in the jobs to do them well. Sixth, the president and other officials diverted much of their attention and time away from official duties to the dispensation of patronage. Finally, the spoils system identified government employment with graft, corruption, and incompetence—an image that lingers even to the present.

Although the disadvantages of the spoils system were considerable, the singularly most important reason for civil service reform was the assassination of President Garfield in 1881 by Charles Guiteau, a disappointed office seeker. This act changed the political scene dramatically. The reformers, who were already preaching in moralistic tones, were able to equate the spoils system with the murder of a president.[25] Thus, civil service reform became a prominent issue in the 1882 congressional election. Many Republican congressmen lost their seats in the election, and many of these defeats were blamed on the Republicans' failure to support civil service reform. Therefore, after the election, Congress was willing to pass the magna carta of the merit system—the Pendleton Act of 1883.

The Pendleton Act established several major features that still exist in present merit systems. First, the act provided for open, competitive examinations designed to measure applicants' ability and competence to do the job. Loyalty to a particular party or political official was no longer sufficient to obtain a position. Second, the act called for a neutral civil service by prohibiting removal for partisan reasons. It also forbade any employee covered by the act to "coerce the political action of any person." Third, the act established an independent, bipartisan commission, composed of three members appointed by the president, to oversee the implementation and administration of the act; no more than two commission members could be from the same party. Although the president could remove commissioners, the reformers hoped that this commission would be a suspicious watchdog that would oppose any attempts to undermine the act.[26]

Although the Pendleton Act was patterned after the British and European civil service systems, there were significant differences. First, the act permitted lateral entry and an open personnel system; that is, new employees could enter at any level of the service if they had the requisite skills. In contrast, Britain had a closed career system in which entry was restricted to the lower positions. Furthermore, the act called for examinations that were "practical in character." In Britain, exams were often of a general nature and were designed for college graduates. Moreover, the act did not provide the security of tenure that was often given to British and European civil servants. These differences assured a more egalitarian U.S. civil service that was less likely to become a closed, elite bureaucracy.

These differences between the British and U.S. systems point to the contrast between the rank-in-person system in Britain and the rank-in-position system in the United States. Under the rank-in-person system, individuals with generalist skills are recruited for entry-level positions and then are promoted through the ranks. Generally, they have a lifetime career in the service and are assigned to a variety of positions over time. Status and rank are in the employee, not in the job or position he or she holds. Conversely, under a rank-in-position system, new recruits may enter at any level for which they are qualified. Emphasis is on the specialized competency necessary to perform a specific function, and rank and status are in the position, not in the individual occupying it.

The Pendleton Act placed only slightly over 10 percent of all federal positions under the merit system to form the classified civil service. The president, however, was given the authority to add more positions to this category. Except for a few exemptions, the president could also remove positions from the classified service. The Congress gave this authority to the president because it would have been administratively impossible in 1883 to apply the merit system to all federal positions.[27] Moreover, the politicians were able to proclaim that they had accomplished reform although they had left 90 percent of the positions subject to patronage. This assured that their patronage power would not be curtailed quickly.

Because the act did allow the president much power to expand the classified service, subsequent presidents gradually expanded the merit system by "blanketing in" incumbents who were not required to take competitive exams to keep their positions. After the Pendleton Act was passed, reformers concentrated on expanding the classified civil service and on developing rules and regulations to systematize selection, promotion, and other aspects of personnel management.[28]

President Chester Arthur brought approximately 1,200 positions into the classified service. When President Grover Cleveland, a Democrat, came into office after twenty-five years of Republican rule, some believed that he might return to the spoils system. Indeed, Cleveland did remove most of the 90 percent of positions in the unclassified category, but he did not remove any classified positions. When he left office, he moved one-third of all federal positions into the classified service.

Although there were pluses and minuses for civil service during William McKinley's administration, on balance, merit pushed ahead. McKinley mandated that classified employees be given a written statement of charges against them before they could be removed. He also increased the number of jobs in the classified service.

Since Theodore Roosevelt had been a civil service commissioner for six years, the merit system had a friend in the White House when he was elected president.[29] He placed more positions in the classified service. Furthermore, he clarified the rules on removals and better defined prohibited political activities.

The reformers emphasized that graft, corruption, and inefficiency were associated with spoils and patronage. They believed that if politics could be removed from public administration, good government would result. Thus, they emphasized neutrality to the exclusion of almost everything else. Personnel reform, therefore, was essentially negative, in that little emphasis was placed on providing a stimulating and dynamic environment designed to maximize personnel satisfaction and efficiency. Instead, the main emphasis was on protecting public employees from the evil effects of politics. Thus, efficiency was equated with neutrality, and the reformers used the politics–administration dichotomy to explain away the problem of how a neutral civil service, protected from the influence of elected politicians, could nevertheless be responsive. According to this dichotomy, public employees are simply neutral tools in the administration of policy; they have no influence on the making of policy. This dichotomy, although unrealistic, served as an intellectual defense for insulating public employees from politicians. Furthermore, as Mosher noted, it encouraged the divorce of "personnel administration from general management—from the executives responsible for carrying on the programs and activities of government."[30]

Scientific Management and Efficiency (1906–1937)

As government budgets increased in size at the start of the twentieth century, more and more citizens became concerned about efficiency in government. The reformers began to conclude that neutrality was not sufficient to assure good government, that both neutrality and efficiency were needed. The efficiency movement started at the local level for several reasons. First, three-fifths of all public expenditures at that time were by local governments. Second, graft and corruption seemed to be most pervasive at the local level. Finally, the activities conducted by cities, such as street maintenance, water supply, refuse removal, and fire protection, were most readily susceptible to the principles and methods used in business.

At the same time, Frederick Taylor's scientific management theories were becoming more popular. Taylor believed that if tasks were studied systematically and quantitatively, a best way or most efficient way to do the task could be discovered. Moreover, Taylor concluded that specialization in materials, tools, equipment, and workers was often necessary to realize the benefits of the one best way. According to Taylor, once the best way was discovered, it should become the standard for all workers doing the task. Taylor's scientific management concept complemented the new search for increased efficiency in government.

Perhaps the major product of scientific management's impact on the public sector was the increased emphasis on job analysis to determine the responsibilities and skills needed to perform tasks. A natural extension of job analysis is job classification or the grouping of jobs into standardized categories that have similar requirements. In 1923, Congress passed the Classification Act, which established broad occupational divisions, called services, that were divided into grades or levels of importance and difficulty.[31] This act was a response not only to a desire for efficiency and orderly management but also to pressure for standardized wages.

As a result of job analysis and classification, examinations could be developed to test for needed skills. According to Mosher, merit then became more than political neutrality and honesty;[32] it also began to denote competence. Furthermore, as jobs were analyzed, training needs and methods were developed and training became an approved personnel function. Job analysis and an emphasis on the best way to do a job also introduced efficiency ratings as a more objective way to manage; they became a major factor in promotions. Thus, personnel management was beginning to involve more than just assuring political neutrality. It was emerging from a primarily negative focus to a greater emphasis on positive, scientific personnel management. The demands for job analyses, examinations, training, and performance evaluation meant that a profession of personnel management was emerging. As a consequence of this development, personnel managers were expected to assist line managers in achieving greater efficiency. At the same time, however, personnel officials were expected to continue to "police" the organization to assure political neutrality. Thus, personnel management obtained two primary functions or goals that often conflict.

The Integration of Personnel Administration and Management (1937–1955)

From 1937 to 1955, there was less emphasis on neutrality as the primary goal of personnel management and greater recognition of personnel management's role in general line management. This trend toward greater integration of personnel administration and line management was most noticeable in the reports of two important groups—the Brownlow Committee and the second Hoover Commission.

The Brownlow Committee

During the Great Depression, government assumed a much more active role in life in the United States. The creation of many government agencies produced considerable confusion and overlapping responsibilities. In 1937, President Franklin D. Roosevelt appointed the Brownlow Committee to recommend solutions to the developing administrative confusion. The committee recommended that the Civil Service Commission become an agency headed by a single administrator who would report to the President. Furthermore, the committee strongly urged that personnel management be integrated with general management. Therefore, the committee supported the continuing development of positive personnel management that would be concerned with much more than obtaining neutral employees.

The Brownlow Committee also recommended that personnel functions be decentralized. Although it recognized that a central personnel agency should establish policy and regulations, it concluded that personnel operations should be decentralized so that it could have a more integrated relationship with middle and lower managers. As a result of this recommendation, President Roosevelt ordered that all major administrative units establish professionally staffed personnel offices. In a similar vein, the Classification Act of 1949 gave line agencies formal responsibility for position classification, performance evaluation, and promotion.

The Hoover Commission

President Dwight D. Eisenhower's most significant influence on public personnel management was his appointment of the second Hoover Commission to study administrative policy. This was the first major study to recommend that the number of political appointees at the top levels not be reduced. The commission also attempted to draw the line between top offices that should be filled by political appointees and those that should be filled by career civil servants. According to the commission, political appointees should fill all positions that have authority to make final decisions on policies, programs, and objectives or that demand public advocacy in defending policies.[33]

The Hoover commission also recommended that top career administrators should not be required to advocate or defend policies and should be part of a special group known as the senior civil service. The senior career officials in this special service should be generalists who could move from one position to another, regardless of the classification of their position. Thus, rank would be in the person rather than in the job. Top career officials would be politically neutral and would serve where they were needed most.[34] In theory, this senior service was intended to assure highly competent senior oficials who would be politically neutral and yet responsive to the needs of their politically appointed superiors. Although this recommendation was not enacted, it did serve to enhance the legitimacy of a rank-in-person system. Much later, the 1978 Civil Service Reform Act included establishment of the Senior Executive Service, which was patterned after the Hoover Commission's recommendation.

To recapitulate, during the period from 1937 to 1955, more officials began to see that a total separation between politics and administration was neither possible nor wise. Also, the trend was toward a single personnel director who would report to the chief executive and away from semi-independent civil service commissions. As a result, personnel management functions were more easily integrated with those of general management. More and more line managers saw the need to have staff with expertise in personnel functions. This was more easily accomplished as personnel functions were decentralized to the agency level.

Professionals, Unions, and Minorities in Public Personnel Management (1955–1978)

Since 1955, three major groups—professionals, unions, and minorities—have had a significant impact on public personnel management. The number of public employees who are in a profession or in a union has increased dramatically since 1955. With this growth has come increased power for these groups over various personnel functions, such as recruitment, promotion, performance evaluation, compensation, and dismissal. Similarly, minorities have obtained increased numbers and influence in personnel management. The emergence of equal opportunity and affirmative action in the 1960s and 1970s has not only affected the traditional personnel functions, it has also introduced new issues, such as quotas, reverse discrimination, comparable worth, and sexual harassment.

The Professionals

Mosher defines a profession as a distinct occupation that requires at least a bachelor's degree and that provides a lifetime career to its members.[35] The number of professionals in government employment has increased dramatically since 1955; today, more than 40 percent of all public employees are engaged in professional and technical duties. Also, more than 36 percent of all professionals work for government. This influx of professionals into public service has affected personnel management in several ways. First, much of the training and orientation a professional receives occurs outside government agencies in institutions of higher education. As a result, public organizations may have less control over the development of their professionals' values. The professionals' loyalty to these values may supersede their loyalty to the agency, and the standards of professional associations and professional schools may replace the standards of the organization. Obviously, such a conflict in allegiance causes additional control problems for the public agency.

The increase in professionalism also affects recruitment. With increasing professionalism, there is a tendency to require credentials (that is, degrees, licenses, certificates, and the like) instead of tests.

The greater number of professionals in government employment also affects salary administration. Separate salary schedules are needed for professionals in engineering, architecture, medicine and nursing, metallurgy, and veterinary medicine, among others.[36]

Perhaps the most important impact of professions on public personnel management has been a greater emphasis on the *person* as opposed to the position.[37] Since 1883, the civil service has concentrated on developing a system of positions that are logically related to one another and on filling these positions on the basis of merit. The emphasis was on the job and the responsibilities associated with it. Since the emergence of professionalism, however, there has been more emphasis on the people filling positions and on their career needs within their professions.[38] In one sense, professionalism has contributed to the development of a rank-in-person system within a primarily rank-in-position civil service.

The power and influence of professionals in the public service can be seen in several ways. First, certain professions dominate particular agencies (for example, educators in the Department of Education and engineers in public works agencies). Second, professionals are influential even in agencies that they do not dominate; for example, most agencies have legal counsel, budgeters, planners, and personnel specialists. Third, professionals inside the public service can persuade their professional colleagues outside the agency to defend their interests.

Unions

Unionization of public employees has accelerated during the last two decades. Although unions have existed in government since the nineteenth century, the real turning point in unionization occurred with the issuance of President Kennedy's Executive Order 10988, which allowed federal employees to organize and engage in collective bargaining. This order encouraged a dramatic growth in unions and collective bargaining at all levels of government. The number (and the percentage) of federal employees covered by formal agreements increased dramatically from 110,000 in 1964 to more than 1.1 million in 1980. At the state and local level, about 1.6 million employees were in unions in 1962; by 1980, the number had climbed to more than 5 million. The development of public unions has had a dramatic impact on public personnel managers. They have been forced to develop expertise in collective bargaining and negotiation. Moreover, they have found it necessary to share some power with unions in the traditional personnel functions, such as selection, evaluation, compensation, and retention. These developments and other issues concerning collective bargaining are discussed in chapter 10.

Minorities

Like professionals and union members, minorities also have had a great influence on public personnel management during the last 25 years. Although the federal government made some attempts to eliminate discrimination in the public service before the 1960s, it was not until the Kennedy administration that equality of opportunity became a major issue in public personnel management. During this time, the civil rights movements was developing into a major political force and a national issue. One product of this movement was the Civil Rights Act of 1964, in which Title VII prohibits discrimination in private employment on the basis of race, sex, national origin, or religion. The prohibitions of Title VII were extended to state and local governments in the 1972 Equal Employment Opportunity Act.

Court decisions also have increased the impact of minorities on personnel management. For example, the 1971 Supreme Court case *Griggs v. Duke Power Company* upheld the equal employment provisions of the 1964 Civil Rights Act. In addition, the *Griggs* decision prohibited selection criteria that appeared to be neutral but were not job-related and excluded minorities in disproportionate numbers. After this decision, a plaintiff no longer had to prove that the employer intended to discriminate; the plaintiff need only prove that the selection criteria were not related to the job and that they excluded a disproportionate number of minorities.

Other laws prohibit discrimination on the basis of age or handicap. As a result of these laws and court decisions, public personnel managers must assure that selection and promotion criteria are job-related. Similarly, since performance evaluations may be used in determining promotions and levels of compensation, they, too, must be based only on performance. Moreover, personnel managers must guard against discrimination in compensation: equal pay for equal work is required by the Equal Pay Act of 1963. A recent, more controversial issue is whether equal pay is required for work of "comparable worth." Some positions that are traditionally held by women often receive lower pay than other positions that are primarily held by men. Although the positions may not involve the same work, they may be of similar worth to the organization's mission. Therefore, some contend that pay for these comparable, yet different, positions should be similar. This issue, which the courts have not yet resolved, is discussed in greater detail in chapter 7.

Federal laws, court decisions, and executive orders require not only that personnel managers prevent discrimination in selection and compensation but that they implement affirmative actions to employ more minorities and women. As a result, the controversial issue of employment goals and quotas has become part of public personnel management. In addition, the possibility of selection, promotion, and retention quotas for minorities and women have produced charges of reverse discrimination by white males. (These contemporary, controversial issues are discussed in chapter 11.)

The Expansion of Merit Systems

By 1980, approximately 90 percent of all federal employees were included in the merit system. It is unlikely that a larger percentage of federal positions can or should be so included. Most of the remaining positions are in seasonal employment, involve sensitive intelligence-gathering activities, or concern policymaking or confidential functions.

Merit systems did not expand rapidly in state and local governments. By 1935, only twelve states had established merit systems. In 1940, however, the Social Security Act mandated that state agencies administering funds authorized by this act must have merit systems. As a result, at least a major portion of the civil service of every state is subject to merit system requirements. In 1980, thirty-six states had comprehensive merit systems, and the rest had partial merit coverage. However, great diversity remains in state personnel systems. Some states provide special systems for some employees; for example, states may have special systems for the state police or for state universities.

Larger cities—of over 100,000 population—generally have merit systems, but counties generally do not. Shafritz, for example, found that only 5 percent of all counties had comprehensive merit systems in 1975.[39]

The Problems of Merit Systems

Although the number and the percentage of employees under merit systems have expanded dramatically during this century, there are numerous problems with these systems. Major criticisms include (1) overprotection of public employees, resulting in poor performance and low productivity; (2) involvement of too many groups in public personnel policymaking; and (3) narrow, detailed, and rigid job classifications. These and other problems often encourage personnel managers and line managers to engage in subterfuges to avoid merit system restrictions. These subterfuges include customizing a job description for a particular candidate, extensive use of temporary appointments, and grade inflation.

Overprotection of Employees

Perhaps the chief problem of merit systems is the that they have done too good a job of protecting public employees. Although the Pendleton Act controlled the "front door" (selection), it left the "back door" (dismissal) open. Over time, however, the back door has also been closed. In recent years, fewer than 300 federal employees of nearly 3 million total were dismissed for inefficiency or incompetence. This extraordinarily small number is a result of several actions that insulate employees from dismissal. First, the Lloyd–LaFollette Act of 1912 states that civil servants cannot be removed until they are given reasons for the dismissal and an opportunity to respond to the charges. Second, the Veterans Preference Act of 1944 requires that the Civil Service Commission review the reasons given for dismissing veterans. This protection was extended to nonveterans by President Kennedy's 1961 executive order. Third, the 1939 and 1948 Hatch Acts prevent the dismissal of any employee for political reasons. Fourth, the courts, have bestowed on public employees considerable due-process rights regarding dismissal.

At the local level, public employees also enjoy considerable protection from removal, including the same procedural due-process protections. Moreover, local civil service commissions that were originally charged with protecting employees against partisan removals have assumed the lawful right to review all the personnel actions of management.[40] In effect, the power to dismiss an employee has shifted from the appointing authority to the civil service commission.[41] Dismissals and disciplinary actions by management have become quasi-judicial: employees are "presumed innocent of incompetence until they are proven otherwise."[42]

Given the often long and laborious process involved in dismissing an employee, public managers often find it preferable to tolerate an incompetent employee. A manager must provide a great deal of documentation to support a dismissal, and it must be developed in detail over a number of months. Managers are reluctant to invest this time when there is a real chance that the dismissal will be reversed and that the employee will return to the workplace. Of course, the continued employment of someone who has been publicly labeled as incompetent destroys the morale of the workforce and the authority of the manager. However, the manager may find easier ways to remove an unproductive employee, such as encouraging a transfer of the employee to another agency. It is usually easier to give a problem to someone else than to remove it. Alternatively, the manager may find it easier to obtain an additional employee to do the work of the ineffective employee—an option that becomes even more attractive if managers are paid according to how many employees they supervise.

Managers often lack sufficient incentives to discipline their employees. If managers are not evaluated or rewarded according to the productivity of their units, they will see little reason to suffer the problems inherent in disciplining incompetent or inefficient subordinates. Why should one manager incur the reputation of being "hard-nosed" when his fellow managers overlook inefficiency? The question becomes even more telling when all managers receive basically the same compensation.

Factionalization of Public Personnel Management

A second major problem of current merit systems is that too many groups are involved in developing personnel policy. Before 1978, federal personnel policy was controlled by the president, Congress, the courts, the Civil Service Commission, the various departments and agencies, and the unions. With so many participants, the federal merit system was often a crazy-quilt of confusing and inconsistent or contradictory rules and regulations. The same problem exists at the local level, where personnel directors, civil service commissions, city councils, city managers, labor unions, civic groups, pension boards, and others are involved in personnel decisions.

Other Problems and the Netherworld of Public Personnel

Other problems also plague many merit systems. For example, many job classifications are too narrowly defined. As a result, employees may be in dead-end positions, and managers may be unable to move employees from one position to another. Rigid, detailed job specifications and descriptions make it impossible to promote an employee; therefore, his or her position must be reclassified to obtain a significant salary increase. Moreover, because the job descriptions are too specific, they are often out of date and fail to reflect what the employees are really doing. Finally, even though the descriptions are too specific, they may fail to specify minimally acceptable standards of performance; that is, they may specify the tasks expected of a position but fail to designate the expected level of performance for these tasks.

Because of the rigidities and problems inherent in many merit systems, line managers and personnel directors often engage in a form of collusion that produces what Shafritz calls the "netherworld of public personnel management."[43] This netherworld is rarely exposed to public view, but any experienced public manager has seen it in action. It involves decisions by both line managers and personnel departments that violate the legal and technical requirements of merit systems. This netherworld exists because there are considerable incentives for bypassing merit system regulations and few punishments for doing so.

Examples of the netherworld can occur in recruitment, selection, and classification. In recruitment, a line manager who knows whom he wishes to select for a position may write the job description in such a way that only the person he wishes to hire can fit the description. During selection, managers may successfully persuade the personnel department to lower the pass point to allow a favored applicant to obtain the position.

Another common occurrence in the personnel netherworld is excessive use of temporary appointments, which can be made through noncompetitive hiring. Merit systems provide for such appointments to resolve emergency situations and to continue operations while a competitive search is conducted for a permanent replacement. Some jurisdictions, however, continue to reappoint temporary employees, thereby avoiding merit regulations. Despite a formal merit system, Mayor Richard Daley of Chicago was able to maintain an effective patronage system through temporary appointments.

Perhaps the most pervasive netherworld occurrence is inflated classifications. Since position classification plans and compensation schedules provide for a specific pay range for each position, regardless of the occupant's level of performance, many employees who are doing good work become frustrated because they have reached the top of the pay scale for their positions. Employees then persuade the supervisor to seek higher classifications for their positions. Of course, the supervisor wants to improve the morale of good workers, so the supervisor and the workers collaborate in inflating the descriptions of the employees' duties to obtain higher classifications and thus, higher salaries. Overclassifications occur because managers see many incentives and no punishment for doing it. Indeed, a manager's own rank and salary may increase because his subordinates have higher classifications.

Because of these problems in the federal merit system, considerable political support for reforming it developed during the 1970s. In 1976, Jimmy Carter campaigned for the presidency as an "outsider" dedicated to "cleaning up" Washington. Part of Carter's agenda included merit system reform to alleviate some of the problems cited here.

The Civil Service Reform Act of 1978

The 1978 Civil Service Reform Act (CSRA) caused dramatic changes in the national merit system. In part, the law was intended to improve efficiency by giving managers more latitude. This goal was revealed in the creation of a pool of senior public executives who are paid on the basis of performance and who can be transferred easily from one assignment to another; the establishment of merit pay which links salary increases to performance rather than to seniority; the development of a performance evaluation system; and the division of the Civil Service Commission into two groups.

Although the CSRA gives management more control over employee rewards, it balances this additional control with more protections for the employee. A major example of this increased protection was the establishment of the Merit Systems Protection Board, which oversees the merit system and guards individual employees against unfair practices. The CSRA also provides a special counsel who can investigate employee complaints. Furthermore, the law provides protections for "whistleblowers" who disclose information concerning bad management, waste, or illegal actions within the bureaucracy.

New Organizational Arrangements

Before the CSRA was passed, all federal personnel management activities were concentrated in the Civil Service Commission (CSC). The CSC established and implemented regulations concerning recruitment, selection, position classification, performance evaluation, and other personnel management functions. The

CSC also exercised a judicial role by hearing employee appeals from the departments and agencies. Critics contended that it was improper for the CSC to serve as the president's chief personnel advisor, on the one hand, and also act as an impartial, quasi-judicial institution, on the other. Furthermore, critics wondered whether the CSC could objectively evaluate the enforcement of legislation it had created? Thus, the critics contended that legislative and judicial roles should not be combined in the CSC. As a result of these concerns, the CSRA abolished the CSC and replaced it with two new organizations—the Office of Personnel Management (OPM) and the Merit Systems Protection Board (MSPB). The OPM is headed by a director who is appointed by the president and confirmed by the Senate. The director reports directly to the president and helps the president manage the federal workforce. The OPM develops programs to improve efficiency and productivity in the workforce, oversees affirmative action efforts, and conducts personnel-related research. The CSRA also requires that the OPM decentralize personnel functions to the greatest extent possible by giving control to the departments and agencies. The purpose of this decentralization is to allow for greater integration of personnel functions (selection, position classification, performance evaluation, and so forth) with those of line management. It is also hoped that decentralization will permit a more rapid recruitment, examination, selection, promotion, and dismissal process.

The MSPB is a three-member bipartisan body appointed by the president with Senate approval. It has responsibility for safeguarding both employee rights and the merit system against abuses and unfair personnel actions. The MSPB not only responds to employee appeals but also reviews OPM regulations to determine whether they might lead to prohibited practices. Within the MSPB is the independent Office of Special Counsel, which investigates and prosecutes allegations of prohibited personnel practices. The MSPB also protects whistle-blowers.

The Senior Executive Service

Another important part of the CSRA is the Senior Executive Service (SES). The SES, composed of managers at grades 16, 17, and 18, is intended to provide a pool of top executives who are assigned, reassigned, and removed on the basis of their performance. The SES is a rank-in-person system, not the usual rank-in-position system. Under this rank-in-person system, SES members may be assigned wherever their skills are needed. The SES was also designed to allow top political executives to select their own management group from among SES members, rather than working only with those already occupying positions. Thus, political responsiveness was another goal of the CSRA.

A key element in the SES is its emphasis on performance and on rewards for good work. When executives enter the SES, they serve a one-year probationary period, during which they can be dismissed from the SES at any time for unsatisfactory performance. After the probationary period, they are evaluated on such criteria as improvements in efficiency, work quality, productivity, and the like. If an SES member receives one unsatisfactory performance evaluation, he or she may be removed. Employees who are dismissed from the SES may return to the regular civil service at no reduction in salary.

As the CSRA provided removal for unsatisfactory performance, it also permitted significant rewards for good performance, allowing for bonuses of up to 20 percent of salary to be given to as many as 50 percent of the SES members. Moreover, the CSRA provided Meritorious Executive awards of $10,000 and Distinguished Executive awards of $20,000.

Is the SES working? The answer is yes and no, depending on which evidence one examines. From the viewpoint of participation of eligible managers in the SES, it is successful. More than 98 percent of the eligible managers have joined the SES. A considerable number of these members, however, are dissatisfied with the operation of the organization. Without question, the issue that is creating the most dissatisfaction among members is the pay and bonus provisions of the SES. Part of this dissatisfaction was caused by the continuation of a pay cap on executive salaries. Most of the SES members' salaries were controlled by a congressionally imposed pay cap. During the first several years of the SES, the pay cap was at Executive Level V, or about $50,000.[44] Since nearly all SES members were at or near that level, the pay cap served as a serious disincentive and undermined the performance pay logic of the SES.

SES members' dissatisfaction with pay also resulted from changes in the SES bonus sytem. As mentioned earlier, the CSRA provided for bonuses of up to 20 percent of salary for as many as 50 percent of SES members. In 1980, however, Congress reduced the number of bonuses that could be given to 25 percent of SES members. The OPM further reduced the number to 20 percent of those eligible. Furthermore, the OPM stated that the full bonus of 20 percent of salary could be given to only 5 percent of those who were eligible.[45] Most members see these changes as a betrayal of the assumptions underlying the SES that makes performance-based compensation a sham.[46]

As a result of the pay cap and bonus changes, more than half of the SES members in a General Accounting Office survey believed that their agency's performance appraisal systems had minimal impact on performance.[47] The respondents also said that the performance appraisal systems had not improved communications and were not worth the cost.

Some critics of the SES are also concerned that political superiors may have too much control over the lives of career SES executives. Fred Thayer notes that political noncareer SES appointees can have considerable control over performance appraisals, bonus decisions, assignments, and other matters that are vital to career executives' futures.[48] Thayer argues that career SES members may be reluctant to engage in any whistle-blowing when their futures are controlled by political superiors. Recent surveys indicate that SES executives believe agencies are being politicized.[49] Supporters of the SES respond, however, by noting that one goal of the CSRA was to make top-level career executives more responsive to their political superiors.

A New Performance Evaluation System

Another major element of the CSRA is a new performance evaluation system. Before the CSRA, employees were rated as outstanding, satisfactory, or unsatisfactory on such traits as initiative, maturity, judgment, loyalty, and the like. Since these traits are difficult, if not impossible, to define operationally, and because they are not necessarily related to performance, both supervisors and employees considered performance evaluation a sham. As a result, most supervisors gave all subordinates a satisfactory or outstanding rating, and few personnel actions used performance evaluations.

The CSRA requires that agencies determine critical elements for each job and establish job-related performance standards that are based on objective criteria and that measure performance on the critical elements. The CSRA encourages employee participation in the process of developing the critical elements and standards. After the new performance evaluation system is in place, it is to be used for all kinds of personnel decisions, including whom to train, select, assign, promote, reward, and dismiss. If the performance evaluations are indeed based on performance, and if employees have participated in the development of the system, personnel actions and management will become much more rational and work-related. Furthermore, employee participation should encourage workers to have more confidence and trust in the evaluation process.

The federal government was successful in developing a new evaluation system for most of its employees by the end of 1981, which was quite an achievement in itself. Nevertheless, there have been considerable problems with the new system. Perhaps the chief problem is the pay cap on executive salaries, discussed earlier. This pay ceiling undermined the linkage between performance evaluation and rewards. Other problems include a reduction in the number of awards, adoption of the system too quickly, and others that are noted in chapter 6.

Although numerous problems are associated with the CSRA, one should remember that it is a major reform that was designed to alter the merit system so that performance is measured and rewarded. Such a major reform cannot be evaluated definitively in only the first few years of implementation. The passage of another fifteen years may be necessary before we know the true impact of the CSRA.

State and Local Civil Service Reform

Many state and local governments initiated civil service reforms after the passage of the 1978 CSRA. Some states moved to create SES systems, while others adopted merit-based, pay-for-performance systems.[50] One very noticeable reform has been the attempt of some state and local governments to improve their performance evaluations.

Even before the 1978 CSRA, many states and cities had initiated civil service reform. For example, the 1970 Model Public Personnel Administration Law of the National Civil Service League suggests that personnel commissions be abolished and replaced by a personnel department that answers to the chief executive. Moreover, it recommends that the rule of three be abolished, that tests be validated, and that political restrictions on employees be reduced. Most states and cities had already adopted these reforms before the CSRA was passed.

Organization for Personnel Management

The personnel commission and the executive personnel department are the two primary organizational arrangements of public personnel systems. Although commissions were very prominent in the early days of civil service reform, they are no longer used in most jurisdictions. Some personnel commissions are independent of the executive in their direction and management of personnel functions. Other commissions are also independent but exercise only quasi-judicial functions by hearing employee complaints and appeals and by assuring that merit principles are protected. Still other commissions have only advisory powers.

The independent, nonpartisan commission was appropriate when personnel administration was concerned primarily with keeping politics out of government. As line managers began to see the vital role of personnel administration in general management, and as personnel administration became concerned about more than just monitoring a neutral bureaucracy, various governments and groups recommended that line managers be given more control over personnel functions. As a result, personnel departments and personnel directors began to report to the chief executive. Most larger cities and those with city managers have personnel departments.

One question about personnel systems (executive or commission) concerns whether personnel functions should be decentralized to the agency level. The acknowledgment that personnel management is a vital element of general line management suggests that decentralization is appropriate because it allows managers more flexibility and control over employees. However, decentralization may also allow for abuse of merit principles and the policies of the central personnel department. Moreover, at the state and local levels, decentralization may not be economically feasible because of the cost of replicating personnel expertise in every agency. Economies of scale often dictate one centralized personnel department.

Conclusion

The history of the merit system reveals that public personnel management reflects larger political forces. The early public service was an extension of the ruling elite (Federalists), with its emphasis on effectiveness. Later, as the newly enfranchised "common man" began to assert political power, the public service began to reflect different values. Responsiveness and loyalty replaced effectiveness as the dominant value in the public service. When the excesses of the spoils period produced new political forces to eliminate patronage, neutrality replaced responsiveness as the overriding concern.

More recently, the growth of government, combined with limited tax revenues and the scientific management movement, restored a concern for effectiveness in the public service. Eventually, the civil rights movement emphasized a representative and a responsive public service. Finally, in the 1970s, many citizens and politicians concluded that the merit system's assurance of neutrality had become a fortress for inefficiency and incompetence. As a result, the most comprehensive reform since the Pendleton Act—the Civil Service Reform Act—was passed in 1978.

Thus, the evolution of the public service reveals that three values—effectiveness, neutrality, and responsiveness—have been dominant at different times. Unfortunately, these values are not always complementary. Emphasis on one generally demands compromise of the others. Therefore, the development of the merit system is cyclical, in that the prominence of one value often creates countervailing forces that eventually elevate a competing value to center stage.

Notes

1. Jay M. Shafritz, *Public Personnel Management: The Heritage of Civil Service Reform* (New York: Praeger, 1975), p. 20.
2. Ibid.
3. Paul P. Van Riper, *History of the United States Civil Service* (Evanston, Ill.: Row, Peterson, 1958), p. 9.
4. Ibid., p. 9.
5. Frederick Mosher, *Democracy and the Public Service* (New York: Oxford University Press, 1968).
6. Ibid.
7. Van Riper, *History of the United States Civil Service*, p. 15.
8. Mosher, *Democracy and the Public Service*, p. 59.
9. Van Riper, *History of the United States Civil Service*, p. 36.
10. Ibid.
11. Matthew A. Crenson, *The Federal Machine: Beginning of Bureaucracy in Jacksonian America* (Baltimore: John Hopkins University Press, 1975), p. 35.

12. Mosher, *Democracy and the Public Service*, p. 62.

13. Sidney H. Aronson, *Status and Kinship in the Higher Civil Service* (Cambridge, Mass.: Harvard University Press, 1964).

14. Herbert Kaufman, "The Growth of the Federal Personnel System," in Wallace S. Sayer, ed., *The Federal Government Service*, 2d ed. (Englewood Cliffs, N.J.: Prentice-Hall, 1965), p. 20.

15. Van Riper, *History of the United States Civil Service*, p. 43.

16. Shafritz, *Public Personnel Management*, p. 19.

17. Kaufman, "Growth of the Federal Personnel System," p. 34.

18. Ibid.

19. Ibid., p. 19.

20. Van Riper, *History of the United States Civil Service*, p. 78.

21. Ibid., p. 81.

22. Shafritz, *Public Personnel Management*, pp. 26–32.

23. Ibid., p. 31.

24. Kaufman, "Growth of the Federal Personnel System," p. 31.

25. Shafritz, *Public Personnel Management*, p. 32.

26. Kaufman, "Growth of the Federal Personnel System," p. 38.

27. Van Riper, *History of the United States Civil Service*, p. 105.

28. Kaufman, "Growth of the Federal Personnel System," p. 41.

29. Ibid., p. 45.

30. Mosher, *Democracy and the Public Service*, p. 70.

31. Van Riper, *History of the United States Civil Service*, p. 299.

32. Mosher, *Democracy and the Public Service*, p. 73.

33. Ibid., p. 87.

34. Ibid.

35. Ibid., p. 106.

36. George Gordon, *Public Administration in America*, 2d ed. (New York: Martin's Press, 1982), p. 307.

37. Ibid.

38. Ibid.

39. Shafritz, *Public Personnel Management*, p. 33.

40. Ibid., p. 50.

41. Ibid.

42. Ibid.

43. Ibid., pp. 105–125.

44. Peter Colby and Patricia W. Ingraham, "Civil Service Reform: The Views of the Senior Executive Service," *Review of Public Personnel Administration* (Summer 1981): 82.

45. Ibid., p. 83.

46. Patricia W. Ingraham and Charles Barrilleaux, "Motivating Government Managers for Retrenchment: Some Possible Lessons from the SES," *Public Adminstration Review* 43 (October 1983): 393–402. Also see Peter Ring and James Perry, "Reforming the Upper levels of the Bureaucracy: A Longitudinal Study of the Senior Executive Service," *Administration and Society* 15 (May 1983): 119–144.

47. "Congress Examines Senior Executive Service," *IPMA News*, April 1984, p. 11.

48. Fred C. Thayer, "Civil Service Reform and Performance Appraisal: A Policy Disaster," *Public Personnel Management* 10 (1981): 20–28.

49. Ring and Perry, "Reforming the Upper Levels of the Bureaucracy," p. 33.

50. R.T. Finkle, H. Hall, and S.S. Min, "Senior Executive Service: The State of the Art," *Public Personnel Management* 10 (Fall 1981): 299–312.

3
Job Evaluation

Key Words

Pay equity

Job analysis

Desk audit

Position description

Job evaluation

Position classification

Position ranking

Factor point

Class breadth

Class specifications

APT employees

Job enrichment

Introduction

Job evaluation is designed to produce an equitable, consistent, understandable, valid, and administratively feasible system for ranking jobs. Such rankings are made for pay differentiations and for other purposes in an organization.[1] Job evaluation begins with job analysis, which involves the determination, using various sources of information, of the tasks comprising a job and the skills, knowledge, and responsibilities required of an employee for successful performance.[2] This chapter explores the crucial importance of job evaluation in other personnel management activities.[3] Various methods of job analysis are reviewed, and the two primary methods of job evaluation used in the public sector—position classification and factor ranking—are examined in greater detail, as are the problems inherent in each approach. The chapter concludes with a discussion of the appropriate evaluation systems for organic versus mechanistic organizations.

Job Evaluation and Public Personnel Management

Job evaluation has the potential to provide valuable information regarding a wide range of personnel functions. If organizations are to cope effectively with change, they need a constant flow of information on the content and requirements of the jobs within them. In addition, Supreme Court rulings and Equal Employment Opportunity Commission guidelines require that selection systems and examinations be job-related. Therefore, job evaluation can be useful in recruitment, in selection, in training, in performance appraisal, in planning, and in meeting other managerial needs. In the public sector, however, job evaluation has traditionally been used primarily to determine pay rates.[4]

Job Evaluation and Determination of Pay Rates

If pay is to motivate performance, employees must believe that their pay is equitable. Pay equity has both internal and external dimensions: internal equity refers to equal pay for equal work inside an organization; external equity refers to equal pay for similar work in several organizations. A good job evaluation process is necessary to assure both types of equity.

Job evaluation determines the tasks involved in a job and the skills, knowledge, and responsibilities required of the job's occupant. This information is essential for the establishment of equal pay for equal work. If a pay plan is based on a sound job evaluation process, employees are more likely to believe that people who perform similar work in the organization receive similar pay, and internal equity is achieved.

External pay equity is achieved through salary surveys of similar positions in other organizations in the labor market. Salary surveys cannot be conducted, however, without information concerning the tasks of a job and the skills and training needed to perform the tasks. This information can be provided by the job evaluation.

The 1963 Equal Pay Act[5] and Title VII of the 1964 Civil Rights Act[6] prohibit wage differentials between similar jobs when the differentials are based on race or sex. A sound and valid job evaluation process is essential to assure that the tasks and requirements of a job—not racism or sexism—determine pay rates. An employer would have considerable difficulty defending a pay plan against charges of racism or sexism without a sound job evaluation process.

Job evaluation is also at the center of the "comparable worth" issue.[7] Critics assert that the great subjectivity in job evaluation practices allows evaluators to give more weight to factors found in presumably "male" occupations, such as heavy lifting or physical labor, and little weight to such traits as "speed and fine motor requirements."[8] Regardless of the truth of this criticism, it notes the central role of job evaluation in equal pay and comparable worth disputes.

Job Evaluation as a Basis for Selection Programs

Job evaluation demands that systematic data be collected about the knowledge, skills, and abilities required to perform each job. This information is essential for constructing appropriate selection processes and intruments. A typical job analysis produces a list of tasks for each job and rates the complexity and importance of each task that is required for successful performance of the total job. This information provides the selection specialist with the necessary information to decide on the education, experience, and skill requirements for each position. Also, this information allows selection tests to be constructed for positions.

Courts require that selection instruments be valid and be related to successful performance by the selected applicant on the job. Good job evaluations and analysis are essential before selection tests can be constructed. One cannot test for a position if one does not thoroughly understand the requirements of the position.

Job Evaluation as a Basis for Candidate Recruitment

Job analysis results in a position description, which describes the tasks involved and the skills required to do them. The description provides the job information needed to prepare recruitment literature, such as brochures, pamphlets, booklets, and classified advertisements in the newspaper.[9] In addition, position classification groups similar jobs into uniform job categories and allows managers to announce and examine for large numbers of positions using one standard job title.

Job Evaluation as a Foundation for Performance Appraisal

Performance appraisals are used for various managerial functions, including salary administration, promotions, and counseling. The 1978 Civil Service Reform Act requires, for example, that every federal agency use performance appraisal as a basis for training, rewarding, reassigning, promoting, reducing in grade, retaining, and removing employees.[10] Objective, work-related performance appraisals are impossible without good job analysis and evaluation. Research reveals that performance evaluations are more valid and more readily accepted by employees when they are based on the actual tasks performed by the employees. Modern performance appraisal formats are moving away from the traditional, subjective trait-rating scales to more objective, job-related formats. This trend toward more objective, task-related performance appraisals demands thorough job evaluations. Also, if employees question the discriminatory impact of a performance appraisal, the courts are likely to conclude that the appraisal is invalid if it is not based on formal job analysis.[11]

Job Evaluation as a Basis for Training and Career Development

Before employees can be trained for a position, the trainer must know the tasks required by the position. A good job analysis can identify the most important skills. Moreover, a good system of job analysis and evaluation provides a framework for the organization and reveals how one position in it is related to others. This information can suggest career paths or ladders that an employee might pursue. Thus, job analysis information is vital not only for recruiting the proper employee for each job but also for providing the necessary training and experience that will allow the employee to make steady progress up the career ladder.

Job Evaluation and Collective Bargaining

Job evaluation can play a significant role in collective bargaining. Although job descriptions are useful for determining the appropriate bargaining unit, the more important role of the job evaluation or classifier in collective bargaining lies in classification grievance arbitration.[12] Unions may seek to define positions in ways that are beneficial to them but not to management. The job description for a supervisor, for example, can be significant in determinig whether supervisors are in the same bargaining unit as the rank-and-file employees. Since the inclusion of supervisors in the same bargaining unit poses serious problems for management, the job analyst and evaluator may be in a crucial position to assist management on such important issues.

Job Evaluation and Budgeting

Job evaluation provides the basic documentation of the numbers and types of positions, with attendant salaries, that will be required for each program. This information is essential for budget formulation. Moreover, the logical grouping of similar positions under meaningful job titles provides a common language for all who are concerned with budgeting—legislators, employees, administrators, and taxpayers.[13] Without clear titles and descriptions, some positions that require relatively routine work might receive comparatively high salaries because of elevated position titles.

The Location of Job Evaluation Authority

Because job evaluation and pay are so closely interwoven in the public sector, there are pressures to upgrade positions. These pressures are exacerbated by many governments' failure to provide adequate pay increases to their employees during recent years of severe inflation and tight budgets. When employees fail to receive pay increases, they may seek to elevate their pay by upgrading their positions. One such inflated position becomes a red flag to others who feel that they have a lower grade for work of equal or greater difficulty and responsibility, and they also may seek to have their positions upgraded.

Supervisors may have several reasons for seeking an inflated grade for a position. They may wish to reward a conscientious or efficient employee with a higher job classification, or they may attempt to keep a good employee from leaving by obtaining a higher grade for his or her position.[14] Supervisors may also believe that their own grade, status, and pay will be affected by the grades of their subordinates. Since a unit with an inflated grade structure gains a competitive advantage in recruiting and retaining employees over other units with a more conservative grade structure, supervisors have strong incentives to seek to upgrade positions in their units.[15]

These pressures to upgrade positions provide the primary argument for centralizing classification authority and operation in a central personnel office. The need for current and accurate job information, however, cautions against over-centralization of job evaluation. Central personnel offices are too far removed from the jobs to obtain current information. Also, central authorities may operate on assumptions of what jobs "should be," rather than on first-hand knowledge of what the jobs are.[16] Furthermore, large, centralized classification operations tend to be slow and unresponsive to operating needs.[17] These considerations suggest that a central personnel office should maintain adequate machinery for coordination and control but should delegate operating authority and the responsibility for job evaluation to lower units.

Whether the delegation of job evaluation authority should be to line managers or to subordinate personnel offices remains in dispute. Since managers often have the authority to commit money and other resources and the responsibility for overall program objectives, some say that managers should evaluate jobs, because such action is a natural extension of their management function. To support this view, examples are given of personnel offices that pursue job evaluation as an end in itself, without regard to the programs it is supposed to serve.[18]

Others, however, note that managers are often more concerned about their immediate programmatic needs and less interested in maintaining an integrated, rational job evaluation system.[19] Also, it is claimed that few managers have the time or interest to master the technical complexity of the job evaluation process. As a result of these concerns, the personnel office generally has central authority for job evaluation, although line managers should be actively involved in the process.

Fact Finding in Job Evaluation: Job Analysis

Job analysis is the fact-finding segment of job evaluation. Job analysis discovers and describes the tasks involved in a job and the employee behaviors that are necessary to perform those tasks.[20] This definition of job analysis suggests that it has two primary focuses: task requirements and worker requirements. Some of the more common fact-finding techniques or job analysis procedures for determining these requirements are interviews with supervisors, desk audits, and questionnaires.

Interviews with Supervisors

If supervisors know in detail what their subordinates do, interviews with the supervisors may yield useful information about the nature of the subordinates' jobs. In addition, protocol and maintenance of good relations between the personnel office and line managers demand that job analysts contact supervisors concerning evaluation of positions under their control. The analyst should prepare for the interview by reviewing all relevant job evaluation standards, existing job descriptions, and descriptions of organizational goals and objectives.[21]

An important difference between an employee interview and an interview with a supervisor is the analyst's opportunity to give management advice concerning the supervisor's unit.[22] Such advice can suggest the impact of various alternatives on the grade levels of positions and on the employees' morale. It might also include advice on job restructuring, excessive layering, work simplification, span of control, and fragmentation.[23] Such contact between the job analyst and the line manager gives the analyst an opportunity to temper the often-negative image line managers have of the personnel office. Close contact between job analysts and managers on a continuing basis—not just when there is a problem—can provide a base of mutual understanding and respect.[24]

Desk Audits

Because supervisors do not always know in detail what their suborinates are doing, and because courts generally require that a valid job evaluation program include actual observation of the work and information from the employee, desk audits are used to obtain more data about a specific position.

A desk audit is the most common form of job analysis in most public organizations. Essentially, it is an interview conducted at the work site or desk to determine the typical tasks and requirements of the job. The desk audit not only yields valuable information about the job, but it also allows the employee to feel involved in the process. The desk audit allows the job analyst to discuss all aspects of the job with the employee and to see examples of the employee's work. The relationship of the individual job to other jobs can also be explored during the desk audit. Job analysts should prepare for desk audits in the same manner they prepared for interviews with supervisor. Analysts should have training in interviewing techniques and should be able to ask appropriate questions without making the employees feel threatened or uneasy.

Desk audits cost considerable time and money. When employees are talking to the analyst, they are not doing their jobs. For this reason, such on-site interviews are often supplemented by questionnaires.

Questionnaires

When a large number of jobs must be analyzed, there may be insufficient money, time, and analysts to conduct desk audits. Questionnaires may be used in such situations if the job analyst has determined that the necessary information can be obtained from employees and supervisors in written form. Questionnaires cause problems, because they are difficult to develop and because ambiguities and misinterpretations can occur. If they are used only to supplement interviews, however, these problems can be reduced.

The format of the questionnaire should be as simple as possible and should be pretested on a group of employees to assure clarity. Advance meetings with groups of employees are necessary to explain the purpose of the questionnaire and to allay employee fears and promote acceptance of it.

Position Descriptions

Position descriptions traditionally contain information about task requirements and about minimal employee qualifications to perform the tasks. Position descriptions generally include a job title, job activities and procedures (tasks performed, interactions with other workers, nature of supervision given or received), working conditions (physical location, heat and noise level, hazardous conditions, and the like), and conditions of employment (hours, payment, fringe benefits, and so forth).[25] In addition, position descriptions often list the minimal employee skills, abilities, training, and education necessary to perform the tasks of the positions.

Job descriptions may be prepared by the employee, by the employee and the supervisor, by the supervisor alone, or by the job analyst.[26] The employee probably is more knowledgeable about the position than anyone else. Also, allowing the employee to contribute to the preparation of the description helps him or her feel involved. Although employees might not always be objective about their jobs, accuracy can be improved if the supervisor accepts the responsibility to review, clarify, and supplement the employee's description of the position.

Most job evaluation experts believe that supervisors should prepare position descriptions, because the activity is a natural extension of their responsibility to plan and assign work.[27] Moreover, supervisors who are involved with and actually write their subordinates' descriptions are more likely to be committed to the operation of the positions as they are described.

Since job analysts must review the position descriptions for technical accuracy, they probably should not write them.[28] Their formal reviewing position would be compromised if they also wrote the descriptions. In addition, if the personnel office devotes valuable time to writing descriptions, it will have less time for the more important task of analyzing and evaluating positions.

Donald Klingner has been critical of traditional job descriptions because they often fail to establish minimally acceptable performance standards for each of the employee's job tasks or duties.[29] Because of this deficiency, Klingner believes that much of the usefulness of position descriptions for the managerial purposes noted at the beginning of this chapter (recruitment, selection, training, performance evaluation, and pay administration) is lost. Klingner suggests that job descriptions should be more results-oriented and should state what the performance expectations are for the position in terms of work quantity, quality, and timeliness.[30]

Keeping job descriptions current and accurate is a persistent problem in most job evaluation systems. Changes in positions occur for numerous reasons. A series of minor changes may occur gradually, eventually culminating in a major change in the position. Also, as employees perform effectively, new tasks or more responsible assignments may be given to them. Conversely, employees who are ineffective may be given assignments of less and less difficulty until, in time, the jobs have changed dramatically. In addition, temporary tasks that are given to employees informally may become permanent merely by usage.[31]

Even when supervisors are aware that positions have changed, they may feel that they are too busy to revise the position descriptions. When changes occur very gradually, the supervisors may not even recognize that change has occurred. Supervisors are generally willing to report changes that may result in an upgrading, but they are reluctant to mention anything that might lower a grade. Classifiers and job analysts may spend much of their time responding to individual cases in which an employee and his or her supervisor are pressing for a reclassification to upgrade a position. The job evaluation office must be careful not to exhaust all its resources on such cases and ignore systematic survey reviews. Although most job evaluation offices do not have sufficient resources to conduct cyclic surveys every twelve to eighteen months, no technique can substitute for such surveys.[32]

The Evaluation System and External Pay Alignment

The compatibility of the job evaluation and pay structure with external pay alignment is a major concern in many evaluation systems. Job evaluation stresses that pay be based on the duties and responsibilities involved in a position. Market forces, however, stress that pay be based on supply and demand. If a shortage exists in an occupation, the organization must pay more to obtain employees for that position. In such cases, there is a temptation to inflate the classification of the position to warrant market wage rates. Such actions, however, distort and subvert the evaluation process. A preferable course is to use special pay rates for occupations that are in short supply, rather than prostituting the job evaluation system.

Classification Appeals

Employees may wish to appeal classification decisions, particularly when they result in downgrading of the employees' positions. The supervisor may also wish to appeal some decisions. A formal appeal process should allow employees and other interested parties adequate opportunity to state, orally and in writing, the facts as they see them. The decision in the appeal should be made by technically competent individuals who were not involved in the original decision. When job evaluation decisions result in downgrading of an employee's position, he or she is often allowed to keep the same salary until a position with a classification to match the employee's abilities and salary is vacant.

Methods of Job Evaluation

Job evaluation is the process of determining the value or rating of each position in relation to the other jobs in an organization.[33] The process begins with the job analyst, who develops job descriptions, and it includes a rating of the descriptions by some job evaluation method to determine the relative values of the jobs. The five main job evaluation methods are position classification, position ranking, rank-in-person, factor point, and factor comparison. McConomy and Ganschinietz provide the following definitions of the five methods:

> *Position Classification:* A method of comparing jobs on a "whole job" basis and grouping together into classes those jobs deemed sufficiently alike with respect to their duties and responsibilities and qualifications as to justify the same descriptive title, rates of pay and qualification requirements. The resultant classes are set forth in written class specifications which define and distinguish the various classes of positions.

Position Ranking: A method of comparing jobs on a "whole job" basis for the purpose of ranking such jobs in a hierarchy from highest to lowest. Usually the basis for ranking is unspecified but frequently includes consideration of organizational level of the position, perceived importance of the position to the organization's mission, personal status of the incumbent, etc.

Rank-in-Person: The method of establishing pay primarily on the basis of an employee's qualifications with less consideration, or none, given to the actual duties and responsibilities performed by the employee.

Factor Point: A quantitative method of evaluating jobs or groupings of jobs on a systematic basis using a predetermined number of factors which are divided into a number of defined levels or degrees, each of which is assigned a value expressed in points. The sum of all the points awarded to the job determines its relative value among the others being evaluated.

Factor Comparison: A method of evaluating jobs on a systematic basis by comparing key jobs with each other on a predetermined number of factors so that each key job is ranked in its relative order of importance on each factor. Factor values are determined by apportioning the current rate being paid for the job among the various factors. Rates for all other jobs are determined by comparison with the key jobs on each factor; the sum of the factor values awarded is the job rate.[34]

Position classification and factor comparison are the primary methods used by public jurisdictions. McConomy and Ganschinietz's 1981 survey of state governments reveals, for example, that most states use either position classification or the factor method for most positions (see table 3–1). Position ranking is used by a few states, and rank-in-person is used by only one state. Indeed, McConomy and Ganschinietz conclude that the rank-in-person system "appears to be extremely limited and almost 'extinct' in these states."[35]

The comparison of job evaluation practices in 1976 and 1981 indicates a dramatic movement toward more quantitative job evaluation methods, such as factor comparison. This shift may reflect the increased judicial pressure on public personnel management to show that job evaluation procedures and the other personnel functions (selection, performance appraisal, and compensation) that are based on job evaluations are actually related to job performance. According to the courts, this often requires increased quantification. An equally important reason for the shift to more quantitative procedures is that in the survey by McConomy and Ganschinietz, the factor method received higher employee acceptance ratings than any other method of evaluation.[36] Moreover, the federal government recently adopted the factor comparison method for classifying approximately 1.3 million white-collar jobs in the general schedule.[37] State and local governments may be following the example of the federal service.

Table 3–1
Utilization of Job Evaluation Methods

	1976		1981	
	N	%	N	%
States Using One Method for All Occupations				
Using position classification/position ranking	29	85	15	88
Using factor point/factor comparison	5	15	2	12
Using other evaluations methods	0	0	0	0
Total	34	100	17	100
States Using Different Methods for Different Occupations				
Executives:				
Position classification	0	0	11	42
Position ranking	3	25	7	27
Factor point/factor comparison	2	17	17	65
Rank-in-person	2	17	1	4
Managers				
Position classification	1	8	14	54
Position ranking	3	25	4	15
Factor point/factor comparison	2	17	17	65
Supervisors:				
Position classification	1	8	19	73
Position ranking	2	17	6	23
Factor point/factor comparison	1	8	14	54
Professionals:				
Position classification	1	8	18	69
Position ranking	0	0	6	23
Factor point/factor comparison	1	8	15	58
Rank-in-person	5	42	0	0
Technicians:				
Position classification	0	0	19	73
Position ranking	0	0	5	19
Factor point/factor comparison	0	0	14	54
Clericals:				
Position classification	1	8	18	69
Position ranking	0	0	4	15
Factor point/factor comparison	3	25	15	58
Labor, Trades and Services				
Position classification	1	8	20	77
Position ranking	0	0	4	15
Factor point/factor comparison	3	25	12	46
Total	12	100	26	100

Source: Steven McConomy and Bill Ganschinietz, "Trends in Job Evaluation Practices of State Personnel Systems: 1981 Survey Findings," *Public Personnel Management* 12 (Spring 1983):5. Reprinted with permission.

Note: Percentages do not always sum to 100 due to states using more than one method.

The Position Ranking Method of Job Evaluation

In the position ranking method, a committee—typically composed of supervisors, department heads, and employee representatives—ranks all jobs in the organization on the basis of their overall worth and importance to the organization.[38] No attempt is made to break the positions into specific parts. Evaluators compare one job to another and determine which is more important or difficult. This is done until each job has been compared to all others. The method is simple, easily understood and easy to install, but problems occur with its use. According to Cascio: "Rankings are often based on the employees performing the job rather than on the job itself, and the evaluations are completely subjective for there are no definite or consistent standards to justify the rankings."[39] In addition, this method reveals only that one job is ranked higher than another, without indicating the distance between the ranks. Finally, the process is impossible to administer for a great number of jobs, because no one is sufficiently familiar with all the jobs to evaluate them.[40]

The History of Position Classification

Although the factor method of job evaluation is becoming more common, position classification remains the dominant job evaluation method—and it is the oldest. The origins of modern position classification techniques date back to the turn of the century.[41] The major impetus for classification was the inequitable distribution of pay and duties to public employees.[42] The federal government first considered establishment of a modern position classification program in 1902 when the Civil Service Commission urged that positions be classified according to the duties performed and that uniform compensation be given for equal duties.[43] The Congress, however, was reluctant to move toward a comprehensive position classification plan. Little progress was made until 1919, when Congress created a special commission to study inequities in salaries in the federal service.[44] The result of this commission's recommendations was the Classification Act of 1923, which established the federal position classification system and the Personnel Classification Board to administer it. The board was abolished in 1932, and its powers were transferred to the Civil Service Commission. Because of lack of uniformity between classification procedures in Washington and in the field service, and as a result of other problems, the Classification Act of 1949 was adopted. Under this act, the Civil Service Commission had authority over all position classification proceedings. Although the commission was empowered to establish and enforce job evaluation standards, the departments actually classified individual positions.[45] Few significant changes occurred in federal position classification until the 1970s.

Congressional dissatisfaction with the ability of position classification to facilitate management goals led to the Job Evaluation Policy Act of 1970.[46] This act resulted in the formulation of the Job Evaluation and Pay Review Task Force, which found that the various uncoordinated job evaluation and pay systems produced serious inconsistencies and inequities in pay and in other personnel practices for federal employees. Furthermore, it found that line managers were not involved in the job evaluation process, nor was job evaluation being used as a management tool.[47] The problems noted by the task force's report led to the development of the factor method of job evaluation and classification in the federal service.

The Process of Position Classification

The first step in position classification is to decide which factors will be used to allocate positions to different classes and grades. Although there is no uniform agreement about which factors should be used, some common ones are (1) difficulty and complexity of duties, (2) nonsupervisory responsibilities, (3) supervisory and administrative responsibilities, and (4) qualification requirements.[48]

After allocation factors have been established, a position classification questionnaire is developed to solicit information about the allocation factors from the occupants of the various positions in the organization. The completed questionnaires are reviewed by the employees' supervisors and returned to the job classifier, who also reviews the questionnaires and then decides how many desk audits are necessary to clarify and amplify the information in them. Although there is no standard number or percentage of positions that should be audited, an audit should occur when there is disagreement among several occupants of the same position concerning the description of the position, or when the employee's and the supervisor's descriptions of the position conflict, or when there is incomplete or unclear information on the questionnaire.

After the classifier has acceptable descriptions of each position in terms of the basic allocation factors, he first groups positions into the same kind of work. For example, all engineers—civil, mechanical, electrical, and so forth—might be grouped into the occupational group of engineers. Next, the positions in a similar occupation are grouped into classes. A controversial problem at this stage is whether these classes should be broad or narrow. Narrow classes are useful if the basic purpose of the classification plan is to define specific salary differences among positions. Also, if the plan is to be used to recruit individuals with highly specialized knowledge and skills, and if little training is to be given to the new employees, narrow, specific classes may be necessary.

If the classification plan is to provide for the recruitment and selection of individuals with general abilities and talents, however, and if the recruits are to receive extensive on-the-job training, broad classes may be appropriate. Broad classes mean fewer classes and fewer examinations. Since the tests will be less job-specific and more difficult to validate, however, they will be subject to greater judicial scrutiny and objection, particularly if they tend to exclude minorities. If selection and judicial concerns were not issues, management would prefer broad classes, because they allow flexibility of assignment and more opportunities to use fully the skills and abilities of each employee.[49] Too often, employees in narrow classes are pigeonholed into a narrowly defined class and must forgo further advancement or try to enter a different class.

After the breadth of a class is defined, class specifications are prepared, including (1) the job title, (2) a description of the work in terms of the basic allocation factors, (3) examples of the work, and (4) requirements of the work (knowledge, abilities, and skills). Great care must be taken to assure that education and experience are really needed to perform the tasks in a class. Some occupations and professions seek such requirements only as a method of excluding others from competition for positions. The classifier must be careful, therefore, that demands for educational requirements are indeed related to successful performance. If the classifier is unsure, such requirements should be stated as "desirable," not "minimum" requirements.

The Factor Method of Job Evaluation

Although, technically, the factor point and factor comparison methods are two separate approaches to job evaluation, elements of each are used in the federal government's factor ranking system.[50] For purposes of this discussion, a review of the steps in the factor ranking system provides sufficient insight into the factor approach to job evaluation:

1. The occupations and positions to be covered by the plan are determined.
2. The factors most appropriate for measuring the positions are selected. Factors are yardsticks used to determine the value of a position. The federal government uses the following nine factors:
   a. The knowledge, skills, and abilities required by the position;
   b. The amount of supervision required by the position;
   c. The nature of the guidelines affecting a position and the judgment needed to apply these guidelines;
   d. The complexity of the task and the difficulty in deciding what needs to be done and how it should be done;
   e. The scope and effect of the activities involved in the position;
   f. The number of personal, face-to-face contacts with people who are not in the formal chain of command;
   g. The nature of contacts (that is, factual information exchanges versus contacts involving controversial issues and differences of opinions);
   h. The physical demands of the tasks;
   i. The nature of the work environment.[51]

3. Key jobs are selected for evaluation. Key jobs are those that can be readily understood and easily described and are not controversial in terms of their pay level.

4. The key jobs are first ranked as a whole by experienced managers who are familiar with a broad range of positions and programs. Although personnel office officials can assist the managers in ranking the jobs, they may have a vested interest in the existing job evaluation system and may therefore be inappropriate as the key evaluators in a new system. Using experienced line managers as raters also helps assure acceptance of the system.

5. After the key jobs have been ranked as a whole, the ranking of each job is compared to the external pay level for such positions. If a considerable discrepancy exists between the ranking given to a job and the pay for that position, more analysis is necessary. For example, if Job A is ranked considerably higher than Job B but the pay level for Job B is considerable higher than that for Job A, additional analysis is necessary. If additional analysis does not eliminate the discrepancy, a separate pay schedule for the deviant positions may be appropriate.

6. Each job is ranked on each factor. This ranking will produce lists of key jobs ranked from top to bottom on each factor.

7. A guide chart that contains a narrative description of each degree or level of each factor and the point value assigned to that degree is prepared. When jobs are ranked on each factor in step 6, natural clusters of positions tend to occur. One factor may have five clusters, while another may have only three clusters. The number of clusters determines the number of levels or degrees of difficulty. The position descriptions for the key jobs in each cluster of each factor are used to write narrative descriptions of each degree or level of each factor.

8. A weight is determined for each factor in each job. For example, if one job has four factors, the first factor might be weighted at 35 percent, the second at 30 percent, the third at 20 percent, and the fourth at 15 percent.

9. Point values are attached to each degree of difficulty, as determined in step 7.

10. Total point values for each job can be obtained by combining the weight of each factor found in a position and the point value attached to the degree of difficulty for that factor in the particular job. If this total point value correlates with the whole-job ranking of that position (as noted in step 4) the guide chart is probably acceptable.

11. The number of skill levels or grades in the system is determined by the whole-job ranking process of step 4. This process produces a clustering of positions and each cluster or group becomes a grade level.

12. The grade levels are converted into point ranges by examining the total point values (see steps 9 and 10) for all positions within the grade.

As the factors of each additional job are compared to the factors of the key jobs, that job becomes another benchmark for the evaluation of the next job. Eventually, all positions in the organization are, in effect, compared to each other. Each job is allocated a place in the classification and pay plan because it was found to rank higher than, lower than, or equal to other positions in the organization.

The factor classification plan should be reviewed periodically. Suskin suggests that at least 10 percent of all positions should be randomly selected, audited, and evaluated according to the factors.[52] If few changes are required, the system may be considered to be functioning effectively. If extensive changes are required, a detailed analysis is necessary.

The Rank-in-Person Method of Job Evaluation

Technically, the rank-in-person method is not a job evaluation method because it does not attempt to measure the job. As the name implies, it evaluates the person, or the occupant of the position, and it is used primarily for professionals. A rank-in-person system is a closed career system into which individuals are recruited for entry-level positions on the basis of their broad competence and potential for advancement in the organization. There is less emphasis on specialized training and skills for a particular job. Moreover, employees may be assigned to a variety of positions without regard to the power and status of the position. Rank and status are in the person, not in the job. Furthermore, promotions come from within the system.[53]

One of the best examples of a rank-in-person system is the Foreign Service of the U.S. State Department. A recent attempt to create such a system is the Senior Executive Service (SES), which was created by the 1978 Civil Service Reform Act. The SES contains more than 8,000 high-level managers who acquire rank and pay not as a result of a particular job classification, but as a result of their qualifications and experience. It was hoped that the Senior Executive Service would become a core of top, neutral, professional, mobile managers who would be generalists capable of moving from one department to another while practicing effective management.[54] Recent evidence indicates, however, that the SES in not performing as intended. Although it allows for greater flexibility in the use of career executives by placing greater emphasis on generalist skills, the realities of federal programs are such that specialization provides greater promise for advancement.[55]

The Impact of Unions on Job Evaluation

In most public jurisdictions, job evaluation and classification have remained in the hands of management. Unions have been concerned primarily with pay, and most public officials oppose collective bargaining about evaluation standards and classification plans. Of course, job analysts and classifiers oppose such bargaining because they view evaluation and classification as technical skills that should not be subject to the political pressures of the bargaining table.

At the federal level (excluding the Postal Service), job evaluation procedures are covered in detail by statute and regulations and are outside the scope of collective bargaining. Under the Civil Service Reform Act of 1978, collective bargaining may not cover job evaluation and classification for both blue-collar and white-collar employees. Job evaluation is subject to negotiation in the Postal Service, but collective bargaining has not resulted in any significant changes in job evaluation plans there.[56] Although most state and local laws do not permit bargaining on position classification, a few jurisdictions do provide for such negotiations. Others treat job evaluation as a function of management but provide for some union/employee involvement and review in the evaluation process.[57]

Although unions have not been enthusiastic about changing job evaluation systems, their interest in and impact on pay may have a dramatic effect on job evaluation and classification. When a jurisdiction has a job evaluation and classification plan that includes employees in several bargaining units, pay negotiations could seriously affect the classification plan. Within each bargaining unit, the union may be as interested as management in a good job evaluation system, with equal pay for equal work. The union may care little, however, about equal pay for equal work *among* the bargaining units. In fact, unions may compete with other unions to provide higher wages for their members. In the face of such competition, it is very difficult to maintain a unified and consistent job evaluation system across several bargaining units.

The increase in the unions' concern for individual classification cases and the increase in arbitration in this area may foretell greater union interest in the future in job evaluation and classification.

Comparisons of Position Classification and Factor Ranking

Position classification remains the most common method of job evaluation. It has the longest history, and jurisdictions often prefer to continue using what they have always used. It also requires the least time to install and can be implemented with less technical background.[58] Along with these advantages, however, come several disadvantages. Classification decisions under position classification are very subjective and the quality of the decision depends heavily on the skill and judgment of the classifier. A typical classifier may need years to acquire the skills needed to make valid judgments. The subjective nature of the process thus results in decisions that are not easily justifiable and convincing to employees, supervisors, and the courts. Position classification is often said to be too rigid and too restrictive of managerial prerogatives, because it does not allow supervisors sufficient discretion in classifying their subordinates. This criticism may be unfair, in that the real problem is the rate of pay, not the classification. Unfortunately, significant increases in pay in the public sector often depend on reclassification. This problem becomes more severe during periods of rapid inflation or tight budgets. Too often, the only way to reward an efficient employee is to reclassify his or her position, even though the employee's duties have not changed. The real problems are inadequate pay increases, invalid performance appraisals, and a failure to link pay and performance. Position classification is often the scapegoat for these endemic problems. Nevertheless, a concern about the problems of position classification has resulted in greater use of the factor evaluation method.[59]

Factor evaluation is becoming popular for several reasons. Although it takes more time to develop and is more expensive to install, once established, it can be applied by trained staff with less extensive classification experience. This method requires less training time for classifiers.[60] Both position classification and factor evaluation are subjective, but the classification decision in position classification rests on *one* comprehensive decision, whereas the classification decision in factor evaluation rests on *many* subjective decisions on a number of different factors. Errors tend to offset one another, and thus the eventual classification decision may be more valid.[61]

Although fear of the unknown and the high cost of installation may generate resistance, once factor evaluation is understood, acceptance appears high, particularly among lower-paid employees.[62] Attitude surveys conducted as part of the federal government's efforts to initiate a factor ranking system revealed a higher degree of acceptability than that obtained by the position classification method.[63] McConomy and Ganschinietz also found that the factor method was accepted well by employees in all the states that used it.[64]

Mechanistic versus Organic Organizations and Job Evaluation

Jay Shafritz's "behavioral critique" of traditional position classification notes its failure to adjust to changing conditions in the "postbureaucratic era."[65] Shafritz believes that position classification is too rigid and too closely tied to the reform and scientific management movements, which supported its birth and growth. As a result, he argues, position classification is overly concerned with control and accountability and is therefore less able to respond to recent changes in the composition of the public service.[66]

Organic organizations are becoming more common, and the environments of these organizations are more turbulent and uncertain. Since this turbulence places a premium on the organization's capacity to adapt quickly and to take risks, roles in such organizations are often flexible and based on the needs of the situation. Such roles are often filled by professional employees who have considerable tolerance for the ambiguity and complexity inherent in their roles.

Shafritz notes that over one-third of all government employees fall into the administrative, professional, and technical (APT) category.[67] According to Shafritz, position classification has been least successful, in dealing with these organic (APT) positions. These jobs require flexibility and a broad definition of roles, but position classification produces rigidity and a narrow specification of roles. In addition, the impact of the incumbent is most significant in the APT position, yet position classification concentrates on the position, not on the incumbent.

Job enrichment is one approach used in organic organizations to improve employee morale, increase productivity, and enable the organization to respond better to its environment. Job enrichment is done in a variety of ways, including increasing the employee's autonomy, increasing the variety of skills used or activities performed, giving the employee the opportunity to perform all aspects of a task rather than just part of it, allowing the employee to participate in management decisions, or increasing feedback about job performance.[68]

In one study, Lawler found that job enrichment improved the quality of the workers' performance and sometimes improved productivity.[69] In another study of ten cases, Lawler concluded that job enrichment improved employee satisfaction in every case.[70] More recent surveys of the job enrichment efforts of state and local governments reveal consistent improvements in job satisfaction.[71] When workers are more satisfied with their jobs, absenteeism and turnover are reduced.

Despite the benefits of job enrichment efforts, particularly for organic organizations, position classification may obstruct such efforts. Position classification often prevents a broad definition of duties and an assumption of new skills and tasks. It also limits the ability to change roles quickly. In short, the specificity and rigidity inherent in position classification are prime obstacles to the successful implementation of job enrichment.

In contrast, mechanistic organizations have calm, stable, and predictable environments. Tasks in such organizations tend to be routine and repetitive, and few APT personnel are needed. Shafritz refers to such mechanistic positions as "service positions," and he suggests that position classification performs a positive service for such positions.[72] These positions require little skill, and the incumbent has little impact on the position. Therefore, position classification can be successful in describing these routine positions and can establish easily understandable benchmark classifications.[73] In addition, these positions do not change often, and the problem of keeping the position description current is less severe.

The rank-in-person system may be more appropriate for APT positions and organic organizations. This system, which emphasizes the person, not the position, assures recognition of the incumbent's impact on any position. It allows the individual to change roles, assume additional duties, and discard others without necessitating extensive changes in the classification plan. It thus allows greater mobility for employees to go where they are most needed.

The rank-in-person approach is not without serious problems, however. Mosher has noted that, in the short run, a rank-in-person system can adapt to certain kinds of changes through quick reassignments and transfers. If sudden needs require completely different kinds of skills, however, the rank-in-person system has trouble adjusting, because it discourages lateral entry.[74] The supply of professionals within the system at any given time is largely determined by who entered the pipeline years before.

Conclusion

Although job analysis and job evaluation demand considerable technical skill and expertise, they should not be viewed as isolated subfields governed by technicians. If job evaluation systems are to serve larger managerial needs, they must complement the organization's environment, structure, technology, and employee characteristics. Furthermore, line managers must be involved in determining the goals and purposes of job evaluation systems. No approach is best for all situations, and selection of the appropriate system demands the attention of top managers. Only in this way can job evaluation be beneficial to the organization.

Notes

1. Robert J. McCarthy and John Buck, "The Meaning of Job Evaluation," In Harold Suskin, ed., *Job Evaluation and Pay Administration in the Public Sector* (Chicago: International Personnel Management Association, 1977), p. 11.

2. Ibid., p. 16.

3. For a discussion of the crucial importance of job analysis in management, see Jai Ghorpade and Thomas J. Atchison, "The Concept of Job Analysis: A Review and Some Suggestions," *Public Personnel Management* 9 (1980): 134–144.

4. Much of this section is based on Robert D. Parsons and Harold Suskin, "Job Evaluation as a Management Tool," in Harold Suskin, ed., *Job Evaluation and Pay Administration in the Public Sector* (Chicago: International Personnel Management Association, 1977), pp. 175–189.

5. *The Equal Pay Act of 1963*, P.L. 88, 77 Stat. 56, 29 U.S.C. Section 206 (1976).

6. *The Civil Rights Act of 1964*, P.L. 88–352, 78 Stat. 241, 28 U.S.C. Section 1447 (1976).

7. The issue of comparable worth is discussed in greater detail in chapter 7. Also see Mary H. Doherty and Ann Harriman, "Comparable Worth: The Equal Employment Issue of the 1980s," *Review of Public Personnel Administration* 1 (Summer 1981): 11–31; and Steven M. Neuse, "A Critical Perspective on the Comparable Worth Debate" *Review of Public Personnel Administration* 3 (Fall 1982): 1–20.

8. See D.J. Treiman, *Job Evaluation: An Analytic Review* (Washington, D.C: National Academy of Sciences, 1979).

9. Parsons and Suskin, "Job Evaluation as a Management Tool," p. 180.

10. Duane Thompson, "Performance Appraisal and the Civil Service Reform Act," *Public Personnel Management* 10 (Fall 1981): 281–288.

11. Hubert S. Field and W.H. Holley, "The Relationship of Performance Appraisal System Characteristics to Verdicts in Selected Employment Discrimination Cases," *Academy of Management Journal* 25 (1982): 392–406. Also see Wayne Cascio and H.J. Bernardin, "Implications of Performance Appraisal Litigation for Personnel Decisions," *Personnel Psychology* 34 (1981): 211–226.

12. Parsons and Suskin, "Job Evaluation as a Management Tool," p. 182.

13. Esther C. Lawton and Harold Suskin, *Elements of Position Classification in Local Government* (Chicago: International Personnel Management Association, 1976).

14. Esther C. Lawton, "Job Evaluation Principles and Problems," in Harold Suskin, ed., *Job Evaluation and Pay Administration in the Public Sector* (Chicago: International Personnel Management Association, 1977), pp. 36–37.

15. H. Alan McKean, "Administering a Job Evaluation Program," in Harold Suskin, ed., *Job Evaluation and Pay Administration in the Public Sector* (Chicago: International Personnel Management Association, 1977), pp. 208–209.

16. Ibid.

17. Ibid.

18. Ibid., p. 210.

19. Ibid., pp. 210–211.

20. Wayne Cascio, *Applied Psychology in Personnel Management* (Reston, Va.: Reston, 1978), p. 132.

21. McCarthy and Buck, "Meaning of Job Evaluation," p. 68.

22. Ibid., p. 72.

23. Ibid.

24. McKean, "Administering a Job Evaluation Program," p. 214.

25. Cascio, *Applied Psychology in Personnel Management*, pp. 135–136.

26. Robert J. McCarthy and John Buck, "Job Analysis," in Harold Suskin, ed., *Job Evaluation and Pay Administration in the Public Sector* (Chicago: International Personnel Management Association, 1977), p. 74.

27. Ibid., p. 75.

28. Ibid.

29. Donald Klingner, "When the Traditional Job Description Is Not Enough," *Personnel Journal* 58 (April 1979): 243–248.

30. Ibid.

31. McKean, "Administering a Job Evaluation Program," P. 199.

32. Ibid., pp. 199–201.

33. McCarthy and Buck, "Meaning of Job Evaluation," p. 16.

34. Steven McConomy and Bill Ganschinietz, "Trends in Job Evaluation Practices of State Personnel Systems: 1981 Survey Findings," *Public Personnel Management* 12 (Spring 1983): 1–12. For an earlier survey, see Gary Craver, "Job Evaluation Practices in State and County Governments," in Harold Suskin, ed., *Job Evaluation and Pay Administration in the Public Sector* (Chicago: International Personnel Management Association, 1977), pp. 427–441.

35. McConomy and Ganschinietz, "Trends in Job Evaluation Practices," p. 9.

36. Ibid., p. 12.

37. For a discussion of the implementation of the factor method in the federal service, see Lawrence L. Epperson, "The Dynamics of Factor Comparison/Point Evaluation," *Public Personnel Management* 4 (January/February 1975): 38–48.

38. Cascio, *Applied Psychology of Personnel Management*, p. 149.

39. Ibid.

40. Ibid.

41. For a discussion of the history of position classification, see Jay M. Shafritz, *Position Classification: A Behavioral Analysis for the Public Service* (New York: Praeger, 1973), pp. 13–22.

42. Paul P. Van Riper, *History of the United States Civil Service: 1789–1957* (Evanston, Ill.: Row, Peterson, 1958), pp. 557–558.

43. Ismar Baruck, *Position Classification in the Public Service* (Chicago: Civil Service Assembly of the U.S. and Canada, 1941), p. 16.

44. Shafritz, *Position Classification*, p. 16.

45. Ibid., p. 20.

46. Ibid., p. 21.

47. U.S. Congress, House Committee on Post Office and Civil Service, Subcommittee on Employee Benefits, *Report of the Job Evaluation and Pay Review Task Force to the U.S. Civil Service Commission*, 22d Cong., 2d Session, January 12, 1972, p. 7.

48. Merrill J. Collett, "The Position Classification Method of Job Evaluation," in Harold Suskin, ed., *Job Evaluation and Pay Administration in the Public Sector* (Chicago: International Personnel Management Association, 1977), pp. 130–174.

49. Ibid., p. 101.

50. Much of this discussion is based on Harold Suskin, "The Factor Ranking System," in Harold Suskin, ed., *Job Evaluation and Pay Administration in the Public Sector* (Chicago: International Personnel Management Association, 1977), pp. 130–174.

51. Ibid., pp. 137–138.

52. Ibid., pp. 160–161.

53. Harold H. Leich, "Rank in Man or Job? Both!" *Public Administration Review* 10 (Spring 1960): 92.

54. Norton Long, "The SES and the Public Interest," *Public Administration Review* 41 (May-June 1981): 305.

55. Peter Ring and James Perry, "Reforming the Upper Levels of the Bureaucracy: A Longitudinal Study of the Senior Executive Service," *Administration and Society* 15 (May 1983): 138.

56. Anthony F. Ingrassia and Charles Feigenbaum, "The Union Impact on Job Evaluation and Pay Administration," in Harold Suskin, ed., *Job Evaluation and Pay Administration in the Public Sector* (Chicago: International Personnel Management Association, 1977), p. 531.

57. Ibid., pp. 532–533.

58. U.S. Office of Personnel Management (OPM), *Position Classification: A Guide for City and County Managers* (Washington, D.C.: U.S. Government Printing Office, November 1979), pp. 6–7.

59. McConomy and Ganschinietz, "Trends in Job Evaluation Practices," p.4.

60. OPM, *Position Classification*, pp. 6–7.

61. Suskin, "Factor Ranking System," p. 171.

62. OPM, *Position Classification*, p.6–7.

63. Suskin, "Factor Ranking System," p. 171.
64. McConomy and Ganschinietz, "Trends in Job Evaluation Practices," p. 7.
65. Shafritz, *Position Classification*, pp. 74–82.
66. Ibid.
67. Ibid., p.77.
68. John M. Greiner and others, *Productivity and Motivation: A Review of State and Local Government Initiatives* (Washington, D.C.: Urban Institute Press, 1981), p. 8.
69. Edward Lawler, "Worker Satisfaction, Job Design and Job Performance," *Good Government* 89 (Summer 1972): 12–18.
70. Edward Lawler, "Job Design and Employee Motivation," *Personnel Psychology* 22 (Winter 1969): 426–435.
71. Greiner and others *Productivity and Motivation*, p. 343.
72. Shafritz, *Position Classification*, p. 77.
73. Ibid.
74. Frederick C. Mosher, *Democracy and the Public Service* (London: Oxford University Press, 1968), p. 151.

4

Recruitment and Selection

Key Words

Human resource planning

Reliability

Validity

Criterion-related validity

Content validity

Construct validity

Adverse impact

Griggs v. Duke Power Company

Uniform guidelines

Four-fifths rule

Connecticut v. Teal

Residency requirement

Aptitude tests

Assessment centers

In-basket test

Eligibility list

Veterans preference

Rule of three

Realistic job previews

Probationary period

Promotion from within

Lateral entry

Introduction

Chapters 1 and 2 introduced three performance criteria that have influenced the organization and operation of public bureaucracies. These criteria—effectiveness, liberalism, and responsiveness—are evident in different expectations concerning the goals and procedures for the recruitment and selection of public employees. The effectiveness criterion stresses merit in the selection of employees. In theory, merit selection procedures should assure that the most competent applicants get the jobs. The liberalism criterion emphasizes that similar people in similar circumstances should be treated equally. According to this criterion, tests and other selection procedures should assure equality of treatment and should prevent favoritism in the selection of employees. These goals are also part of the merit concept.

In contrast to the liberalism and effectiveness criteria, the responsiveness criterion stresses that the bureaucracy should be responsive to and representative of citizens. This criterion emphasizes affirmative action, and it suggests selection procedures that assure the representation of minorities and women in public bureaucracies. In theory, these minorities and women in the bureaucracies are more concerned about minority and female clients; therefore, the bureaucracies are more responsive and representative.

The responsiveness criterion can also be seen in patronage and spoils systems. Under patronage, the recruitment process is heavily influenced by partisan politics; a job applicant's political affiliation is more important than his or her professional qualifications. Patronage systems place a premium on loyalty to the winning party. In theory, such loyalty assures that the bureaucracy is responsive to political executives and to the citizens who elected them.

The three criteria of responsiveness, liberalism, and effectiveness produce considerable controversy concerning recruitment goals and procedures in the public sector. Regardless of the procedures a public agency pursues, some elements of the community are likely to be dissatisfied.

Recruitment becomes even more controversial as a result of the various purposes of public employment. One obvious function of public employment is to produce products or a service. When this purpose is primary, merit procedures may be dominant, because they seek to assure that the applicant who is best able to produce the products or services is selected. When the private economy is weak and private-sector unemployment is high, government is often expected to be the employer of last resort. During such times, the primary purpose of government employment is not to accomplish a service or produce a product but to employ the unemployed. Similarly, government employment has been used to provide a form of retirement to veterans. When such purposes are primary, merit is compromised.

As government has employed an ever-increasing percentage of the workforce, the conflicting purposes and criteria of government employment and recruitment have become more apparent. If only a few were employed by government, little controversy would surround recruitment; however, since one out of six workers is employed by government today, controversy is high because the stakes are high.

This chapter examines the controversial and important personnel function of recruitment and selection, beginning with a discussion of the major problems in human resource planning. When organizations have used human resource planning to determine the types of personnel they need, they must use various selection instruments to find the right employees. The advantages and disadvantages of instruments—including biographical data, tests, references, interviews, and assessment centers—are reviewed here. Also, the concepts of the reliability and validity of the instruments are explained. If such instruments do not have validity, they might discriminate against some candidates. Discrimination in selection and its adverse impact are defined and discussed.

As with selection of new employees, promotion of present employees presents many problems. The major problems concerning promotions are noted, and the relationship of promotions to other personnel functions is reviewed. The chapter concludes with a discussion of the differences in recruitment, selection, and promotion criteria for organic and mechanistic positions.

Human Resource Planning

Human resource planning forecasts the types of skills and people needed by the organization, and it predicts the availability and sources of such skills and people. Good planning allows the organization to adjust to changes in technology and labor markets.[1] The human resource planning process involves several steps.

First, the organization must link future program goals to the demand for personnel. Public organizations are often unable to predict future goals, however, because enabling legislation often does not contain a clear statement of goals and because future program priorities are heavily dependent upon the changing preferences of legislators, citizens, and clients. Because of these restraints, public organizations may find it difficult to plan for long-term personnel needs. Planners may be able to offer only a rough prediction of future program goals by analyzing predicted changes in demographic and social statistics that could affect the demands on the public agency.

Assuming that future program goals are known, planners must estimate the number and types of personnel needed to achieve the goals. In addition, planners must predict the probable future budget allocations to the organization, because the number of personnel depends on the size of future budgets. Once the planners have decided on the number and types of personnel needed, they must determine which of these needs can be met by personnel who are already in the organization.

Forecasting Internal Supply

A skills inventory is an essential ingredient in projecting the supply of labor within the organization. A skills inventory provides up-to-date information concerning the qualifications of personnel.[2] When this inventory is compared to the forecast for needed personnel, planners can determine what skills must be developed from present personnel via training and what personnel must be recruited from outside the organization.[3]

One key to predicting future internal personnel supply is predicted turnover rates: the number and types of employees who leave the organization as a result of voluntary retirement, medical or disability retirement, resignation, or death.[4] If the organization is stable, historical averages of turnover for various personnel categories may be useful.

Forecasting External Supply

Public organizations must fill many positions with new employees. Therefore, personnel specialists must be able to predict the availability of personnel outside the organization. A number of factors affect the public organization's ability to attract personnel, including economic conditions, population shifts, and the general image of government employment. During periods of recession and high unemployment, personnel are readily available, except in a few specialized fields. Conversely, during periods of high employment, public agencies have more difficulty attracting the most talented personnel. Population shifts also affect the general availability of labor. In the last twenty years there has been a dramatic increase in the labor force with the entry of the "baby boom" generation and more women. By 1990, however, the labor force will decline, and employers may find it increasingly difficult to find new personnel.

The general image of the government and public employment also affects public organizations. If the image is positive and attractive, the public organization can more easily attract good recruits. If the image deteriorates—particularly if it does so during periods of low unemployment—the public organization may experience more pronounced problems in recruiting the best personnel. The image of government employment in the United States has generally been negative in comparison to the image of private employment. This is particularly true in the better-educated, higher-income segment of the population.[5] Because of this negative image, governments have difficulty attracting more highly educated professionals, such as doctors, accountants, computer scientists, and engineers.

Recruitment

The primary goal of recruitment is to provide a sufficiently large pool of candidates from which to select qualified employees. Traditionally, recruitment has been a rather simple task in government. Civil service rules generally required that job openings be announced for some period in advance of testing for the positions. Recruitment often consisted of no more than formal posting or announcement of the position. As government employment increased dramatically during the 1960s, and as more professionals were recruited, governments found it more and more important to engage in active recruitment of applicants. Also, affirmative action required more active recruitment procedures, because governments could not rely on announcements of openings to produce a sufficient number of qualified minority applicants.

More active recruitment involves a variety of attempts to publicize job vacancies. For example, recruiters may go to college campuses in search of such professionals as engineers, accountants, and nurses. Position announcements may be placed in professional journals to elicit more applicants. Similarly, recruiters may make special efforts to attract more minority applicants. Announcements may be placed in media that minorities are more likely to use, and recruiters may go directly to minority high schools in an effort to attract more minority applicants.

The high unemployment in recent years has resulted, however, in numerous applicants for government's blue-collar and clerical jobs. Such jobs tend to offer more security and pay than similar jobs in the private sector. In addition, applicants for such jobs, who usually have little education, have a more positive image of government employment. Therefore, governments generally have few problems attracting a sufficient number of qualified applicants for such positions. This may explain why government recruitment continues to be relatively haphazard when compared to recruitment by private corporations. Most government employment expenditures continue to be in testing and selecting applicants rather than in recruiting and attracting applicants.

Selection Instruments

The selection process attempts to provide an informed estimate or prediction of which applicants have the greatest likelihood of performing their jobs successfully. Selection instruments or devices include (1) biographical data or minimum qualification requirements, (2) references and background information, (3) tests, (4) interviews, and (5) assessment centers. Each instrument has both advantages and disadvantages and different positions require different selection instruments. The combination of instruments selected for a particular position should include those that best measure the various qualifications demanded by the position. These qualifications are known only after a thorough job analysis has been conducted, as described in chapter 3. Every instrument should be both reliable and valid, and the extent to which the instruments accurately predict the applicant's capacity to do the job determines their reliability and validity.

Reliability

A selection instrument's reliability is the consistency with which it produces the same score throughout a series of measurements: that is a test given to the same person at different times should yield similar scores. One method of determining the reliability of a test is to administer it to a group of persons at two different times and compare the scores for consistency. Another method of determining reliability is to compare scores on all odd-numbered questions to scores on all even numbered questions. If the test is reliable, the scores on the two halves should be similar.

Validity

The validity of a selection instrument is the degree to which it measures what it is intended to measure. A valid selection instrument is one that accurately predicts job success. The three basic types of validity are as follows:

1. Criterion-related validity, including
   a. Concurrent validity
   b. Predictive validity
2. Content validity
3. Construct validity

Criterion-Related Validity. Criterion-related validity refers to the correlation of scores on the selection instruments with quantitative measurements of actual job performance. Concurrent validity is determined by comparing the scores on selection instruments of a group of *present* employees with some measure of their job performance, including quantity and quality of work performance, attendance, and supervisors' ratings. Concurrent validity has several internal weaknesses. Primarily, current employees are not a truly representative sample of all applicants for the position. Current employees have passed a probationary and training period, and unsatisfactory employees have already resigned or have been removed. Therefore, current employees will score higher on a test than untrained applicants, and the employees' scores will not vary as much as the scores of applicants. This narrow range of scores makes it more difficult to obtain meaningful correlations between employees' scores on the instruments and their job performance scores.

Predictive validity addresses the weaknesses of concurrent validity by comparing the scores of applicants on selection instruments with their subsequent job performance scores. If applicants who have high scores on selection instruments are hired and later perform their jobs successfully, one can assume that the selection instruments are valid. A major problem with both concurrent and predictive validity is that the measures of job performance that are used to validate selection instruments may be invalid. For example, supervisors may vary greatly in the evaluations they give of the same performance. Therefore, if supervisory ratings do not actually measure job performance, high correlations between selection instruments and supervisory ratings may indicate little about actual job performance.

Content Validity. Content validity reveals how well the subject matter or behavior required in selection instruments represents all the important aspects of the job. Content validity is not measured by correlation of scores on the selection instruments and job performance. Instead, it rests on the collective judgment of a group of experts who are supposed to know the essential behaviors required to perform a job and how these essential behaviors can be measured by selection instruments. The behaviors necessary for successful job performance may range from those that are directly observable, such as typing, to those that are highly abstract. The higher the level of abstraction, the more difficult it becomes to show validity by the content validity approach. Content validity is therefore most appropriate for achievement tests, such as typing and mechanical tests. It is least appropriate for selection procedures that seek to measure intelligence, aptitudes, and personality.

The experts who judge the content validity of selection instruments might be occupants of the positions for which the selection instruments are used, or they might be outside consultants, such as industrial psychologists or professors, who supposedly can determine whether the tests are reasonably related to the jobs. Although rigorous methods have been used to collect the judgments of experts, the fact remains that content validity rests on composite opinions, not on direct correlations between tests and job performance.

Construct Validity. Construct validity is one of the more difficult and controversial types of test validation. It attempts to measure the psychological constructs underlying job performance. For example, an employer might believe that the capacity for creativity is an important requirement for successful job performance in a particular position. Therefore, the employer may seek a test to measure an applicant's capacity for creativity. Before this can be done, however, several requirements must be met. First, the construct "capacity for creativity" must be a reasonably well-established, understood, and operationalized concept in psychological literature. Second, a careful job analysis must demonstrate that capacity for creativity is a basic element in the successful performance of the job. Third, there must be proof that the selection instrument actually measures the construct. Since construct validation is more difficult than the other validity tests, its use in the public sector is limited.

Limits of Validation. No test or selection instrument correlates perfectly with successful job performance. A comprehensive review of testing studies has revealed that the average selection test can predict only 25 percent of the differences among employees' job performance.[6] One should also remember that test scores can never firmly predict what will happen if a specific individual is hired. At best, test scores indicate that a greater proportion of applicants above a certain point will be successful than those who score below that point.

The fact that most selection instruments are unable to predict much about the differences in applicants' subsequent job performance is particularly significant when the same instruments tend to exclude minorities or women from particular jobs. The courts have been suspicious of tests and other requirements that seem to exclude minorities and are unrelated to job performance. Moreover, the courts have required that selection instruments that tend to exclude minorities and women, or have an adverse impact on minorities and women, must be validated.

Discrimination in Selection

The first occasion for the Supreme Court to look closely at the discriminatory impact of an apparently neutral selection instrument occurred in the case of *Griggs v. Duke Power Company* in 1971.[7] The Duke Power Company operated the Dan River Steam Station at Draper, North Carolina, which was organized into five departments. The lowest paying jobs were in the Labor Department, in which all the black employees of the station worked (fourteen out of ninety-five total employees). The traditional criterion for promotion was seniority. In 1965, however, the company initiated a high school education requirement for all departments except the Labor Department. This effectively meant that most of the black employees could not move out of the Labor Department.

The Duke Power Company later relaxed the high school education requirement, but it began to require passing scores on two general aptitude and intelligence tests that had no specific relationship to job performance. These tests were more restrictive than the high school graduation requirements. Thirteen of the fourteen black employees at the Dan River Steam Station, who had been denied promotion because they failed the tests, sued Duke Power Company for violating Title VII of the Civil Rights Act of 1964. The Supreme Court found in favor of the black Employees and said that Title VII prohibited not only overt discrimination but also tests that have a discriminatory impact and that are not related to job performance.

In *Albemarle Paper Co. v. Moody*, the Supreme Court again defined discrimination in employment selection as "adverse impact."[8] The Court said that an employer may use any selection instrument he or she wishes, unless the instrument results in an adverse impact by selecting applicants in a racial pattern significantly different from that of the pool of applicants. In 1978, after extensive negotiations, the Equal Employment Opportunity Commission (EEOC), the Civil Service Commission, and the Departments of Justice and Labor agreed on the *Uniform Guidelines on Employee Selection Procedures*. The *Uniform Guidelines* also incorporated the adverse impact definition of discrimination.

Establishing Adverse Impact

Plaintiffs claiming discrimination have made two basic statistical comparisons in efforts to establish a prima facie case of adverse impact.[9] In the first comparison, plaintiffs compare the percentage of minority applicants successfully passing the test or criteria with the percentage of majority applicants successfully passing the test or criteria. The second kind of comparison involves measuring the percentage of minority persons employed in the specific job for which the test or criteria is required against the percentage of minority persons in the relevant geographical labor market.[10] The courts have been hesitant, however, to rely on comparisons of population statistics, because they realize that the percentage of minorities who have the necessary requirements for a particular job may be quite dissimilar to the percentage of minorities in the general population.

The courts generally use the comparison of pass/fail rates of minority and majority applicants to determine adverse impact, but it is not clear how much adverse impact must be demonstrated to establish a prima facie case. Although the courts have not clearly defined adverse impact, the *Uniform Guidelines* use the 80 percent rule or four-fifths rule, to define it. According to this rule, adverse impact is established when the selection rate of the protected group is less than four-fifths of that of the majority group or the group with the highest rate. In other words, adverse impact is measured by comparing the percentage of the applicants from like groups that are selected (that is, hired, promoted, fired, and so on).[11] For example, if twenty of forty white applicants for a position are selected and only two of ten black applicants are selected, adverse impact occurs because the rate of acceptance of blacks (0.20) is not four-fifths of the rate of acceptance of whites (0.50).

In situations where the number of minority or majority job candidates is insufficient to establish a statistical case, the Supreme Court has specified four criteria for establishing a prima facie case of unfair discrimination:

1. The plaintiff belongs to a racial minority;
2. He/she applies for and is qualified for a position for which the employer is seeking applicants;
3. He/she is rejected despite the qualifications; and

4. After the rejection, the position remains open and the employer continues to seek applicants from persons of the complainant's qualifications.[12]

Defense Against Finding Of Adverse Impact

When a plaintiff has shown that an employer's selection instrument has had an adverse impact on a minority, the burden of proof shifts to the employer, who must show that the selection instrument is related to job performance. The employer can use a combination of the validation methods described in this chapter to show a significant relationship between the selection instruments and job performance. If the employer proves that the selection instrument is related to job performance, the burden shifts back to the employee to prove that other tests or selection instruments would not have had such a discriminatory effect on minorities, that the instruments were available, and that it would have been reasonable for the employer to use them.[13]

Before the Supreme Court case of *Connecticut v. Teal,* it was generally agreed that if an employer's total selection process did not have an adverse impact, the courts would not expect the employer to validate the individual components of the process.[14] The key factor was how many minorities were hired, not the legitimacy and validity of each step in the selection process. In other words, the courts and the enforcement agencies emphasized protection of groups (that is, minorities) rather than the rights of any individual. If an employer hired a satisfactory number of blacks, it was not deemed judicially important that particular blacks might have been discriminated against by the employer.

In *Teal,* however, the Supreme Court said that Title VII protects individuals, not groups. Consequently, if one element of an employer's selection process discriminates unfairly against an individual, the employer may find it necessary to validate that one element even though the selection process as a whole has no adverse impact on a minority. The *Teal* decision may make the employer's validation efforts considerably more difficult. The employer may be forced to validate every step of a selection process, even when the overall selection process has no adverse impact. Therefore, the employer's strategy may shift from hiring more minorities, to escape a finding of adverse impact and the necessity to validate tests, to hiring more psychologists, to prove that tests are valid.[15] If such shifts do occur, the impact of *Teal* will be rather paradoxical, indeed.

Biographical Data, Minimum Qualifications, and the Application Form

The completion of an application form is the first step for most people who seek government employment. The application form seeks information concerning the minimum requirements for the job, such as previous education (subjects, degrees, and grades) and previous work experience, including duties, salary, length of time on the job, and reasons for leaving. The application form may also contain questions about professional associates, health histories, and leisure time activities of the applicant. In addition, the applicant may be asked to describe his or her goals and interests.

Federal laws and guidelines prevent inquiries in a number of areas. For example, the application form should not ask about the applicant's age, sex, race, religion, marital status, ancestry or national origin, or credit ratings.[16] Although the employer must collect data on the race and sex of applicants for reporting to the EEOC, the application form should not contain these questions: the information must be obtained on another form that is not used in any personnel selection activity.

The application form serves several purposes. First, it is a record of the application. The information collected is important because such a record may be needed to answer a charge of discrimination. The application also reveals the applicants' abilities to write, to organize their thoughts, and to present facts clearly and succinctly. Finally, the form provides information that the employer can use in the interview.

The information given on an application form may not always be accurate. One study found that applicants overestimated both the duration of their prior employment and their previous salaries.[17] Other studies, however, indicate substantial agreement between reported and verified biographical data.[18] Some information can be verified by requiring a transcript from the applicant's school or college, and an applicant's work history can be verified, although the exact nature of the applicant's work experience may be more difficult to discover.

If an employer has minimum education or experience requirements, he or she should be able to validate them. This is particularly important if these requirements tend to exclude minority or female applicants. Most reviews strongly support the validity of biographical data.[19] In fact, personal biographical data as predictors of future work behavior may be superior to any known alternative.[20]

Cities that have residency requirements may be particularly interested in the home address of the applicant. Several major cities (Atlanta, Boston, Chicago, Detroit, Miami, Pittsburgh, and St. Paul) have residency requirements.[21] Cities defend such requirements by claiming that workers who live in the city feel a greater commitment to their city and to their jobs. Another reason for the requirement is to provide more job opportunities for residents of the city, particularly black and minority residents, thus promoting greater racial and ethnic balance in the city's workforce. Although municipal unions and employees tend to oppose these requirements, the courts have upheld the right of cities to impose them. Since such requirements are bitterly opposed by employees, however, the benefits of the requirements may be offset by their detrimental impact on employee morale. If a city does institute a residency requirement, it should be uniform for all employees. Top officials or employees in special fields should not be given exemptions, because the morale problem becomes more severe when exceptions are allowed.

References and Background Investigation

At first glance, a background investigation appears to be a reasonable procedure for obtaining more information about an applicant. Previous employers and school officials should be able to provide valuable insights into an applicant's potential and the best guide to what a person may do in the future is what he or she has done in the past. This maxim assumes, however, that an employer can obtain accurate accounts of the applicant's work history from references and past employers. This is a risky assumption, as anyone who has read many letters of reference can readily attest.[22] Most reference letters are overwhelmingly positive, because reference sources are reluctant to give a negative reference, especially in written form. Most studies of the validity of reference checks reveal little correlation between references and job performance criteria. The validity of reference checks can be improved, however, by using the telephone to check an applicant's background. This allows the employer to ask more questions and to follow up questions that indicate problems.[23] Also, the employer may be able to read between the lines of what is said and detect areas in which more investigation is necessary.

Tests

Tests have been a major part of the merit system; to many people, employee selection in the public sector implies tests. Many types of tests exist, but the major types are written tests, performance tests, and oral tests.[24]

Written Tests

Written tests include both achievement and aptitude tests. Achievement tests measure the applicants' mastery of the knowledge necessary for successful job performance, whereas aptitude tests are used to determine the applicants' ability to learn the skills and information necessary to perform the job. Intelligence and personality tests can be considered aptitude tests. Employers may use intelligence tests on the assumption that more intelligent people can learn almost any job more quickly and perform it more efficiently. Several problems occur with intelligence tests, however. First, psychologists cannot agree on what intelligence is and how it can be measured. Second, although intelligence tests may measure several factors, such as verbal comprehension and reasoning, it is difficult to know which specific factor is related to job performance. Third, many people believe that a number of intelligence tests measure familiarity with the majority culture and therefore are culturally biased against minorities.

Whereas intelligence tests purport to measure one's *ability* to learn, personality tests seek to measure one's *willingness* to learn. Personality factors may be crucial in the performance of some jobs; for example, willingness to assume responsibility and a tolerance for ambiguity and stress may be important traits for managerial positions. Typical personality tests seek to measure these traits and others, such as ambition, self-confidence, decisiveness, optimism, and patience.

Unfortunately, some of the problems accompanying intelligence tests also occur with personality tests. First, psychologists have considerable difficulty agreeing on an operational definition of many traits and on how to measure them. Second, employers may have difficulty showing that a particular trait is a necessary element in successful job performance. Thus, construct validity, with all its attendant problems, is required for personality tests. If personality tests discriminate against minorities or women, the tests invite immediate attack because they usually lack content, or self-evident, validity; that is, the average person or test taker is unable to see how some personality tests are related to job performance. Most written tests are multiple-choice, so that more material can be covered in a short period of time and evaluators can grade them more easily and quickly than essay tests. In addition, there is less subjectivity in grading a multiple-choice exam. Critics of multiple-choice exams contend, however, that these tests often measure vocabulary and reading skills, rather than the knowledge or skills needed for the position.

Performance Tests

The simplest type of test is to require the applicant to perform a sample of the work required by the job. The more a test simulates job content and tasks, the more it becomes a performance test. Although performance tests for typists or machinists may be constructed easily, however, performance tests for managers are difficult to construct.

Oral Tests

Oral examinations are not the same as job interviews, which generally take place after the applicants have passed a test and are certified as qualified by the personnel department. Whereas the job interview is generally conducted by the line supervisor of the position to be filled, the oral examination is part of the testing process to determine whether the applicant is qualified. The personnel department often conducts oral exams to measure such factors as the applicants' oral communication skills, interpersonal relations skills, personality characteristics, and ability to think under pressure. Examiners may give oral tests to individuals or to groups. For a group oral test, a problem is given to a group of candidates who must resolve it within a specified time period. Such exams are supposed to reveal a candidate's ability to work within a group.

The reliability of oral exams is often less than satisfactory, and different examiners may score exams differently. To reduce such inconsistencies, oral exams should be well planned and structured. Examiners should know what behaviors they wish to measure and how they intend to do it. Reliability is also improved if the examiners have received training in the conduct of an oral exam.

Interviews

The interview remains the most popular selection instrument, primarily because it satisfies several needs of both the interviewer and the applicant.[25] The interviewer seeks information about applicants that will help predict their future performance on the job and wishes to inform applicants about the nature of the job and the organization and attract them to the organization. The interviewer may also wish to determine the "personal chemistry" between the applicants and the people with whom they would work.[26] Applicants seek to present themselves favorably and sell themselves to the interviewer.[27] They also seek information about the job and the organization to determine whether they really want to work for the organization.

The objectives of the interviewer and the applicant may conflict during the interview. For example, the interviewer is attempting to make an accurate estimate of the applicant's future performance, but this is difficult when the applicant is attempting to sell himself or herself. Similarly, the interviewer must ask demanding and penetrating questions in an attempt to obtain an accurate impression, but such questioning may undermine the interviewer's goal of selling the organization.

These conflicting objectives during the interview may explain the chief problem of interviews—low reliability and validity. All comprehensive surveys of research literature on interviewing reveal that interviews have the lowest reliability and validity of any selection instrument.[28] Often, different interviewers disagree in their assessments of the same applicant. In addition, there is little correlation between interviewers' assessments and the subsequent job performance of applicants. This low reliability and validity are due, in part, to other problems and weaknesses of interviews.

One major problem is the interviewer's poor planning and preparation for the interview. Too often, the interviewer is a personnel specialist or a line supervisor who views interviewing as a secondary appendage to another major task or activity. As a result, he or she may rush into an interview without sufficient preparation. A good interviewer prepares for the interview by obtaining a thorough understanding of the job to be filled. Thus, a good job analysis is an essential ingredient of a good job interview.

Good planning generally points to a structured rather than an unstructured interview. In a structured interview, the interviewer has a list of questions that he or she has prepared before the interview and follows closely during the interview. Research has consistently shown that structured interviews have greater reliability and validity than unstructured interviews.[29]

Structured interviews also help the interviewer avoid another common problem in interviews—making an assessment too early in the interview. Interviewers often reach a final decision quite early in the interview—typically within the first four minutes.[30] Of course, when interviewers make such snap judgments, they may overlook much of the information the interview is supposed to elicit.

Another common problem in interviews is placing too much weight on negative information. Research has shown that interviewers give roughly twice as much weight to negative information as they do to positive information. A single negative characteristic can bar an applicant from a job.[31] Structured interviews reduce this tendency to give undue weight to negative information.[32]

Another problem is that interviewers may allow their biases to influence their assessment of the interviewee. Studies of interviewing indicate, for example, that women are generally rated lower by both male and female interviewers.[33] It is surprising, however, that not many studies have investigated the impact of the applicant's race on the interviewer's evaluation. The few studies that have been done indicate little evidence of racial bias in interviews.[34] Similarly, only a few studies have examined the impact of the applicant's age on the interviewer's evaluation.[35] Unlike race, however, the applicant's age does appear to affect the evaluation; older employees are often considered less suitable for a job than younger ones.[36]

Thus, a well-planned, structured interview is the best way to reduce the traditional problems associated with interviews. In addition, the interview should be as directly related to actual job performance as possible. Moreover, interviews conducted by a board or panel of interviewers appear to have higher reliability and validity than interviews conducted by a single interviewer,[37] although panel interviews are much more costly.

Assessment Centers

The term *assessment center* refers to a group-oriented, standardized series of activities that provide multiple measures for predicting or evaluating job performance.[38] The unique role of assessment centers is to simulate the behaviors required on the job.[39] The simulations are based on a thorough job analysis of the positions to be filled. A group of participants, generally ten to fifteen, goes through as many as four days of simulations and exercises, and the behavior of the participants is evaluated by assessors or judges.

Assessment procedures were first used by German military psychologists during World War II.[40] They were first used in the United States by the Office of

Strategic Services for the selection of spies during World War II.[41] AT&T was the first industrial firm to make extensive use of assessment center procedures. Later, other large firms, such as IBM, General Electric, Ford, J.C. Penney, and Sears began to use assessment center techniques. Today, more than 2,000 companies have used or currently are using assessment center methods.[42] Governments have also turned to assessment centers; a 1980 survey revealed that 196 of the 208 state and local jurisdictions surveyed had used assessment center methods.[43]

Assessors are often line managers who occupy positions above the ones to be filled. They should receive extensive training in recognizing examples of behavior patterns that are required on the job. They should also receive training in interviewing and recording their observations. In addition, the assessors should not know any of the participants to be evaluated.

Before any assessment center exercises or simulations are developed, the positions to be filled must be analyzed. This job analysis should establish dimensions, or activities, needed to perform the job, such as interpersonal skills, oral communication skills, and organizational skills.

Two common assessment center techniques used to measure such skills are the leaderless group discussion (LGD) and the in-basket test. In the LGD, a group of participants talks about some topic for a period of time. No one is appointed leader, and the assessors observe but do not participate in the group. Each participant may be required, for example, to make a five-minute oral presentation of a candidate for promotion and then defend his or her candidate. The assessors judge the participants' aggressiveness, persuasiveness, oral communication, self-confidence, and interpersonal skills.

The in-basket test is a simulation for an individual participant. The in-basket contains materials on problems that the participant might face on the job; it could include letters, memos, notes of incoming telephone calls, and other material. The participant is given some information about the background of the organization and is asked to respond to the in-basket material. The participant actually writes letters and memos as though he or she were on the job. This simulation measures participants' organizational and planning abilities, written communication skills, and decision-makng capabilities. It also measures their ability to delegate authority and establish priorities.

Assessment centers have become popular for several reasons. First, most studies reveal that they have high validity.[44] They appear to be excellent procedures for predicting the promotion potential of candidates. There is a high correlation between the evaluation of participants in the assessment centers and subsequent promotions of the candidates. Moreover, the predictive validity of the centers appears high for both minorities and women. Because the centers have high validity, and because they do not discriminate against minorities and women, the courts have viewed them with considerable favor.[45] Assessment centers are also popular with the participants. Most people who go through the exercises believe that they do represent the kinds of behavior required on the job.[46]

Although assessment centers are popular, they do have some problems. In particular, they are expensive; a cost of $600 per participant is not unusual. Part of this high cost results from the necessity to customize assessment programs for each organization. In 1980, the average yearly cost of operating an assessment center was almost $90,000.[47]

While some criticize the costs of assessment centers, others question their validity.[48] Most of the high validity claims for assessment centers rest on correlations between their evaluations of participants and the participants' subsequent promotions or salary increases. Critics note, however, that such correlations do not compare assessment center evaluations to actual performance. Thus, instead of predicting performance, the assessment centers may only be predicting which participants will impress their superiors in the organization. This criticism becomes more acute when one considers that many of the assessment center evaluations are given to the superiors in the organization. The evaluations thus may become self-fulfilling prophecies, since supervisors who have seen the evaluations may expect more of high-scoring participants and give them more responsibilities.

Test Administration and Eligibility Lists

Tests are generally conducted by the civil service commission or the central personnel department of the jurisdiction, although, in some cases, the line agencies administer the tests. The number of different tests required depends on the specificity of the job classes (see chapter 3). Narrow, specialized classes demand a larger number of more specific tests. Wide, broad classes require fewer, more general tests. Tests are given as often as necessary to maintain a list of eligible candidates. After the tests are scored, a list is created of eligible candidates who have passed the tests. Those who make the highest scores are placed at the top of the list, although the scores often include extra points that are given to veterans.

Veterans Preference

The practice of adding additional points to veterans' scores is known as veterans preference. At the federal level, disabled veterans receive ten points and other veterans receive five extra points. The widows and mothers of veterans who lost their lives receive similar preferences, as do the wives and mothers of disabled veterans. Veterans preference is also practiced in many state and local governments. As a result, veterans often clog the top of eligibility lists, even though many nonveterans have higher scores.

Veterans preference has been defended in several ways, the major defense being that veterans should receive preference to compensate for the service they gave their country. This defense is more persuasive when the draft is operative or when the veteran has been in combat, but it seems less persuasive when the veteran joined the armed services during peacetime and never was near combat.

A major criticism of veterans preference has been that it violates the merit principle.[49] The person with the highest score on the tests might not be selected if he or she is not a veteran. Supporters of veterans preference are quick to note, however, that extra points are generally added to passing scores; thus, although the veteran might not be the *best* qualified, he is qualified. Also, veterans note that the validity of most entrance tests is not sufficiently high to predict, with certainty, that the candidate who scores a few points higher on an entrance exam will automatically be a better employee than the veterans who have slightly lower scores.

Women's groups are the primary opponents of veterans preference. Since most veterans are men, veterans preference results in women being excluded from employment, even though they may have higher scores. Thus, some contend that veterans preference is a denial of equal protection of the law and that it discriminates against women. The Supreme Court has held, however, that veterans preference applies equally to male and female veterans and, therefore, does not discriminate against women.[50] Of course, this decision ignores the fact that nearly all veterans are men.

Although it is intellectually stimulating to debate veterans preference, the political facts are that veterans groups and organizations have sufficient influence in legislatures to prevent any fundamental change in the procedure.

The Rule of Three

When agencies have vacant positions, they request names of applicants from the central personnel office. The personnel office consults the eligibility list for the particular class of positions in which the vacancies occur and certifies a list of candidates for the positions. Sometimes, however, the personnel office finds that the people on the top of the list have already found jobs and are no longer available. This is very likely to occur when tests are given infrequently and when considerable time has elapsed between the tests and the requests from the agencies. Good people at the top of eligibility lists are particularly likely to have found employment during the interim.

The central personnel office generally does not give the entire eligibility list to an agency. Often, only the names of the top three candidates are given. This is known as the rule of three. The rule is justified as a defense of merit, because it prevents agencies from hiring a less-qualified applicant who is further down on the eligibility list. Of course, it also assures the selection of a veteran who, with the help of the extra points, may be among the top three candidates.

Agencies tend to dislike the rule of three. They generally want greater latitude in selecting employees. Sometimes, an agency will not hire any of the top three candidates and will leave the position vacant. The agency might hope that another unit or department will hire the present top three, and that the next top three might be more acceptable. This is a risky strategy, however, because the agency might lose the vacant position or the next top three might be even less attractive.

Although the federal government uses the rule of three, some jurisdictions do not. Some allow more latitude, such as the rule of six or ten, and some even send the entire list to an agency. In a few jurisdictions, only the top name on the eligibility list is provided, and the agency has no choice but to hire the top candidate.

Orientation and Probation

After a candidate is hired, he or she receives an orientation and serves a probationary period. Orientation really begins before the new employee starts to work, since the position announcement/description and the selection interview provide the new worker with a view of his or her new position. Although agencies may be inclined to present a very good but possibly unrealistic image of the organization and the position during the interview and selection process, considerable research has indicated that a more realistic and balanced presentation is preferable.[51] Candidates who receive a more realistic job preview are more likely to self-select themselves out of consideration for a job that they feel is not right for them.[52] In the long run, such self-selection is a major benefit to the organization, because a mismatched employee is likely to be unhappy and not very productive and is also likely to leave the organization at the first opportunity.[53] As a result, the organization will lose the money spent on recruiting and training the employee. Realistic job descriptions and interviews also lower the new employee's job expectations, thereby reducing dissatisfaction once the employee starts to work.

An orientation program can have several goals. A primary goal, which may often be overlooked, is to reduce the anxiety of the new employee.[54] New employees worry about their ability to do their jobs and they are concerned about acceptance by their new work group supervisor. Also, new employees may be subject to some hazing and initiation rites by other employees. Orientation should attempt to reduce all of these concerns.

The employee's anxiety can be reduced considerably if his or her supervisor is actively involved in the orientation. The immediate supervisor should help the new employee learn the specific duties of the position. The supervisor should also attempt to give the new employee interesting first assignments and shelter him or her from demands outside the work group.[55]

Another goal of orientation is to explain the "big picture" or overall organization to the new employee. The employee should learn the primary mission of the organization, who the key people are, and how his or her job fits into the overall mission.

A third general goal of orientation is to explain the many rules, policies, procedures, and benefits of the organization, including policies about sick leave, vacations, absences, insurance, parking, grievances, and retirement. This information is best provided in an employee handbook or folder.

Following orientation, most new employees in public organizations serve a probationary period that generally lasts from several months to a year. Even with very good selection procedures, there is no substitute for observing the employee on the job to determine whether he or she can perform it satisfactorily. The probationary period is intended to serve as this final test. Unfortunately, most supervisors do not view the probationary period in this way. Even though probationary employees do not have the procedural rights of regular employees and can be dismissed much more easily, very few are released. Supervisors dislike firing anyone, particularly if other supervisors are not doing so. As a result, the probationary period is often pro forma. Some employees who should be removed survive their probations and become long-term employees, making them much more difficult to remove.

Promotions

Many of the instruments used for selecting new employees—biographies, references, tests, interviews, and assessment centers—are also used to identify candidates for promotion. In addition to these selection devices, performance evaluations and seniority may also be used to determine promotions. Formal tests probably play a less important role in the promotion of employees than they do in the selection of new employees. Conversely, interviews and assessment centers may play a larger role in promotion than in selection. Regardless of which instruments are used, the same reliability and validity requirements that govern selection instruments also apply to promotion procedures. Moreover, employers must avoid adverse impact on minorities and women when making promotions.

Promotion from Within versus Lateral Entry from Outside

Every public organization faces a fundamental issue concerning potential candidates for promotion: whether is is better to promote from within the organization or to allow for lateral entry from outside. Arguments can be made for both options. Employees and their unions generally press for promotion from within. Indeed, a major defense of promotion from within is that appointments from outside have a negative impact on employee morale. Promotions from within provide career ladders for employees and increase their job satisfaction and loyalty to the organization. Furthermore, if due care has been taken in the design of career ladders, occupants of positions just below the vacant ones may have the most appropriate skills and experience for the positions.

Although the advantages for promotion from within are considerable, the disadvantages are not minor. Promotions from within encourage inbreeding and the development of an "organization view" that may help the agency resist criticisms from the public and control by elected political superiors.

Promotions from within also discourage mobility among agencies within a jurisdiction. Some believe that such mobility provides employees with a wealth of experience that can be very beneficial to government. Also, employees with experience in different agencies may be better able to see the big picture and may be less governed by narrow departmental perspectives.

Promotion from within may cause serious harm to merit systems, in that the best available candidate is not sought. Some critics contend that promotion from within also encourages favoritism and cronyism among supervisors and superiors who decide which employees are to be promoted. This fear is the major reason why unions favor promotion from within, with seniority as the primary criterion for promotion. Critics of promotion from within, however, point to this emphasis on seniority as another reason to provide lateral entry. These critics note that seniority does not necessarily correlate with competence and merit. Although seniority may be an appropriate criterion for promotion to some clerical and blue-collar positions, it may be inappropriate for determining promotions to supervisory and managerial positions, since the necessary talents for success in such positions may or may not reside in the candidate with the most seniority.

Public organizations that rely on a career type, rank-in-person system have opted for a predominantly promotion-from-within system. As noted earlier, rank-in-person means that rank and attendant salary and status belong to the individual, not to the position the individual may occupy at any particular time. For example, an Army captain has appropriate salary and status regardless of the position he or she may occupy. In contrast, rank-in-position means that rank and attendant salary and status go with the position; one has the rank, status, and salary as a result of occupying the position. Examples of rank-in-person systems are the police and firefighting forces of local governments and such departments as the Foreign Service, the Forest Service, the National Park Service, and the military at the national level. These organizations place more emphasis on recruiting talented individuals at the entry level who have general potential for promotion and leadership. The entry tests are less job-specific and more related to general abilities and talents. In comparison, the more numerous rank-in-position organizations recruit at all levels, and they recruit for specific jobs. Therefore, these organizations look for individuals with more specific talents for particular positions.

Announcements of vacancies may occur in several ways in public organizations. In some agencies, particularly in rank-in-person systems, the vacancy may not be announced. Superiors and supervisors in such organizations may already know who the eligible candidates are within the organization. In most organizations, however, the vacancy is at least announced within the department in which it occurs. In addition, the announcement of a vacancy may be sent to the central personnel office, which will send it to other public agencies in the the jurisdiction. In other cases, the central personnel office not only announces the vacancy in other public agencies in the jurisdiction but also makes an announcement to the general public.

After the announcement, potential candidates may apply. Some jurisdictions may require that candidates go through a process very similar to that of selecting new employees; they submit biographical data to show that they meet minimum requirements, take exams, and go through other selection techniques. The names of those who pass all the hurdles are placed on an eligibility list, which might be ranked or unranked. Seniority and performance evaluations may be used as part of the determination of candidates' overall scores.

Other jurisdictions, particularly those that emphasize promotion from within the organization, downplay formal tests. These organizations place more emphasis on the candidates' past performance, interviews, and assessment center results.

Promotions and Other Personnel Functions

Promotions cannot be considered an isolated part of the selection process. They are directly related to human resource planning, job design and classification, performance evaluation and counseling, and training and development. Moreover, promotions are critical considerations in efforts to produce a representative bureaucracy and in collective bargaining.

Many of the future personnel resources in an organization will come from within via promotions. Therefore, human resource planners must consider the kinds of personnel that will be needed in the future and must determine how promotions can occur to meet these needs. To do this, human resource plans may include projected career ladders that outline the probable movement of an individual from one position to another and the length of time between promotions.

Promotions are also related to job design, analysis, evaluation, and classification. For example, promotions are obviously related to the decision to develop either a rank-in-position system or a rank-in-person system. Each system makes very different assumptions about how promotions should occur. Also, assumptions about career ladders and promotions affect how a job is designed. If a position is to serve as a training ground for a higher post, this expected relationship (promotion from one position to another) has or should have a great deal of influence on how both positions are designed and classified.

Performance evaluations and counseling are intimately associated with promotions. First, a supervisor's evaluation of an employee may significantly affect the employee's beliefs about his or her ability to perform more complex duties. Thus, evaluations may determine who applies for a higher position. Similarly, supervisors' evaluations may determine who receives a promotion. Therefore, evaluations should not only consider past behavior for the immediate purpose of salary administration but should also consider the future promotability of the employee. Counseling should also assist the employee in preparing for future promotions.

Promotions in organizations are related to training and development efforts, since much training is directed at employees who wish to improve their skills and prepare for more complex duties and responsibilities. If organizations have considered possible promotional or career ladders, they are better able to plan and target their training efforts to prepare the personnel resources they will need in the future.

Promotions are also related to the representativeness of public bureaucracies in the United States. As noted in chapter 11, although many minorities and women are in public bureaucracies, they tend to be concentrated at the lower levels. If bureaucracies are to be truly representative of the U.S. populace, more women and minorities must occupy higher-level positions, and this will happen only if promotion policies contain specific goals and strategies to promote more women and minorities. Public organizations must identify promotable minority and woman employees early in their careers within the organization. Then these employees must be encouraged to engage in training and developmental activities that can better prepare them for promotion.

Another personnel activity that concerns promotions is collective bargaining. Unions often push for promotion from within and seek seniority as a primary criterion for promotion. Within the federal service, the determination of who is promotable is a management right that is nonnegotiable.[56] Most states and local governments have also resisted union attempts to control who is promoted. Although unions emphasize seniority and promotion from within, such union pressure probably has little impact, since most public organizations already tend to promote from within and give due consideration to seniority.

Selection and Promotion in Organic and Mechanistic Organizations

Many of government's administrative, professional, and technical (APT) positions are organic, that is, they require occupants who are flexible, educated, and tolerant of the considerable ambiguity inherent in the position. Often, it is difficult to construct specific tests or performance tests for such positions. When they are recruiting for these jobs, recruiters may be more interested in future potential than in immediate, specific job knowledge. Therefore, the recruiters may look for general abilities, education, and experience that indicate future potential. Biographical data, references, interviews, and assessment centers may be more important selection instruments for these positions.

Whereas organic positions demand one group of selection instruments, mechanistic positions require others. Mechanistic positions are routine, highly structured, and repetitive, and performance tests can be designed for them. Employees are hired for such positions because of their immediate ability to perform a specific job, and there is less concern about their future potential. Most are not expected to move into managerial or professional positions, so selection instruments that attempt to gauge future potential and managerial skills are less appropriate. Assessment centers would be inappropriate and prohibitively expensive for these numerous mechanistic positions. Also, extensive educational requirements are rarely necessary for these positions, although considerable experience in the specific job may be required. An extensive education might be counterproductive for these positions, because highly educated employees would quickly become frustrated with the routine, repetitive tasks.

As organic and mechanistic positions require different selection instruments, so they demand different validation procedures. Selection instruments for mechanistic positions are more easily validated. Since the tests and requirements are more job-specific, it is easier to show a relationship between test results and job performance. Content validation is easier because the selection tests tend to be samples of the actual job; for example, it is easy to validate a typing test for a clerk-typist position.

In contrast, the selection instruments for organic, APT positions may be considerably more difficult to validate, because the selection instruments are not samples of actual job behavior. These instruments are designed to measure more generic skills, abilities, and potentials that are assumed to be related to successful performance on the job. One might assume that a B.A. degree is essential for some supervisory positions, for example, but it might be difficult to prove or validate that a degree is necessary. Similarly, certain general personality tests purport to measure attitudes and predispositions that are essential for leadership positions. Showing that the tests are related to effective job performance, however, may require construct validation, which is one of the most difficult types.

The promotion process, like selection instruments and validation, differs in organic and mechanistic organizations. The development of career ladders may be more important in organic, APT positions. Since employees may be recruited because of their general skills and future potential, considerable emphasis must be devoted to developing that potential in a logical, sequential fashion in a number of positions. In APT positions, it is particularly important that employees not feel they are in dead-end jobs. Development of career ladders for APT positions implies that most promotions will be from within, provided that competent individuals are available. It does not imply, however, that seniority should be the primary criterion for promotion. In contrast, seniority may play a larger role in movement from one mechanistic position to another. Often, promotions among mechanistic positions imply a greater level of proficiency and experience in a particular skill, rather than a capacity to assume new and different responsibilities and tasks. One might be promoted from a Clerk Typist I to a Clerk Typist II, for example, but the duties might remain very similar. For such promotions, seniority can be a significant criterion.

Conclusion

Recruitment and selection may be the most important of all personnel functions. The best management techniques, the most insightful compensation policies, and the most gifted leaders cannot save a public organization that has given little attention to the personnel it has chosen. Recruitment and selection are also very important because the stakes involved are high. Since governments employ one of every six workers in the United States, government recruitment policies can have a dramatic impact on the U.S. labor force. Finally, the centrality of these functions demands that recruitment and selection be examined not as isolated activities but as integral parts of other personnel concerns.

Notes

1. A good review of human resources planning can be found in Elmer H. Burack, *Strategies for Manpower Planning and Programming* (Morristown, N.J.: General Learning Press, 1972)

2. Dale Beach, *Personnel*, 4th ed. (New York: Macmillan, 1980), p. 188.

3. Ibid., p. 189.

4. Albert C. Hyde and Torrey S. Whitman, "Workforce Planning—the State of the Art," in Jay M. Shafritz, ed., *The Public Personnel World* (Chicago: International Personnel Management Association, 1977), p. 68.

5. Charles T. Goodsell, *The Case for Bureaucracy* (Chatham, N.J.: Chatham House Publishers, 1983), pp. 104–109.

6. Edwin Ghiselli, *The Validity of Occupational Aptitude Tests* (New York: Wiley, 1966).

7. *Griggs v. Duke Power Company*, 401 U.S. 424 (1971).

8. *Albemarle Paper Co. v. Moody*, 422 U.S. 405 (1975). Also see James Ledvinka and Lyle F. Schoenfeldt, "Legal Developments in Employment Testing: 'Albemarle' and Beyond," *Personnel Psychology* 31 (1978): 1–13.

9. Duane E. Thompson and Patricia S. Christiansen, "Court Acceptance of Uniform Guidelines Provisions: The Bottom Line and the Search for Alternatives," *Employee Relations Law Journal* 9 (Spring 1983): 591.

10. Ibid.

11. Karen Ann Olsen, *Equal Employment Opportunity and Affirmative Action* (Washington, D.C.: Labor Management Relations Service, 1979), p. 6.

12. *McDonnell Douglas Corp. v. Green*, 411 U.S. 792 (1973).

13. Thompson and Christiansen, "Court Acceptance of Uniform Guidelines Provisions," p. 598.

14. *Connecticut v. Teal*, USLW 4716 (1982).

15. This is the conclusion of Alfred W. Blumrosen, "The 'Bottom Line' After *Connecticut v. Teal,*" *Employee Relations Law Journal* 9 (Spring 1983): 572–586.

16. Clifford M. Koen, "The Pre-Employment Inquiry Guide," *Personnel Journal* 59 (October 1980): 825–829.

17. I.L. Goldstein, "The Application Blank: How Honest Are the Responses?," *Journal of Applied Psychology* 55 (1971): 491.

18. J.N. Mosel and C.W. Cozan, "The Accuracy of Application Blank Work Histories," *Journal of Applied Psychology* 37 (1953): 365–399.

19. W.A. Owens, "Background Data," In M.D. Dunnette, ed., *Handbook of Industrial and Organizational Psychology* (Chicago: Rand McNally, 1976); J.J. Asher, "The Biographical Item: Can It Be Improved?" *Personnel Psychology* 25 (1972): 251–260; Richard Reilly and Georgia Chao, "Validity and Fairness of Some Alternative Employee Selection Procedures," *Personnel Psychology* 35 (1982): 1–62.

20. Wayne Cascio, *Applied Psychology in Personnel Management* (Reston, Va.: Reston, 1978), p. 202.

21. Steven L. Hayford, "Local Government Residency Requirments and Labor Relations: Implications and Choices for Public Administrators, *Public Administration Review* 38 (September-October 1978): 482–486.

22. For a review of the validity of references, see Reilly and Chao, 'Validity and Fairness of Some Alternative Employee Selection Procedures."

23. Robert B. Best, "Don't Forget Those Reference Checks," *Public Personnel Management* 6 (November-December 1977): 422–426.

24. O. Buros, *Eleventh Mental Measurements Handbook* (Highland Park, N.J.: Gryphon Press, 1981).

25. James G. Goodale, *The Fine Art of Interviewing* (Englewood Cliffs, N.J.: Prentice-Hall, 1982), p. 22.

26. Ibid.

27. Ibid.

28. R. Wagner, "The Employment Interview: A Critical Summary," *Personnel Psychology* 2 (1949): 17–46; E.C. Mayfield, "The Selection Interview: A Reevaluation of Published Research," *Personnel Psychology* 17 (1964): 239–260; L. Ulrich and D. Trumbo, "The Selection Interview Since 1949," *Psychological Bulletin* 67 (1965): 100–116; N. Schmitt, "Social and Situational Determinants of Interview Decisions: Implications for the Employment Interview," *Personnel Psychology* 29 (1976): 29–79; R.D. Arvey and James E. Campion, "The Employment Interview: A Summmary and Review of Recent Research," *Personnel Journal* 61 (1982): 281–322.

29. Ibid.

30. Schmitt, "Social and Situational Determinants of Interview Decisions," pp. 29–79.

31. Ibid.

32. Mayfield, "Selection Interview."

33. R.D. Arvey *Fairness in Selecting Employees,* (Reading, Mass.: Addison-Wesley, 1979), pp. 174–176.

34. Ibid.

35. Ibid.

36. J.E. Haefner, "Race, Age, Sex and Competence as Factors in Employer Selection of the Disadvantaged," *Journal of Applied Psychology* 61 (1977): 199–202; B. Rosen and

T.H. Jerdee, "The Influence of Age Stereotypes on Managerial Decisions," *Journal of Applied Psychology* 60 (1976): 428–432.

37. Arvey and Campion, "Employment Interview," p. 293.

38. W.C. Byham, "Assessment Centers for Spotting Future Managers," *Harvard Business Review* 48 (1970): 150–160.

39. Joyce D. Ross, "A Current Review of Public Sector Assessment Centers: Cause for Concern," *Public Personnel Management* 8 (January-February, 1979): 42.

40. Cascio, *Applied Psychology in Personnel Management,* p. 250.

41. Ibid.

42. C.W. Millard and Sheldon Pinsky, "Assessing the Assessment Center," *Personnel Administrator* 25 (May 1980): 85.

43. Louise F. Fitzgerald, *The Incidence and Utilization of Assessment Centers in State and Local Governments* (Washington, D.C.: International Personnel Management Association, 1980).

44. W.C. Byham and C. Wettengel, "Assessment Centers for Supervisors and Managers: An Introduction and Overview," *Public Personnel Management* 3 (1974): 352–364; S.L. Cohen, "Validity and Assessment Center Technology: One and the Same?" *Human Resource Management* 19 (1980): 2–11.

45. Frederick Frank and James Preston, "The Validity of the Assessment Center Approach and Related Issues," *Personnel Administrator* 27 (June 1982): 87–95.

46. Kenneth S. Teel and Henry DuBois, "Participants' Reactions to Assessment Centers" *Personnel Administrator* 28 (March 1983): 85–91.

47. B. Friedmand and R.W. Mann, "Employer Assessment Methods Assessed," *Personnel Psychology* 34 (November-December 1981): 73.

48. R.J. Klimoski and W.J. Strickland, "Assessment Centers: Valid or Merely Prescient," *Personnel Psychology* 30 (1977): 353–361. Also see P.R. Sackett, "A Critical Look at Some Common Beliefs about Assessment Centers" *Public Personnel Management* 11 (Summer 1982): 140–147.

49. Charles Davis, "Veteran Preference and Civil Service Employment: Issues and Policy Implications," *Review of Public Personnel Administration* 2 (Fall 1982): 57–65.

50. *Personnel Administrator v. Feeney,* 434 U.S. 884 (1978).

51. D.P. Schwab, "Organizational Recruiting and the Decision to Participate," in K. Rowland and G. Perris, eds., *Personnel Management: New Perspectives* (Boston: Allyn and Bacon, 1982).

52. J.P. Wanous, *Organizational Entry: Recruitment, Selection and Socialization of New Comers* (Reading, Mass.: Addison-Wesley, 1980).

53. M.S. Taylor and D.W. Schmitt, "A Process-Oriented Investigation of Recruitment Source Effectiveness," *Personnel Psychology* 36 (1983): 343–354.

54. Daniel C. Feldman, "A Socialization Process That Helps New Recruits Succeed," *Personnel Psychology* 33 (March-April 1980): 11–23.

55. Ibid., p. 22.

56. George T. Sulzner, *The Impact of Labor-Management Relations upon Selected Federal Personnel Policies and Practices* (Washington, D.C.: U.S. Government Printing Office, 1979).

5
Motivation and Performance

Key Words

Content theories

Need hierarchy

Herzberg's two-factor theory

Process theories

Expectancy

Valence

Instrumentality

Equity theory

Reinforcement theory

Feedback

Intrinsic and extrinsic motivators

Job satisfaction

Consideration

Initiating structure

Situational leadership

Path–goal theory

Introduction

Assumptions concerning the motivation process are at the heart of such personnel activities as performance appraisal, compensation, training and development, and productivity improvement. In discussing motivation, this chapter provides an appropriate and necessary introduction to the further consideration of these personnel activities in chapters 6 through 9. Discussion of the motivation process also accentuates and clarifies the contingency approach to personnel management.

The motivation process is explained here in terms of three major contemporary theories of motivation—content, process, and reinforcement—which explain what energizes an employee's behavior and how this bahavior can be channeled and sustained. The three theories are integrated in a model of the motivation process that explains the associations between motivation, job satisfaction, and performance.

The motivation model stresses the important role of the leader in motivation and performance. Moreover, it reveals that although one leadership style may be appropriate for one situation, another may be required for different circumstances. Therefore, various leadership styles are reviewed, and the situational—or contingent—nature of leadership is explained. The thesis that the situational nature of motivation and leadership requires different approaches to motivation and rewards in mechanistic and organic organizations provides an appropriate conclusion to the chapter.

Definition of Motivation

Motivation is a complex concept, and different motivation theorists have focused on different facets of the concept. Dessler, for example, sees motivation as a "person's desire to fulfill certain needs."[1] Kelly states that it "has to do with the forces that maintain and alter the direction, quality and intensity of behavior."[2] Jones claims that is is concerned with "how behavior gets started, is energized, is sustained, is directed, is stopped, and what kind of subjective reaction is present in the organization while all of this is going on."[3] These different definitions highlight three parts of the motivation process:

1. Motivation is concerned with what *incites* or *energizes* a person's behavior.
2. Motivation is *process-oriented* and is concerned with how behavior is directed or channeled.
3. Motivation is concerned with how behavior is sustained.

These three aspects of the motivation process provide a framework for discussion of the three major contemporary theories of motivation—content, process, and reinforcement—and for development of a basic model of motivation.

Content Theories of Motivation

Content theories of motivation concentrate on what arouses or triggers individual behavior, and they attempt to establish individual needs or motives that account for behavior. Needs are defined as internal drives for external incentives, such as pay. The two most important content theories are Maslow's need hierarchy and Herzberg's two-factor theory.

Maslow's Theory of Needs

Maslow postulated that everyone has five basic needs.[4] In ascending order, starting with the most basic, they are (1) physiological needs, (2) safety needs, (3) social needs, (4) esteem needs, and (5) self-actualization needs.

Maslow's theory is based on several basic assumptions:

1. People have needs that activate their behavior.
2. These needs are arranged in a hierarchy (see figure 5–1).
3. Only after a lower-level need is satisfied will an individual seek satisfaction of a higher-level need.
4. A satisfied need is not a motivator.
5. The need framework is complex; several needs may affect a person's behavior at any one time.

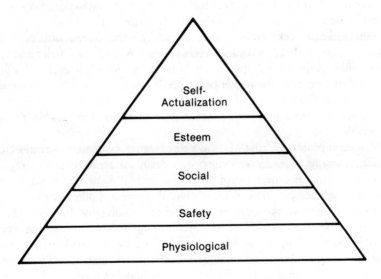

Figure 5–1. Maslow's Need Hierarchy

6. Higher-level needs can be satisfied in more ways than lower-level needs.

Physiological needs include such physical requirements as food, clothing, and shelter. They are the primary human needs and are represented in the workplace by a desire for salary, job tenure, and adequate basic working conditions, such as heating and eating facilities.

Safety needs include the desire for security, stability, and absence from pain. These needs are often satisfied in organizations by job security or tenure, medical insurance, retirement programs, unemployment insurance, disability insurance, and other regulations and procedures that protect the worker's safety.

Social needs include the desire for affection, love, and belonging. These needs are often satisfied within organizations by informal work groups and by supervisors who recognize their role in making an employee feel wanted and part of a larger social scene.

Esteem needs include both a need for a feeling of achievement, or self-worth, and a need for recognition, or respect from others. The internal parts of this need include such personal feelings as self-confidence, achievement, knowledge, and competence. The external need for recognition involves status, recognition, and respect.

Self-actualization needs refer to the desire for self-fulfillment or the realization of one's full potential. Before an individual can realize this need—indeed, before he or she will even seek to realize it—the other needs must be at least partially met. Most people never achieve this level of satisfaction, because they remain preoccupied with satisfying their lower-order needs.

One of the problems with the need hierarchy is that there is little evidence to support the concept of five distinct levels of need. A study by Lawler and Suttle, for example, identified only two levels of need—a biological level and a global level that encompasses the higher-order needs.[5] Furthermore, it is questionable whether the fulfillment of one need must occur before another need is activated. Indeed, several needs may be operational at the same time within the same individual.

A second problem is that Maslow's theory gives inadequate attention to the differences among individuals. Some people desire job tenure over status, power, and money, whereas others accept less job security if there is a chance for more esteem and self-actualization. Research has also revealed different needs among and between rural workers and urban workers, among and between Mexican workers and workers in the United States, among and between young workers and older workers, among and between black and white workers, among and between workers in large and small organizations, and among and between line managers and staff managers.[6] The list of individual differences could go on and on, but the crucial point is that differences do exist among employees' needs. Therefore, managers should not assume that a similar need hierarchy exists for all employees. Rather, they should be empirical and attempt to find which needs exist among their subordinates and how these needs can be utilized to accomplish the organization's goals.

A third criticism of Maslow's theory is that some outcomes or rewards could satisfy more than one need. Money is perhaps the best example of a ubiquitous reward that satisfies several levels of needs simultaneously—such as the needs for security, esteem, and self-confidence.

A fourth and fundamental criticism of Maslow's theory is that it is basically a normative theory, not an empirical one. Maslow's adherents often speak in terms of what *should* be as opposed to what *is*. Self-actualization, for example, remains a fuzzy, ill-defined concept. Although managers may understand self-actualization intuitively, they may not know how to provide it to those employees who seek it.

A fifth criticism is the assumption that individuals look to the workplace for fulfillment of their needs. A whole world exists apart from the workplace, and individuals may look to other areas of their lives for fulfillment of their basic needs. For example, some workers may desire a shorter workweek and more money rather than self-actualization on the job, because more money and more free time may allow them to pursue other hobbies or interests that have a more significant impact on their feelings of self-actualization.

Finally Maslow's theory provides a rather convenient, benign justification for extensive involvement of the individual in the organization. Although such involvement may be very beneficial for the organization, it may not be good for the employee or for individuals in the external environment of the organization. For example, citizens might not want CIA employees to be totally dedicated to the CIA.

Although criticisms of Maslow's theory are numerous, it continues to have great popularity because of its simple, commonsense appeal to managers. It provides a ready, simple explanation of individual needs and how managers should respond to them.

Herzberg's Two-Factor Theory

A second popular content theory of motivation, closely related to Maslow's need hierarchy, is Frederick Herzberg's two-factor theory of motivation, also known as the motivator-hygiene theory.[7] Herzberg and his associates asked respondents to describe periods in which they were exceedingly happy or unhappy about their jobs. Subsequent analysis of the data revealed that intrinsic factors (motivators)—those related to the work itself—were most often associated with good or happy feelings. Extrinsic factors (hygienes)—those related to the job environment—were most often associated with bad or unhappy feelings about the job. The motivators were achievement, recognition, the work itself, responsibility, and advancement. The hygiene factors were company policy and administration, supervision, working conditions, and relationships with peers and subordinates.

Herzberg concluded that satisfaction and dissatisfaction do not exist on a single continuum but, rather, that job satisfaction is composed of two unipolar traits. The absence of motivators produces a condition of "no satisfaction" but does not contribute significantly to dissatisfaction. Similarly, the presence of hygiene factors causes a condition of "no dissatisfaction" but does not contribute significantly to satisfaction.

Herzberg believed that hygienes are provided by many organizations, but motivators are not. According to Herzberg, management should become motivator-oriented. Herzberg also recommended that organizations enrich jobs by increasing the complexity and responsibility associated with them. He thought that enriched jobs would provide more motivators and job satisfaction. (For further discussion of job enrichment, see chapter 9.)

Considerable research on Herzberg's theory has produced several major criticisms of it, one of which concerns the research methods on which the theory is based. Since people usually attribute good results to their own efforts and blame others for bad results, Herzberg's interviewees may have attributed their satisfaction to their own achievements and accomplishments, and they may have attributed their dissatisfaction not to personal deficiencies but to variables in the work environment that are under the control of management. In other words, workers may take credit for the good times but blame management for the bad times.

Other critics suggest that satisfaction and dissatisfaction may not be two separate dimensions—that some factors may contribute to both satisfaction and dissatisfaction.[8] A final criticism is that Herzberg's theory concentrates on satisfaction, not on performance. It does not suggest why certain factors should affect performance or bahavior in a particular way. Furthermore, satisfaction does not always lead to improved performance. Therefore, since Herzberg concentrates on satisfaction, not on behavior, his theory is not a complete explanation of motivation.

Process Theories of Motivation

The content theories of motivation provide managers with a better understanding of their employees' needs, but these theories provide little understanding of why employees choose certain behaviors to satisfy their needs or of how managers can structure the job environment so that employees can satisfy their needs through improved performance. The process theories give more attention to an employee's selection of one behavior over another to obtain a desired reward. This section will examine two major process theories—expectancy and equity.

Expectancy Theory

Perhaps the best-known process theory is expectancy theory, which can be traced to earlier works by Tolman[9] and Lewin[10] but is most closely associated with such current researchers as Vroom,[11] Lawler,[12] and Hackman and Porter.[13] Expectancy theory suggests that individuals are rational, thinking creatures who make behavioral choices according to their expectations about the outcomes or results of such choices. According to Vroom, there are three major elements in expectancy theory—expectancy, valence, and instrumentality.

Expectancy is an individual's perceived probability that effort by him or her will result in a certain level of work-related performance. For example, a caseworker in a welfare office may believe that if he makes a great effort, he can process a high number of welfare cases in one day. This expectancy, or perceived probability, that effort will result in the desired performance can range from zero (no chance that effort will lead to performance) to one (certainty that effort will produce performance).

Valence is the value an employee attaches to a particular goal or outcome. This value could be either positive or negative; in an organization, however, one would expect that most outcomes offered as rewards to the employee would be valued positively. The outcomes could include pay increases, promotions, vacations, rest breaks, and a variety of other rewards.

Instrumentality refers to the employee's perceptions of the probability that performance will produce a particular outcome. If a particular performance or level of performance always leads to a particular outcome, the instrumentality is one; if there is no relationship between the performance and the outcome, the instrumentality is zero. For example, if the caseworker believes that processing a great number of cases always produces a pay raise, the instrumentality of processing a great number of cases for a pay increase approaches one. Thus, the employee chooses from a considerable number of behaviors according to his or her perception of how these behaviors will produce particular outcomes and the value the employee attaches to the outcomes.

Vroom states that expectancy and valence combine multiplicatively to determine *force* or *motivation*. If valence or expectancy is near zero, there will be no force or motivation. Before the caseworker will process more cases, he must believe that his efforts will result in more processed cases and that processed cases will produce a pay increase. (Vroom's model is illustrated in figure 5–2.) Thus, the effort that an individual exerts on the job is a function of (1) the perceived expectancy that certain outcomes result from particular behaviors and (2) the valence for these outcomes. The valence of an outcome is, in turn, a function of its instrumentality for obtaining other outcomes and the valence of these outcomes.

Researchers would like to know more about the effort-to-performance (E → P) expectancy. Some factors that seem to influence it are self-esteem, past experience in similar situations, role perceptions, and the individual's ability. Additional factors may also affect the E → P expectancy. Also, the performance-to-outcomes (P → O) expectancy may be affected by the attractiveness of the outcomes, by E → P expectancies, and by past experience in similar situations.[14] Other variables probably affect the P → O relationship, and these need addi-

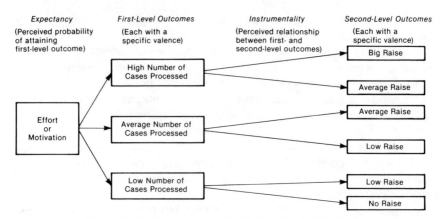

Figure 5–2. Expectancy Model for a Social Worker

tional research. As research on expectancy theory continues, the theory becomes more complex and more difficult to test. Lawler and Suttle note that expectancy theory "has become so complex that it has exceeded the measures which exist to test it."[15] Few studies have tested all the variables within the theory, and much of the research is based on survey questionnaires that have not been validated scientifically.[16]

Although the expectancy model has become complex, the manager should not discard it as merely another academic exercise in "splitting hairs." Motivation is a complex phenomenon, and any theory that is capable of explaining it will be complex. Expectancy theory stresses the manager's responsibility in clarifying the E $\rightarrow$ P expectancy by providing additional training and counseling to employees. The theory also emphasizes the manager's important role in establishing the P $\rightarrow$ O expectancy; that is, the manager must strive to make outcomes or rewards contingent upon the desired performance.

Equity Theory

Equity theory states that if employees perceive an imbalance between their contributions and the rewards they receive for their contributions, they will attempt to achieve a balance by obtaining more rewards or by reducing their contributions, or they will leave the organization. The perceived imbalance is a result of the employees comparing their contributions–rewards ratios with those of others—fellow employees in the work group or the larger organization or individuals outside the organization. Contributions include the employees' effort, performance, training, skills, and education; rewards include pay, promotion, recognition, achievement, and status.

Much of the research on equity theory has been in laboratory experiments. Several such experiments have revealed strong support for the theory's contention that employees become dissatisfied when they perceive that they are victims of an inequity.[17] Some field studies in actual organizations have supported this finding.[18]

Another area of equity research focuses on how employees attempt to resolve perceived inequity by altering their performance. Reviews concur that research on underpaid subjects supports the predictions of equity theory.[19] Research findings in situations of overpayment are mixed, however, and there is a need for additional study in this area. Research does reveal that turnover and absenteeism may result when withdrawal is the only alternative to inequity.[20]

Although research tends to confirm parts of equity theory, problems remain. First, the individual's perception of equity is often based on an internal, socially derived standard of inputs and outcomes, rather than on a comparison with a particular person.[21] Second, research on equity theory has focused on pay and has ignored other rewards. This oversight is particularly significant because many of the content theories of motivation emphasize the limitations of pay as a motivator. Also, equity theory research must examine not only the amount of pay but also the system of allocating pay and rewards in an organization. Some employees may believe that their present pay is equitable but that the system for administering pay is unfair.

Despite these problems, equity theory provides useful insights for managers. Managers must be concerned about more than the absolute amount of money they pay an employee; they must also be concerned about comparative levels of pay, because employees are very sensitive to comparisons of their pay with the pay of their fellow employees. If tenured public employees perceive a reward–contribution imbalance, and if they do not leave the organization, they may significantly decrease their contributions and rationalize their behavior as entirely acceptable and appropriate. The cumulative, aggregate effect of such decisions could populate entire organizations with employees who occupy positions but display little enthusiasm, interest, or energy in their work.

Reinforcement Theory

Whereas content theories of motivation describe what incites or energizes a person's behavior, and process theories are concerned with how an individual selects behavior through motivation, reinforcement theory—or behavior modification—is concerned with how behavior is sustained.

Reinforcement theory, which is based in the work of B.F. Skinner, contains several basic assumptions.[22] First, it is assumed that individuals are relatively passive and that their behavior is determined by their environment. Second, the theory contends that only behavior is observable and that such factors as needs, goals, and drives cannot be validated empirically; that is, behavior can be explained only in terms of the consequences surrounding it, not by searching for unseen inner drives.

The consequences or the contingencies of behavior are the types of reinforcement that occur after a particular behavior and serve to encourage or extinguish the behavior. These include positive reinforcement, punishment, avoidance, and extinction.

Positive reinforcement increases the likelihood that a particular behavior will be repeated. When a supervisor compliments a subordinate for an excellent report and states that a pay increase will result, positive reinforcement has been provided for the excellent work.

Punishment is used to decrease behavior. When a supervisor reprimands an employee for being late to work, punishment has followed the undesired behavior, and it is hoped that the behavior is thereby reduced.

Avoidance occurs when an employee behaves in a particular way to avoid punishment. When workers arrive on time for work to avoid punishment and, as a result, do not receive punishment, their behavior is reinforced by the absence of undesired consequences.

Extinction occurs when a previously desired response or behavior is no longer positively reinforced. The withdrawal of a positive reinforcer will eventually extinguish the behavior. For example, if employees had been accustomed to receiving a vacation day for every ten unused sick days but the agency found that this policy was too expensive and discontinued it, the employees would fail to see as much reward for not using their sick days, and sick days would increase.

Criticisms of Behavior Modification in Organizations

Critics of behavior modification contend that it is a threat to personal autonomy and individuality. These critics say that the use of behavior modification on people is mechanical, dictatorial, and dehumanizing,[23] and they question the right of anyone to manipulate and mold another person into some ideal shape. Supporters of behavior modification reply that employees in any organizational environment are being controlled and manipulated by someone and that behavior modification merely makes the control more visible and predictable. They argue that openly recognizing the control is more defensible than pretending that control and manipulation do not exist. Argyris, however, is critical of behavior modification's emphasis on making the individual more aware of what the reinforcer expects, rather than an emphasis on the growth and development of the individual.[24]

Other critics of behavior modification claim that cognition and introspection by individuals do influence the individual's behavior. Edwin Locke, a leading proponent of goal-directed behavior theory, flatly rejects the deterministic nature of behavior modification theory. According to Locke, studies of actual practices of behavior modification in organizations show that the techniques used implicitly contradict the main premises of behaviorism because they assume that employees are introspective and rational.[25]

Argyris contends that if behavior modification is to be successful in organizations, the controlled environment of the laboratory must be transferred to real-world organizations. For this transferral to be successful, however, one must assume that employees are passive—that they will not think about what is happening, talk to anyone about it, focus on the long-term implications, or consider their own goals.[26] Whyte also has several criticisms concerning the application of behavior modification to actual organizations.[27] First, positive reinforcement is difficult to dispense in work organizations, because behavior and environment in an applied setting are difficult to define and measure. Second, conflicting stimuli are often present in the work environment; the supervisor is not the only reinforcer. Third, contingencies are difficult to manage because of time lags between performance and rewards.

Another criticism concerns worker participation in decision making under behavior modification. During the last decade, employee participation has become popular in management theory, as revealed in the literature on job involvement, job enrichment, and organizational development literature; these orientations, however, are in opposition to behavior modification, at least in theory. Of course, one could allow employees to participate in the choice of reinforcers and the schedule of reinforcement, but such practices would seem to depart from reinforcement theory.

Others criticize behavior modification for placing too much emphasis on external rewards or reinforcement. Behavior modification does recognize, however, that reinforcement can come from the job itself. Indeed, one goal of behavior modification is to shift from external to internal reinforcement, because the feedback from the latter is constant and occurs immediately after the performance; theoretically, this is the best schedule of reinforcement to strengthen performance.

The Application of Behavior Modification in Public Organizations

Behavior modification may be most applicable to lower-level positions that can be easily structured and whose occupants tend to be relatively passive. It may be difficult to apply in many government agencies, however, because civil service regulations, seniority, grievance procedures, tenure, and other variables make it extremely difficult to control all or even most of the contingencies of behavior. Some basic concerns of organizational behavior modification should be noted, however, by contemporary public managers.

Perhaps behavior modification's chief contribution to management is its emphasis on data and information. Also, behavior modification is behavior- or performance-oriented. Thus, managers can focus on the performance-related behavior of workers. Managers need not be clinicians who can decipher the attitudes or inner needs of workers; rather, they must determine and communicate specific performance objectives and definitive plans of action. Managers also must conduct performance audits to determine baseline data against which subsequent interventions and changes in performance can be compared.

Organizational behavior modification also resists the use of punishment, which is believed to be inappropriate because it might result in undesirable side effects, such as anxiety, aggressive acts toward the punishing agent, passivity, or withdrawal, and because it might remove the undesireable response only temporarily. Since punishment has been a major method of behavior control in some organizations, behavior modification's rejection of it may prove to be a significant benefit.[28]

Organizational behavior modification emphasizes positive feedback to the worker. The emphasis on a schedule or timing of reinforcement may offend some who stress individual needs and differences, but it does ensure that workers will be provided with feedback concerning the correct behavior.[29]

A Model of the Motivation Process

Motivation is too complex to be explained by a single theory; each theory explains only part of the whole motivation process. The model in figure 5–3 incorporates elements from all of the theories discussed in this chapter: (1) the content theories of motivation (Maslow and Herzberg), which provide insight into what incites or energizes a person's behavior; (2) expectancy and equity theory, which reveal the process by which employees choose one behavior over another to obtain a reward; and (3) behavior modification or reinforcement theory, which provides insight into how behavior is sustained. Each theory is useful because it examines or focuses on one facet of the complex subject of motivation.

The chief focus of the model is effort. First, effort is a result of the belief that it will lead to performance and that performance will lead to an outcome (expectancy theory). Second, effort is a result of the value attached to an outcome. Outcomes are valued according to the needs of individuals (Maslow's need theory) and according to the perception that the outcome is equitable (equity theory). Third, effort is a result of the intrinsic value of the performance; that is, employees will exert more effort if they enjoy the work itself. As the model indicates, feedback from the individual's attempt to perform influences his or her belief that effort will produce performance, and feedback from the reward or punishment for performance influences the individual's estimate that performance will lead to a certain outcome (reinforcement theory).

Managers can influence the model most dramatically in the two feedback loops. First, through their efforts to provide training and support to their employees, they can influence the employees' perception that effort will lead to per-

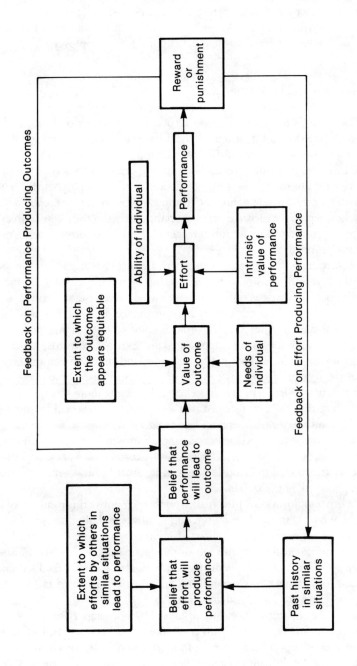

Figure 5–3. Model of the Motivation Process

formance. Second, by careful and systematic administration of rewards, managers can affect employees' perception that performance will result in rewards. Thus, a knowledge of employees' needs will assist managers in predicting the types of outcomes or rewards that may appeal to the employees.

Satisfaction and Performance

Studies of motivation are often concerned with how performance and satisfaction are related to motivation.[30] Behavioral scientists assumed for many years that employees who were satisfied with their jobs were more productive employees. Therefore, according to this assumption, organizations could improve productivity by improving the job satisfaction of their employees. Reviews of the research literature investigating the relationship between satisfaction and productivity, however, have revealed little association between the two variables.[31] Thus, the assumption that greater job satisfaction leads to improved performance has been undermined.

According to Lawler and Porter, performance may cause satisfaction, rather than the reverse.[32] This positive relationship between performance and satisfaction will occur, however, only when employees perceive that intrinsic and extrinsic rewards are associated with their performance. Intrinsic rewards include the employees' feelings that they have accomplished challenging and worthwhile tasks that require the use of important skills. Extrinsic rewards, which are given by the organization, include pay, promotion, and status. When the organization makes the receipt of rewards contingent on performance, employees with superior performance levels receive more rewards and are more satisfied. If employees also believe that the extrinsic rewards are equitable, they will be more satisfied. Thus, when superior performance leads to desired extrinsic and intrinsic rewards that are contingent on performance, employees will be more satisfied and satisfaction and performance will be positively correlated. When superior performance does not lead to intrinsic or extrinsic rewards, however, performance and satisfaction will not correlate.

When employees are dissatisfied with their jobs, the result is often withdrawal, which is most often reflected in turnover and absenteeism. Most studies of absenteeism reveal that job dissatisfaction is a major causal factor.[33] Research has also indicated that overall job dissatisfaction is consistently and negatively related to turnover.[34] Job dissatisfaction may also result in conflict among employees, complaints about supervisors, incorrectly performed tasks, sabotage of equipment and products, and drug use.[35]

Employee dissatisfaction can be caused by poor supervision, unsafe or poor working conditions, conflict with co-workers, inequitable pay, lack of job security, or lack of opportunity for promotion, recognition, or challenge. Management may find it difficult to isolate causes of dissatisfaction if there is a considerable amount of distrust and fear in the organization. An anonymous questionnaire can be a useful method of discovering causes of employee dissatisfaction. Once the causes are found, management can attempt to reduce the dissatisfaction in several ways. One method to improve job satisfaction is to transfer dissatisfied employees to other jobs that better fit their needs, interests, and abilities. Another method is to change the perceptions of dissatisfied employees. Management can attempt to correct misperceptions by providing factual and accurate information—a task that is difficult, of course, when employees distrust management.

Astute managers will prevent job dissatisfaction by implementing selection and training programs that assure close matches between employees' needs, interests, and abilities and the demands and responsibilities of their positions. Giving job applicants accurate descriptions of what the positions are really like prevents subsequent employee frustration with jobs that are not as they were described in the job selection and interviewing process. During recruitment, too many organizations exaggerate the good points of jobs and understate their disadvantages. Thus, implied promises are made that cannot be kept. As a result, employees' expectations cannot be met, and they become frustrated and dissatisfied.

Styles of Leadership and Motivation

Most researchers believe that the leader's behavior and his or her leadership style can affect the motivation and performance of subordinates. Because there are so many possible leadership behaviors and styles, an early goal of leadership research was the identification of a few relatively distinct and meaningful categories. Perhaps the best-known early research on leadership styles was done at Ohio State University,[36] where researchers developed a questionnaire to investigate the different types of leader behavior. Responses to the questionnaire from hundreds of people revealed two basic dimensions of leader behavior: "consideration" and "initiating structure."[37] Most of the other research on leadership styles has revealed categories roughly equivalent to these two.

Consideration is the degree to which leaders act in a warm, supportive, friendly, and respectful manner toward their subordinates. Some examples of consideration are being warm and approachable, being open to suggestions, listening to subordinates' problems, treating subordinates as equals, defending subordinates, and consulting with subordinates before making important decisions.

Initiating structure is the degree to which leaders organize and define tasks, assign work, establish communication networks, and evaluate subordinates' performance. Some examples of initiating structure are letting subordinates know what is expected of them, critiquing subordinates' performance, suggesting methods of improvement, establishing deadlines for completion of work, coordinating activities, and assuring adherence to rules and operating procedures.

Researchers at the University of Michigan, who were investigating leadership styles at about the same time as the Ohio State study, found two leadership dimensions that closely parallel consideration and initiating structure: the "production-centered" style and the "employee-centered" style.[38] The production-centered leader is similar to the leader who emphasizes initiating structure; the employee-centered style is very similar to the consideration dimension.

Although the Ohio and Michigan studies were able to identify and describe the two primary behaviors displayed by leaders, they found no universally superior leadership style. Rather, they concluded that leadership style varies with the situation. This recognition prompted a concern about the appropriate leadership styles for different situations.

The Situational Nature of Leadership

One of a leader's most important tasks is to diagnose a situation and determine the appropriate leadership style for that situation. This diagnosis demands that the manager examine four important areas: (1) managerial characteristics, (2) subordinate characteristics, (3) group structure and the nature of the task, and (4) organizational factors.[39]

Managerial Characteristics

A leader's style reflects his or her personality, needs, values, motives, and past experiences. The degree of confidence a leader has in his or her ability influences his or her willingness to delegate decision making. A self-confident, secure leader may seek subordinates' involvement in decision making, whereas a manager with high security needs may keep tight control over subordinates. A manager's past experiences also affect his or her leadership style; for example, managers who trained under task-oriented, successful leaders are likely to adopt a task-oriented style themselves.

Subordinate Characteristics

The needs, personalities, and values of subordinates affect the manager's choice of a successful leadership style. Managers can give more freedom to their subordinates if the subordinates (1) need independence, (2) can tolerate ambiguity, (3) are ready to accept responsibility for decision making, (4) are interested in the problem, (5) have the knowledge and experience to deal with the problem; and (6) identify with the organization's goals.

Group and Task Factors

The dynamics within the work group and the task itself affect a leader's style. A work group that is not cohesive and that contains much internal bickering cannot be given decision-making responsibility. If the group has worked together effectively for a long time, however, the leader can delegate decisions to it.

The nature of the task also affects the leader's relationship with the work group. If a task is structured in such a way that the group can complete it in a logical sequence, the manager can forgo close supervision of task completion. Conversely, a task that is very unstructured and ambiguous demands the active involvement of the leader. In such cases, the work group may expect the leader to produce initiating structure.

Organizational Factors

Organizational characteristics that have a significant impact on leadership style include (1) the power base of the leader; (2) the rules, procedures, and informal norms of the organization; and (3) the time available to make a decision.

A leader can have several sources of power. Legitimate power is derived from the formal authority of the leader's position. Coercive power is based on employees' fear that failure to comply will result in some form of punishment. Reward power is based on the leader's ability to control distribution of rewards. Expert power is based on the leader's expertise and knowledge. Referent power derives from the leader's charisma, or personal attraction. A leader who has little legitimate, coercive, reward, or expert power must depend more on referent power. This power source implies a more employee-oriented leadership style.

The organization's rules and informal norms may dictate certain leadership styles. Superiors are often impressed with and expect subordinate managers to be task-oriented and to direct and "take charge." If such norms and expectations are strong, a manager may experience problems when practicing an employee-oriented style of leadership.

Finally, the time available for making a decision also affects the style of leadership. If a decision must be made within a very short time, the manager will probably have to make it without much involvement by subordinates.

The Path–Goal Theory of Leadership

The path–goal theory of leadership incorporates many of the situational variables just discussed and complements the motivation model presented in figure 5–3. The theory, developed by Robert House, is based on expectancy theory.[40] According to the path–goal theory, a leader's primary task is to (1) clarify the tasks to be performed by subordinates, (2) remove obstacles that might prevent accomplishment of the task, (3) enhance subordinates' intrinsic satisfaction with their tasks, and (4) provide valued extrinsic rewards based on performance.

The path–goal theory indentifies four specific kinds of leadership behavior or styles:

1. *Directive leadership* occurs when the leader organizes, controls, and structures subordinates' activities.
2. *Supportive leadership* is characterized by a leader who supports and is concerned about the needs, well-being, and welfare of subordinates and who is approachable and friendly.
3. *Participative leadership* occurs when the leader shares information and decision making with subordinates.
4. *Achievement-oriented leadership* is characterized by a leader who sets challenging goals and seeks the highest levels of performance from subordinates.

The appropriate leadership style is determined by the subordinates' needs and the nature of the environment or situation. When the task is highly ambiguous and complex, directive leadership may be appropriate and welcomed by subordinates. When work is basically routine, however, any attempt by the leader to clarify the task may be viewed as unnecessarily close control. Usually, supportive leadership is more effective in situations with well-defined goals and assignments. When subordinates strive for high performance and are confident of their abilities, achievement-oriented leadership is appropriate. Finally, participative leadership is appropriate when employees understand the problem, are interested in it, and wish to be involved.

The Motivation Process and the Management of Other Personnel Functions

The motivation process dramatically affects the personnel functions discussed in the next four chapters. The motivation model emphasizes the importance of feedback to employees concerning their performance. This feedback involves both rewards for appropriate behavior and advice concerning how the employees' behavior should change for them to obtain valued rewards. Similarly, the two primary functions of performance appraisal are to allocate rewards and counsel employees (see chapter 6). Thus, an understanding of feedback in the motivation process can help managers develop sound evaluation systems, and an understanding of the goal-directed behavior of employees can assist organizations in developing goal-based forms of evaluation, such as management by objectives.

The motivation process is also intimately associated with the administration of pay and benefits (chapter 7). First, understanding the motivation process allows one to recognize the conditions under which pay can motivate performance. Some employees value intrinsic rewards (a challenging job) more than pay; therefore increases in pay for such employees might produce little change in performance. Moreover, equity theories of motivation explain why pay increases that are not viewed as equitable by employees fail to produce improved performance. Finally, the motivation model shows that pay cannot improve employee performance unless it is based on performance.

A knowledge of the motivation process is also necessary for selecting and implementing various training and development techniques (see chapter 8). An understanding of motivation helps managers create the proper conditions for learning to occur. From the motivation model, they know, for example, that good feedback is essential for training and that employees will learn more readily when what is learned is useful for obtaining desired rewards. The motivation model also explains why some of the development techniques discussed in chapter 8 (grid organization development, team building, intergroup interventions, and so on) are appropriate in some situations but not in others. The model also explains why the productivity techniques discussed in chapter 9 (job enrichment, quality circles, and flexitime) may be useful in some circumstances but not in others.

The Contingency Approach, Motivation, and Rewards

Employees in mechanistic and organic organizations have different needs. Mechanistic organizations have relatively routine, highly structured tasks that require employees with comparatively little education and little desire for independence and autonomy in the workplace. Such employees are generally more concerned with the lower-order needs in Maslow's need hierarchy or the extrinsic hygienes in Herzberg's theory. They are less concerned with finding a sense of achievement in the work itself, or self-actualization on the job. Therefore, managers in mechanistic organizations may waste resources if they attempt to enrich the workers' jobs by making them more challenging. First, the nature of the positions and of the organization may make such job enrichment efforts prohibitively expensive. Second, even if job enrichment can occur, the workers may not desire it. They may be more interested in their pay, fringe benefits, peer group relationships and relationships with their supervisors.

Because the tasks in mechanistic organizations are relatively simple, routine, and structured, leaders need not attempt to superimpose a structure. Such attempts are superfluous and are viewed as close supervision and control by subordinates. Rather, the leaders should be more concerned that rewards valued by employees are contingent on performance. In addition, leaders should emphasize supportive leadership. They should show employees that they are concerned about their needs, well-being, and welfare, and they should be approachable and friendly.

Organic organizations have more complex technologies and require employees who are more educated, professional, and able to perform nonroutine, highly unstructured tasks. These employees often seek greater fulfillment in the work itself and are more concerned that opportunities for individual growth and development are available in the workplace. When organic organizations provide these more intrinsic rewards, they not only satisfy their employees' higher-order needs, they also develop more creative employees who can better help the organization adapt to its dynamic environment and complex technology.

Since tasks in organic organizations are often unstructured, ambiguous, and complex, the process by which the tasks can be completed is not self-evident. Therefore, employees may expect the leader to help clarify paths (path–goal theory) to task completion. Furthermore, employees who are performing such tasks often desire some participation in decision making.

Conclusion

The model presented in this chapter incorporates three major motivation theories: content, process, and reinforcement theories. These theories explain how behavior is started, channeled, and sustained. The motivation model also notes the relationship between motivation and performance and emphasizes the situational or contingent nature of motivation and leadership. According to the model, the effective leader must perform the following functions to motivate his or her subordinates:

1. Identify the needs and abilities of employees.
2. Match employee needs and abilities with task demands.
3. Identify rewards that are under the leader's control and valued by employees.
4. Make the receipt of valued rewards contingent on successful task performance.
5. Recognize both the opportunities and the constraints inherent in the characteristics of employees, the nature of the task and the work group, the formal and informal rules and norms of the organizations, and the leader's personal background, values, and needs.

Notes

1. Gary Dessler, *Organization and Management: A Contingency Approach* (Englewood Cliffs, N.J.: Prentice-Hall, 1976), p. 206.

2. Joe Kelly, *Organization Behavior,* rev. ed. (Homewood, Ill.: Richard D. Irwin, 1974), p. 279.

3. M.R. Jones, ed., *Nebraska Symposium on Motivation* (Lincoln: University of Nebraska Press, 1955), p. 14.

4. Abraham H. Maslow, *Motivation and Personality,* 2d ed. (New York: Harper & Brothers, 1954).

5. Edward E. Lawler and J.L. Suttle, "A Casual Correlational Test of the Need Hierarchy Concept," *Organizational Behavior and Human Performance* 8 (1972): 265–287.

6. Lyman W. Porter, "Job Attitudes in Management: Perceived Deficiencies in Need Fulfillment as a Function of Size of Company," *Journal of Applied Psychology* 47 (1963): 386–397; Lyman W. Porter, "Job Attitudes in Management: The Perceived Importance of Needs as a Function of Job Level," *Journal of Applied Psychology* 47 (1963): 141–148; C. Altemis and R. Tersine, "Chronological Age and Job Satisfaction: The Young Blue-Collar Worker," *Academy of Management Journal* 16 (1973): 28–33; J. Slocum, P. Topichak, and D. Kuhn, "A Cross-Cultural Study of Need Satisfaction and Need Importance for Operative Employees," *Personnel Psychology* 24 (1971): 435–445.

7. Frederick Herzberg, Barnard Mausner, and Barbara Snyderman, *The Motivation to Work* (New York: Wiley 1959).

8. Robert J. House and Lawrence A. Wigdor, "Herzberg's Dual-Factor Theory of Job Satisfaction and Motivation: A Review of the Evidence and a Criticism," *Personnel Psychology* 20 (Winter 1967): 385–386.

9. Edward C. Tolman, *Purposive Behavior in Animals and Men* (New York: Century, 1932).

10. Kurt Lewin, *A Dynamic Theory of Personality* (New York: McGraw-Hill, 1935).

11. Victor Vroom, *Work and Motivation* (New York: Wiley, 1964).

12. Edward L. Lawler, *Motivation in Work Organization* (Monterey, Calif.: Brooks/Cole, 1973).

13. J. Richard Hackman and Lyman W. Porter, "Expectancy Theory Predictions of Work Effectiveness," *Organizational Behavior and Human Performance* 4 (November 1968): 417–426.

14. Lawler, *Motivation in Work Organization.*

15. Edward E. Lawler and J.L. Suttle, "Expectancy Theory and Job Behavior," *Organizational Behavior and Human Performance* 9 (1973): 482–503.

16. F. Schmidt, "Implications of a Measurement Problem for Expectancy Theory Research," *Organizational Behavior and Human Performance* 10 (1973): 243–251.

17. W. Austin and E. Walster, "Reactions to Confirmations and Disconfirmations of Expectancies of Equity and Inequity," *Journal of Personality and Social Psychology* 28 (1974): 208–216; L.A. Messe, J.E. Dawson, and I.M. Lane, "Equity as a Mediator of the Effect of Reward Level on Behavior in the Prisoner's Dilemma Game," *Journal of Personality and Social Psychology* 26 (1973): 60–85; T.L. Radinsky, "Equity and Inequity as a Source of Reward and Punishment," *Psychonomic Science* 15 (1969): 293–295.

18. P.S. Goodman, "An Examination of References Used in the Evaluation of Pay," *Organizational Behavior and Human Performance* 4 (1968): 340–351; J.R. Schuster and B. Clark, "Individual Differences Related to Feelings Toward Pay," *Personnel Journal* 49 (1970): 591–604; C.S. Telly, W.L. French, and W.G. Scott, "The Relationship of Inequity to Turnover Among Hourly Workers," *Administrative Science Quarterly* 16 (1971): 164–171.

19. J.S. Adams and S. Freedman, "Equity Theory Revisited: Comments and Annotated Bibliography," in L. Berkowitz, ed., *Advances in Experimental Social Psychology* (New York: Academic Press, 1976); M. Carrell and J. Dittrich, "Equity Theory: The Recent Literature, Methodological Considerations and New Directions," *Academy of Management Review* 3 (April 1978): 202–210.

20. Telly, French, and Scott, "Relationship of Inequity to Turnover,"; M. Carrell and J. Dittrich, "Employee Perceptions of Fair Treatment," *Personnel Journal* 55 (1976): 523–524.

21. Carrell and Dittrich, "Equity Theory," pp. 202–210.

22. B.F. Skinner, *Beyond Freedom and Dignity* (New York: Knopf, 1971); B.F. Skinner, *Contingencies of Reinforcement* (New York: Appleton-Century-Crofts, 1969).

23. Fred Luthans, *Organizational Behavior: A Modern Behavioral Approach to Management* (New York: McGraw-Hill, 1973).

24. C. Argyris, *"Beyond Freedom and Dignity, by B.F. Skinner: A Review Essay,"* *Harvard Educational Review* 44 (1971): 550–567.

25. E. Locke, "The Myth of Behavior Modification in Organizations," *Academy of Management Review* 2 (1977): 544.

26. Argyris, "Beyond Freedom and Dignity," 550–567.

27. W.F. Whyte, "Skinnerian Theory in Organizations," *Psychology Today* 6 (1972): 66–68.

28. For a somewhat more benign view of punishment in organizations, see Richard D. Arvey and John Ivancevich, "Punishment in Organizations: A Review, Propositions and Research Suggestions," *Academy of Management Review* 5 (1980): 123–132.

29. For a recent review of organizational behavior modification, see Donald Fedor and Gerald Ferris, "Integrating Organizational Behavior Modification with Cognitive Approaches to Motivation," *Academy of Management Review* 6 (1981): 115–125.

30. Anne H. Hopkins, *Work and Satisfaction in the Public Sector* (Totowa, Rowman and Allanheld, 1983).

31. A.H. Brayfield and W.H. Crockett, "Employee Attitudes and Employee Performance," *Psychological Bulletin* 57 (1955): 396–424; J.H. Vroom, *Work and Motivation* (New York: Wiley, 1964).

32. E. Lawler and L.W. Porter, "The Effect of Performance on Job Satisfaction," *Industrial Relations* 6 (October 1967): 20–28.

33. R.M. Steers and S.R. Rhodes, "Major Influences on Employee Attendance: A Process Model," *Journal of Applied Psychology* 2 (August 1978): 391–407.

34. W.H. Mobley, S.O. Horner and A. Hellingsworth, "Review and Conceptual Analysis of the Employee Turnover Process," *Psychological Bulletin* 81 (May 1979): 493–522.

35. P. Spector, "Relationships of Organizational Frustration with Reported Behavioral Reactions of Employees," *Journal of Applied Psychology* 59 (October 1975): 635–637.

36. E.A. Fleishman, "A Leader Behavior Description for Industry," in R.M. Stogdill and A.E. Coons, ed., *Leader Behavior: Its Description and Measurement,* (Columbus: Ohio State University, Bureau of Business Research, 1957).

37. Ibid.

38. D. Katz, N. Maccoby, and N. Morse, *Productivity, Supervision and Morale in and Office Situation* (Ann Arbor: University of Michigan, Survey Research Center, 1950).

Also see Rensis Likert, *New Patterns of Management* (New York: McGraw-Hill, 1961).

39. J.M. Ivancevich, A.D. Szilagyi, and M.J. Wallace, *Organizational Behavior and Performance* (Santa Monica, Calif.:Goodyear, 1977), p. 282.

40. Robert J. House, "A Path–Goal Theory of Leadership Effectiveness," *Administrative Science Quarterly* 16 (September 1971): 321–338; Robert J. House and Terrence R. Mitchell, "Path–Goal Theory of Leadership," *Journal of Contemporary Business* 3 (Autumn 1974): 81–97.

6
Performance Appraisal

Key Words

Graphic rating scale

Halo effect

Leniency

Central tendency

Interpersonal bias

Behaviorally anchored rating scales (BARS)

Forced distribution

Forced-choice checklist

Essay

Management by objectives (MBO)

Appraisal interview

Performance appraisal requirements of the 1978 Civil Service Reform Act

Introduction

Supervisory feedback to employees about their job performance is the crucial component of the motivation model discussed in the preceding chapter (see figure 5–3), and performance appraisal is a major component of that feedback. Accurate appraisals are essential for linking the distribution of the organization's rewards (pay, promotions, recognition, and the like) to job performance. Furthermore, appraisals can provide counseling and development feedback to employees, thus increasing the probability that an employee's efforts will result in continued and improved performance.

The importance of performance appraisal can be seen in the various purposes of evaluation in public organizations, which are described in this chapter. A central thesis of this chapter is that performance appraisal can be improved only when the entire evaluation process is viewed as a system. Therefore, a model of the process is presented, and the various components of the model are described, as are the interrelationships among the components. Since the appraisal interview is a crucial element in successful performance appraisal, various issues in and components of interviews are discussed, including frequency, employees' roles, and goal identification.

Improved performance appraisals are an important part of the attempt of the 1978 Civil Service Reform Act to link rewards to performance and to improve productivity, and an evaluation of the appraisal systems required by the Act is included in this chapter. Also, because the 1978 Act requires the use of performance appraisals in salary administration, promotions, demotions, layoffs and dismissals, the legal issues surrounding performance appraisals have multiplied. Therefore, a brief description of the legal requirements for performance appraisal is presented. After a discussion of the role of performance evaluation in organic and mechanistic organizations, the chapter concludes with a reemphasis of the need to approach performance appraisal from a total-system or process perspective.

The Purposes of Appraisal

Performance appraisal is a crucial function of public personnel management that can provide numerous benefits to employees and their employers. For example, employees can obtain valuable feedback from appraisals, and such feedback can help employees and their supervisors prepare training and development plans. In addition, performance appraisals are used by managers when they are making decisions concerning pay increases, promotions, and dismissals. The various purposes of performance appraisals are as follows:

Employment development: Performance appraisals may indicate employee weaknesses that can be corrected by training or counseling, or they may identify potential strengths that can be developed by additional training.

Promotions: Performance appraisals can identify individuals who are prime candidates for promotion and they can identify the training that will be needed before promotion.

Salary increases: Accurate performance appraisals are essential for the smooth functioning of merit or performance-based salary systems.

Demotions and dismissals: Although performance appraisals may be useful in identifying those who should be demoted or dismissed, their primary value in this area is to provide the needed documentation for these extreme actions.

Layoffs: Although most layoffs in the public sector are based on seniority, in recent years the federal government and some local governments have increased the weight of performance evaluations in layoff decisions.

Communication between supervisors and subordinates: Unfortunately, formal performance appraisals may be the only opportunity for supervisors to give any systematic performance feedback to employees, although such communication should occur on a continuing basis. A good performance appraisal system, however, will encourage and support such communication.

Human resource planning: Part of any human resource plan is an accurate assessment of the strengths and weaknesses of the present workforce. Performance appraisals can assist in providing this information.

Validation of selection procedures: Both legal necessity and good management demand that organizations examine the adequacy of their selection tests and minimum qualifications requirements. One way to do this is by comparing applicants' scores on entrance exams with their subsequent performance appraisals.

In several recent surveys of state and local governments, a majority of the respondents indicated that they used performance appraisals for these purposes.[1] The purposes most frequently mentioned were merit raises, promotion, dismissal, and demotion. Performance appraisals are used less frequently for employee development and validation purposes.

One reason for the less frequent use of appraisals for employee development is the inherent conflict in using the same process for administering rewards and for developing employees. Employee development demands open, frank discussion between employees and their supervisors. When performance appraisals are used to determine salaries, promotions, and dismissals, however, both supervisors and employees may enter the evaluation session with considerable anxiety and reluctance. This environment does not promote the openness and communication necessary for effective employee development. Because of this inherent conflict, some experts suggest that separate performance appraisals be used for administering rewards and for developing employees; the same process may not satisfy both purposes.

The Performance Appraisal Process

Figure 6–1 presents a model of the performance appraisal process. As noted in the figure, the adequacy and accuracy of the performance appraisal depend on two primary variables: (1) the motivation and ability of the evaluator and (2) the appraisal methods or formats. If either of these variables is insufficient, the appraisal may be inadequate and incapable of accomplishing its purposes. Moreover, these variables are interrelated; a well-designed appraisal format is of little use if the evaluator lacks sufficient training or motivation to use it. Too often, management seeks to solve performance appraisal problems by changing only one element of the process. Generally, problems can be corrected only when attention is given to the entire process.

The Evaluator's Motivation and Ability

As shown in figure 6–1, several factors affect an evaluator's motivation and ability to provide adequate and accurate appraisals: the organization's policies and procedures, the purposes and results of the appraisals, the personal characteristics of the evaluator and the employee, the training of the evaluator, and the appraisal method or format used. Before we discuss each of these factors in more detail, we must know who the evaluator is in most public agencies.

Who Evaluates? Although peers, subordinates, or the employee could act as the evaluator, supervisors generally do performance appraisals in public organizations. Tyer found that in all states in his survey, the supervisors were the primary evaluators.[2] Lacho, Stearns, and Villere found that in 93 percent of the cities in their survey, the supervisor was the rater.[3] Norms and traditions within most public organizations, plus legal requirements, often dictate that supervisors evaluate their subordinates. Moreover, employees usually expect their supervisors to evaluate them, especially when rewards, such as increased pay and promotions, are linked to the evaluation.

Although supervisors generally conduct performance appraisals, they can be done by subordinates, or peers, or as self-evaluations. Subordinate's evaluations of their superiors are used in a few organizations. If the superior–subordinate relationship is crucial to a supervisor's task, subordinates' ratings may be useful for identifying competent superiors, but there are serious problems with subordinate evaluations. Some supervisors might fail to provide proper leadership by trying to be "nice guys" with their subordinates. Furthermore, employees might not give accurate appraisals because they fear reprisals from their supervisors. In addition, subordinates might not be familiar with all aspects of their superiors' jobs; for example, they might know little about their relationships with other supervisors and higher-level managers.

Evaluation by peers is an option that is most widely used by professors in

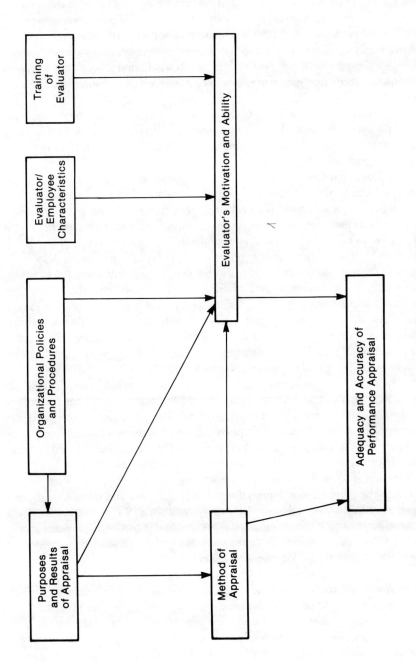

Figure 6–1. The Performance Appraisal Process

colleges and universities for promotion and tenure decisions and in the military. Peer ratings are rare, however, in public organizations. Peer appraisals tend to work (1) when there is a high level of trust among peers, (2) when the appraisals are not used to divide rewards, and (3) when employees are knowledgeable about their peers' performance. If peer ratings are to work, employees must not view appraisals as zero-sum games in which one employee's gain is another employee's loss.

Self-evaluation is not common in public organizations, although employee participation in the appraisal process is being emphasized more than in the past. Management by objectives, for example, requires the active participation of employees in goal setting.

Employee participation in performance appraisals also helps reduce a significant problem in many appraisals—employee distrust of the system. This distrust is a result of several factors. The evaluation is often the only indicator employees receive about management's view of them. Therefore, evaluations are important to employees not only because they may determine salaries and promotions but also because they indicate management's evaluation of their worth. Also, most public employees do not perform work that can be easily quantified. As a result, much subjectivity surrounds evaluations, and supervisors may allow numerous non-work-related variables (race, sex, and so on) to affect their evaluations of employees. When this occurs, employees are likely to distrust the whole system. Thus, employee participation in the performance appraisal process is essential for reduction of this distrust. A performance appraisal system will work only if employees believe it to be accurate, fair, and equitable.

The most accurate appraisals may involve several evaluations, because different individuals in an organization have different and unique perspectives of employees' performance. Supervisors might see one dimension, while peers can see a second. A composite asessment by the different groups can provide a comprehensive view of the employees' performance, although collecting and integrating data on all employees from all groups would be time-consuming.

Having discussed who serves as evaluator in public organizations, we can return to the performance appraisal model of figure 6–1 and investigate the factors that influence the evaluator's motivation and ability to provide accurate performance appraisals: (1) organizational policies and procedures, (2) the purposes and results of the appraisal, (3) evaluator/employee characteristics, (4) the training of the evaluator, and (5) appraisal methods.

Organizational Policies and Procedures. Perhaps the chief influence on evaluators' motivation and ability is the organization's policies on and procedures for performance appraisals. Supervisors learn very quickly whether the organization and their superiors take appraisals seriously. In some organizations, everyone knows that the evaluations are a joke and that no one pays much attention to them. Supervisors also know whether other supervisors tend to give high ratings to all their subordinates, and no supervisor wants to be the only "hard-nose" in the organization. If an organization wants accurate performance appraisals, it must communicate this goal by both word and deed. Organizations must reward supervisors who take the time and effort required for comprehensive appraisals.

The organization's policies on performance appraisal must also be consistent with its dominant management philosophy. In a mechanistic organization with a highly structured autocratic organization, for example, a participative performance appraisal method, such as management by objectives, would probably not be successful.

Purposes and Results of the Appraisals. The organization's performance appraisal policies determine the purposes and results of the appraisals, which in turn, affect the evaluator's motivation. If supervisors believe that their appraisals will actually be used to distribute rewards in the organization, they may invest more effort and thought in those appraisals. If seniority is the only basis for salary increases, however, supervisors may show little interest in formal appraisals. Similarly, if collective bargaining establishes across-the-board pay increases for both efficient and inefficient employees, supervisors may show little interest in formal appraisals.

The separation of salary administration from performance appraisal may encourage supervisors to be more accurate, because no punishment is involved.[4] When rewards are connected to appraisals, supervisors are often too lenient in their assessments, thus leading to the problem of leniency or inflation of ratings that is found in many performance appraisal systems.[5] In such situations, supervisors assign inaccurate ratings because so few benefits result from accurate ratings and so few penalties result from inaccurate ones.[6]

Evaluator/Employee Characteristics. The characteristics of the evaluator and the employee also affect the evaluator's motivation in the appraisal session. White supervisors who are prejudiced against blacks, for example, may give higher evaluations to white employees, and some white supervisors may be overly lenient when evaluating black employees to avoid any hint of racism. Research has indicated that, in general, whites rate whites higher and blacks rate blacks higher.[7]

Like race, the sex of supervisors and employees may affect the accuracy of the appraisal. For example, if a supervisor (male or female) believes that a particular position should not be occupied by a woman, the supervisor may give lower evaluations to any woman occupying the position. In general, studies have shown that females in positions that are generally perceived to be men's jobs tend to receive less favorable evaluations than men in the same positions.[8]

Although age differences between the evaluator and the employee may also affect the accuracy of the appraisal, research results have been unable to find any statistically significant variations in evaluations based on age differences.[9] The same conclusion applies to differences in educational level between the evaluator and the employee.[10]

Regarding the two leadership styles described in chapter 5—the employee—centered style and the production—centered style—research has indicated that production—oriented supervisors tend to give lower ratings to their subordinates.[11] Additional research has noted that supervisors who are highly considerate of employees give higher evaluations to their subordinates than supervisors who are more concerned about structuring the tasks to be accomplished by their subordinates.[12]

The impact of the various evaluator/employee characteristics (race, sex, age, and so forth) indicates a larger problem in performance appraisal. These characteristics would have little effect on evaluations if productivity and performance standards could be easily quantified. Unfortunately, the goals and missions of public organizations are not easily measured. (Reasons for this are given in chapters 1, 2, and 9.) Therefore, supervisors must make subjective judgments, which allow biases to enter evaluations. To reduce these biases, public agencies should train supervisors to recognize them and learn how to overcome them during appraisals. Such training should also help supervisors arrive at common definitions of what is excellent, average, or bad performance. Even in the absence of bias, different evaluators may use different standards in evaluating employees who are doing the same work. It is imperative, therefore, that evaluators agree to common definitions of performance levels.

Training of Evaluators. Training supervisors for performance appraisal can reduce many of the problems associated with evaluations, thereby improving the accuracy of the appraisal. First, supervisors should be informed of the purposes of performance appraisal, and they should know the linkage between a particular performance appraisal system and the purpose or purposes for which it is used. Second, the training should involve agreement on common standards of performance, and the supervisors should learn to apply these standards to case studies or sample situations. Third, the training should help supervisors recognize and control their own biases. Such training could involve role playing like that described in chapter 8.

Training has also helped to reduce other more technical problems in performance appraisal, including the halo effect (the tendency of an evaluator to allow one good or bad element of an employee's performance to affect the entire evaluation), central tendency (the tendency to give all employees the same rating), recency (the tendency to give greater weight to recent performance), and the contrast effect (the tendency to compare one employee to another rather than against a predetermined standard).

Supervisors should also receive training in giving bad news—including how to give feedback and how to develop nondefensive climates. Unfortunately, this requires considerably more time and skill than may be available in many performance appraisal training programs.[13] Nalbandian suggests that superiors, supervisors, and subordinates should all engage in evaluation training sessions together.[14] Although most training programs are deliberately designed to avoid this mix and to concentrate on supervisors only, Nalbandian contends that such training rarely affects supervisory behavior and that more attention must be given to the training of vertical slices of an agency's personnel—subordinates, supervisors, and supervisors' superiors—on problems generated by all participants.[15]

Appraisal Methods

As figure 6–1 notes, there are two primary influences on the accuracy of performance appraisals. We have discussed one—the evaluator's motivation and ability. The second is the appraisal method or format. The following are the most common appraisal methods:

1. Rating scales
   a. Graphic rating scales of personal traits and behavior
   b. Behaviorally anchored rating scales (BARS)
2. Interpersonal comparisons
   a. Ranking
   b. Forced distribution
3. Forced-choice checklists
4. Essay
5. Management by objectives

These methods can be categorized according to the concept underlying each method. First, some methods, including rating scales and checklists, compare employee performance against standards. The standards may be descriptions of various levels of behavior or they may consist of numerical scales. In the second category, which includes ranking and forced distribution methods, the evaluator makes interpersonal comparisons of employees against other employees in the unit on an overall basis. No specified standards of performance are used. In the third approach, management by objectives, an employee's performance is compared against objectives agreed to by both the employee and his or her supervisor. Finally, in the fourth approach, an evaluator prepares a general essay describing and evaluating an employee's performance.

Graphic Rating Scales. The oldest and most widely used appraisal method in government is the graphic rating scale. With this method, the direct supervisor of employees is supplied with one printed form for each employee to be evaluated. The form contains a number of characteristics to be assessed. Some of the common characteristics for nonsupervisory public employees include quantity and quality of work, personal appearance, dependability, cooperativeness, initiative, job knowledge, and attitude. Characteristics for supervisory employees might include leadership, decision-making ability, initiative, judgment, job knowledge, analytical ability, fairness, creative ability, and emotional stability.

Rating scales are provided for each characteristic; the scales can be continuous—in which the rater places a mark somewhere along a numbered line—or they can have a number of discrete steps for each characteristic, so that the rater must select one. Figure 6–2 is an example of a conventional rating scale that uses five discrete rating steps. Some forms also allow the supervisors to insert written explanations of their selections.

There are numerous problems with rating scales. First, the scales appear to be objective and scientific, when, in truth, they are often very subjective. The employee characteristics that are rated on the forms are generally traits that are difficult to define. Furthermore, the traits may not be related to performance. In addition, different evaluators may have very different standards in mind when they are evaluating their employees on the same traits. Also, because the traits may be unrelated to performance, they cannot be used for purposes of counseling and employee development.

Rating scales often encourage greater employee mistrust and defensiveness. For example, if a supervisor rates an employee low on responsibility because he was late to work several times, the employee's reaction to the supervisor's statement that he is not responsible will create more animosity than a more factual statement concerning the number of times the employee was tardy. In other words, it is preferable to comment on actual behavior than to evaluate general employee traits that are supposedly the cause of behavior.

Graphic rating scales are also subject to some of the common errors of appraisal, such as the halo effect, leniency, central tendency, and interpersonal bias. The *halo effect* refers to the tendency of raters to give the same or similar ratings to all behavior or personality dimensions on a scale. If the rater does not really know how to define each trait or behavior pattern and cannot see a direct link between the scale and performance, he or she may tend to rate all dimensions similarly. This problem might be reduced if the rater assessed all employees on a single dimension, rather than rating a single subordinate on all dimensions before rating the next subordinate. In this way, the rater could assess all employees on a common trait.

Leniency refers to the rater's tendency to be too lenient when rating a subordinate. Since many supervisors are uncomfortable when they must appraise their subordinates, they compensate by being too lenient. This may be particularly true with trait rating scales that are not directly linked to performance.

Some supervisors are reluctant to rate people at the outer end of the rating scale, and some raters attempt to play it safe by sticking to the middle of the scale. Rating scales tend to accentuate this common appraisal problem, which is known as *central tendency*.

Job Knowledge

[1]	[2]	[3]	[4]	[5]
Serious gaps in his knowledge of essentials of job	Satisfactory knowledge of routine aspects of job	Adequately informed on most phases	Good knowledge of all phases of job	Excellent understanding of his job. Extremely well-informed.

Judgment

[1]	[2]	[3]	[4]	[5]
Decisions often wrong or ineffective	Judgment often sound but makes some errors	Good decisions resulting from sound analysis of factors	Sound, logical thinker	Consistently makes sound decisions, even on complex issues

Oral and Written Communication

[1]	[2]	[3]	[4]	[5]
Unable to express ideas clearly. Often misunderstood	Expresses ideas satisfactorily on routine topics	Generally expresses thoughts adequately	Consistently expresses thoughts clearly	Outstanding in written and oral expression

Attitude

[1]	[2]	[3]	[4]	[5]
Uncooperative, resents suggestions, no enthusiasm	Often cooperative, often accepts suggestions	Satisfactory cooperation, accepts new ideas	Responsive, cooperates well, helpful to others	Excellent in cooperation, welcomes new ideas, very helpful and enthusiastic

Quantity of Work

[1]	[2]	[3]	[4]	[5]
Falls below minimum requirements	Usually meets minimum requirements	Satisfactory quantity	Usually well exceeds minimum	Consistently produces superior quantity

Quality of Work

[1]	[2]	[3]	[4]	[5]
Poor quality, many errors or rejects	Quality usually O.K. Some errors or rejects	Satisfactory quality	Quality exceeds normal standards	Consistent, high-quality work

Overall Evaluation

[1]	[2]	[3]	[4]	[5]
Poor	Fair	Satisfactory	Good	Excellent

Source: Dale S. Beach, *Personnel*, 4th ed. (New York: Macmillan, 1980), p. 297. Reprinted with permission.

Figure 6–2. A Conventional Rating Scale Form That Uses Five Discrete Steps for Each Factor Being Rated

Interpersonal bias refers to the impact supervisors' feelings about subordinates could have on their appraisals of those subordinates. Bias may have a greater impact when traits, rather than actual job performance, are assessed. Given the number of problems with graphic rating scales, it is surprising how many public agencies continue to use them. Rating scales remain the most popular method of appraisal. Tyer, for example, found that 40 percent of the states in his survey use graphic rating scales (see table 6–1).[16] Similarly, a recent survey of appraisal methods used by cities reveals that a large majority continue to use rating scales as the primary method of appraisal.[17]

There are several reasons for the popularity of rating scales. First, they are easy and inexpensive to construct. Second, one form can be applied across a large number of different positions. Third, they can be administered quickly: therefore, supervisors can dispense with the unpleasant task of evaluation quickly. Fourth, the numerical nature of the scales allows for easy comparison of employees for the purpose of determining salary increases.

Behaviorally Anchored Rating Scales (BARS). The BARS system is relatively new in the field of performance appraisal. The development of a typical BARS system includes five steps:

1. Persons with knowledge of the job to be appraised are asked to describe specific illustrations of effective and ineffective performance (critical incidents).
2. The developers of the instrument then cluster the incidents into a smaller set of performance dimensions, which they define. Typically, there are five to ten dimensions.
3. Another group of individuals who also have knowledge of the job to be appraised are asked to reallocate the critical incidents to each dimension. It is typical that incidents are retained if 50 to 80 percent of this group assign the incident to the same dimension as did the group in step 2.
4. The second group is then asked to rate (seven to nine-point scales are typical) the behavior described in the incident regarding how effectively or ineffectively the incident represents performance on the appropriate dimension.
5. Six or seven incidents per dimension are then arranged in the final instrument as behavioral anchors or benchmarks of effective and ineffective performance on the dimension.[18]

The presumed advantage of a BARS system is that it involves rigorous developmental procedures and high levels of participation by people who are familiar with the job to be appraised. Moreover, these are the same people who will ultimately use the system, presumably producing an evaluation that is highly job-related and that reflects actual performance. Helping to develop the instrument

Table 6–1
Types of Appraisal Formats Used in State Governments

	Number of States	Percentage
Graphic rating scales	21	40
Management by objectives	20	39
Essays	8	15
Behaviorally anchored rating scales	3	6

Source: Compiled from data in Charlie B. Tyer "Employee Performance Appraisal in American State Governments," *Public Personnel Management* 11 (Fall 1982):203.
Note: The number of states totals fifty-two because some use more than one format.

also may encourage greater use and acceptance of the instrument. Again, some think that BARS reduces leniency and central tendency error because the incidents represent actual job behavior characteristics, not personal traits.

The extensive time and expense needed to develop a BARS system and the variations that are required for different jobs probably account for the lack of interest in the BARS approach within government. Only one city in the survey by Lacho, Stearns, and Villere used a BARS system,[19] and Tyer found only three states using it.[20] Recent research indicates that this lack of enthusiasm for BARS systems is well justified. A review of research by Schwab, Heneman, and Decotiis indicates that there is little reason to believe that the BARS system is superior to other appraisal formats.[21] A subsequent review of research by Jacobs, Kafry, and Zedeck also found that the BARS system is no better or worse than other evaluation systems.[22]

Ranking. The ranking method requires that raters, who are usually supervisors, rank their subordinates on a global basis, according to their job performance and value to the organization. One system requires that the supervisor pick the best employee, then pick the worst employee, and so on, until all employees have been ranked. This is called *alternative ranking.*

Paired-comparison ranking involves ranking each subordinate against all other employees, one at a time. An employee's final rank-order is based on the number of times he or she is chosen over the other individuals in all the paired comparisons. One major problem with ranking is that it does not reveal the amount of difference between persons in adjacent ranks. Since the method is not job-specific and the employee is judged without any direct standards of performance, it provides little guidance for developmental counseling of employees. Also, it is difficult to make intergroup comparisons with this method, because it is impossible to tell how the top person in one group really compares to the top person in another group.

Forced Distribution. With the forced distribution method, supervisors are forced to distribute their ratings according to some predetermined distribution—generally, a normal frequency distribution (bell-shaped curve). This approach is designed to prevent supervisors from clustering their employees at the high end of the scale (leniency effect). The biggest problem with this approach is that it would be sheer coincidence if it coincided with actual job performance. Forced distribution is not a widely accepted technique when ratings must be discussed with employees. Given that such discussions are an important factor in the success of a performance appraisal process, this is a serious disadvantage.

Forced-Choice Checklists. In a forced-choice checklist system, supervisors must choose from among a set of alternative descriptors (usually four items) some subset that is most characteristic of each employee. Each descriptor isolates a component of employee behavior. Although all statements may appear favorable, only some are actually characteristic of high performers. The purpose of this approach is to reduce rater bias, because the rater is not actually assessing the employee but is selecting from a group of positive descriptive statements.

Contructing items for the forced-choice technique requires a trained technical specialist and a different set of items for each occupation. Also, with this system, supervisors must assess employees without knowing whether they are giving one person a more favorable rating than another. Such a method severely limits supervisor–employee discussion of the appraisal, and it would be difficult for the subordinate to obtain counseling or developmental information from such a process.

Essays. The essay method involves a single written statement describing the employee's performance. It can be written by the supervisor, by the employee, by peers, or by a combination of raters. The essay is more effective if it is based on actual job performance and if it cites facts about that performance as they relate to understood standards.[23] To do adequate evaluations, supervisors must devote considerable time and thought to writing the essays, and they must be more observant of their subordinates' performance. Because the essay often demands more time than the average supervisor is willing to devote to it, it is often combined with a graphic rating scale. Lacho, Stearns, and Villere found that a combination of the essay and the graphic rating scale was the main appraisal format in 68 percent of the cities in their study.[24] Tyer found that the essay was used in 15 percent of the states in his survey.[25]

Management by Objectives (MBO). Management by objectives (MBO) has become a popular management tool in both private and public organizations since Peter Drucker popularized the concept in his book, *The Practice of Management*, in 1954.[26] Designed to overcome some of the inherent problems of traditional graphic rating systems, MBO is much more than a performance appraisal format; it actually constitutes a new way of managing.

MBO is based on two key concepts: (1) the clearer the idea one has of what one is trying to accomplish, the greater the chances are of accomplishing it; and (2) progress can only be measured in terms of what one is trying to make progress toward.[27] Several key features are necessary to implement these basic concepts:

1. The superior and the subordinate agree upon and list the principal duties of the subordinate's job.
2. They agree upon a number of goals that the subordinate will attempt to attain in a certain time period.
3. They agree upon methods to measure progress toward the goals.
4. They agree upon resources that the subordinate may need to accomplish the goals.
5. They evaluate performance toward the goals at some regular interval.

It appears that MBO is gaining popularity in state and local governments. Moore and Staton, for example, found that 40 percent of the cities in their survey used MBO,[28] and Tyer found that 20 states used an MBO/performance-standards approach to appraisals.[29]

MBO is intended to produce a number of benefits. Because superiors and subordinates must confer about the nature of the subordinates' tasks and goals and how they interrelate with the unit's goals, the MBO process is said to ease communication within the organization. Since employees have a better idea of what they are trying to accomplish, their motivation and sense of responsibility are increased. As specific goals are developed and methods for measuring progress toward the goals are agreed upon, much of the subjectivity in the appraisal process is eliminated. Because the employees are appraised according to goals and standards in whose development they have had a part or toward whose development they have made a significant contribution, they are less likely to be defensive at evaluation time. Because the supervisors are applying criteria that were agreed upon in advance of the evaluation, they too, can enter the evaluation process with less stress and anxiety. The emphasis in such appraisals is on performance, not on personality traits.

MBO has some disadvantages, however. First, it requires more time and attention from the supervisor than other methods do. Because goal setting and attainment are so individualized, comparing the performance of one person with that of another or with some common standard is difficult. Also, lack of information may make it difficult for the supervisor to assess the feasibility of objectives. In addition, MBO may overstress short-run goals and easily quantifiable objectives, and important objectives may be neglected because of the difficulty in quantifying results. Despite these disadvantages, however, Tyer found that the states rated the MBO appraisal process as considerably more effective than other forms of evaluation.[30] Similarly, Moore and Staton found considerable satisfaction among the cities that were using MBO.[31] They found that the method's capacity for improving communication, increasing motivation, and enabling managers to better assign priority to tasks were among its most important benefits.

Selecting an Appropriate Appraisal Format. Keeley suggests that the choice of an appropriate appraisal format is contingent upon the employee's need for independence and the nature of the job.[32] He recommends the following: (1) behavior-based evaluation procedures—those that define specific performance expectations—for employees who perform highly routine jobs and need little independence; (2) goal-based procedures—those that define less-specific performance expectations—for employees who perform moderately routine jobs and need a moderate degree of autonomy; (3) multiple subjective judgments—those that define performance least specifically—for highly independent employees in decidedly nonroutine tasks.[33] For example, an MBO approach would not be appropriate for clerical employees, but it would be most appropriate for professionals and managers. Moore and Staton found this to be exactly the case in their survey of MBO use in the cities.[34] The higher up the bureaucratic ladder a position is, the more the evaluation of the occupant of the position becomes highly judgmental, subjective, and complex.

The Performance Appraisal Interview

The interview is an important part of a performance appraisal system. Perhaps the first question relating to the appraisal interview is what its purpose should be. The two main purposes of the interview are (1) counseling along with development and (2) the evaluation and a discussion of administrative decisions. Some argue that interviews that attempt to accomplish both functions force the superior into the conflicting roles of counselor and judge, cause subordinate defensiveness, and usually become salary discussions, with little influence on the subordinate's future performance.[35]

Expectancy motivation theory and path–goal leadership theory suggest, however, that development and salary functions should be combined in appraisal interviews. Some research has revealed that when rewards are tied to the performance appraisal system, employees' motivation to improve is enhanced and their satisfaction with the appraisal process is heightened. Perhaps a way out of the dilemma is to have one or more developmental sessions in which the supervisor talks about the problems of the employee, discusses methods of resolving them, and suggests goals that the employee might seek to accomplish in the future. These developmental sessions would act as preparation for the evaluation interview, which would be concerned with salary, promotion, and other rewards. This approach would allow for some development and would minimize employee surprise and possible resentment about eventual decisions.[36]

Frequency of Interviews

Most performance appraisal interviews occur annually. Tyer found that forty-three states require annual performance appraisals,[37] and in the Lacho, Stearns, and Villere survey, 80 percent of the cities appraised annually.[38] There are no clear guidelines regarding how often appraisal interviews should occur, but one can assume certain approximate intervals. Developmental interviews for employees in discretionary, nonroutine jobs should be conducted relatively frequently—generally, more than annually. Maintenance appraisals for satisfactory employees in more routine jobs could be conducted annually. Low performers may demand more frequent reviews, and new employees need more frequent appraisals than long-term employees.

Goal Setting in the Appraisal Interview

Goal setting by or for the subordinate during the appraisal interview has been consistently associated with positive appraisal interview results. Goal setting is directly related to greater mutual understanding and perceived fairness.[39] Also, when critical appraisals are revised into goals, they are much more likely to result in improved performance.[40] Useful goal setting may be limited, however, by the degree of control employees have in routine jobs and by the less quantifiable components of performance in very nonroutine jobs. For nonroutine, unstructured tasks, relatively open-ended, directional goals might function more effectively than fixed, specific goals.[41]

Subordinate Participation in the Appraisal Interview

The appraisal interview generally produces more positive results when there is more subordinate participation, because participation reduces defensiveness and increases employee satisfaction with the appraisal. Supervisors can encourage participation by asking questions and by not interrupting the subordinates or by requesting that subordinates appraise themselves or set and discuss their own goals. Greater employee participation is most effective, however, if the subordinates perceive the appraisals as nonthreatening. This perception is more likely if the employees are accustomed to participating with the supervisors in activities other than the appraisal process, if they are longer tenured subordinates who have previously been in appraisal interviews with their supervisors, and if they are relatively independent and knowledgeable about the issues to be discussed in the interviews.[42]

A Situational Approach to Performance Appraisal Interviews

The foregoing discussion of appraisal interviews suggests a situational approach to the interviews. Interviews with high performers in nonroutine positions should be directed toward development and should be conducted at necessary intervals. For long-term employees who have performed satisfactorily in routine jobs, interviews should be more concerned with deviation from prior acceptable performance. Such interviews should occur less frequently, at set intervals or as warranted by either outstanding or substandard performance. Frequent developmental and evaluative interviews should be held with new or low-performing employees.[43]

Appraisal interviews should be structured for high participation by the subordinates when the interviews are likely to be nonthreatening to them, when the subordinates are independent and knowledgeable about the issues, or when they are longer-term employees who are accustomed to participation with their superiors.[44] Some goal setting is recommended for most situations, but it should be limited to those components of jobs that are under the employees' control.[45]

The 1978 Civil Service Reform Act and Performance Appraisal

The 1978 Civil Service Reform Act (CSRA) requires that every federal agency (excluding military intelligence and security-related agencies) develop at least one system for periodic, objective appraisal of employees' job performance. All critical elements of the employees' positions must be identified in advance, and objective performance standards must be developed and communicated in writing to the employees at the beginning of the performance period. Also, federal agencies must encourage employees to participate in the establishment of performance standards. The CSRA also specifies that performance appraisal results must be used as a basis for training, rewarding, reassigning, promoting, reducing in grade, retaining, and removing employees.[46]

This new performance appraisal program began for the 8,000 Senior Executive Service (SES) officers in July 1979, for the 120,000 merit-pay managers and supervisors in October 1980, and for most of the 1.7 million rank-and-file employees in October 1981.[47] Although there has been insufficient time to make a definitive evaluation of the impact of the reform, recent studies indicate problems. In particular, the studies found that employees are less likely to believe that pay is based on performance after the implementation of the CSRA than before it was implemented.[48]

The federal government attempted to install the new performance appraisals too rapidly. As a result, little time was available to correct problems in the new evaluations before they were used to determine pay and other rewards. Employees are often wary of appraisals even in the best of circumstances, but when the appraisal system has been adopted quickly, is untried, and is tied to rewards such as pay, they are particularly suspicious.

Perry and Pearce note a "fatal contradiction" in the new performance appraisals.[49] On the one hand, the appraisals must be accurate reflections of performance, but, on the other hand, they must be addressed by pay-pool managers to maintain salary equity across the pay pools. This manipulation of ratings to achieve agency merit-pay goals undercuts the perceived validity of the entire performance appraisal system.

There are also signs of "gaming," or attempting to look good on the appraisals by concentrating on the quantitative criteria. For example, the Social Security Administration's evaluation criterion "processing-time" was manipulated by allowing a claimant to fill out an application but not allowing it to be signed until the earnings record and proofs were received.[50] Therefore, the two weeks it took to obtain the documents were not counted in the processing-time statistic. Such concentration on quantitative criteria also may have reduced risk taking and innovation in some agencies.

Some of the federal employees' negative reactions to the new performance appraisals may have been caused not by the evaluations but by other problems. Although the CSRA allowed bonuses for up to 50 percent of all SES members in a pay pool, Congress later reduced the ceiling to 25 percent, and the Office of Personnel Management further reduced the maximum to 20 percent. Career executives who entered the SES with the expectation that many above-average performers would receive bonuses felt betrayed.

The continuation of the pay cap on executive salaries generated more employee suspicion. The general pay increase of 9.1 percent in 1981 added to the pool another 46,000 executives who had reached the pay ceiling of $50,112.[51] Executives at or near the ceiling view the linkage between performance and pay as empty rhetoric. They know their performance will have little impact on their pay.

If the new performance appraisals are to be effective, several changes are required. The validity of the appraisals must be improved, and supervisors need additional training in developing standards and in giving appraisal feedback to employees. If performance and pay are to be linked, Congress and the Office of Management and Budget (OMB) must assure adequate funding for pay increases. Otherwise, employees will continue to see the pay-for-performance connection as empty rhetoric.

Performance Appraisal and the Law

Since the performance appraisal may be used for rewarding, promoting, retaining, and removing employees, it can be crucial in discrimination cases.

Duane Thompson's review of recent court decisions suggests that performance appraisals should have the following characteristics if they are to withstand judicial examination successfully:

1. They should be based on formal job analyses.
2. The entire appraisal process should be formal and as objective as possible.
3. Administration and scoring of appraisals should be standardized and controlled.
4. Evaluators should have written directions and training in the use of appraisal methods, and they should have considerable daily contact with those they are evaluating.
5. If the appraisal includes different measures of performance, the proportion that each measure represents in the total assessment should be fixed and stated.
6. Subjective supervisory ratings are permissible as one part of an entire process.
7. Employees should be informed of inadequate performance ratings as measured.[52]

Perhaps it is not coincidental that what the courts require is generally what researchers suggest as most effective and valid in performance appraisals.

The Contingency Approach and Performance Appraisal

The contingency approach suggests that mechanistic and organic organizations require different performance appraisal methods. Employees in highly mechanistic organizations perform highly routine jobs for which performance indicators are comparatively clear, unambiguous, and objective. For these employees, specific performance expectations and objective evaluation procedures seem most appropriate. Mechanistic organizations often have hierarchical management structures and their norms may dictate that supervisors perform the evaluations. Since measures of performance are often self-evident, there is little desire or need to engage in self-appraisals or peer appraisals. Appraisal interviews for long-term employees who have performed satisfactorily in the routine jobs of mechanistic organizations need not be held frequently—perhaps only when warranted by outstanding or substandard performance.

Employees in highly organic organizations are often professionals who desire considerable independence and perform decidedly nonroutine tasks that cannot be easily quantified and evaluated. More subjective and comprehensive performance appraisals are necessary for these positions, and self-ratings and peer appraisals are more acceptable and appropriate. Appraisal interviews for these employees should be directed toward development and should be conducted more frequently. Since employees in organic organizations generally are more knowledgeable about the issues of their jobs, and since they desire more independence, the appraisals should allow for considerable participation by the subordinates.

Conclusion

The discussion of performance appraisals in this chapter suggests that more performance-based systems are required. The 1978 Civil Service Reform Act requires performance-based appraisals for federal agencies, and surveys of state and local governments indicate that performance-based systems are becoming more common in the states and cities. The courts also are requiring performance-based systems.

This apparent shift to performance-based systems should not be interpreted to mean that appraisals will henceforth operate without problems. Defining performance objectives for some complex positions may be difficult, since not all components of any position can be quantified. Even though an organization is concerned about the methods for accomplishing its objectives, conditions may change and undermine the feasibility of previous objectives.

There are also many important components of a given job that cannot be defined as performance objectives. For example, supervisors often hope that their subordinates will take the initiative to solve problems that are not formally the responsibility of the subordinates. Also, supervisors hope that their subordinates are cooperative with colleagues and that eagerness to accomplish specified objectives does not produce divisive competitiveness. Some subordinates are valuable not for their productivity but because they encourage group cohesion and make the workplace much more sociable and enjoyable.

Nalbandian has noted that trust plays an important part in any successful appraisal system.[53] He states: "Even where work standards are clear, without organizational trust, employees will view performance evaluation with suspicion and defensiveness."[54] In other words, the quality of the appraisal process depends on the nature of the day-to-day supervisor–subordinate relationship. A good relationship implies that the supervisor is providing daily feedback and counseling; thus, the appraisal interview is merely a review of issues that already have been discussed.[55] If there is mutual trust, subordinates will be more willing to discuss performance problems and less defensive about negative evaluations.

Performance appraisal must be viewed as an entire process. Attempts to improve isolated elements without considering the dynamics of the entire process are destined for limited success. Before any changes are attempted in performance appraisal, organizations must identify their goals and purposes for appraisal. All changes should hinge on what the organization seeks from the process. Once an organization has clearly delineated its goals, it should ensure that its policies and procedures complement them. If an organization wants salary increases to be based on accurate performance appraisals, for example, it must demand that this policy be carried out, and it must reward supervisors who invest the time necessary for complete and accurate appraisals.

Public managers should also realize that the supervisor's motivation and ability to perform accurate appraisals is as important as the design of the appraisal format. Public organizations should help supervisors recognize how their biases can influence their performance appraisals. Moreover, supervisors must be trained to avoid common problems in evaluation, including the halo effect, central tendency, and leniency. The success of performance evaluation also demands that supervisors receive training in the proper conduct of appraisal interviews. Good interviews are particularly necessary to achieve the counseling and development goals of performance appraisal.

Finally, an organization's selection of an appraisal format must be based on more than just convenience or ease of administration. Good evaluation systems require time to design and administer; there is no cheap and easy route to accurate and useful appraisals. Although supervisors often prefer simple methods (graphic rating scales), such formats often provide only the appearance of evaluation. Substantive and useful appraisals require that supervisors recognize the importance of evaluation and that they commit the necessary time to do it properly.

Notes

1. Hubert S. Feild and William H. Holley, "Performance Appraisal—An Analysis of Statewide Practices," *Public Personnel Management* 4 (May-June 1975): 145–150; Charlie B. Tyer, "Employee Performance Appraisal in American State Governments," *Public Personnel Management* 11 (Fall 1982): 199–211; Kenneth J. Lacho, G. Kent Stearns, and Maurice F. Villere, "A Study of Employee Appraisal Systems of Major Cities in the United States," *Public Personnel Management* 8 (March-April 1979): 111–125.

2. Tyer, "Employee Performance Appraisal."

3. Lacho, Stearns, and Villere, "Study of Employee Appraisal Systems."

4. Thomas Decotiis and Andre Petit, "The Performance Appraisal Process: A Model and Some Testable Propositions," *Academy of Management Review* 3 (July 1978): 637.

5. For a discussion of this behavior, see C.J. Bartlett and A.T. Sharon, "Effect of Instructional Conditions in Producing Leniency on Two Types of Rating Scales," *Personnel Psychology* 22 (1969): 251–263; J.C. Dwyer and N.J. Dimitroff, "The Bottoms Up/Top Down Approach to Performance Appraisal," *Personnel Journal* 55 (1976): 349–353.

6. Decotiis and Petit "Performance Appraisal Process," p. 638.

7. W.J. Bigoness, "Effect of Applicants Sex, Race and Performance on Employer Performance Ratings: Some Additional Findings," *Journal of Applied Psychology* 60 (1976): 80–84.

8. N. Schmitt and T. Hill, "Sex and Race Composition of Assessment Center Groups as a Determinant of Peer and Assessor Ratings," *Journal of Applied Psychology* 61 (1977): 261–264.

9. F.J. Landy and J.L. Farr, "Performance Rating," *Psychological Bulletin* 87 (1980): 72–107.

10. Ibid.

11. E.K. Taylor, J.W. Parker, L. Mortens, and G.L. Ford, "Supervisory Climate and Performance Ratings, An Exploratory Study," *Personnel Psychology* 11 (1959):453–468.

12. M.S. Klores, "Rater Bias in Forced-Distribution Ratings," *Personnel Psychology* 18 (1966): 411–421.

13. John Nalbandian, "Performance Appraisal: If Only People Were Not Involved," *Public Management Review* 10 (May-June 1981): 392–396.

14. Ibid.

15. Ibid.

16. Tyer, "Employee Performance Appraisal," p. 203.

17. Lacho, Stearns, and Villere, "Study of Employee Appraisal Systems," p. 115.

18. D.P. Schwab, H.G. Heneman, and T.A. Decotiis, "Behaviorally Anchored Rating Scales: A Review of the Literature," *Personnel Psychology* 28 (1975): 550–551.

19. Lacho, Stearns, and Villere, "Study of Employee Appraisal Systems," p. 115.

20. Tyer, "Employee Performance Appraisal."

21. Schwab, Heneman, and Decotiis, "Behaviorally Anchored Rating Scales," p. 557.

22. Rich Jacobs, Ditsa Kafry, and Sheldon Zedeck, "Expectations of Behaviorally Anchored Rating Scales," *Personnel Psychology* 33 (1980):595–629.

23. Robert G. Pajer, U.S. Office of Personnel Management (OPM), Intergovernmental Personnel Programs, *Employee Performance Evaluation* (Washington, D.C.: U.S. Government Printing Office, 1979), p. 17.

24. Lacho, Stearns, and Villere, "Study of Employee Appraisal Systems," p. 115.

25. Tyer, "Employee Performance Appraisal," p. 210.

26. Peter Drucker, *The Practice of Management* (New York: Harper & Brothers, 1954).

27. W.S. Wikstrom, *Managing By-and-with Objectives,* Personnel Policy Study No. 212. (New York: National Industrial Conference Board, 1968).

28. Perry Moore and Ted Staton, "Management by Objectives in American Cities," *Public Personnel Management* 10 (Summer 1981): 223.

29. Tyer, "Employee Performance Appraisal," p. 210.

30. Ibid., p. 210.

31. Moore and Staton, "Management by Objectives in American Cities," p. 230.

32. Michael Keeley, "A Contingency Framework for Performance Evaluation," *Academy of Management Review* 3 (July 1978): 428–438.

33. Ibid., p. 436.

34. Moore and Staton, "Management by Objectives in American Cities," p. 223.

35. H.H. Meyer, E. Kay, and J.R.P. French, "Split Roles in Performance Appraisal," *Harvard Business Review,* 43 (1965): 123–129; Douglas Cederblan, "The Performance Appraisal Interview: A Review, Implications, and Suggestions," *Academy of Management Review* 7 (1982): 220.

36. L.L. Cummings and D.P. Schwab, "Designing Appraisal Systems for Information Yield," *California Management Review* 20 (1978): 18–25.

37. Tyer, "Employee Performance Appraisal," p. 205.

38. Lacho, Stearns, and Villere, "Study of Employee Appraisal Systems," p. 116.

39. M.M. Greller, "The Nature of Subordinate Participation in the Appraisal Interview," *Academy of Management Journal* 21 (1978): 646–658.

40. J.R.P. French, E. Kay, and H. Meyer, "Participation and the Appraisal System," *Human Relations* 19 (1966): 3–20.

41. Cederblan, "Performance Appraisal Interview," p. 223.

42. Ibid., p. 225.

43. Ibid., p. 226.

44. Ibid.

45. Ibid.

46. Duane Thompson, "Performance Appraisal and the Civil Service Reform Act," *Public Personnel Management* 10 (Fall 1981): 281–288.

47. Robert W. Brown, "Performance Appraisal: A Policy Implementation Analysis," *Review of Public Personnel Administration* 2 (Spring 1982): 69–85.

48. Jone L. Pearce and James L. Perry, "Federal Merit Pay: A Longitudinal Analysis," *Public Administration Review* 43 (July-August 1983): 315-325. Also see Peter Ring and James Perry, "Reforming the Upper Levels of the Bureaucracy: A Longitudinal Study of the Senior Executive Service," *Administration and Society* 15 (May 1983): 119–144; Patricia Ingraham and Peter Colby, "Individual Motivation and Institutional Changes Under the Senior Executive Service,' *Review of Public Personnel Administration* 2 (Spring 1982): 101–117.

49. James L. Perry and Jone L. Pearce, "Initial Reactions to Federal Merit Pay," *Personnel Journal* 62 (March 1983): 230–237.

50. Pearce and Perry, "Federal Merit Pay," p. 321.

51. Brown, "Performance Appraisal," p. 80.

52. Thompson, "Performance Appraisal and the Civil Service Reform Act," p. 285. Also see Hubert S. Feild and W.H. Holley, "The Relationship of Performance Appraisal System Characteristics to Verdicts in Selected Employment Discrimination Cases," *Academy of Management Journal* 35 (1982): 392–406; G.B. Giglioni, J.B. Giglioni, and J.A. Bryant, "Performance Appraisal: Here Comes the Judge," *California Management Review* 23 (Winter 1981): 14–23; Wayne Cascio and H.J. Bernardin, "Implications of Performance Appraisal Litigation for Personnel Decisions," *Personnel Psychology* 34 (1981): 211–226; Lawrence S. Kleeman and Richard L. Durham, "Performance Appraisal, Promotion and the Courts: A Critical Review," *Personnel Psychology* 34 (1981): 103–121.

53. Nalbandian, "Performance Appraisal," pp. 392–396.

54. Ibid., p. 394.

55. Michael Beer, "Performance Appraisal Dilemmas and Possibilities," *Organizational Dynamics* (Winter 1981): 24–36.

7
Compensation: Pay and Benefits

Key Words

Determinants of pay satisfaction

Consequences of pay dissatisfaction

Salary surveys

Pay plan

Pay ranges or grades

Pay-for-performance system

Equal pay for equal work

Equal pay for comparable worth

Equal Pay Act of 1963

County of Washington v. Gunther

System rewards

Sick leave

Replacement rates

Early retirement

Cost-of-living adjustments

Actuarial funding

Unfunded accrued liability

Introduction

Since compensation is the largest expense of all governments, it is hoped that it contributes to performance and effectiveness. This chapter examines the role of compensation in promoting organizational effectiveness and discusses the importance of pay to public employees and their perception of pay equity. Various salary surveys and pay plans are described, and the linkage between pay and performance and the problems in establishing a pay-for-performance system (merit pay) are revealed through an analysis of the 1978 Civil Service Reform Act. Because the comparable worth issue is a major problem in pay administration, recent court decisions and opposing points of view on this controversial issue are explored. Finally, fringe benefits, which comprise more than 30 percent of total compensation to public employees, are examined at length.

Compensation and Organizational Effectiveness

An organization provides pay and fringe benefits to its employees to promote the organization's effectiveness. Katz and Kahn list the patterns of employee behavior that are required for organizational effectiveness:

1. Joining and staying in system
   a. Recruitment
   b. Low absenteeism
   c. Low turnover
2. Dependable behavior: role performance in system
   a. Meeting or exceeding quantitative standards of performance
   b. Meeting or exceeding qualitative standards of performance
3. Innovative and spontaneous behavior: performance beyond role requirements for accomplishment of organizational functions
   a. Cooperative activities with fellow members
   b. Actions protective of system or subsystem
   c. Creative suggestions for organizational improvement
   d. Self-training for additional organizational responsibility
   e. Creation of favorable climate for organization in the external environment[1]

It is obvious that sufficient employees must remain in the organization to perform the essential functions. High turnover and absenteeism are always costly to organizations. Furthermore, the employees must meet or exceed minimal qualitative and quantitative standards. The organization also needs employees who are innovative and who perform activities that are beneficial to the organization. As Katz and Kahn note: "The resources of people for innovation, for spontaneous behavior and creative behavior are vital to organizational survival and effectiveness."[2] Wages encourage the kinds of behavior noted by Katz and Kahn only under the following conditions: (1) pay is important to the employee; (2) the employee views his or her pay as equitable; and (3) pay is related to the employee's behavior.

The Importance of Pay

If pay is to motivate behavior, employees must desire it. Some organizational behavior researchers believe that money is most important to employees, while others believe that interesting work is of the utmost importance. Both groups are able to find examples to support their beliefs. Pay tends to be more important to the young male employee.[3] Employees in industrial organizations also value pay most highly. Workers in government agencies, however, place less emphasis on pay; and people who work in hospitals and social service organizations place the least emphasis on pay.[4] Since people tend to work for organizations that they feel will satisfy their most important needs, people who enter public careers may value money less than those who pursue careers in private organizations.[5] Indeed, Rawls and his associates found that students about to enter the nonprofit sector valued economic wealth to a lesser degree than did students entering the profit sector.[6] Studies of the preferences of public employees consistently indicate that high wages are not their top objective.[7] Public employees' lower desire for high pay should caution those who expect merit pay or more pay to dramatically increase the productivity of those employees.

Although public employees do not rate pay as highly as their private-sector counterparts do, and although pay may not be their most prized reward, they do value it. In fact, public employees often voice considerable dissatisfaction with their pay.[8] Pay is valued because it is a ubiquitous reward that can satisfy several needs simultaneously: the needs for security, esteem, and self-confidence. In addition, the level of pay may be the only indicator of the employee's value to the organization. In other words, pay is important because of the message it conveys to the employee.

Pay and Equity

If pay is to motivate employee behavior, the employees must see their pay as equitable. Equity theory (see chapter 5) states that if employees believe that their pay does not equal their contributions (effort and performance), they may reduce their contributions or leave the organization (turnover and absenteeism).

Edward Lawler has developed a model of the determinants of pay satisfaction (see figure 7–1). According to this model, pay satisfaction depends on the employees' perception of their pay as equitable. Moreover, employees' perception of what their pay should be depends, in part, on their perception of what others receive. Therefore, public employers must conduct salary surveys to determine whether their employees receive pay comparable to that received by similar employees in other organizations.

The model also shows that employees' perception of what their pay should be depends on (1) the skills, abilities, and training the employees bring to their jobs; (2) the responsibilities and skills required by the jobs; and (3) the employees' perception of their own effort and performance versus other employees' effort and performance. Therefore, the public employer must have a sound pay plan or schedule that assures the same general level of pay for positions of similar difficulty and responsibility. Also, the public employer must assure that employees' pay is based on performance. If the public employer fails to do these things, the employees may be dissatisfied with their pay, leading to the consequences noted in figure 7–2.

Government Salaries and Salary Surveys

Government agencies compete for labor with other public employers and with private companies. In the past, government salaries were lower than salaries for similar positions in the private sector. The Federal Salary Reform Act of 1962 and the Federal Pay Comparability Act of 1970, however, established the principle that salaries for federal white-collar workers should be comparable to those paid to similar private-sector workers. Today, salaries for many government jobs equal or exceed salaries for similar positions in the private sector. A 1978 study reported, for example, that federal wages were 152 percent of private wages for similar jobs.[9] Higher salaries are not the case, however, for all government employees. Pay rates vary widely among state, local, and county governments; in some areas of the country, public employees make more than their private-sector counterparts, while in other areas, they make less. Moreover, compensation for executives at all levels of government has never equaled that of private executives. Since citizens are opposed to big salaries for bureaucrats, politicans are reluctant to increase salary ceilings, particularly during election years. When salary ceilings remain unchanged for several years, pay scales are compressed, and executives, with more responsibilities, are paid little more than their subordinates. This, of course, creates salary inequity, pay dissatisfaction, and turnover.

Governments conduct salary surveys in an effort to determine appropriate salaries for their employees. The surveys concentrate on collecting data for key classes of jobs that include large numbers of employees and that occur in substantial numbers in the workforce.[10] After the jobs to be included in the surveys

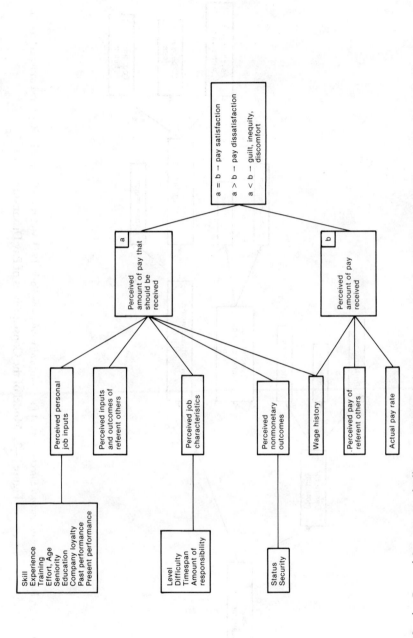

Edward Lawler, *Pay and Organizational Effectiveness: A Psychological View* (New York: 1971 McGraw-Hill), p. 215. Reprinted with permission.

Figure 7–1. Model of the Determinants of Pay Satisfaction

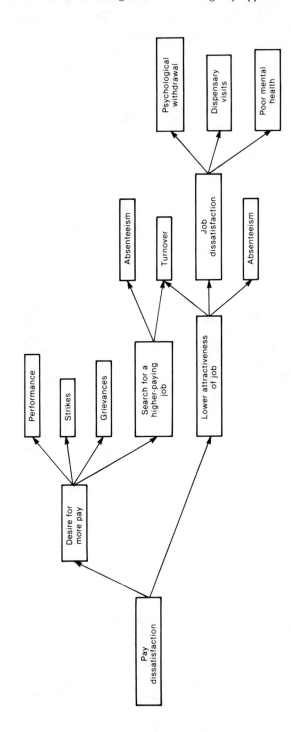

Edward Lawler, *Pay and Organizational Effectiveness: A Psychological View* (New York: 1971 McGraw-Hill), p. 233. Reprinted with permission.

Figure 7–2. Model of the Consequences of Pay Dissatisfaction

are selected, the appropriate geographic area to be covered by the salary surveys must be determined. State and local governments' surveys generally cover only the area within which the government must compete for workers. The federal government uses local surveys to establish pay rates for blue-collar workers, but it uses national surveys for general-schedule, white-collar positions. Some believe that this practice fails to recognize that the appropriate labor markets for white-collar employees are local or regional, and that reliance on a national survey results in some employees being overpaid in one locale and other employees being underpaid in another. Presidents Ford and Carter attempted to rectify this problem, but Congress refused to act.

After the geographic area for a survey is selected, the government must determine which employers should be in the survey. Employers with large workforces that contain key jobs similar to those of the government employer should be selected, but some small employers should also be included to provide balance in the survey. Large firms tend to pay higher salaries than small companies do, so a survey of only large firms would indicate an average salary higher than what is actually paid. The federal surveys exclude most small firms, however, and thus produce inflated average salaries. The federal surveys also fail to include state and local employees. Since these workers perform functions similar to those of federal employees, failure to include them compromises the reliability of the federal surveys.

Some salary surveys include fringe benefits, but others do not. The federal surveys compare only wages. Since benefits are generally higher in government, failure to include them in comparisons of compensation may result in serious distortions. The problem of defining benefits remains problematic, however. Which benefits should be included? How should the benefits be measured? Comparisons could be made on the basis of the cost of each benefit to the employer, but the cost of a particular benefit may differ across occupations. Also, benefit levels may be influenced by the demographic characteristics of the workforce (for example, older employees require more health care).[11] Since employees are interested in the level, not the cost, of benefits, surveys should compare the level of benefits provided by different organizations. The benefits that should be compared include pensions and health care, disability and life insurance plans, and the number of paid holidays, vacation days, and sick leave days.[12]

The public employer can use good salary surveys to establish competitive pay scales for employees. By paying competitive salaries, the public employer can obtain talented personnel who will remain in the organization. Competitive salaries will not ensure, however, that employees will be satisfied with their pay. Pay satisfaction is a product of both external and internal comparisons, and salary surveys provide only the external comparison. Even if a public agency pays significantly higher salaries than its competitors, its employees may remain dissatisfied with their salaries because they dislike the internal process of allocating salaries. Thus, pay satisfaction requires both external and internal equity.

Internal Equity: Establishing a Pay Plan

A pay plan for a specified group of employees indicates that pay levels have been established that are related to the relative worth of the different kinds of positions and that are based on prevailing pay rates for similar jobs in the relevant job market.[13] A good pay plan serves several purposes. First, it ensures that there is the same general level of pay for positions of similar difficulty and responsibility, and it provides the proper differences in salaries among positions that differ in difficulty and responsibility.[14] A pay plan also allows employees to know what their present and future salaries may be. Finally, those who are responsible for raising revenue and administering public funds can use pay plans to predict probable future financial obligations.[15]

A sound pay plan requires a good classification plan that provides information concerning the skills, effort, and responsibility required for each position. (See chapter 3 for a discussion of classification plans.) Because the classification of positions is essential for the development of a sound pay plan, jurisdictions may prepare the two plans concurrently.[16] If the jurisdiction has a comprehensive, up-to-date classification plan, immediate development of the pay plan can begin.

Pay plans include pay schedules which consist of several pay ranges or grades, each of which includes several pay rates or steps. Table 7–1 is an example of a pay schedule that has four pay ranges, with five pay rates within each pay range. Pay ranges may vary in width and should be tailored to fit the job classes assigned to them. For example, more complex jobs that require a longer time to master should have wider pay range than routine, quickly learned jobs. Ranges of 25 to 35 percent for lower-level jobs and up to 50 percent for managerial and executive positions are normal.[17]

After the width of the pay range is decided, the differential between successive pay rates or steps in each range must be selected. This selection will, in turn, establish the number of pay rates needed in each pay range. A 5 percent differential is commonly used. Many believe that if the differential is less than 5 per-

Table 7–1
Sample Pay Schedule

	Pay Rate				
Pay Range	A	B	C	D	E
1	$644	$676	$710	$746	$783
2	$708	$743	$781	$820	$861
3	$779	$818	$859	$902	$947
4	$857	$900	$945	$992	$1042

cent, there is no incentive for better performance. On the other hand, larger differentials may result in too few pay rates or pay ranges that are too wide.

There is considerable variation in the number of pay ranges or grades in pay schedules. Some schedules have only four or five ranges as in figure 7–2, whereas others contain more than twenty. Also, larger jurisdictions may have more than one pay schedule; for example, a city may have one schedule for police, another for firefighters, and a third for general employees in the remaining departments.

Pay ranges are based on the job analysis and evaluation used to develop the classification plan, which groups jobs into classes or grades on the basis of numerous factors, including complexity of tasks, level of responsibility, degree of judgment, level of difficulty, supervision received and exercised, and working conditions. These grades are then located within each pay range in the pay plan. The pay for any particular range is determined by conducting salary surveys for major jobs found within the pay range.

Because it is necessary to maintain an integrated pay schedule in which there are set differentials among the pay ranges, salary surveys cannot completely dictate pay for particular ranges. In general, community pay rates are too erratically spaced to be used directly in deciding the pay for each range. A salary survey might reveal, for example, that one range should go up 9 percent, another should go up 4 percent, another should remain the same, and yet another should decrease by 3 percent. If this were done, however, all semblances of an integrated pay schedule would disappear. Furthermore, these changes would not be politically acceptable. Therefore, a payline is developed by statistical techniques in such a way that the regular salary intervals of the pay plan are maintained while still providing the best approximation of community pay rates.

Once pay ranges, their widths, and the number of rates or steps within each range are established, the administrator must decide how to award within-range pay increases. Seniority often dictates such increases within the pay range. For example, new employees generally start at the minimum salary of the pay range for their position. After completing the probationary period, they may move to the next step. The employees may then move up one step or rate increase per year until they are at the top of the pay range for their position. These within-range step increases often come to be viewed as automatic employee rights. Once employees have reached the top of the pay plan, they may ask that their positions be reclassified and placed in a higher pay range, and the process starts over again. Critics of this typical case suggest that pay increases should be permissive, rather than automatic, and should depend on the employees' performance, not on their seniority.

Pay and Performance

The foregoing discussions of job evaluation, internal pay equity, and pay plans stress that people in equal positions should receive equal compensation. However, different people who occupy the same position may perform the job with different degrees of skill. Therefore, a good pay plan must provide some latitude for discrepancies in pay according to performance. Furthermore, the patterns of behavior required for organizational effectiveness are more likely to occur if pay is linked to performance. Both the expectancy and the reinforcement theories of motivation (see chapter 5) emphasize that behavior is contingent on rewards. If rewards are to motivate the desired behavior, pay should be based on performance.

Another reason for basing pay on performance is that more achievement-oriented individuals are attracted to organizations that base pay on performance.[18] These good performers expect more pay than poor performers; therefore, the public agency that seeks to retain them must pay for their good performance.[19] Poor performers generally stay in an organization because they cannot obtain more pay elsewhere. Therefore, if pay is not based on performance, good performers will leave or become discouraged, and poor performers will remain, build additional seniority, and demand more pay, a situation that results in an irrational distribution of scarce money. These advantages of pay for performance may explain why a recent survey of state and local governments found that 54 percent of the states and 48 percent of the local governments utilize programs linking monetary rewards with superior performance ratings.[20]

Pay for Performance and the 1978 Civil Service Reform Act

Despite the advantages in basing pay on performance, organizations find it difficult to do so. Some of the problems inherent in pay-for-performance systems are revealed in the implementation of the 1978 Civil Service Reform Act, which required several pay-for-performance programs. Among these were $10,000 and $20,000 presidential awards for senior executives whose performance was judged outstanding over several years. Senior executives also became eligible for annual bonuses of up to 20 percent of their salaries, based on performance appraisals. The pay-for-performance program that includes the largest number of employees is merit pay, which was established for managers and supervisors in grades 13 through 15 of the general schedule.[21]

The implementation of the CSRA has produced some problems. Merit pay cannot produce improved performance if employees value pay less than other rewards that are not contingent on performance, yet this is apparently the case for some federal employees. Pearce and Perry's longitudinal study of the impact of the CSRA on employees in five federal agencies reveals, for example, that employees value challenging work responsibilities and retirement benefits more highly than pay.[22] Since these rewards are not necessarily contingent on high performance, the merit-pay provisions of the CSRA may have only limited influence in improving performance.

The introduction of merit pay is more successful when employees accept the principle that there may be legitimate differences in compensation among employees who hold the same job title. Many public employees, however, have come to expect within-range longevity increases as automatic adjustments for seniority rather than rewards for performance. This expectation is even more pronounced when inflation is severe and many employees expect a cost-of-living adjustment. Cost-of living adjustments can absorb most of the money available for salary increases, leaving comparatively little for merit-based increases.

Merit-pay programs can be introduced more easily if the employees have considerable trust in the process of salary administration within the organization. Some early studies of the acceptance of merit pay in the federal service indicate that there is insufficient trust for an easy acceptance of merit-based pay. For example, 65 percent of 250 senior executives at a Federal Executive Institute seminar felt that Senior Executive Service (SES) bonuses were not given fairly.[23] Colby and Ingraham found that almost as many SES members thought the CSRA reforms made the linkage between pay and performance worse (23 percent) as thought they made the linkage better (27 percent).[24] Similarly, Pearce and Perry discovered that employees in five federal agencies were less likely to believe that pay was based on performance after the implementation of the CSRA than before it was implemented.[25]

Trust is more readily developed when the performance criteria on which employees are evaluated are clear and objective. In the white-collar work of government, however, objective performance measures are difficult to formulate. Therefore, performance appraisals may emphasize the more easily measured quantitative job dimensions and ignore the qualitative ones. Moreover, employees in public organizations that have multiple goals may not know which goals to pursue. In addition, managers complain about being held responsible for things over which they have little or no control.

The CSRA recognizes the critical importance of the performance appraisal in a merit-pay system. It requires that every federal agency develop objective performance appraisals and communicate the performance standards in writing to employees at the beginning of the performance period. The CSRA also specifies that the performance appraisal be used as a basis for training, rewarding, promoting, reassigning, reducing in grade, retaining, and removing employees.[26] Unfortunately, several problems have developed in the implementation of these CSRA performance appraisal requirements. First, too much was attempted too quickly. The federal government established a new performance appraisal system throughout the government in less than two years. Thus, no time was available to experiment and correct problems before the appraisal was accepted as the critical link in the merit-pay process.[27] Employees are naturally apprehensive about performance appraisal, even under the best of circumstances. When the appraisal system is new and untried, and when much of the employees' welfare rests on the new process, their suspicion and apprehension are more pronounced.[28]

Additional problems plagued the new CSRA performance appraisal system. The CSRA allowed bonuses for up to 50 percent of all SES members in a particular pay pool; however, after NASA provided bonuses to 46 percent of its SES members, Congress reduced those eligible for bonuses from 50 percent to 25 percent.[29] Executives who had entered the SES with the expectation that many above-average performers would receive bonuses felt betrayed. Additional mistrust of the pay-for-performance system of the CSRA was caused by the continuation of the cap on executive salaries. The 1980 pay raise of 9.1 percent increased the number of executives who had reached the annual salary ceiling of $50,112. Employees whose salaries had already reached the ceiling before the general salary increase, and who had more difficult responsibilities, may have viewed the pay-for-performance concept as empty rhetoric.[30]

Suspicion of the system is also caused by what Perry and Pearce call a "fatal contradiction" in the new federal performance appraisal process: although appraisals must be accurate reflections of employees' performance, they must also be managed by pay-pool managers and personnel specialists to maintain equity across pay pools.[31] Perry and Pearce note that this contradiction is based on several assumptions:

1. All pay pools include equal percentages of high, average, low performers.
2. The natural distribution of performance permits high performers in each pool to receive salary increases several times greater than those of low performers.
3. The only reason supervisory ratings do not reflect this is because the supervisors, either purposely or through ignorance, distort their ratings.[32]

These assumptions are dubious at best, and such manipulation of ratings contributes to further employee distrust of the whole process. If the evaluations are accurate, why should they require manipulation?

Finally, the CSRA was passed because President Carter had capitalized on the public's antibureaucracy attitude. Both Presidents Carter and Reagan ran as outsiders against the federal bureaucracy, and neither president has had many kind words for bureaucrats.[33] Thus, the political rhetoric surrounding the passage of the CSRA did little to ensure a receptive and fertile organizational climate for its implementation.[34]

Obstacles to Implementation of the Pay-for-Performance System

In their review of state and local attempts to implement pay-for-performance systems, John Greiner and his associates identify several barriers to the introduction of such incentives.[35] The first barriers they note are legal ones. Some state and local governments have laws that prohibit their giving employees any rewards except regular wages and salaries. In addition, some appropriation ordinances prescribe in detail the pay rates for government employees.

Second, civil service practices and procedures are often barriers to merit pay. These procedures may limit the frequency with which rewards can be granted or they may require that an employee remain at a given step for a given amount of time. Such regulations may tightly control the amounts of rewards given to employees and may require that certain pay differentials be maintained. Similarly, civil service laws obstruct experimentation with pay-for-performance systems and restrict the gradual introduction of such systems because these laws are usually written to emphasize uniformity in compensation.

Greiner also notes political barriers to the introduction of pay-for-performance programs.[36] City councils may be reluctant, for example, to give supervisors and city managers wide discretion in awarding merit increases. Monetary incentives are often viewed by the public as a giveaway of tax funds, and legislators are hesitant to proceed with a merit plan that could increase costs.

These problems suggest that before an organization introduces merit pay, it should carefully review its own needs and climate. If the organization's employees do not value pay as highly as other rewards, the organization may produce little change by linking pay to performance. Employees should desire pay and also believe that pay should be based on performance before a pay-for-performance system is introduced.

A pay-for-performance system may not be appropriate for organizations that place a premium on group effort and cooperation and value risk-taking and innovation. Often, pay-for-performance occurs in a zero-sum game context; that is, what one employee receives, another must lose. Such situations undermine cooperation and group efforts and employees under pay-for-performance plans might play it safe and forgo risk taking and innovation by concentrating on "what counts" in the performance appraisal—which may be a reflection of "what is quantifiable." Thus, essential but nonquantifiable behaviors may be ignored.

If an organization decides that a pay-for-performance plan is appropriate for its needs, it should establish the proper climate for the introduction of the system. Accusations that bureaucrats are lazy and that a system is needed to force then to work do not create a receptive environment. Such antibureaucracy rhetoric should be avoided. Furthermore, organizations should not attempt to implement a merit-pay plan over a short period of time. Considerable time is needed to explain the purposes and procedures of a new plan, and additional time is necessary to correct problems in the performance appraisal.

The performance appraisal is the crucial link in any pay-for-performance system. If merit pay is to be effective, employees must have confidence in the appraisal. This confidence is more easily developed if the employees have been intimately involved in the development of the appraisal. Moreover, employees are more likely to develop confidence when they do not view the new system as a potential threat to their welfare. Therefore, problems in the performance appraisal system should be eliminated before it is used to determine salary increases.

Equal Pay for Comparable Worth

As Doherty and Harriman note: "The problem of equal pay for equal worth occurs when women are paid less for doing the same job as men; the problem of equal pay for comparable worth occurs when whole classes of jobs, those that are traditionally held by women, are relegated to low pay and low status."[37] Studies have shown that one-third to one-half of women workers are in occupations that are 80 percent female, and that these occupations are low paying and low in status.[38] Some say that women are discriminated against when primarily female occupations receive lower salaries than male-dominated occupations, even though both are of equal worth to the organization.

Differences in pay for different occupations in the public sector are rooted in job evaluation procedures. Since job evaluation is inherently subjective, evaluators may give more weight to such factors as heavy lifting and physical labor, which are associated with "male"occupations, and little weight to such traits as speed and fine-motor requirements, a characteristic that is more common to "female" jobs. Another criticism of job evaluation procedures concerns the use of multiple systems within the same organization. Supporters of multiple systems say that unitary job evaluation systems would result in "comparing apples and oranges." The typical practice, therefore, is to have one system for primarily male occupations in the organization and another for female occupations—for example, one system for blue-collar workers and another for clerical employees.

Another major criticism of job evaluation in the public sector is that it relies too heavily on the worth of comparable occupations in the private labor market. This criticism rests on several complaints. First, the geographic areas covered by surveys for different occupations in the same organization may differ. A wage survey of blue-collar jobs may cover an area that is significantly different from the area surveyed for wages of clerical workers. Similarly, the sizes of the organizations covered by the surveys might differ. Such differences can contribute to significant variations in the average salaries determined by the surveys.

Second, even if the salary surveys were conducted uniformly across all positions in the organization, they would continue to reflect the history of discrimination that has existed in private-sector markets. Historically, women were encouraged to become nurses, clerks, librarians, and teachers. Employers paid lower wages for these occupations because women were in them and because the employers assumed that the wages of women were used only to supplement their husbands' salaries. Also, unions chose to organize predominantly male occupations. As a result, although primarily female occupations may be as important to organizations as primarily male occupations, and although the market rates may not reflect the true availability of labor because of union influence, women in primarily female occupations continue to be paid less in the marketplace. The salary surveys used by the public sector, therefore, may simply perpetuate and transfer the historical discrimination in the private labor market to the public sector.

The Equal Pay Act of 1963 prohibits discrimination in wages within the same occupation on the basis of sex. It could not be used, therefore, to prohibit discrimination in pay for work of comparable worth in dissimilar jobs. However, Title VII of the 1964 Civil Rights Act also prohibits discrimination in wages and fringe benefits based on sex. Whether Title VII prohibits wage discrimination only between equal jobs or whether the prohibition extends to unequal wages among dissimilar jobs of equal worth is subject to considerable disagreement. In most cases, the courts have held the Title VII allows suits involving wage discrimination claims for equal jobs only. However, in *County of Washington v. Gunther,* the Supreme Court did hear an appeal by four matrons in the Washington County jail who claimed that their wages were illegally lower than the wages of male guards in the same facility.[39] In a five-to-four decision, the Court seemed to say that plaintiffs could bring suits under Title VII even though the relevant comparisons were not between equal jobs. The Court wrote a very narrow decision, however, and said specifically that it was not based on comparable worth. Although the Court said that jobs need not be equal or substantially similar before a claim of sex discrimination in pay can be brought to court, it appeared to say, also, that mere proof of job comparability in sex-segregated jobs is not sufficient to make a prima facie comparable-worth case. The Court appeared to allow an employer to continue to use a neutral procedure—that is, one that is not *intended* to discriminate against women—even if the procedure results in pay differences between jobs of comparable worth. Such neutral procedures include seniority, merit, quantity or quality of work, and salary surveys.

In 1983, a federal district judge ruled that substantial pay increases are necessary for nearly 15,000 female employees of Washington state because they have the same levels of skills and responsibilities as men in more highly paid jobs. Data collected by the American Federation of State, County and Municipal Employees (AFSCME) show, for example, that secretaries, most of whom are women, receive $500 per month less than truck drivers, most of whom are men. AFSCME contends that the jobs are comparable and should receive the same pay rate. Estimates of the costs necessary to equalize pay rates in Washington range as high as $500 million, however, and the district court decision is being appealed. A definitive answer must come from the Supreme Court. Although additional Supreme Court decisions are necessary before the legal issues in the comparable-worth controversty can be clarified, the Court is unlikely to order sweeping changes in the present wage determination mechanisms or to issue decisions that will have a massive impact on the economy.[40] Courts would have great problems deciding pay rates in the absence of market guidelines.

Although much of the difference in wages between "male" and "female" occupations is a result of discrimination, all differences cannot be so explained. Simply because all wage differences cannot be statistically explained by econometric models does not necessarily mean that the unexplained portion must be a result of discrimination. As Neuse notes, the difficulty here is that "none of the models include direct measures of discrimination and too much is assumed in concluding that all unknown factors are discriminatory."[41] The sloppy measures of discrimination are evidenced by varying claims that anywhere from 12 percent to 75 percent (a 63 percent variance) of male–female wage differences are a result of discrimination.[42] If the models are accurate and reliable, there should not be so much disagreement and variance concerning the true impact of discrimination on male–female wage differences.

Neuse describes several realistic methods by which differences in male–female wages can be reduced.[43] First, women must become more actively involved in the job evaluation process. They should not accept the claim that job evaluation is a totally neutral, scientific procedure. Second, broad pay ranges within job grades should be established. Broad ranges would more nearly recognize the equal worth of jobs, yet would allow personnel managers to continue to be sensitive to supply and demand in the marketplace. Finally, the comparable-worth issue will disappear when occupational segregation disappears. Vigorous affirmative action programs are necessary to accomplish this end.

Benefits in the Public Sector

Fringe benefits—paid vacations and holidays, sick leave, life, health, and disability insurance, and pensions—are system rewards. System rewards differ from individual rewards, such as pay, in that they are allocated to everyone in the organization, despite differences in effort and performance. The major basis for differential allocation of system rewards is seniority in the system. Since these rewards are often based on the length of service in the organization, and people want to stay to receive them, system rewards are most effective for keeping employees within the organization, thus reducing turnover. System rewards may also be useful in attracting employees to the organization, since high-quality employees may be attracted to an organization with good fringe benefits.

Since system rewards are either given equally to all employees or differentially in terms of seniority, workers are not motivated to do more than meet the standards for remaining in the system. Although system rewards may generate more positive employee atitudes about the organization, the linkages between system rewards, more positive attitudes, and greater productivity are unclear. Employees may seek to remain in an organization with system rewards, but they will not necessarily express their gratitude by working harder for the organization.[44]

The Growth of Fringe Benefits

Fringe benefits are no longer extras; most public employees view these benefits as essential and as a major portion of their compensation. Today, benefits comprise more than 30 percent of the compensation of the typical public employee. In contrast, in the early 1930s, benefits were often less than 10 percent of typical payroll costs. In the decade from 1967 to 1977, benefit costs tripled.[45] This growth is a result of several factors.

First, most governments assume a social responsibility, which requires that they provide benefits to their employees. Second, the public employer may believe that more benefits will improve employee morale. Third, more public employees have joined unions which have demanded more benefits. Governments have sometimes been willing to accede to union pressure for benefits because costs of some benefits can be pushed far into the future (for example, pensions). Fourth, employees want the public employer to provide the benefits because they are purchased with before-tax dollars, which thus reduces the employee's taxes. Employees also realize that the mass purchasing power of the public employer can buy insurance and benefit programs more cheaply.

Finally, inflation is a prime reason for the dramatic increase in benefit costs in recent years. Inflation in medical costs, which has exceeded general inflation, has greatly increased the cost of health insurance. In addition, most pension plans have some form of cost-of-living adjustment, which greatly increases the cost of pension benefits during times of rapid inflation.

Vacations and Holidays

Over time, public employees have received more and more time off with pay. Many states provide twelve to fifteen days of paid vacation and ten or more paid holidays. Given holidays and vacations, a typical employee may work about forty-seven weeks per year. (In addition, public employees are generally entitled to ten to fifteen days of paid sick leave per year.) Usually, restrictions are imposed on the number of vacation days that may be accumulated; vacation time is often limited to thirty days. Accumulated vacation can be important when employees are terminated, because in some jurisdictions they are paid for the accumulated days.

Sick Leave

Many public organizations provide paid sick leave for employees. Several studies have indicated that paid sick leave programs may increase employees' use of sick leave.[46] Since approximately two-thirds of all absences are due to sick leave,[47] the annual cost of such absences for U.S. business and government is approximately $18 billion.[48] Traditionally, paid sick leave programs allow sick leave to accrue over time and to be paid when employees are absent from work because of short-term illnesses. Generally, no compensation is given for accrued sick leave when an employee leaves the organization.[49]

Several costs are associated with the abuse of paid sick leave programs:

1. Expenses of overtime and extra work for employees who must do the work of the absent employee.
2. Continued fringe benefit costs for the absent employee.
3. Supervisory time devoted to correcting the impact of absenteeism (most of which is unscheduled and with short or no notice).
4. The resentment of co-workers who must do the work of the absent employee.
5. A drop in productivity, caused by inexperienced personnel performing the work of the absent worker.[50]

Some public organizations have tried a variety of "well pay" plans, which provide bonuses to employees who stay well. Other organizations have combined sick days with vacation days and holidays to provide a "personal time bank" for employees to use in any way they desire. The costs of sick leave absences have been reduced by both types of programs, and employee satisfaction with the sick leave programs has increased.

After reviewing the absenteeism policies of nearly 1,000 corporations, Scott and Markham made the following suggestions for reducing absenteeism:

1. Identify and analyze the methods used to control absenteeism within the organization.
2. Centralize absenteeism records and determine whether employees are receiving consistent treatment from supervisors. Termination or disciplinary actions for absenteeism may be overturned by a judge or arbitrator if the absenteeism policy is not established clearly and administered consistently.
3. Do not overlook the value of using positive inducements to reduce absenteeism. Positive inducements include bonuses for attendance plus public recognition for good attendance.
4. Control absenteeism with a comprehensive strategy, rather than relying on one or two methods to solve the problems.[51]

Health Insurance

Most public employees receive a variety of insurance benefits, such as health, life, and disability insurance. These benefits are generally covered by plans that are provided by private carriers, such as Blue Cross/Blue Shield health insurance, but the government pays most or all of the insurance premium in most jurisdictions. The cost of health insurance has been increasing rapidly because of inflation and increased coverage. Over the past thirty years, health-care costs have risen an average of 20 percent per year; whereas these costs were 4.5 percent of the gross national product (GNP) in 1955, today they are 10 percent of the GNP, or approximately $230 billion.[52] The various reasons for this increase include more sophisticated and more expensive technology, increased labor costs, inappropriate services, and the competition among hospitals for the most modern equipment. The increase is also caused by consumers ignoring the cost of health care because a third party—the government or the insurance company—is paying the bill.

Because of these rapidly increasing costs, public employers must give more attention to methods of reducing health-care costs. The first step is preparing a good database, including data on the number of employees making claims, the frequency of claims, the rates being charged, and the diagnoses relating to the claims.[53] Second, public employers should encourage employees to check their health-care bills for accuracy and reasonableness.

Third, employers should have claims units to audit claims. A claims audit can make sure that a reported claim can actually be charged; it can also determine whether the charge has been paid by another employer, since employees' spouses are often covered by other insurance carriers, which may also pay the claim. Coordination of benefits (COB)—that is, checking whether someone else has already paid the claim or should pay it—is a first requirement in claims processing.[54] A claims review can also check to see that charges are appropriate and that the services were actually delivered.

Fourth, public employers can reduce health-care costs by instituting preventive medicine or pro-health programs for their employees. Such programs could include programs to reduce or eliminate smoking and alcoholism, weight-reduction programs, exercise activities, blood pressure control programs, cholesterol-reduction programs, and stress management programs.[55]

Fifth, large public employers might consider self-funding of their health-care benefits. Self-funding allows a company to pay health claim costs for its employees from its own funds, thereby reducing the employer's costs for insurance agency commissions and profits.[56]

Finally, public employers could encourage the development of a health maintenance organizations (HMOs) for their employees. HMOs have provided significant savings for some employers.[57]

Pensions

The first pensions for public employees in the United States were those established for disabled veterans of the Revolutionary War. In 1855, Congress provided retirement benefits for over-age naval officers, extending such benefits to regular army officers in 1861.[58] Municipal pensions for police were first provided in 1878.[59] The early municipal plans covered police, firefighters, and teachers. From the 1930s to the 1970s, the percentage of public employees covered by pension plans increased from 75 percent to over 90 percent of all federal employees and from 30 percent to over 70 percent of all state and local employees.[60]

As the number of employees within pension plans increased, the costs of these plans escalated. Expenditures increased as employees matured, as retirees accumulated on the rolls, and as retirement benefits were liberalized. Also, as inflation increased benefits for plans in which annuities were based on final pay (or on averages of the highest years) or included cost-of-living escalators, costs increased dramatically.[61] Total expenditures for public retirement systems in 1950 were approximately $800 million, including $500 million for federal systems and $300 million for state and local systems. In 1980, these costs totaled $39 billion.[62]

Reasons for Pensions. The first occupations to receive pensions were those involving hazardous work, such as military service, policing, and firefighting. The primary reason for retirement plans in these occupations was to remove the older employees from the ranks and to maintain an able and efficient workforce. The offer of attractive retirement benefits was also used as a tool to retain experienced, able personnel that the employer wanted to keep in the workforce. In addition, pensions have been given as rewards for long and faithful service to government, which bespeaks public employers' perception of their social and moral obligation to provide support in old age to those who have committed their working lives to government employment. Finally, pensions are provided to defer income and to reduce or avoid taxation. Employee contributions to pension plans are deferred until retirement, and employer contributions, which are part of the employee's compensation, are not taxed.

Replacement Rates. The ratios of retirement benefits to salaries at retirement are known as replacement rates or replacement ratios. Replacement rates are not true measures of total retirement income, however. First, they do not include social security benefits which many public employees start receiving at age 62. Second, the replacement rates do not acknowledge that the retirees' income taxes, social security payroll taxes, and pension contributions are dramatically reduced or nonexistent during retirement.[63] In other words, the amount of money needed to equal the employee's preretirement standard of living is less than the employee's final salary. Moreover, most states and local governments that provide both a staff pension plan and social security coverage have not integrated the two plans. As a result, some replacement rates that include both pensions and social security benefits exceed 100 percent.[64]

The same problem also occurs in public organizations that do not provide social security coverage but do have early-retirement programs. Under such programs, an employee can retire early from one job and take another job under the social security system. The salary from the new job combined with the pension probably exceeds the employee's final salary at retirement. Moreover, the employee eventually retires from the second job and receives social security benefits. Thus, the combined pension and social security benefits are probably larger than the retiree's final salary. Failure to integrate social security benefits and pensions encourages competent public employees to retire early, requires the employment of another employee to replace the early retiree, and increases the costs of pension plans and the social security system.

Although a replacement rate goal of 100 percent is attractive, it is costly. The cost of a 100 percent replacement rate could equal 30 percent of an employee's annual salary. Currently, most state and local employees pay approximately 11 percent of their salaries for pensions and social security benefits, and it is unlikely that employees would be able to assume a larger share of the costs. Therefore, the public's share of the costs to provide 100 percent replacement rates would be very high.[65]

Retirement Age. Early-retirement provisions are one of the primary causes of high costs in retirement systems. Greater life expectancy, lower birthrates, and a growing proportion of the population in the ranks of the elderly bring into serious question the wisdom of retiring workers before the age of 65. Moreover, early-retirement provisions and high wage-replacement rates encourage people to stop being productive and place heavy demands on taxpayers.[66]

Early-retirement provisions are most common for firefighters and police. They are provided to ensure the maintenance of youthful and vigorous forces. However, this is an extraordinarily expensive method to maintain effective personnel. Because the cost of some police and firefighter pensions are close to 50 percent of payroll, governments should consider moving middle-age police officers and firefighters out of physically demanding jobs and into jobs that they could perform effectively until they reach the normal retirement age for most employees.[67]

Cost-of-Living Adjustments. Cost-of-living adjustments (COLAs) that are directly tied to the consumer price index (CPI) can dramatically increase pension costs during periods of high inflation. Although protecting retirees from the effects of inflation is a laudable goal, it may be prohibitively expensive during years of high inflation. Moreover, actuaries have been unable to predict the impact of inflation on pension costs twenty or thirty years in the future. Because of the open-ended nature of COLAs, only a few private companies provide them, and they have low limits. Most state and local governments also place limits on their COLAs. The federal government's COLA, however, is set at 50 percent of the CPI for all federal retirees under age 62 and 100 percent for all retirees age 62 and older.

Another reason for placing limits on COLAs is to discourage early retirements. Employees who do not have CPI-based COLA guarantees are less inclined to retire early and risk seeing their retirement benefits emasculated by inflation.

The Salary Base on Which Pensions are Based. A factor contributing to the rapidly increasing costs of public pensions is the practice of basing benefits on the average salary for the highest three or five years. Many private pension plans base benefits on the average salary for the last five or ten years. In contrast, some public employers base benefits on the highest salary year, which is generally the last year. Since employees' supervisors are not responsible for paying the pensions, and because their departments or agencies have no direct responsibility for the payments, supervisors may help the employees amass the largest possible income for the base period.[68] Special assignments, overtime, or unwarranted provisions may be used to inflate an employee's salary in the final year. Jurisdictions should guard against such maneuvers by basing pensions on the average salary over a minimum of three to five years.

Funding Pension Costs. Critics have suggested that pension costs have escalated dramatically because legislators do not realize the total costs of what they are asked to approve or because they are able to hide the full costs from citizens until long after the increase in benefits has occurred.[69] Whenever retirement benefits are extended, liabilities are incurred for all present employees who may be eligible for the benefits. Although the government jurisdiction incurs the liability whenever the benefits are extended, payment of the liability is deferred until the employee retires. If governments have not developed proper funding for future claims, sudden, huge increases in operating costs could occur when large numbers of employees retire and claim their benefits.

To avoid such a financial crisis, employers should fund benefits as they accrue—a practice known as *actuarial funding*.[70] The actuarial part of such funding is the process of estimating what the pension costs will be at some future date. The actuary must predict whether the employee will quit; when the employee will retire; whether and when the employee will become disabled; the age at which the employee will die; the employee's salary progression; and the rate of interest earned on invested funds.[71] With so many assumptions to make, actuaries often arrive at different estimates of long-term pension costs.

Unfunded accrued liabilities (that is, liabilities for which there are as yet no costs) trouble many critics of public pension plans. A sound funding plan usually includes provision for spreading the unfunded accrued liability over several years. According to Bernard Jump, an expert on public pensions, a jurisdiction's record in funding its accrued liabilities and in limiting the growth of the liabilities is a "better indicator of the adequacy of its pension funding program than is the absolute size of unfunded accrued liabilities at a single point in time."[72]

The Contingency Approach and Compensation in Organic and Mechanistic Organizations

Employees in organic organizations tend to value pay less than employees in mechanistic organizations do. This may reflect, in part, the higher salaries of employees in organic organizations. Since they have more money, they may value salary increases less than those whose incomes are lower. A more likely explanation, however, is that employees in organic organizations receive more satisfaction from other rewards. The work itself may give considerable satisfaction, and they may realize a considerable sense of accomplishment and self-worth from their work. In contrast, employees in mechanistic organizations may receive little sense of self-worth from their work and may concentrate on the size of their paychecks for their job satisfaction.

Employees in organic organizations are more likely to believe that pay should be based on performance, whereas employees in mechanistic organizations generally want their pay to be based on seniority.

Pay ranges for the more complex jobs in organic organizations are wider, because such jobs take longer to master and because there may be greater variation in how occupants of similar positions perform their tasks. The wider pay ranges allow for greater variation in pay for similar jobs. Pay ranges in mechanistic organizations tend to be relatively narrow, because there may be little variation in the performance of relatively simple jobs.

Conclusion

A good compensation plan attracts competent employees, encourages skilled energetic performance, promotes employees' commitment to the organization, and reduces turnover and absenteeism. To be successful, a pay plan must be perceived as equitable by employees. Public employers can assure equity by providing equal pay for equal work and by basing pay on performance. Equal pay for equal work is possible only if sound and up-to-date job evaluation and position classification procedures are in place. Similarly, pay can be based on performance only if the employer and the employees are able to define and measure performance. Thus, good pay plans are based on good performance evaluation procedures.

An increasing percentage of total compensation costs is applied to fringe benefits. Rapid increases in benefits pose two dangers. First, governments may buy employee support by increasing fringe benefits but deferring the costs of the benefits to the future. Although this strategy is politically appealing, it is financially unsound. The second danger is that governments are allocating almost one-third of their total compensation costs to system rewards (fringe benefits), which provide little direct incentive to improve performance. It is unwise for governments to pay huge sums of money as rewards that have relatively little influence on productivity. Rather, governments should attempt to maintain or increase the percentage of their total compensation costs that can have a more direct effect on the employee behavior needed for organizational effectiveness.

Notes

1. Daniel Katz and Robert Kahn, *The Social Psychology of Organizations* (New York: Wiley, 1966), p. 337.

2. Ibid., p. 338.

3. Edward Lawler, *Pay and Organizational Effectiveness: A Psychological View* (New York: McGraw-Hill, 1971), pp. 47–51.

4. Ibid., p. 55.

5. Ibid., p. 56.

6. J.R. Rawls and O.T. Nelson, "Characteristics Associated with Preference for Certain Managerial Positions," *Psychological Reports* (1975): 911–918; J.R. Rawls, R.R. Ulrich, and O.T. Nelson, "A Comparison of Managers Entering or Reentering the Profit and Non-Profit Sectors," *Academy of Management Journal* 22 (1979): 616–622.

7. John M. Greiner and others, *Productivity and Motivation: A Review of State and Local Government Initiatives* (Washington, D.C.: Urban Institute Press, 1981), p. 17.

8. Ibid.

9. George J. Borjas, *Wage Policy in the Federal Bureaucracy* (Washington, D.C.: American Enterprise Institute for Policy Research, 1980), p. 7.

10. Robert Trudel, "Preparing and Maintaining a Pay Plan," in *Job Evaluation and Pay Administration in the Public Sector* (Chicago: International Personnel Management Association, 1977), p. 280.

11. Wendy M. Geringer, "Indentification and Evaluation of Data Necessary to Establish 'Equitable' Pay Scales for Federal Government Employees," *Public Personnel Management* 10 (Summer 1981): 211.

12. Trudel, "Preparing and Maintaining a Pay Plan," p. 285.

13. Robert Trudel, "Principles of Pay Administration," in Harold Suskin, ed., *Job Evaluation and Pay Administration in the Public Sector* (Chicago: International Personnel Management Association, 1977), pp. 246, 247.

14. Ibid.

15. Ibid., p. 248.

16. Ibid., pp. 253 and 254.

17. Ibid., p. 271.

18. Edward Lawler, *Pay and Organization Development* (Reading, Mass.: Addison-Wesley, 1981), p. 81.

19. Ibid.

20. Greiner and others, *Productivity and Motivation*, p. 31.

21. J.L. Perry. C. Hanzlik, and J.L. Pearce, "Effectiveness of Merit-Pay-Pool Management," *Review of Public Personnel Administration* 2 (Summer 1982): 65.

22. Jone L. Pearce and James L. Perry, "Federal Merit Pay: A Longitudinal Analysis," *Public Administration Review* 43 (July-August 1983): 317.

23. "1981 Survey of Top Executives Shows SES Discontent," *Public Administration Times*, July 1, 1981, p. 2.

24. P.W. Colby and P.W. Ingraham, "Civil Service Reform: The Views of the Senior Executive Service," *Review of Public Personnel Administration* 2 (Summer 1981): 86.

25. Pearce and Perry, "Federal Merit Pay," p. 318.

26. Duane Thompson, "Performance Appraisal and the Civil Service Reform Act," *Public Personnel Management* 10 (Fall 1981): 281–288.

27. James Perry and Jone L. Pearce, "Initial Reactions to Federal Merit Pay," *Personnel Journal* 62 (March 1983): 236–237.

28. Ibid.

29. Robert W. Brown, "Performance Appraisal: A Policy Implementation Analysis," *Review of Public Personnel Administration* 3 (Spring 1982): 80.

30. Ibid.

31. Perry and Pearce, "Initial Reactions to Federal Merit Pay," p. 237.

32. Ibid.

33. Kenneth W. Kramer, "Seeds of Success and Failure: Policy Development and Implementation of the 1978 Civil Service Reform Act," *Review of Public Personnel Administration* 3 (Spring 1982): 5–20.

34. For additional criticisms of the CSRA, see Frank Sherwood, "Wrong Assumptions, Wrong Strategies," *Bureaucrat* 11 (Winter 1982–83): 22–27.

35. Greiner and others, *Productivity and Motivation*, pp. 96–105. This section is based in large part on Greiner's discussion.

36. Ibid., p. 103.

37. Mary H. Doherty and Ann Harriman, "Comparable Worth: The Equal Employment Issue of the 1980s," *Review of Public Personnel Administration* 2 (Summer 1981): 13.

38. Ibid.

39. *County of Washington v. Gunther*, 101 S. Ct. 352 (1980).

40. Steven M. Neuse, "A Critical Perspective on the Comparable Worth Debate," *Review of Public Personnel Administration* 3 (Fall 1982): 1–20. For additional clarification of the comparable worth issue, see John R. Schnebly, "Comparable Worth: A Legal Overview," *Personnel Administrator* 27 (April 1982): 43–48, 90; George L. Whaley, "Controversy Swirls over Comparable Worth Issue," *Personnel Administrator* (April 1982): 51–61, 92.

41. Neuse, "Critical Perspective on the Comparable Worth Debate," p. 10.

42. Ibid., pp. 10, 11.

43. Ibid., pp. 16–19.

44. Katz and Kahn, *Social Psychology of Organizations*, p. 356.

45. George Strauss and Leonard Sayles, *Personnel* (Englewood Cliffs, N.J.: Prentice-Hall, 1983), p. 154.

46. R.E. Ropelman, G.O. Schueller, and J.J. Silver, "Parkinson's Law and Absenteeism: A Program to Rein in Sick Leave Costs," *Personnel Administrator* 26 (May 1981): 57–63.

47. J.N. Hedges, "Absences from Work: Measuring the Hours Lost," *Monthly Labor Review* 100 (October 1977): 18.

48. The estimated total annual cost of absences in the nation's workforce is over $26 billion. See Richard Steers and Susan Rhodes, "Major Influences on Employee Attendance: A Process Model," *Journal of Applied Psychology* 31 (1978): 391–407.

49. Barron H. Harvey, "Two Alternatives to Traditional Sick Leave Programs," *Personnel Journal* 62 (May 1983): 374–378.

50. Barron H. Harvey, Jerome Rogers, and Judy Schultze, "Sick Pay vs. Well Pay: An Analysis of the Impact of Rewarding Employees for Being on the Job." *Public Personnel Management* 12 (Summer 1983): 218–224.

51. Dow Scott and Steve Markham, "Absenteeism Control Methods: A Survey of Practices and Results" *Personnel Administrator* 28 (June 1983): 73–84.

52. John. F. Wagner, "What Business Can Do to Cut Health-Care Cost," *S.A.M. Advanced Management Journal* (Summer 1980): 12–20.

53. Ibid.

54. K. Per Larson, "Taking Action to Contain Health Care Costs," *Personnel Journal* 59 (August 1980): 640–645. For more information on coordination of benefits, see Thomas Fannin and Teresa Fannin, " Coordination of Benefits: Uncovering Buried Treasure," *Personnel Journal* 62 (May 1983):386–391.

55. For a discussion of management-sponsored pro-health programs, see Andrew Brennan, "Worksite Health Promotion Can Be Cost-Effective," *Personnel Administrator* 62 (April 1983): 38–42.

56. For more information on self-funding of insurance, see Ronald Bujan, "A Primer on Self-funding Health Care Benefits," *Personnel Administrator* 62 (April 1983): 61–64.

57. For an analysis of HMOs and cost containment, see C. Carl Pegels, "Health Care Cost Containment Potential for Employers," *Public Personnel Management* 9 (1980): 208–213.

58. Michael S. March, "Retirement Benefits for Public Employees" in Steven Hays and Richard C. Kearney, eds., *Public Personnel Administration* (Englewood Cliffs, N.J.: Prentice-Hall, 1983), p. 154.

59. Ibid.

60. Ibid., p. 155.

61. Ibid., p. 156.

62. Ibid., pp. 156, 157.

63. Bernard Jump, "Compensating City Government Employees: Pension Benfit Objectives, Cost Measurement and Financing," in Donald E. Klinger, ed., *Public Personnel Management* (Chicago: Mayfield, 1981), pp. 293–391.

64. Ibid.

65. Ibid.

66. March, "Retirement Benefits For Public Employees," p. 169.

67. Jump, "Compensating City Government Employees," p. 303.

68. William N. Thompson, "Public Pension Plans: The Need for Scrutiny and Control," *Public Personnel Management* 6 (July-August 1977): 216.

69. Jump, "Compensating City Government Employees," p. 304.

70. Ibid., p. 306.

71. Ibid.

72. Ibid., p. 307.

8
Training and Development

Key Words

   Training

   Development

   Organizational analysis

   Operations analysis

   Person analysis

   On-the-job training (OJT)

   Supervisory coaching

   Job rotation

   Lecture

   Programmed instruction (PI)

   Case study

   Incident process

   Role playing

   T-groups

   Organization development (OD)

   Role analysis technique (RAT)

   Grid OD

   Control group design

   Time-series design

Introduction

Training and development programs perform vital functions within public organizations. Few new employees in an agency or department can immediately perform the tasks for which they were hired. Also, employees must acquire new skills and abilities to meet new demands and responsibilities. Training and development programs include any planned efforts by the organization to foster and enhance the learning of job-related behavior by employees.[1] *Training* generally refers to the teaching of relatively narrow or structured material that has an immediate job application. *Development* refers to attempts to improve the decision-making abilities, interpersonal skills, self-awareness, and motivation of employees. The crucial difference between training and development is their mission within the organization. As Warren notes: "Participants are chosen for training because they lack skills, knowledge, or attitudes needed to satisfy job requirements; for management development, they are chosen because their performance demonstrates a potential for further responsibilities."[2] Training efforts generally have specific, short-term, task-related goals. In contrast, development programs have broad, long-term, organization-related goals.

Although training and development programs can contribute to organizational effectiveness, public organizations traditionally have spent comparatively little on such programs. When public agencies have lean budgets, they often conclude that training and development are luxuries that should be eliminated.[3] As a result, many training and development programs within the public sector lack continuity. During cutbacks, trainers are released and training programs cease. Later, during better budget years, new training and development programs are started. Such instability, of course, undermines the effectiveness and status of training and development programs in public organizations.

In recent years, however, public agencies have been investing more resources in training and development. Several factors may account for this. Employees and their unions have demanded more training and development programs to upgrade and improve their skills. Also, dissatisfaction with the public education system and the inability of many high school graduates, and even some college graduates, to read and comprehend and to write and communicate clearly have required that public agencies pay more attention to training. In addition, changing technologies, such as microcomputers and word processors, have demanded more training. Finally, affirmative action efforts have required that training play an even larger role in preparing minorities and women for roles and positions they have not held in the past.

Training and development are related to other personnel functions. First, recruitment and selection procedures affect the amount of training required for new employees and the capacity of employees to benefit from training. If good recruitment and selection provide good hires, there is less demand for training, because more employees enter with the skills necessary to do the job. Good recruits who have the basic intellectual and motivational talents are better able to understand training materials and benefit from development programs.

Second, job analysis is directly related to training and development. Before a training program for a position can be prepared, the employer must know what is required for successful performance of the job. Job analysis can assist in providing this information. Job analysis and job classification also can suggest the kinds of development programs that are needed to help employees progress from one position to another within the organization.

Third, performance appraisals are very important in designing and evaluating training and development efforts. Good performance appraisals can identify employee weaknesses that might be alleviated through training and development. Also, objective, performance-based appraisals can provide evaluations of the impact and worth of training and development programs. Finally, good performance appraisals can provide feedback to employees concerning the effects of training efforts on their performance. Such feedback is a crucial component of the learning process.

Finally, training and development are related to organization development (OD), which is concerned with the organization's overall health and effectiveness. In its OD efforts, an organization often invites a consultant, or change agent, to diagnose problems within the organization and develop intervention strategies to bring about lasting change. Training and development differ from OD in that they are concerned primarily with increasing the skills, self-awareness, and motivation of *individuals* in the organization. Although OD is also concerned with individual development, it is only a part of OD's primary goal of improving the cooperation and effectiveness of all units within the total organization. Thus, OD places great emphasis on changing the attitudes, behavior, and performance of organizational groups or teams, rather than individuals. Some OD techniques, such as survey feedback and grid OD, may also be used by trainers to develop individual managers. These OD techniques, and others, are discussed in this chapter.

The training and development process is composed of three major phases or steps: (1) the assessment phase, (2) the implementation phase, and (3) the evaluation phase. In the assessment phase, the need for training and development efforts is determined, and the goals and objectives of such efforts are specified. In the implementation phase, appropriate training and development strategies are selected and implemented. Finally, the evaluation phase focuses on measuring how well the training and development strategies accomplish the objectives specified in the first phase. The three phases of the process are examined in this chapter, including descriptions of several training and organization development techniques. First, however, we examine the factors that affect learning in training and development.

Factors That Affect Learning in Training and Development Programs

Training and development programs are more likely to be successful when certain conditions exist in an organization. First, employees must be motivated to learn. The motivation model that was described in chapter 5 and expectancy theory suggest that employees' motivation to excel in training and development programs increases when they see valued rewards associated with such programs. Thus, employees must believe that training and development programs actually improve their performance and that management will reward them for the improvements. If this linkage among training, performance improvement, and additional rewards is not perceived by employees, management can expect minimal employee interest in training and development.

Too often, training and development programs are initiated because they are popular in other organizations or because an organizational consultant is able to sell a particular technique to management. Also, managers may believe that they know what employees need and want. A better approach, however, is to involve employees in determining and designing the training and development programs. This involvement allows the employees to see the relevance of the programs to their needs and interests.

The motivation model of chapter 5 and reinforcement theory suggest the importance of feedback to learning in training and development programs, because trainees must know when and how they have done things correctly. Feedback is necessary to show trainees how to adjust their behavior. It also leads to the establishment of specific goals for maintaining or improving performance. Feedback can be given in the form of verbal praise, test scores, or performance measurements. According to behavior modification theory, most feedback should be positive and should follow the trainees' behavior as soon as possible. Negative feedback is also useful, so long as it is interspersed with positive feedback and provided that it is not considered punitive by trainees.[4] Besides such extrinsic feedback, trainees also obtain intrinsic feedback from results of the training task itself. The best training programs include both extrinsic and intrinsic feedback.

Learning is also affected by the spacing of training and development sessions—whether they are held in one or two long periods or spaced over a number of days. Research has indicated that practice distributed over a number of hours or days is clearly superior for most learning. Why, then, do many organizations cram training and development programs into a few days? One reason is that management is eager to have the employees trained to some minimal competency as quickly as possible. Another reason is that such cramming tends to minimize job disruptions, since a few days away from work may be preferable to several hours per day spread over twenty days. Also, many development programs for supervisors and managers occur away from the work site and are offered only in two- or three-day sessions.

Assessment of Training and Development Needs

William McGehee suggests that three types of analyses are necessary to determine training and development needs in an organization.[5] First, *organizational analysis* is necessary to determine where training is needed in the organization. Second, *operations analysis* is necessary to determine what employees need to know to do their jobs effectively. Third, *person analysis* is necessary to find out who needs training and what kind of training they need.

Organizational Analysis

Organizational analysis involves several kinds of investigations. One aspect of organizational analysis is the estimation of how many people need to be trained to accomplish the future goals of the organization. To make this estimate, one must know the goals of the organization and the abilities of present personnel. Good human resources planning involves personnel audits (see chapter 4) that take inventory of the skills and talents available in the organization and project the kinds and numbers of employees that will be needed in the future. Personnel audits consider anticipated future technological and organizational changes. These future needs can be met by both recruitment of needed individuals and training of present employees to assume new duties.

Another type of organizational analysis examines various indices to see where training might improve performance. These indices include reports on productivity, safety, quality control, absenteeism, and turnover. Such indices can signal where problems may be occurring and why, but further investigation is necessary to determine whether additional training and development can solve the problems.

A third type of organizational analysis investigates the climate within an organization, which is composed of the members' attitudes and feelings about the organization, about others in it, and about their own roles. This type of analysis can pinpoint problems that might be alleviated by more training and development. Also, such analysis can indicate whether there is a good environment for training. This analysis of the organization's climate generally is conducted by means of attitude surveys of all employees. Personnel reports on grievances and absenteeism may also be used, as may exit interviews with employees leaving the organization.

Operations Analysis

Operations analysis is very similar to task analysis, which was described in chapter 3.[6] Operations analysis is useful in determining which tasks employees must perform to do their jobs effectively. This analysis also indicates the level of performance expected of position occupants, and it determines any differences between the incumbents' actual performance and expected performance. Operations analysis can also suggest whether a performance deficiency can be corrected by training and whether the cost of the deficiency exceeds the cost of the training necessary to correct it.

Person Analysis

Person analysis focuses on the individual employee. One type of person analysis uses performance appraisals of employees as a guide to their need for training and development.[7] Unfortunately, the use of performance appraisals for salary administration purposes complicates their use for counseling and training. If they are objective, however, and if they are performance-oriented, not trait-oriented, they can be useful in determining training needs.

Another method of determining the training needs of employees is simply to ask them. Given the expense and complexity of the other more sophisticated methods of determining needs, surveys of employees may be a good, cost-effective option. Also, employee interest and enthusiasm are significant factors in the success of training and development programs.[8]

Assessment Problems

The foregoing assessment methods may reveal numerous needs in the organization, but managers must not assume too quickly that all needs can be alleviated by training and development. Some needs may be the result of inadequate human resource planning, improper recruitment, poor job design, or insufficient pay. Training may reduce problems caused by poor recruitment, but it cannot seriously alleviate them. Similarly, low employee morale that is caused by pay dissatisfaction is not correctible by training and development. Therefore, managers must be certain that their training and development programs are appropriate for the identified needs before they invest considerable resources in such programs.

Even if a training and development program is appropriate for resolving a need, it may not be efficient or effective. Since it is unlikely that a training and development program will completely correct a problem, the costs of the program should be considerably less than the cost of the problem. The costs of a training and development program generally are easier to calculate than the costs of the problem. Training costs include the salaries and benefits paid to the trainers who assess the needs, establish the objectives, and implement the program and the salaries paid to employees for the time spent in training. Training costs also include incidentals such as room rental and supplies. If a training and development program takes place away from work, additional expenses for travel, lodging, and food must be included. On the other side, the costs of the problem can include low productivity, turnover, absenteeism, and poor-quality service or goods. If these costs do not considerably exceed the costs of the training or development program, the program should not be implemented.

Training and Development Methods

Training and development methods can be divided into two broad categories: on-site methods and off-site methods. On-site methods include on-the-job training (OJT), supervisory coaching, and job rotation. Off-site methods include lectures, programmed instruction, case studies, incident processes, role playing, and sensitivity groups.

On-the-Job Training

On-the-job training (OJT) occurs when the training and development of new employees are assigned to experienced employees and supervisors. The primary advantage of OJT is that knowledge learned during training is easily transferred to the job. In addition, training can be more individualized for each trainee, and the trainees learn by doing, which is the most effective way to learn. OJT is less expensive than other training methods for two reasons. First, trainees produce as they learn, thus offsetting part of the training costs. Second, money is not spent on off-site facilities, trainers, and instructional equipment and materials. Finally, OJT allows greater involvement of supervisors in training. As a result, supervisors may feel more responsible for their employees' development, which, in turn, may increase the trainees' motivation to learn.

Problems do occur, however, with OJT. The chief concern is that, too often, training may be overlooked because it is not a distinct activity with specific objectives for which someone is directly responsible. OJT might turn out to be no more than a supervisor telling an experienced employee to "teach Sally her job," and there may be little concern for the trainer's willingness or ability to train a new employee.[9]

An OJT program is most effective when the following conditions exist:

1. The employees who act as trainers believe that the time they spend training others can assist their own careers, pay, and status.
2. The employees who are selected as trainers have both the ability and the willingness to teach others.
3. The trainers receive instruction in training.
4. The trainers and the trainees are well matched in terms of background, age, and attitudes.
5. The organization understands that learning takes precedence over production during training periods.

Supervisory Coaching

Supervisory coaching occurs when supervisors conduct periodic reviews of trainees' performance and counsel the new employees about how to improve. Coaching allows subordinates to know what their supervisors think of their performance and to work cooperatively on improving it. Thus, communication is improved, as is collaboration between supervisors and employees. This provides a framework for establishing short- and long-term personal career goals.

Coaching is often not as effective as it could be because supervisors and subordinates fail to communicate or exchange much information. Because the supervisors often evaluate employees' performance for the purpose of determining salary increases and promotions, employees may withhold information that reflects unfavorably upon themselves. As a result, deficiencies cannot be discussed in an open constructive way. This problem can be reduced if the following conditions exist:

1. Employees are able to participate in the evaluation process.
2. Supervisors listen as well as instruct.
3. Specific improvement goals are mutually agreed upon.
4. Supervisors maintain a constructive, supportive attitude.
5. Criticism is kept to a minimum.
6. Feedback occurs on a regular, frequent schedule.[10]

Job Rotation

Job rotation involves giving trainees a series of job assignments in different parts of the organization for specific time periods. Job rotation is particularly useful for training employees to assume general managerial duties that involve coordinating different parts of the organization. It provides trainees with an overall perspective of the organization and an understanding of the interrelationships among the various organizational units.

Lecture

The lecture is the oldest and most often used method of instruction. It is particularly effective in transmitting large amounts of straightforward, factual information.[11] Training by lecture, however, often ignores important differences among members of the audience. Moreover, the learners are in a passive position and do not actively participate in the training. This passive approach complicates the transfer of knowledge from the lecture to the job. Because of these problems, research evidence indicates that the lecture is not as appropriate as more participatory methods for modifying attitudes, developing problem-solving skills, or improving personal competence.[12] Training objectives can determine whether the lecture method is appropriate. If the objective is to transmit information, the lecture can be effective, but it is less effective for increasing motivation or changing behavior.

Programmed Instruction

Programmed instruction (PI), or programmed learning, is a self-instruction method of learning. For PI, material that is to be learned is divided into discrete steps that are related in a logical sequence. Learners control their own pace in progressing through the steps, and they receive immediate feedback on whether they have successfully mastered each step. When one step is learned, the trainees can move on to the next. Behavior modification (stimulus, response, feedback) provides the theoretical foundation for PI. Programmed learning generally reduces the time required to learn information, but it does not seem to result in greater retention of knowledge over time than with conventional lecture methods.[13]

Case Study

The case study method is a prominent training technique, particularly for the development of managerial skills. A case is a written description of an organizational problem, presenting pertinent facts in detail but often omitting the solution to the problem. The trainer assists the trainees by asking questions and by encouraging participation and group discussion. The case method brings realism to training, thereby encouraging the transfer of knowledge to the job. This method also demands the active involvement of the learners. Trainees can see that there are few pat answers to complex problems, and they thus learn to tolerate other viewpoints, opinions, and values. Moreover, trainees gain experience in analyzing complex situations and searching for acceptable solutions.

The case study is a slow way of learning, however. Case selection, analysis, and discussion can take a great deal of time, and any one case can teach only one or two general principles. Also, the nondirective method of teaching cases requires very competent trainers who are patient, can think quickly, and are not threatened by questions they cannot answer.

A variant of the case study method is the in-basket exercise described in chapter 4. In this exercise, the trainee assumes the role of a manager who is confronted with a stack of memos, notes, letters, phone calls, and problems that require action. After receiving a brief description of the organization and his or her role in it, the trainee must respond relatively quickly to the in-basket material. This exercise is used to teach such topics as decision making, time management, establishment of priorities, and delegation. The exercise provides realistic, hands-on experience, particularly if the examples are taken from the actual organization in which the employee works.

Incident Process

The incident process is a variation of the case study. However, unlike the case study, which gives all the relevant facts in a case, the incident process gives only a brief description of a crucial incident from the case situation.[14] Instructors provide additional information in response to questions from trainees. Supporters of this process believe that it is more realistic than the case study because trainees, like real managers, must discover the facts by asking the right questions. Comments from participants who have used the incident process approach are extremely positive. There is little evidence, however, that such training actually improves managerial decision-making behavior.[15]

Role Playing

Instead of discussing a problem, as in the case study and incident process methods, role playing allows trainees actually to respond to specific problems. Trainees are told to respond as though they were participants in a case. The case or situation that is presented to them might be imaginary or it might be an actual problem from a real organization. Role playing permits trainees to discover their own behavior and, from reactions of others, the relative effectiveness of different behaviors in a given situation. It is an effective method for showing trainees that others do not always interpret their actions and statements as they intended them. As a result, trainees' sensitivity and insights into interpersonal relationships are enhanced. Role playing may be particularly useful in resolving conflict. A trainee might be asked to assume the role of someone with whom he or she is in conflict and to approach a situation from that person's point of view and position and with that person's values and attitudes. This type of role reversal could be used, for example, to reduce conflicts between two departments in an organization.

Although role playing is a popular training method, it does have several disadvantages. First, it takes considerable time to plan and conduct the role-playing exercise. Second, the method demands highly competent and trained instructors. Finally, some trainees may regard role playing as childish play acting, and some may feel uncomfortable and threatened if they have to perform before others.

Sensitivity-Training Groups (T-Groups)

Sensitivity-training groups, or T-groups, are difficult to explain because they are conducted in many different ways. Huse had identified three types of T-groups: (1) a "stranger" group, in which members have never met and know nothing about each other; (2) a "cousins" group, in which members may be part of the same organization but are not in the same work unit; and (3) a "family" group, which is composed of members of the same work unit.[16] T-groups can be either structured or unstructured. Structured groups follow a predetermined schedule that includes role playing, games, and other exercises designed to accomplish specific outcomes. Unstructured groups function according to whatever agenda is spontaneously agreed upon by the members. T-group sessions can last from several hours to several days.

T-groups seem to develop through four stages.[17] First, members in the groups tend to compete for status in the group. Second, the members become upset with the leader or coordinator because he or she does not fulfill their expectations of what a leader should do. Third, the group begins to develop cohesiveness. Finally, individual assessment and group problem-solving skills are developed. T-groups are intended to increase self-insight, self-understanding, and self-awareness about one's behavior and its impact on others. They are also supposed to increase understanding of and sensitivity to the behavior of others. Also, T-groups may help trainees understand the conditions that inhibit or promote effective group functioning. Finally, T-groups attempt to improve trainees' diagnostic skills in interpersonal and intergroup situations.

The use of T-groups has declined significantly in recent years because of concerns surrounding them. First, T-groups are difficult to understand because their major purpose is to produce emotional understanding, rather than cognitive learning. Second, the specific results of T-groups are difficult, if not impossible, to measure. There is no uniform agreement regarding what the objectives of sensitivity training should be, let alone agreement on a system to measure accomplishment of objectives. A third concern about T-groups is the poor selection processes used to decide who may or may not attend sensitivity-training sessions. For example, individuals with histories of psychological problems should probably not attend T-groups. Finally, participants' privacy has been invaded by some T-group members who believe that everyone in the group has some problem and that the group must find it and correct it. Therefore, they badger each person into confessing some problem. This possible invasion of privacy becomes even more problematic when one recognizes the fine line between voluntary participation in a T-group and the coercive pressure that is applied when an employer asks an employee to participate.

Organization Development

Organization development (OD) can be better understood if one knows the assumptions on which OD strategies are based. French and Bell note that OD makes assumptions about people as individuals, about people as group members, and about people as members of organizational systems.[18] First, OD assumes that if people have a challenging and supportive work environment, they will seek personal growth and development. Second, it assumes that people want to and can make greater contributions to organizational goals than the organization permits. Too often, according to OD theory, organizations squelch their employees' growth and constructive contributions by not rewarding or encouraging them.

Furthermore, OD assumes that work groups are pivotal to organizational effectiveness. This belief is based on the following assumptions:

1. The work group is very important in determining individuals' feelings of competence and satisfaction.
2. Most people want to be accepted by their work group, and the group can work more effectively if the members work together more cooperatively.
3. The group leader cannot perform all of the leadership functions, and the group can work more effectively if members perform some of the leadership functions.
4. Suppressed feelings adversely affect problem-solving ability, personal growth, and job satisfaction.
5. Too often, feelings are suppressed in organizational work groups, and the level of interpersonal trust, support, and cooperation is much lower than that which is desirable.
6. These problems can be resolved if all parties resolve their mutual relationships.

Finally, OD makes the following assumptions about people in organizational systems:

1. The leadership style at the top of the organization is transmitted to lower teams. If top management displays trust, openness, support, and teamwork, this style will influence the style of lower managers.
2. Resolving conflict between individuals and groups in a way that permits clear winners and losers does not promote the long-term health of the organization.
3. OD efforts designed to improve trust, openness, cooperation, and performance must be supported by other organizational subsystems, such as performance appraisal, training, recruitment, selection, and compensation.

OD Interventions

Team Building. Because it assumes that effective work groups are the crucial elements in a healthy organization, OD is particularly concerned about developing work teams. The "family" sensitivity-training group discussed earlier is one method of developing a more open, supportive work group. Another is the role analysis technique (RAT), which is designed to improve team effectiveness by clarifying the role obligations and expectations of team members. First, all members' expectations of each role in the team are clarified. If there are conflicting expectations, they are revealed and resolved. Then each team member must summarize the various expectations concerning his or her position. This process helps reduce intragroup conflict by providing all members with a common set of expectations concerning each role.

Intergroup Interventions. A central tenet of OD is that intergroup conflict and competition can undermine the effectiveness and health of the organization. OD attempts to reduce this conflict by using intergroup intervention.[19] The intervention begins when two conflicting groups meet in separate rooms, and each group makes two lists. On one list, the group notes its perceptions, attitudes, and feelings about the other group. On the second list, the group predicts what the other group is saying about them. Then the two groups are brought together to share the information on their respective lists. The only questions allowed at this time are for clarification. Next, the two groups return to their individual meeting places to discuss what they learned about themselves, and about the other group. Often, groups begin to see at this stage that many of the disagreements and conflicts between them are based on erroneous perceptions and communication breakdowns. After this is realized, each group must construct a list of priority issues that still need to be resolved between the two groups. Next, the two groups are brought together again to share their priority lists. After comparing lists, one overall priority list is created, and action steps are formulated for handling each item on the list.

Survey Feedback. Some OD interventions go beyond work groups or units to encompass the entire organization. Survey feedback is a total organizational intervention that seeks to improve relationships between managers and their employees at all levels of the organization. Survey feedback includes two distinct phases. In the first phase, a questionnaire is designed to collect data on the current state of the organization. The questionnaire can be a standardized instrument or one that is tailored to the specific needs of the organization. The questionnaire may include questions concerning leadership, communication, motivation, decision making, control, coordination, and satisfaction in the workplace. All members of the organization receive the questionnaire and are encouraged to respond.

In the second phase, data collected from the survey are shared with the top executives of the organization. Subsequently, each executive presides at a meeting of his or her subordinates at which the collected data are discussed. The subordinates are asked to help interpret the data and to suggest constructive changes. Plans are also made for introducing the data to the next lower level of employees. A consultant often helps prepare managers for the feedback sessions with subordinates. The consultant also acts as a neutral expert and resource person to help the work group interpret the data.

Although survey feedback for an entire organization is costly and requires a great deal of time to implement, it can be an effective intervention. The effectiveness of survey feedback is supported by the most comprehensive and elaborate evaluation of OD interventions to date, in which David Bowers compared data from almost 15,000 respondents in twenty-three organizations in which various OD interventions were tried.[20] He found that survey feedback was more effective than other interventions in improving organizational climate, leadership behavior, and job satisfaction.

Grid OD. Perhaps the most thorough and comprehensive OD intervention is that designed by Robert Blake and Jane Mouton.[21] The program consists of six phases, which take three to five years to implement fully. At the center of the grid program is the concept of the managerial grid, also developed by Blake and Mouton, which is a two-dimensional scheme for examining and improving the managerial styles of individual managers. The two dimensions of the grid are "concern for production" and "concern for people." Each dimension contains nine degrees ranging from 1, low concern, to 9, high concern. In addition, there are five basic management styles. Grid OD rests on the premise that the most effective managers use the 9,9 style (that is, high concern for both production and people). The six phases of grid OD are designed to help managers achieve a 9,9 style.

Phase 1, the grid seminar, is essentially a seminar for the organization's managers in which they assess their own grid styles and work to develop better communication, problem-solving, and critiquing skills.

Phase 2, team development, concentrates on the development of actual work teams (that is, a manager and subordinates). Again, the objective is to have each team analyze and improve its problem-solving, planning, goal-setting, and communication skills. In addition, each manager receives feedback about how his or her behavior affects the team's behavior.

The major goal of phase 3, intergroup development, is to improve coordination and communication among groups who must work together. The groups discuss what an ideal relationship between the groups would be. Then, each group separately develops action steps to move toward the ideal situation that was defined jointly by the two groups.

During phase 4, development of an ideal strategic plan, which may take up to a year, the top management group develops an ideal overall strategic plan.

During phase 5, implementation of the ideal strategic plan, which may take two or three years, the organization attempts to implement the ideal plan. Various planning teams may be established throughout the organization to determine exactly what needs to be done to implement the plan.

In phase 6, the systematic critique, the results of the grid OD program are measured. Progress is evaluated, barriers are identified, and further action steps are determined.

Although grid OD is popular and has been used for some time, little evaluative research has been conducted on it using control or comparison groups. Without such controls, it is difficult to determine whether improvements attributed to grid OD programs were caused by the programs or by other factors.

Evaluation of Training and Development

Training and development programs must be evaluated to determine whether the objectives for the programs have been accomplished. Otherwise, the organization has no way to know whether the benefits of the program justify its costs. Also, evaluation can provide useful data for improving training and development efforts. The effectiveness of training and development efforts can be measured in terms of four criteria: (1) reactions, (2) learning, (3) job behavior, and (4) results.[22]

Reaction criteria measure how well the participants liked the program, the trainer, the methods used, and the surroundings in which the program occurred. These reactions can help trainers improve their programs by noting which program elements are particularly effective for different types of participants.

Learning criteria measure the knowledge and skills participants obtained from the training or development program. Trainees might have favorable reactions to a program but not learn any new knowledge or skills. Tests that are given after completion of a program to determine what the participants learned should be based directly on the program's learning objectives, which were determined by the needs assessment process discussed earlier.

Whereas learning criteria measure the trainees' acquisition of new knowledge or skills, job behavior criteria measure the transferability of that new knowledge or skills to the actual job, since there can be a big difference between knowing facts and using them on the job.[23] The appraisal of job behavior should be made several months after the training or development program to give the participants adequate opportunity to put what they have learned into practice. Appraisals of job behavior can be collected from supervisors, co-workers, and/or subordinates.

Most organizations adopt training programs to produce tangible results, such as reduced absenteeism or turnover and improved quality and quantity of production. Unfortunately, it is often difficult to obtain such measurements, or the data are contaminated by changes unrelated to the training or development program, such as increased pay, changes in management, or better selection methods.

After the appropriate criteria have been selected for measuring the effectiveness of a training or development program, the proper design or procedure for conducting the measurement must be chosen. The best procedure is the pretest–posttest control group design, in which trainees are assigned at random to a training group or to a control group. Both groups are measured on the criteria that will be used to evaluate the program. Then, after the training program, both groups are again measured on the same criteria. If the performance of the trainees shows significantly more improvement than performance of the control group members, one can assume that the program had a positive impact on the evaluation criteria.

The control group design is often difficult to implement in public organizations. Management may be unwilling to assign employees randomly to training programs. Often, participants are selected for training and development because management believes they will benefit most from it. Also, employees may volunteer for training. Although some public organizations may use the control group design to evaluate training programs, few, if any, use such procedures to determine the effectiveness of OD development programs. Most OD interventions are accepted on faith, because it is too difficult to construct a control group design for an OD intervention, which is aimed at the total organization.

Because of the problems in establishing control group designs, many evaluations use a time-series design, in which data on the evaluation criteria are collected for a number of years or time periods before the training or development program is implemented. These data are then compared to postprogram data on the same criteria. If the data show significant improvement, and if all other possible causes for the improvement can be excluded, there are reasonable grounds for concluding that the training or development program has been successful. Of course, even successful training and development programs might not be cost-effective. The benefits derived from a program must always be compared to the costs of the program to determine whether the program should be continued.

Effectiveness of Training and Development Methods

Few studies have compared the relative effectiveness of the various training and development methods; most have compared only two methods for producing one or more types of learning. Nigro and DeMarco asked local government personnel directors which training techniques they used and which were most effective.[24] The most utilized techniques were OJT, supervisory coaching, and lectures (see table 8–1); comparatively few used case studies, programmed instruction, role playing, and sensitivity training.

Charles Watson, who has reviewed a great deal of research on the effectiveness of various training methods, notes that some methods are especially appropriate for particular objectives.[25] The lecture, for example, is more effective for knowledge acquisition, but role playing is more effective for developing interpersonal skills. The selection of a particular training method depends upon the objective of the training and the amount of time and money that can be invested in the effort.

Although Nigro and DeMarco found that only 17 percent of the personnel directors in their study had used OD in their jurisdictions, Golembiewski, Proehl,

Table 8–1
Effectiveness and Utilization of Training Techniques

Training Technique	Effectiveness, as Perceived by Respondents[a]	Percentage Utilizing the Technique
On-the-job training	8.9 (N = 216)	80 (N = 386)
Supervisory coaching/counseling	7.2 (N = 213)	63 (N = 380)
Job rotation	5.3 (N = 211)	33 (N = 377)
Assigned readings/correspondence study	2.4 (N = 207)	25 (N = 376)
Lectures and discussions	5.9 (N = 214)	63 (N = 380)
Case study/in-basket	4.5 (N = 207)	17 (N = 376)
Programmed instruction	3.2 (N = 206)	11 (N = 372)
Simulation/role playing	3.7 (N = 206)	18 (N = 373)
Sensitivity training	1.8 (N = 206)	11 (N = 372)
OD	N.A.	17 (N = 407)

Source: Lloyd Nigro and John J. DeMarco, "Training in Local Governments: Attitudes and Practices" *Southern Review of Public Administration* 3 (March 1979), p. 479. Reprinted with permission.
[a]Median ranking. Scale: 9, most effective; 1, least effective.

and Sink found that almost half of all reported OD efforts between 1945 and 1980 occurred in the public sector.[26] They also found that over 80 percent of the public-sector applications had positive effects. Most of the OD applications were used to develop skills in giving and receiving feedback, listening, and resolving conflict. Other purposes of the OD applications were to develop teams and improve intergroup relations.[27]

Training and Development in Mechanistic and Organic Organizations

Some training techniques are appropriate for both organic and mechanistic organizations. Lectures, OJT, job rotation, and supervisory coaching can be equally effective in both kinds of organizations. Some methods work best, however, in a particular type of organization. Programmed instruction, for example, may be more effective in mechanistic organizations because it is best for learning factual, sequential information. It is not effective, however, in developing problem-solving or interpersonal skills, which are not so crucial in mechanistic organizations as they are in organic ones.

Other training techniques, such as case studies, incident process, role playing, and T-groups, are most appropriate for organic organizations. All of these methods improve problem-solving skills, which are vital in the more dynamic, unstable conditions that surround organic organizations and positions. Role playing and T-groups develop interpersonal skills that are essential in organic organizations. As noted in chapter 1 (appendix 1A), control processes in organic organizations involve interpersonal contacts, suggestions, persuasion, and consensus building, all of which place a premium on interpersonal skills.

Organization development's emphasis on personal growth, team building, trust, and openness complements the more flexible, participatory nature of organic organizations, whereas OD methods and goals may conflict with the more hierarchical, nonparticipatory, and impersonal style found within mechanistic organizations.

Notes

1. Kenneth Wexley and Gary Latham, *Developing and Training Human Resources in Organizations* (Plainview, Ill.: Scott, Foresman, 1981), p. 3.

2. Malcolm W. Warren, *Training for Results: A System Approach to the Development of Human Resources in Industry*, 2d ed. (Reading, Mass.: Addison-Wesley, 1979), p. 6.

3. A. Hyde and J.M. Shafritz, "Training and Development and Personnel Management," *Public Personnel Management* 8 (November-December 1979): 344–349.

4. Wexley and Latham, *Developing and Training Human Resources in Organizations*, pp. 61–63.

5. William McGehee, "Training and Development Theory: Policies and Practices," in Dale Yoder et al., eds., *ASPA Handbook of Personnel and Industrial Relations. Vol. V: Training and Development* (Washington, D.C.: Bureau of National Affairs, 1977), pp. 5–9.

6. K.L. Vinton, A.O. Clark, and J.W. Seybolt, "Assessment of Training Needs for Supervisors," *Personnel Administrator* 28 (November 1983): 45–51.

7. Dennis Daley, "Performance Appraisal as a Guide for Training and Development," *Public Personnel Management* 12 (Summer 1983): 159–166.

8. E.J. Mitchell and A.C. Hyde, "Training Demand Assessment: Three Case Studies in Planning Training Programs," *Public Personnel Management* 8 (November-December 1979): 360–373.

9. Wexley and Latham, *Developing and Training Human Resources in Organizations*, p. 107.

10. Ibid., pp. 114–117.

11. Charles Watson, *Management Development Through Training* (Reading, Mass: Addison-Wesley, 1979), p. 157.

12. S.J. Carroll, F.T. Paine, and J.J. Ivancevich, "The Relative Effectiveness of Training Methods—Expert Opinion and Research," *Personnel Psychology* 25 (1972): 495–510.

13. Wexley and Latham, *Developing and Training Human Resources in Organizations*, p. 137.

14. P. Pigors and F. Pigors, *The Incident Process: Case Studies in Management Development* (Washington, D.C.: Bureau of National Affairs, 1955).

15. Wexley and Latham, *Developing and Training Human Resources in Organizations*, p. 195.

16. Edgar F. Huse, *Organizational Development and Change* (St. Paul: West, 1975), pp. 252–253.

17. Ibid.

18. W. French and C. Bell, *Organizational Development*, 2d ed. (Englewood Cliffs, N.J.: Prentice-Hall, 1978), pp. 30–37.

19. Ibid., pp. 132–135.

20. D.G. Bowers, "O.D. Techniques and Their Results in 23 Organizations: The Michigan ICL Study," *Journal of Applied Behavioral Science* 9 (1973): 21–43.

21. R.R. Blake and J.S. Mouton, *The New Managerial Grid* (Houston: Gulf, 1978).

22. Donald G. Kirkpatrick, "Four Steps to Measuring Training Effectiveness," *Personnel Administrator* 25 (November 1983): 19–25. Also see Irwin L. Goldstein, "the Pursuit of Internal and External Validity of Training Programs," *Public Personnel Management* 8 (November-December 1979): 416–428.

23. Ronald W. Clement, "Testing the Hierarchy Theory of Training Evaluation: An Expanded Role for Trainee Reactions," *Public Personnel Management* 11 (Summer 1982): 179–184.

24. Lloyd Nigro and John DeMarco, "Training in Local Governments: Attitudes and Practices," *Southern Review of Public Administration* 3 (March 1979): 473–487.

25. Watson, *Management Development Through Training*, pp. 211–216.

26. R.T. Golembiewski, C.W. Proehl, and D. Sink, "Success of OD Applications in the Public Sector: Toting Up the Score for a Decade, More or less," *Public Administration Review* 41 (November-December 1981): 679–682.

27. Ibid.

9
Retrenchment and Productivity

Key Words

Across-the-board cuts versus targeted cuts

Hiring freezes

Last hired, first fired

Bumping rights

Bona fide seniority system

Retroactive seniority

Efficiency

Effectiveness

Job enlargement

Job enrichment

Flexitime

Quality circles (QCs)

Labor–management committees (LMCs)

Productivity bargaining

Firefighter Local 1784 v. Stotts

Introduction

Declines in tax revenue during recessions, citizen opposition to tax increases, and successful movements to reduce taxes have imposed severe fiscal constraints on many governments. Because state and local governments spend over 70 percent of their operating budgets on pay and benefits, a most obvious consequence of these fiscal constraints is pressure to reduce the number of personnel in government.[1] Therefore, retrenchment management has become a more visible, if not more popular, topic in public personnel management.

This chapter notes the crucial role of human resource planning in preventing retrenchment and explores the problems and strategies associated with retrenchment. One method of reducing the pains of retrenchment is to increase the productivity of public employees; however, numerous obstacles impede productivity improvement efforts in the public sector. The chapter discusses the nature and impact of these obstacles and examines several techniques for improving public employees' motivation and productivity that have been popular in recent years. The potential of these techniques for productivity improvement is also evaluated. The chapter concludes with an analysis of retrenchment and productivity improvement efforts in mechanistic and organic organizations.

Retrenchment and Personnel Planning

In one sense, retrenchment suggests a failure of human resource planning. Effective planning can predict a decline in revenues, thus cautioning managers against adding units and employees during good economic times that cannot be sustained under more austere conditions. Unfortunately, human resource planning receives little attention or funding in public organizations, and human resource plans are too often viewed as requests for increased personnel.[2] Even where human resource plans are developed, they probably are not the primary determinants of workforce size. Workforce changes, which occur incrementally, are tied closely to budgetary considerations and often reflect political negotiations, rather than human resource planning, even where such planning exists.[3]

Public managers often have little reason to economize in the number of positions in their organizations. Prestige and power go to the growing organization, and conserving positions results in few rewards for public managers. Indeed, such behavior is often illogical, because positions conserved by a frugal manager may be used to offset excesses of less self-sacrificing managers. Moreover, savings remaining at the end of the fiscal year are taken away. Thus, managers must spend all of their budgeted resources to show that their budgets should be increased in subsequent years. Because of these disincentives to conserve, public managers see little value in planning for possible retrenchment.

Problems of Retrenchment

Denial of Crisis

Public administrators and public employees are generally unaccustomed to real budgetary reductions. Although they expect politicians to call for greater efficiency in government, they generally assume that such talk is rhetoric intended to appeal to voters, not a serious intent that retrenchment should actually occur. Therefore, many public administrators and employees refuse to believe that there is a crisis during the initial stages of retrenchment.[4] Many assume that they can cut a little here and there, stretch resources, and survive until better days.[5] If the retrenchment is temporary or minor, this approach is reasonable.[6] The organization can postpone filling some positions, delay other expenditures, and perhaps survive the crisis. This response is not appropriate, however, when big, permanent cuts are necessary.[7] In such situations, the organization's leaders must explain to employees that major cuts are necessary.[8] One or two memorandums explaining the cuts are not sufficient; leaders must make it clear; with many speeches and reports, that the retrenchment is real and unavoidable.

The Need for Analytical Skills during Retrenchment

During retrenchment, managers need information and analytical capacity more than at any other time. Management information systems can provide performance criteria, service levels, projected future attrition rates, and much other information that is necessary for contingency planning. It is precisely during retrenchment, however, that management may be least willing to spend money for the "luxury" of analytical staff. Analytical personnel may actually be removed to avoid cutting personnel who deliver services. Thus, a paradox exists. The management information systems and policy analysis capabilities that are developed during good times are not used extensively, because there are sufficient resources and there is no perception that long range planning is needed. Thus, when an agency has analytical support, it fails to use it; and when it needs it, it does not have it.[9]

The Decline of Morale during Retrenchment

The dramatic drop in employee morale is the most serious problem during retrenchment. Retrenchment destroys the hope of future expansion and threatens each employee's belief in his or her own worth.[10] When the organization cannot control its own future, this inevitably affects the employees' confidence in their ability to control events.[11]

Rumors concerning possible layoffs spread rapidly in an organization. Many of the most talented employees, who are most valued by the organization, may become frustrated and seek other job opportunities. Since they are often the most mobile, the organization may lose its best employees. Moreover, younger employees, who may correctly assume that seniority will determine retrenchment, may leave as quickly as they can find another job. Thus, a distinct "graying" of the organization may occur.

As some employees leave, the motivation of the remaining employees declines. The insecurity and the lack of advancement opportunities often leads to demoralization and pessimism among the employees.[12] Because of the detrimental effect of retrenchment on morale, the employees must be able to believe that management is controlling the crisis, not that the crisis is buffeting the organization. Only in this way can employees regain confidence in their futures.

Across-the-Board Cuts versus Targeted Cuts

A major problem facing managers during retrenchment is whether to cut equally across the board or to target cuts. Most employees prefer across-the-board cuts, because they are viewed as most equitable and as an attempt to share the burden. Although such cuts may reduce immediate organizational conflict, they may compromise the organization's future survival. Not all units contribute equally to the functioning of the organization. Moreover, some units may have been frugal before the retrenchment crisis and thus have few excess resources that can be cut easily, whereas other units may have considerable surplus resources that can be eliminated without great sacrifice. Efficient units often find that productivity improvement during retrenchment is more difficult because they have already utilized the obvious techniques.[13]

Hiring freezes, like across-the-board cuts, may affect organizational units in an irrational, haphazard way.[14] Units that have more attrition than others are severely affected by a hiring freeze. Moreover, frugal units suffer greater harm than inefficient units that enter the retrenchment crisis with excess personnel. In addition, if vacancies occur among the most crucial positions, whose occupants are the most mobile, a hiring freeze could result in these vital positions remaining vacant.[15]

Seniority and Layoffs

Seniority is often used to determine which employees are released during retrenchment, because most employees believe it is the fairest way to decide who should be fired. Seniority is also preferred by unions, which are fearful that the use of other criteria for cuts would give too much discretion to management. Moreover, many public managers follow the politically safe course of using seniority because it avoids painful decision making; that is, the managers do not have to decide who stays and who leaves. Although employees, managers, and unions may prefer to use seniority in making retrenchment decisions, however, it assures neither rational nor equitable decisions.[16] Units with high concentrations of younger employees are hurt when retrenchment is based entirely on seniority. Furthermore, managers are unable to target cuts and orchestrate the general direction and impact of retrenchment.

When retrenchment decisions are based on seniority, public agencies may lose their best employees, because good workers with little seniority may be released while less-productive employees are retained. Fear of this possibility has encouraged the federal government to place greater weight on job performance in future retrenchments.[17] Federal unions have opposed this change, however, claiming that the use of performance evaluations permits too much managerial discretion during retrenchment.

When seniority is used to decide the order of layoffs, there is a question of whether it should be calculated according to the number of years in the organization, in a unit within the organization, or in a particular position. The answer to this question affects the "bumping" rights of employees during retrenchment. Bumping refers to the right of a more senior employee to take the job of, or bump, an employee who has less seniority. When seniority is based on the number of years in the organization, bumping can occur across the entire organization, and it may require multiple job changes to produce only a few reductions. These changes can create considerable record-keeping and bookkeeping problems. Moreover, some workers may be moved from jobs they can do well to positions in which their performance may be marginal. Calculating seniority within units also presents problems; it discourages mobility, because employees are afraid that they will lose seniority when they switch from one position to another.

Layoffs and Equal Opportunity

Women and minority employees are often the first to be released when reductions are based on seniority.[18] During recent retrenchments, for example, the New York Police Department discharged 74 percent of the women on the police force but only 24 percent of the men.[19] This is why minority groups often oppose the last-hired, first-fired method of determining reductions. Of course, this opposition results in considerable conflict between minorities and the unions, which favor seniority-based retrenchment.

Much of the progress made by minorities and women in gaining employment is based on Title VII of the 1964 Civil Rights Act, although section 703(h) of this act indicates that Congress intended to protect otherwise neutral seniority systems, even when such systems continue the effects of past discriminatory employment practices.[20] Moreover, in three recent Supreme Court decisions, *American Tobacco v. Patterson, Pullman-Standard v. Swint,* and *Firefighters Local 1784 v. Stotts,* the Court has said that Congress did intend to provide special protection to bona fide seniority systems.[21] These decisions raise the question of what constitutes a bona fide seniority system. Court cases have indicated that such a protected seniority system must indeed be neutral and must not be intended to perpetuate segregation.[22] Conversely, the courts are likely to find that a seniority system is not bona fide and is therefore invalid when the following conditions exist:[23]

1. The agency is divided into units in a way that does not reflect common practice.
2. Minorities or women are concentrated within certain units in the agency.
3. The agency determines seniority on the basis of years within the unit.
4. The agency prohibits transfer of seniority from one unit to another.

The *Stotts* decision states that a bona fide seniority system cannot be displaced during retrenchment to avoid terminating minorities and women with comparatively little seniority. (More information on the *Stotts* case can be found in the appendix to this chapter.) Some women and minorities, however, may have an opportunity to keep their positions through retroactive seniority, a procedure for giving employees who are victims of discrimination the approximate place on the seniority list they would have if the agency had used job-related hiring criteria.[24] The courts are likely to uphold retroactive seniority whenever minority or female employees can show they would have attained their positions earlier if discrimination had not occurred.[25] These employees must show that they applied for their positions and were rejected because of discriminatory requirements or tests, or that they did not take the employment exams because they believed them to be discriminatory.[26]

Productivity

Because layoffs are highly injurious to employee morale and trust, it is imperative that public agencies minimize them. Organizations have used numerous methods to avoid layoffs, including hiring freezes and early retirement.[27] Another method to avoid the pains of retrenchment, however, is to improve the productivity of the organization's workforce.[28]

Although productivity improvement has received much attention in recent years, considerable confusion surrounds its meaning. Also, in recent years, several productivity improvement techniques have been popular, including job enlargement and quality circles.

The Meaning of Productivity

Productivity means many things to many people. Katzell and Yankelovich found little consensus on the meaning of the term.[29] Definitions range from efficiency to effectiveness of output measures, including client or customer satisfaction, rates of turnover and absenteeism of employees, and such intangibles as employee morale, loyalty, and job satisfaction. Although there are many definitions of productivity, however, most measurements of it involve efficiency and effectiveness.[30] *Efficiency* refers to the ratio of outputs (goods, products, or services) produced or delivered by a public agency to the inputs (equipment, money, and personnel) used by the agency. *Effectiveness* indicates the real service of the agency or the actual impact of the service. For example, a productivity study that compares the number of trainees completing a job training program to the costs of the training is an efficiency study. Such a study can reveal the efficiency of the training program, but it can not indicate the program's effectiveness, which can be measured only by determining how many of the trainees obtained jobs as a result of the program. Similarly, a study of the costs of treating a certain number of clients in a health center can show the efficiency of the center—that is, the cost per client treated—but it cannot reveal the effectiveness of the treatment—that is, the improvement in the health of the clients. Effectiveness measurements of productivity are concerned with the *quality* of the service delivered. Therefore, such measurements often include surveys of client attitudes about service, which can measure the timeliness, accessibility, courtesy, and equity with which each service is performed.[31] Although the concepts of efficiency and effectiveness seem straightforward, numerous problems surround their measurement and the improvement of public-sector productivity.

Obstacles to Productivity Improvement

Productivity improvement is difficult for numerous reasons. First, there are few incentives to improve productivity in the public sector. Money saved by a manager is taken away at the end of the fiscal year, and the existence of leftover funds may adversely affect the size of the agency's next budget. Also, although managers realize that achieving productivity improvement generally takes a long time, the managers are judged in the short term. Charles Perrow notes that the successful public manager is often judged according to the growth of his or her agency, the size of its budget, and its power over other organizations.[32] Although it is often difficult to measure the effectiveness of an agency's programs, the agency's size and power are more easily perceived, if not measured. Successful public executives usually know this and act accordingly.

A second obstacle to productivity improvement is that legislators are often more concerned about political realities than about financial realities. A board of directors for a private corporation may be interested in the financial impact of its actions, whereas a city council may be much more concerned about the political repercussions of its decisions. The council members or legislators depend on support from their constituencies and must react to the general desire for a larger slice of pie. Rarely is there an organized, important constituency that is providing sustained political support for improved productivity. Moreover, elected officials are more concerned with short-term, politically attractive benefits than with the long-term investments of time, finances, and support that are required for most productivity improvement efforts.[33]

A third obstacle to productivity improvement is the line-item budget used by many governments. A line-item budget lists expenditures for a wide array of categories, including personnel, equipment, supplies, and so forth. Line-item budgeting concentrates on the inputs or resources used to produce a service or output but ignores the impact or effects of the service. There is little opportunity to compare inputs and outputs in line-item budgeting, so this type of budgeting encourages legislators to focus on the small details of expenditures, thus overlooking the impact of those expenditures on the community.

A fourth obstacle to productivity improvement concerns the nature of goals in the public sector. Public organizations often have broad, ambiguous goals that are difficult to measure, such as "to promote the safety of the community" (police), "to provide leisure opportunities" (recreation), and "to promote the health of the community" (health service). Each broad goal demands multifaceted measurements that, even in total, fail to provide a complete picture. The difficulty in measuring broad goals often tempts evaluators to concentrate on what is quantifiable rather than what is significant. This concentration on quantifiable elements may produce some unintended consequences. For example, a concentration on the number of clients served may encourage social service workers to rush clients through the system without providing proper assistance. Similarly, a focus on the number of tons of garbage collected may overlook how the garbage is collected—whether there is spillage and whether the cans are damaged. Also, when they are evaluated according to the number of tons collected, garbage collectors have been known to water down loads.

A fifth obstacle to productivity improvement is the inability, in many instances, to link a specific performance indicator to the actions of a particular employee. For example, reported crime rates are used as measures of the effectiveness of police departments' efforts at crime prevention. There is no way, however, to relate this indicator to the job behavior of any specific police officer. This problem is part of a larger issue. Indicators of the effectiveness of a public service point out whether the service is effective or not, but they rarely can explain *why* the service is or is not effective. This is analogous to a test that indicates whether or not a student is failing but cannot answer the more important question of why the student is failing. Knowing why is the key to improving productivity.

A sixth obstacle to productivity improvement is that many governments lack the analytical capacity to measure their productivity. Small local jurisdictions often do not have the technical staff or computer capability to engage in extensive measurements. Also administrators often lack training in sample selection, measurement, data analysis, and evaluation of the strengths and weaknesses of conclusions drawn from data.[34]

A seventh obstacle to productivity improvement is the lack of a common database among different jurisdictions. Such a database could provide a basis for comparisons of productivity data in different governments. At present, the only national database is the FBI's collection of national statistics on crime. Although the Urban Institute and the International City Management Association have suggested productivity measures for various municipal functions, few cities gather the same data for the same activities. Even if governments did invest the extensive effort needed to gather data on the same measures, however, comparison of the data would be difficult. Governments differ widely in such characteristics as race, household income, type of city (central city, suburban, or rural), and form of government (manager-council versus elected executive). These characteristics, and others, can affect the efficiency, effectiveness, and productivity of different local services.

The lack of valid comparisons among governments makes it difficult to determine whether productivity data in any particular jurisdiction are good, bad, or mediocre. For example, a police department might gather a great deal of productivity data, but the city's executives do not have valid national police productivity standards with which to compare their department's data. Thus, the executives may know little about how their police department compares to others. As a result of such problems, most comparisons are of data from one year to another in the *same* jurisdiction.

Productivity Improvement Efforts

Governments spend 70 percent of their budgets on personnel pay and benefits. Therefore, government productivity improvement efforts naturally focus on personnel. In the private manufacturing sector, the most efficient method of improving labor's productivity is to replace it with capital equipment (automation). Automation is much more difficult in service industries, however, than in manufacturing industries. Because 95 percent of the personnel expenditures in government are for service personnel, government's productivity improvement efforts are considerably more difficult than those in private manufacturing. Moreover, such government efforts cannot rely on automation but must concentrate on improving the motivation and performance of personnel. Some of the popular techniques now being used by governments to improve their employees' motivation and productivity include management by objectives, merit pay and monetary incentives, job enlargement, job enrichment, flexitime, quality control circles, labor–management committees, and productivity bargaining. Management by objectives and merit pay were discussed in chapters 6 and 7. The other productivity improvement efforts are described here.

Job Enlargement. Job enlargement increases the number of tasks, responsibilities, and operation performed by an employee but does not increase the skill levels or autonomy associated with the work. Most job enlargement efforts in the public sector have involved programs that establish public safety officers.[35] Under these programs, firefighters provide certain police patrol and support functions when they are not needed for fighting fires, and police provide some fire suppression activities at the scene of a fire. A few job enlargement programs have involved the training of inspectors to scrutinize several areas (plumbing, heating, fire, public health, and so on).

Although these job enlargement efforts produce savings in some cities, they also generate intense opposition from police and firefighters and their unions.[36] Many police and firefighters believe that the public safety officer programs are intended to save money rather than to enrich jobs. The employees conclude, often correctly, that the real purpose of job enlargement is to reduce the total number of positions, rather than to improve or enrich jobs or make them challenging and enjoyable.

Job Enrichment. Unlike job enlargement, job enrichment does not simply add more of the sames kinds and levels of task requirements to a position (horizontal expansion of the job); rather, it attempts to expand the position vertically. Job enrichment usually includes the following elements:

1. Workers are given an entire piece of work to perform, rather than a fragmented task.
2. Workers are given more autonomy in deciding how the entire task is to be done.
3. Workers perform a greater variety of job responsibilities.
4. Workers receive more immediate feedback on their performance.

Job enrichment is based largely on Herzberg's two-factor theory of motivation, which (as presented in chapter 5) focuses on two factors—hygiene factors and motivators. When hygiene factors (pay, working conditions, and so forth) are not present in the job, workers are dissatisfied. When the hygiene factors are present, however, workers' dissatisfaction is reduced to zero, but the workers are not satisfied. Satisfaction occurs only when motivators (for example, challenge, autonomy, responsibility, and achievement) are present in the job. Job enrichment, therefore, is intended to create jobs with motivators, thus producing greater job satisfaction and improved performance and productivity.

Job enrichment programs are rare in the public sector. A national survey by Greiner and his associates, for example, found only thirty-six job enrichment programs in state and local governments.[37] Job enrichment in the public sector is hampered by several factors. First, position classification systems are often too detailed and rigid to allow for significant job enrichment. Second, unions may oppose efforts at job enrichment or demand that higher pay accompany the job enrichment program. Union leaders are often suspicious of job enrichment, viewing it as a form of manipulation designed to divert employees' attention away from their economic problems. The adversarial nature of collective bargaining makes it difficult to handle the problem of worker dissatisfaction with job design. Also, if job enrichment makes workers more satisfied and more like managers, they may see less need for unions. Third, job enrichment efforts may require the existence of slack resources that could pay for the changes. In recent years, however, few governments have had slack resources to invest in enrichment programs. Moreover, governments are hesitant to enrich jobs when the immediate costs are considerable and the benefits are mixed and difficult to predict.

Although there have been few job enrichment attempts in the public sector, the few that have been tried have produced results similar to those in the private sector. Most studies of job enrichment programs in private industry have revealed that employee job satisfaction increased significantly with the installation of the program. As a result of this greater job satisfaction, turnover, absenteeism, and grievances decreased.[38] The quality of production improved in some but not all cases. There is little evidence, however, that job enrichment programs increased *quantity* of production.

It is difficult to determine the actual impact of job enrichment programs, because most efforts have lacked meaningful controls or methodological rigor.[39] Many job enrichment applications have involved simultaneous changes in the nature of the work, supervision, relationships with peers, and pay. When job enrichment programs have produced positive effects, it has been difficult to determine which changes accounted for the good results.

Job enrichment is more likely to be successful when several conditions are present. First, the remedy should fit the disease. Problems of absenteeism, turnover, grievances, and poor performance may result from the rate of pay, the nature of supervision, the physical working conditions, or outdated equipment. These factors can be changed without engaging in the complex process of job enrichment. Therefore, management should be sure that their problems are caused by conditions that job enrichment is designed to correct.

Second, job enrichment is successful only when employees really want more challenging jobs. Some workers may prefer to remain in highly repetitive, low-skill jobs. They are primarily concerned about such factors as pay, job security, congenial fellow workers, proximity of their work to their homes, and attitudes of supervisors. Such workers often do not seek or want enriched jobs.

Third, successful job enrichment efforts demand the active support of top management and middle- and lower-level supervisors. Managers should recognize that job enrichment indicates a change in traditional bureaucratic, hierarchical practices. In theory, work systems that are designed around enriched jobs are more flexible, open, and employee-centered. In such systems, supervisors may feel less secure in their jobs because their subordinates assume many of the activities for which the supervisors were formerly responsible. These changes should be recognized before a program is implemented, and supervisors should receive training in adjusting to the new environment. Changes in recruitment, performance appraisal, and pay policies should also be anticipated.

Fourth, job enrichment programs are more successful when unions support the changes. Unions are more likely to support job enrichment when union–management relations have been good in the past, when there is mutual trust,

212 Public Personnel Management—A Contingency Approach

and when union members are compensated fairly for the enriched jobs. Unions should be involved in the enrichment programs from the inital planning stages through final implementation.

Flexitime. Flexible work schedules—flexitime—are beginning to gain popularity in the public sector. Flexitime usually consists of a core time (a time during which all employees are to be present, excluding lunchtime) and flexible time, which is determined by the employer. The core time is often six hours (9 A.M. to 3 P.M.) in the middle of the traditional work schedule, coinciding with the period of greatest activity in the agency. The flexible time allows the workers to determine their own starting times (generally between 6 A.M. and 9 A.M.) and quitting times (generally between 3 P.M. and 6 P.M.), so long as they are at work during the core time.[40]

The degree of flexibility in a flexitime system depends on several variables; the amount of freedom management is willing to give to employees; the amount of interdependence necessary among employees and units in the organization; and the nature of civil service laws and collective bargaining agreements covering the workforce.[41]

Golembiewski and Proehl's survey of seventy-four applications of flexitime in the public sector reveals overwhelming support for the benefits of flexitime.[42] First, the flexitime programs have reduced tardiness, absenteeism, and sick leave. Tardiness is virtually eliminated, and absenteeism is reduced because workers no longer need to use sick leave and personal leave to conduct personal business, such as medical appointments. If a worker must be late one morning, he or she need not call in sick and take the whole day off. Second, Golembiewski and Proehl found changes in employee morale to be overwhelmingly positive in the seventy-four flexitime applications they reviewed.[43] This improvement in employee morale leads to lower turnover rates and advantages in recruiting new workers.

Although attempts to measure changes in productivity after the introduction of flexitime systems are rare, the few evaluations that have been done indicate improvements.[44] Even if productivity does not increase, there is no evidence that it decreases. Given that flexitime is a no-cost or low-cost system, and given a stable level of productivity, the benefits of improved employee morale and decreased absenteeism encourage its use.[45]

Although flexitime provides some very positive benefits, a few problems may accompany its implementation. Supervisors may encounter some problems adjusting to flexitime, because much of the burden for oversight of the system falls on them. They must solve the greater coordination and communication problems accompanying flexitime. They also lose some authority under flexitime, because they cannot be supervising during both flexible hours and core hours; therefore, they must delegate some supervisory authority. Despite these concerns, Golembiewski and Proehl found that supervisors were generally supportive of flexitime and wanted to continue it.[46]

Another problem with flexitime is that unions and employees may be concerned about possible decreases in overtime under such a system. In most flexitime systems, however, if an employee is asked by the employer to work longer hours, these hours are credited as overtime.[47] Thus, employees can continue to obtain overtime if the employer requests it.[48]

Quality Circles. Quality circles (QCs)—voluntary study groups dedicated to solving job-related problems[49]—are being used by some public organizations to improve productivity. Although QCs can be established at any level of the organization, they usually are first established at the bottom. Workers in the same area or in the same kind of position volunteer to form a QC. The foreman is generally included in the group and may serve as group leader. The organization also provides a facilitator for each group, who is specially trained in the implementation of QCs. This person assists the group leader in training the members to use QC problem-solving techniques, to assure that the QC meeting adheres to the prescribed structure, and to act as a liaison between the QCs and management.[50] The facilitator obtains information, data, and support from management and seeks to assure that any suggestions from the QC are accepted and implemented by management.

The first few QC meetings are used to teach members techniques for identifying, analyzing, and solving problems. Members are encouraged not to criticize one another and to arrive at decisions by consensus. After some initial training meetings, the members identify a problem and suggest a plausible solution. In general, QCs do not discuss problems concerning wages, benefits, promotions, grievances, interpersonal disputes, and issues covered by the union contract.[51] After a group has analyzed a problem and has developed a solution, it presents the analysis and solution to management. According to Roll and Roll: "It is a general rule that management always accepts and implements the Circle's solutions."[52]

The QC system generally includes a steering committee, composed of facilitators, union leaders, and representatives from middle and upper management, that is headed by a top management official. The steering committee, which often meets weekly, decides how to evaluate the QC program, discusses problems, and develops plans for the expansion of the program.[53]

After QCs were introduced in Japan in 1962, they expanded dramatically to more than 100,000 by 1980.[54] In 1974, Lockheed was the first U.S. corporation to initiate a large-scale QC program, and more than 1,000 corporations in the United States now use the concept.[55] The number of QCs in government is also increasing.[56] They are used in some parts of the Air Force, Army, and Navy and in the Federal Aviation Administration. Some state and local governments have also used QCs.[57]

QCs have apparently produced a number of positive results in Japanese industry. According to a 1979 survey of Japanese managers and QC leaders, QCs have improved worker morale, strengthened teamwork, and improved safety and product quality.[58] They have also improved communication within the organization, increased problem awareness, and improved the working environment. About 80 percent of the managers in the 1979 survey reported that their companies also gained monetary benefits as a result of QCs, ranging annually from $12,000 to $1.2 million per business unit.[59]

Many of the U.S. companies using QCs report productivity improvements similar to those of the Japanese, and published accounts of public organizations' use of QCs, though few in number, provide additional evidence of positive results from QC programs. Cost savings may be overestimated, however, because they are often calculated as savings in employees' time, which is then assumed (but not demonstrated) to be spent doing more productive work, rather than resting or performing some other nonproductive activities.[60] Some critics caution against hurried adoption of QCs and inflated expectations of what QCs can produce.[61] A primary concern of critics is the transferability of the QC concept from the Japanese to the American culture. Gary Helfand has noted that, as a result of the extremely homogeneous Japanese society, Japanese workers have a heightened sense of mutual understanding and intimacy.[62] He states: "This is thought to make possible a more intense identification of the individual with the immediate work group and with the organization as a whole."[63] As a result of this identification with the group, the Japanese worker may perceive his or her performance as directly reflecting upon the honor or integrity of the group and the organization. In contrast, individualism is the accepted norm in the heterogeneous U.S. society. Individuals are judged on the basis of their own behavior, rather than on that of the group. Thus, identification with and concern about group performance is less apparent in U.S. society,[64] and QCs may therefore be less successful in the United States.

Although a definitive evaluation of QCs in the Unites States cannot be made at this time, research does indicate the conditions under which QCs are likely to be successful. Organizations under stress, where there is considerable union–management conflict or where high levels of distrust exist between employees and management, are not good candidates for QCs.[65] Organizations that do not have a reputation for candor with their employees will find it difficult to convince them that QCs are in the employees' interest.

Organizations should not attempt to implement QCs unless their top management is committed to the system and thus willing to pay the considerable costs of starting the system. These costs include the time spent by employees in quality control meetings and the money needed to hire facilitators and other support staff. Top management support is also needed to ensure implementation of the groups' suggestions, since failure to implement these suggestions is fatal for most QC systems.

Before the introduction of QCs in organizations, the support of the union and the supervisors must also be assured. Union representatives should be involved early in the planning of the program, and management should assure the unions that the QCs will not meddle in areas covered by contracts. Also, supervisors who must be group leaders in the QCs should be supportive of the concept, and they should receive extensive briefings on the nature and potential of QCs.

Finally, management should remember that improvements resulting from a QC program may not occur quickly and may be limited to improvements in employee morale. A long period of organization and training is necessary before QCs operate efficiently. Also, improvements may not be as dramatic as expected. In many cases, QCs may do little more than improve the quality of the work life of the group, thus improving job satisfaction but not necessarily improving productivity.[66]

Labor–Management Committees. Labor–management committees (LMCs) exist in many public agencies to create an environment in which labor and management can discuss problems of mutual concern in a casual, nonadversarial manner.[67] LMCs have several purposes, including improvement in productivity, improvement in labor relations, and improvement in the working environment (that is, making the workplace more humane, safer, and more satisfying).

Generally, LMCs consist of managers with decision-making authority and union officers for the bargaining unit.[68] If more than one bargaining unit exists within an agency, members from each unit may be on the committee. Middle managers may feel threatened by LMCs, because their authority appears to be undercut when employees have the opportunity to talk with top management. Therefore, middle managers are often included on LMCs.[69] Of course, if too many middle managers and representatives from different bargaining units are on LMCs, it is difficult to find common subjects to discuss.

A problem encountered by some labor–management committees is an overlap of collective bargaining issues with productivity issues.[70] Most LMCs do not discuss matters that are covered in the union contract. Indeed, most committees in the public sector are created to discuss issues that both sides believe cannot or should not be bargained over. If LMCs become involved in contractual issues, the union is very likely to believe that its turf is being invaded and that management is attempting to bypass the union by using LMCs. Because union skepticism is a major stumbling block to the successful operation of LMCs, considerable care must be exercised when selecting issues for discussion.

Because there have been few systematic evaluations of LMCs, it is difficult to determine their true impact on productivity, although many LMCs, appear to have had a distinctly positive impact on union–management relations.[71] Primarily, LMCs have allowed for the resolution of some issues early, before they could lead to confrontation. Although the LMCs have produced some improvements in job satisfaction, the actual extent to which they have enriched the jobs of employees is difficult to determine. Greiner and his associates conclude their evaluation of LMCs by noting that the "fears of management and the wariness of labor indicate that the establishment of and operation of successful joint labor–management committees are likely to continue to require a considerable measure of good faith and trust and . . . broader involvement by line employees."[72]

Productivity Bargaining. Under a productivity bargaining system, management and labor agree on a formula to be applied to cost savings that result from productivity improvement projects.[73] In the public sector, work rules (for example, job classifications, work schedules, staffing levels, pace or work quotas, safety precautions, and grievance procedures) evolve to protect the various interests found in the public service—that is, the public, public officials, management, employees, clients, and suppliers. Productivity bargaining attempts to change work rules that are obsolete and improve others for the sake of efficiency, quality, and dependability of the service.[74] The process may also attempt to reduce employee dissatisfaction in the hope of improving attendance, effort, and work quality. The bargain may include a buy-out—a wage increase in return for changes in work rules—monetary incentives that are contingent upon increased productivity and are calculated on dollar savings.

Although there has been no definitive study of the impact of productivity bargaining, scattered evidence indicates considerable problems with the concept. First, most cities and other jurisdictions resort to productivity bargaining because of large wage gains won by unions without any corresponding increase in productivity—a situation that develops because of an imbalance in power between strong unions and weak management. Raymond Horton correctly notes, however, that productivity bargaining will not necessarily alter preexisting bargaining or power relationships.[75] Therefore, the very conditions that make productivity bargaining necessary politically (such as powerful unions) also tend to reduce its utility to public managers. In other words, a powerful union that is able to obtain big wage increases before productivity bargaining probably will continue to fare rather well under such a system.

Another difficulty with productivity bargaining is determining the methods for measuring the extent of productivity improvements and the savings produced by such improvements. As noted earlier, productivity standards for various public services and comparative productivity data rarely exist in the public sector. Productivity incentives in bargaining often demand more data, more analysis, better understanding of operations, and better management than many public jurisdictions can provide.[76] Even if there are no technical problems in developing standards, there are special problems in detailing all of the standards in a collective bargaining contract.[77] Furthermore, the application of standards assumes good managerial performance. For example, a refuse collection crew should not be penalized if trucks are not available or if they break down in service.

Because comparative standards cannot be found or cannot be agreed upon by management and unions, the base for measuring productivity improvements may often be the existing level of performance at the time productivity bargaining is introduced. Since, as noted earlier, management often seeks productivity bargaining because of its past inability to bargain successfully with powerful unions, it is questionable whether existing productivity levels should become the baseline.

Another problem with productivity bargaining is that formulas that emphasize rewards for productivity improvement cannot provide the rewards after initial gains, because the possibility of continued improvement year after year becomes smaller and smaller. Therefore, as the years pass, employees and their unions become increasingly frustrated with meager gains and rewards.

Finally, particularly in periods of economic difficulty, taxpayers resent paying productivity bonuses to public employees to do what citizens think they should be doing anyway.

Productivity Improvements in Mechanistic and Organic Oranizations

When productivity is defined as efficiency (that is, the ratio of inputs to outputs) mechanistic organizations can usually attain more significant improvements more rapidly than organic organizations can, because mechanistic organizations often involve functions that can be mechanized or automated. For example, considerable productivity improvements are possible in clerical positions with the introduction of microcomputers and word processors into office systems. Automation may also hold considerable hope for productivity improvements in sanitation and garbage collection and in maintenance and repair of streets and roads. The benefits of automation are less likely in organic organizations, which have a considerable number of administrative, technical, and professional (APT) positions.

Productivity bargaining is also more appropriate in mechanistic organizations, not only because unions are more visible and influential in such organizations but also because productivity improvements are generally more easily measured in mechanistic organizations. Therefore, the formula for distributing productivity savings can be more readily incorporated into the contract. Conversely, productivity in APT positions generally involves the effectiveness of quality of service delivery in addition to the efficiency of service delivery, and it is often difficult to measure.

Job enrichment is an appropriate productivity improvement strategy for organic organizations. Indeed, many of the jobs in such organizations may already be enriched. Job enrichment may not be appropriate, however, for most mechanistic positions. First, it can be prohibitively expensive to enrich some mechanistic jobs. Also, employees in mechanistic positions may not desire more challenging jobs. Moreover, the additional autonomy that is granted employees through job enrichment may not complement the hierarchical, centralized style of management that is common in mechanistic organizations. The APT positions in organic organizations can be more easily enriched, and the occupants of APT positions are more likely to desire job enrichment. In addition, the increased autonomy given to employees through job enrichment complements the more consensual, decentralized management style of organic organizations.

Although the use of labor–management committees and quality control circles in the public sector has been limited to mechanistic organizations, they could also be used in organic organizations. These techniques do seem more appropriate for mechanistic organizations, however, because employees in APT positions within organic organizations may already have considerable influence on how their positions are structured and on how the work is done. Thus, the formation of quality control circles and labor–management committees may duplicate what is already occurring in organic organizations.

Flexitime can be useful in both mechanistic and organic organizations, although many employees in APT positions may already operate on an informal flexitime arrangement. For example, some administrators may take longer lunch breaks but work later in the evening, and many APT employees are more concerned with completing particular tasks than with putting in so many hours. Flexitime may have a greater impact on mechanistic employees, who traditionally have had little influence over the hours they work. Therefore, improvements in employee morale as a result of flexitime may be most dramatic in mechanistic organizations.

Most of the productivity improvements discussed in this chapter (job enrichment, quality control circles, flexitime, labor–management committees) imply a movement away from the directive, centralized hierarchical managerial style that is typical of most mechanistic organizations. Therefore, managers—particularly middle-level managers—and supervisors may have considerable difficulty in adjusting their management style to the participatory tendencies implicit in most of these techniques. Organizations should be aware that supervisors may resist giving up the controls and responsibilities they have traditionally held.

Conclusion

It is important to remember that effectiveness is only one of several competing cultural values that affect the U.S. public bureaucracy. As noted in chapters 1 and 2, public administration in the United States must also respond to two other values—liberalism and responsiveness. Quests for greater productivity and reduced costs should not obscure our concern for assuring basic fairness and due process to public employees. Similarly, retrenchment efforts that might promote efficiency but that also do great harm to the realization of a representative bureaucracy should be used only when absolutely necessary.

Finally, it is unfortunate that calls for retrenchment and for Japanese-style productivity efforts are often made in the same breath. The Japanese productivity improvements are based on job security, which increases employees' trust and commitment to the corporation. This trust and commitment contributes, in turn, to the employees' flexibility, energy, cooperation, and productivity. Retrenchment, however, is a great destroyer of employee trust. It promotes insecurity, competitiveness, and despondency. Therefore, it is difficult to think that Japanese productivity improvement efforts can be transplanted successfully to U.S. public bureaucracies that are undergoing retrenchment. If better economic conditions and improved human resource planning can again assure considerable job security for the public employee, U.S. public bureaucracies may yet prove to be fertile environments for the techniques that have been successful in Japan.

Notes

1. Donald Klinger and John Nalbandian, "Human Resource Administration and Cutback Management—A Symposium," *Review of Public Personnel Administration* 4 (Fall 1983): 1–11.

2. Arthur Johnson, "Cutback Strategies and Public Personnel Management: An Analysis of Nine Maryland Counties," *Review of Public Personnel Administration* 3 (Fall 1982): 41–55.

3. Ibid., p. 47.

4. Charles H. Levine, "More on Cutback Management: Hard Questions for Hard Times," *Public Administration Review* 39 (March–April 1979):179–183.

5. Robert C. Wilburn and Michael A. Werman, "Overcoming the Limits to Personnel Cutbacks: Lessons Learned in Pennsylvania," *Public Administration Review* 40 (November–December 1980): 609–612.

6. Levine, "More on Cutback Management," p. 181.

7. Robert D. Behn, "Leadership for Cutback Management: The Use of Corporate Strategy," *Public Administration Review* 40 (November–December 1980): 613–620.

8. Ibid., p. 615.

9. Levine, "More on Cutback Management," p. 180.

10. Behn, "Leadership for Cutback Management," p. 617.

11. Ibid.

12. Carol Lewis, W. Wayne Shannon, and G. Donald Ferree, "The Cutback Issue: Administrators' Perceptions, Citizen Attitudes and Administrative Behavior," *Review of Public Personnnel Administration* 4 (Fall 1983): 12–26.

13. Levine, "More on Cutback Management," p. 181.

14. Charles Levine, "Organizational Decline and Cutback Management," *Public Administration Review* 38 (July–August 1978): 322.

15. Robert P. Biller, "Leadership Tactics for Retrenchment," *Public Administration Review* 40 (November–December 1980): 604–609.

16. Levine, "Organizational Decline and Cutback Management," pp. 316–315.

17. "RIF Rules Downgrade Seniority Protection," *Public Administration Times*, November 11, 1983, p. 1.

18. "RIF Rules Challenged By Treasury Union," *Public Administration Times*, December 1, 1983, pp. 3, 4.

19. Robert Roberts, "Last Hired, First Fired and Public Employee Layoffs: The Dilemma," *Review of Public Personnel Administration* 2 (Fall 1981): 29–48.

20. Ibid., p. 31.

21. *American Tobacco Co. v. Patterson*, 102 S.Ct. 1534 (1982); *Pullman-Standard v. Swint*, 102 S.Ct. 1781 (1982); *Firefighters Local 1784 v. Stotts*, Docket Nos. 82–229 (June 12, 1984).

22. *Sears v. United Transportation Union*, 102 S.Ct. 2045 (1982).

23. For an excellent discussion of bona fide seniority systems, see Marcia Graham, "Seniority Systems and Title VII: Reanalysis and Redirection," *Employee Relations Law Journal* 9 (Summer 1983): 81–97.

24. Hindy L. Schachter, "Retroactive Seniority and Agency Retrenchment," *Public Administration Review* 43 (January–February 1983): 77–81.

25. Ibid., p. 79.

26. Ibid., p. 78.

27. For an examination of legal problems involved in reduction in force, see Gary R. Siniscalco, "Reductions in Force: Minimizing Exposure to Contract, Tort, and Discrimination Claims," *Employee Relations Law Journal* 9 (Autumn 1983): 209.

28. For a discussion of other methods to reduce the trauma of retrenchment, see R. Fuller, C. Jordan, and R. Anderson, "Retrenchment: Layoff Procedures in a Nonprofit Organization," *Personnel* 29 (November–December 1982): 14–24.

29. R. Katzell and D. Yankelovich, *Work, Productivity and Job Satisfaction* (New York: New York University Press, 1975).

30. Harry Hatry, "The Status of Productivity Measurement in the Public Sector," *Public Administration Review* 38 (January–February 1978): 28–33.

31. Harry Hatry, "Performance Measurement: Principles and Techniques," *Public Productivity Review* 4 (December 1980): 312–339.

32. Charles Perrow, "Demystifying Organizations," in R.S. Sarri and Y. Hasenfeld, eds., *The Management of Human Services* (New York: Columbia University Press, 1978), p. 113. If Perrow's assessment is correct, it should not be surprising that surveys of local managers reveal that productivity improvement is not a high priority. See David N. Amonons and Joseph C. King, "Productivity Improvement in Local Government: Its Place Among Competing Priorities," *Public Administration Review* 32 (March–April 1983): 113–120.

33. D.R. Ballantyne, *Improving Local Government Productivity* (New York: John Jay College of Criminal Justice, Center for Productive Public Management, 1977).

34. Seymour Mann, "The Politics of Productivity: State and Local Focus," *Public Productivity Review* 4 (December 1980): 360.

35. John M. Greiner and others, *Productivity and Motivation: A Review of State and Local Government Initiatives* (Washington, D.C.: Urban Institute Press, 1981), p. 294.

36. Ibid., p. 307.

37. Ibid., p. 309.

38. E. Lawler, "Job Design and Employee Motivation," *Personnel Psychology* 22 (Winter 1969): 426–435.

39. M. Fein, "Job Enrichment: A Re-evaluation," *Sloan Management Review* 20 (Winter 1979): 69–88.

40. R.S. Rubin, "Flexitime: Its Implementation in the Public Sector," *Public Administration Review* 39 (May–June 1979): 277–282.

41. Ibid.

42. R. Golembiewski and C. Proehl, "Public Sector Applications of Flexible Work-hours: A Review of Available Experience," *Public Administration Review* 40 (January–February 1980): 72–85.

43. Ibid., p. 78.

44. Ibid.

45. Ibid.

46. Ibid., p. 81.

47. Ibid.

48. Rubin, "Flexitime," p. 277.

49. Hirotaka Takeuchi, "Productivity: Learning From the Japanese," *California Management Review* 23 (Summer 1981): 9.

50. J. Roll and D. Roll, "The Potential for the Application of Quality Circles in the Public Sector," *Public Productivity Review* 7 (June 1983): 125.

51. Ibid., p. 126.

52. Ibid.

53. Ibid.

54. Takeuchi, "Productivity," p. 9.

55. J.D. Blair, S. Cohen, and J.V. Hurwitz, "Quality Circles: Practical Considerations for Public Managers," *Public Productivity Review* 6 (March–April 1982): 10.

56. S. Bryant and J. Kearns, "Workers' Brains as Well as Their Bodies: Quality Circles in a Federal Facility," *Public Administration Review* 42 (March–April 1982): 144–150.

57. Ibid.

58. Takeuchi, "Productivity," p. 10.

59. Ibid.

60. Blair, Cohen, and Hurwitz, "Quality Circles," p. 13.

61. J.S. Sullivan, "A Critique of Theory Z," *Academy of Management Review* 8 (1983): 132–142.

62. G. Helfand, "The Applicability of Japanese Management Techniques in the American Public Sector: Some Cultural Considerations," *Public Productivity Review* (June 1983): 105–111.

63. Ibid.

64. Ibid., p. 110.

65. Blair, Cohen, and Hurwitz, "Quality Circles," pp. 16, 17.

66. Ibid.

67. Greiner and others, *Productivity and Motivation*, p. 265.

68. Susan Clark, *A Guide to Labor–Management Committees in State and Local Governments* (Washington, D.C.: Public Technology, 1980), p. 33.

69. Ibid., p. 7.

70. A.C. Goldoff and D.C. Tatage, "Joint Productivity Committees: Lessons of Recent Initiatives," *Public Administration Review* 38 (March–April 1978): 184–186.

71. Greiner and others, *Productivity and Motivation*, p. 336.

72. Ibid.

73. Ballantyne, *Improving Local Government Productivity*, p. 71.

74. D.R. Layden, "Productivity and Productivity Bargaining: The Environmental Context," *Public Personnel Management* 9 (1980): 251.

75. R.D. Horton, "Productivity and Productivity Bargaining in Government: A Critical Analysis," *Public Administration Review* 36 (July–August 1976): 109.

76. F. Hayes, *Productivity in Local Government* (Lexington, Mass: Lexington Books, D.C. Heath, 1977) p. 239.

77. Ibid.

Appendix 9A: *Firefighters Local 1784 v. Stotts*

As the manuscript for this book was being prepared for the publisher in June 1984, the Supreme Court delivered a significant decision on seniority and affirmative action. The case, *Firefighters Local 1784 v. Stotts*, originated in Memphis, Tennessee. In 1980, the city signed a consent decree to settle a class-action race-discrimination lawsuit brought by Carl Stotts, a black captain in the Memphis Fire Department. Under the terms of the consent decree, the city agreed to increase the proportion of minority representation in the fire department. Although the city signed the decree, it never admitted to any discrimination, and no finding of discrimination was ever made against the city.

Approximately one year after the city signed the consent decree, it faced a budgetary crisis and, to reduce expenditures, announced the layoffs of some personnel. The reductions were to be based on the last-hired, first-fired rule, as required by the union contract. As a result, the newly hired black firefighters could see that their recent victory would be emasculated by retrenchment, and they asked the federal district court to stop the layoffs. The district court enjoined the city from proceeding with the layoffs because they would thwart the basic purpose of the consent decree, which was to increase minority representation in the fire department. The district court's injunction resulted in the release of several white firefighters who had more seniority than some black firefighters who were not released.

The firefighters local union and the city appealed the district court's decision to the Sixth Federal Circuit Court of Appeals, which upheld the district court's opinion, and the union and the city then sought review of the case by the Supreme Court. The city's position on appeal was based not only on the seniority rights of its employees but also on a court's power to modify a consent decree. The city contended that it had never admitted to discrimination in the consent decree and that it had agreed only to two specific affirmative action provisions involving hiring and promotion goals. Thus, the decree contained no provision regarding the method of layoffs within the fire department. The city contended that a court could not subsequently alter a consent decree by adding provisions that were not negotiated or agreed upon by the parties. Moreover, the city and the union asserted that the Memphis seniority system was a bona fide system protected by section 703(h) of Title VII and, therefore, that a court could not overturn it without a finding of discrimination.

The Supreme Court held that a bona fide seniority system cannot be modified by a Title VII consent decree without the agreement of the union and noted that Section 703(h) of Title VII expressly protects bona fide seniority systems, provided that there is no intention to discriminate. Furthermore, the Supreme Court said that a consent decree could be modified by a court only to protect actual, specific victims of discrimination. Moreover, the Court said that a court may not grant preferential treatment to any individuals or groups simply because the class to which they belong is adversely affected by a bona fide seniority system. The Court's emphasis on compensating identified victims of discrimination rather than an entire class of individuals has prompted some to suggest that the case represents a major retreat from affirmative action. Indeed, some people in the Justice Department have been predicting the end of affirmative action. There are several reason, however, to support a more restricted interpretation of the *Stotts* decision.

First, it was a six-to-three decision; only four justices were able to agree to the majority opinion. Therefore, it is unclear whether a Court majority can agree to a decision overturning the concept of affirmative action goals or quotas. Second, the only issue before the Court was whether a bona fide seniority system could be set aside to promote affirmative action goals. In the absence of a finding of discrimination, the Court said no. The issues of affirmative action in hiring and promotion were not before the Court.

What can we safely conclude about the impact of the *Stotts* decision? First, the case does not affect hiring goals, since seniority is generally not a consideration in filling entry-level positions. Therefore, there is little conflict between seniority rights and affirmative action hiring goals or quotas. Second, specific victims of discrimination who prove their cases in court can obtain retroactive seniority. Third, if a court finds that a class of individuals has been a victim of discrimination, the court may order hiring goals, but it may not override a bona fide seniority system. Fourth, voluntary modification of seniority policies for affirmative action goals are permissible, provided that the union agrees.

It is more difficult to predict the impact of *Stotts* on promotion decisions. If seniority is the sole criterion for determining promotion, and if the seniority system is bona fide, the *Stotts* decision would seem to preclude affirmative action promotion goals for a class of individuals when such goals conflict with seniority. If specific individuals can prove in court, however, that they have been victims of discrimination, they will receive retroactive seniority for promotional purposes.

A more difficult case occurs when seniority is only one of several criteria used for making promotion decisions. The more applicable Supreme Court decision in this circumstance is *United Steelworkers v. Weber,* in which the Court upheld a voluntary affirmative action plan that provided racial preferences for entry into an apprenticeship program. Although the *Weber* decision concerned entry into an apprenticeship program, entry was based upon seniority. The Court upheld the plan because it did not preclude the promotion of whites nor require their discharge. The Court is likely to uphold modifications of seniority in promotions when seniority is only one of several criteria for promotion and if such modifications do not constitute an absolute bar to the promotion of whites.

10
Public-Sector Labor Relations

Key Words

American Federation of State, County and Municipal Employees (AFSCME)

Elastic versus inelastic demand

Federal Labor Relations Authority (FLRA)

Public Employee Relations Board (PERB)

Bargaining unit

Exclusive recognition

Union shop

Agency shop

Right-to-work laws

Abood v. Detroit Board of Education

Whipsawing

Bona fide supervisor

Certification election

Fragmentation of management

End run

Scope of bargaining

Bargaining impasse

Mediation

Fact-finding

Voluntary arbitration

Compulsory arbitration

Final-offer arbitration

Sovereignty doctrine

Management-rights clauses

Introduction

A chapter on labor–management relations would not have been an important chapter in a public personnel text twenty years ago. The dramatic growth of public employee unions, however, and the substantial increase in collective bargaining in the public sector have moved labor–management relations to the forefront of public personnel management. These recent developments and their causes are investigated in this chapter, and the political and legal environments of collective bargaining are reviewed. Methods are presented by which public management can organize to implement collective bargaining, and steps in the negotiation process—from preparing for negotiations to developing strategies at the bargaining table—are discussed. Since some negotiations end at an impasse, the various methods of resolution are discussed, with particular attention to the controversial impasse resolution of compulsory arbitration. Because impasses may result in strikes, the pros and cons of legalization of public employee strikes are examined. The chapter also reviews the impact of collective bargaining on wages, fringe benefits, and other personnel management functions, such as selection, promotions, position classification, discipline, and reductions in force. Finally, the chapter concludes with a consideration of the impact of public employee unions on democracy and the public interest.[1]

The Development of Unions in the Public Sector

The first public service union of any importance emerged in the U.S. Postal Service during the 1880s.[2] Police and firefighters also began organizing at the local level at about the same time. These unions, however, operated primarily as mutual benefit societies to provide pension and insurance programs for their members. Few significant developments in public-sector unionization occurred until the 1960s.

Several factors account for the slow development of unions in the public sector. Perhaps the primary factor was the generally unfavorable political environment. Many people believed that the doctrine of sovereignty precluded public employee unions because collective bargaining would be tantamount to an illegal delegation of legislative power to a nongovernmental body—the unions. The second factor was the civil service merit system. Public employees had job security and were protected against arbitrary adverse actions, and unions found it difficult to organize workers who were relatively secure and who did not have any major complaints against management. A third reason was the anti-union bias of public white-collar employees. Unionization was most difficult among white-collar employees, who saw themselves not as workers but as part of management. Union membership was considered unprofessional by many public employees, who identified with middle-class values and who often opposed all unions. A fourth reason was the unfriendly legal environment for unions. Few states had laws permitting public employee unions and collective bargaining, and most states prohibited strikes by public employees. Moreover, the courts were generally hostile to public unions.

The Growth of Public-Sector Unions

Membership in public-sector unions increased rapidly during the 1960s and 1970s. This growth was particularly impressive in comparison to the decline of union membership in the private sector. From 1956 to 1976, union membership in the private sector dropped from one-fourth to one-fifth of all employees, while in the public sector it increased from one-tenth to over one-third.[3] Moreover, public unions represented employees who were not actually members of the unions. As a result, over half of all government employees in the early 1980s were represented by unions,[4] including over 70 percent of all firefighters and teachers; approximately half of all police, sanitation workers, and highway employees; and approximately 60 percent of all federal civilian employees.[5]

There are several reasons for this dramatic growth. First, the rapid expansion in government employment during this period provided fertile soil for union recruiters. Between 1951 and 1980, government employment increased by more than 10 million new workers—a 227 percent increase. In comparison, the gain in private employment was only 89 percent. Much of the growth in the private sector was in areas that were traditionally difficult to unionize (finance, insurance, real estate services). Moreover, the number of traditional, unionized blue-collar jobs began to decrease. Therefore, unions viewed public employees as potential new recruits to offset setbacks in the private sector. This increase in competition among unions for new members from the public sector encouraged the growth of public unions. For example, when the National Education Association (NEA) saw the success of the American Federation of Teachers (AFT) in gaining new members and in achieving good salary increases, the NEA had to support collective bargaining to remain competitive.

As government services expanded during the 1960s, agencies increased in size and became more mechanistic (see chapter 1). Relationships between employees and their managers became more impersonal, and more rules and regulations were developed to control the larger bureaucracies. As a result, many government employees felt that they had little influence in their organizations, and they looked to the unions to give them a larger voice in the operation of their agencies. Particularly the professional employees, such as teachers, nurses, and social workers, may have been so motivated.

Another important reason for the growth of public unions was the change in public employees' attitudes. Until 1960, many public employees believed that the sovereignty argument precluded unions in the public sector. Also, many white-collar public employees viewed unions as nonprofessional organizations for lower-status, blue-collar workers. These attitudes began to change in the 1960s as public employees found unions more useful and less threatening to their self-images. Some possible explanations for this attitude change are the civil rights movement, the student demonstrations, and the antiwar movement, which contributed to the general tendency for public employees to become more militant, which, in turn, enhanced unionization.[6] In addition, white-collar public employees could see that many blue-collar employees were making more money and that the unions were responsible for the improvement.

The dramatic growth in the number of public employees in the 1960s also produced a powerful political force, which led to less political resistance to public employee unionization and collective bargaining. One result of the political power of the public employees was President Kennedy's Executive Order 10988. Although this order continued many restrictions on bargaining, it did recognize the right of public employees to join a union. The symbolic importance of this recognition was most important in that it provided respectability to public employee unions. At the state level, legislatures began to remove restrictions on public employee unionization and collective bargaining.[7] Reapportionment of state legislatures by the Supreme Court during the early 1960s also reduced their control by primarily rural, anti-union interests. As metropolitan areas gained more influence in the legislatures, the unions from these areas also gained power. As a result, by 1982, thirty-seven states had given public employees the right to organize and bargain collectively.

Although public-sector unions experienced dramatic growth in the 1960s and 1970s, they have suffered declines during the early 1980s. Recessions, taxpayer revolts, and public hostility toward public employees and unions have encouraged management to resist unions and union organizing. The situation is particularly bad for teacher unions. Taxpayer resistance to tax increases and a decline in the number of school-age children have led to school closings and teacher layoffs, which have, in turn, reduced the ranks of the American Federation of Teachers and the National Education Association. Similarly, President Reagan's cuts at the federal level have reduced the number of nondefense federal employees. In addition, Reagan's successful decertification of PATCO, the air traffic controller's union, was a significant restraint on federal unions.

Public-Sector Unions

Federal unions do not have as much power as private-sector unions and many state and local unions. At the federal level, the scope of bargaining is very restricted, and there is a strong no-strike policy. Moreover, federal unions cannot force employees to join the union (union shop) or pay dues to the union (agency shop). At present, the largest federal unions are the American Federation of Government Employees, the National Federation of Federal Employees and the National Treasury Employees Union.

At the state and local levels, the largest general-purpose union is the American Federation of State, County and Municipal Employees (AFSCME). It is one of the most progressive and liberal public unions in the nation, perhaps because blacks and women make up a majority of the union's membership. The Service Employees International Union (SEIU), another large, general-purpose union, concentrates on employees in hospitals and social service agencies and on non-teaching personnel in schools.

As mentioned earlier, two public unions—the National Education Association (NEA) and the American Federation of Teachers (AFT)—compete for most teachers. The NEA is older, larger, and more conservative. For many years, the NEA opposed collective bargaining on salaries. In 1961, however, New York City teachers selected an affiliate of the AFT as their bargaining agent. After that loss, the NEA began to change its policies and later adopted collective bargaining.

Municipal firefighters are the most highly organized public employees; the International Association of Firefighters (IAFF) represents a large majority of firefighters. Unlike the firefighters, police officers are represented by several general-purpose unions, including AFSCME, SEIU, and the Teamsters.

The Political Environment of Public-Sector Collective Bargaining

One major difference between public-sector and private-sector collective bargaining is that the latter is more subject to demands of the economic market. In the private sector, the union's trump card is its ability to withhold its labor and cause serious economic loss to a company. The company is fearful that, without a large inventory, its plants will stand idle, customers will move to alternative products, and the company may suffer long-term losses in its share of the market.

In the public sector, however, the chief fear of the employer is not that the union may withhold its labor and cause economic damage but that the union will cause political damage to the image of the government, its elected leaders, and its top managers. A strike in the public sector might not cause severe economic losses—indeed, it might produce short-run economic gains because of savings in wages—but it can embroil the government in controversy, attract media attention, and embarrass elected officials and public managers.

In the private sector, union-forced wage hikes may increase product prices. In a competitive market, such increases may encourage customers to switch to substitute products or simply do without the product. These customer responses may lower demand for the higher-priced products, which, in turn, may lead to higher unemployment. This specter of higher unemployment acts as a restraint on private-sector union wage demands. In the public sector, however, there are few competing sources for government products or services. Therefore, public unions have less fear that customers or citizens will switch to another product. Usually, the only way for the customer of public services to switch is to move to another jurisdiction.

Also, public unions know that there is inelastic demand for most public services. A change in the price of fire or police protection, for example, does not decrease citizens' demand for protection. In contrast, the demand for many private products is elastic; customers may choose to do without a product if its price increases too much. Public unions may recognize that the inelastic demand for public services mitigates any unemployment that might result from higher prices for the service, especially if citizens do not pay directly for services when they consume them, as is true for most government services. Thus, citizens may not see a direct association between, for example, an increase in the wages of police or firefighters and an increase in the costs of protection. In such a situation, demand becomes even more inelastic, and the union's power increases.

When the potential political power of the unions to pressure elected political leaders (which will be discussed later) is combined with the foregoing factors, it is possible that unions will become stronger in the public sector than in the private sector. There are arguments, however, for expecting the reverse. To the extent that existing legal barriers inhibit union organization, collective bargaining, and strikes in the public sector, union power is reduced.[8] Also, public employers may enjoy an advantage in that they employ a large number of workers whose duties and skills have few direct counterparts in the private sector. It is not easy for such public employees as firefighters and police to transfer their skills to the private sector. In addition, recent research suggests that differences in elasticity of demand for labor between the public and the private sectors are not nearly so great as is implied by the elasticity-of-demand argument, which was presented earlier.[9] If this is true, a major reason for expecting greater union power in the public sector would be undermined.

A second major difference between public-sector and private-sector collective bargaining is the political influence that public unions can have on government management. Although some jurisdictions attempt to prohibit political activity by public unions, the very existence of unions is a political act, and restrictions of union political activity have not been effectively enforced.[10] The primary long-term political strategies of public unions are election campaign activity and lobbying. In election campaigns, publics unions can provide manpower, a voting bloc, money, information, endorsements, and other supports for candidates. These resources become even more significant if a candidate's political party is weak and if there are few competing, well-organized, and visible special-interest groups concerned about the outcome of the election—as is often the situation in local elections. There are considerable risks, of course, in a public employee union openly supporting a candidate. If the union's candidate were to lose, the union would then have to negotiate with the victorious opponent.

Lobbying—another long-term political strategy of public unions—has several goals. The first purpose of union lobbying is to maintain continuous and direct contact with elected politicians to ensure that sympathetic attention is given to the union's concerns. Second, union lobbyists seek to supply legislators with data that support union-backed legislation. Although legislators realize that much of this information is self-serving for the unions, they often must rely on it because they lack the time or expertise to gather comparable data for themselves.[11]

If a union's members comprise a significant portion of a legislator's constituency, the union's lobbyist will remind the legislator of that fact and advise him or her of the intensity with which the union supports a particular bill. Local employee groups that have common interests with similar employee groups on a statewide basis, such as police, firefighters, and teachers, are particularly effective in applying this sort of political pressure in support of their common interests.[12] The most active efforts of public employee union lobbyists at the state level have been to obtain and strengthen collective bargaining laws. Public unions also lobby against antistrike legislation.

At the local level, union lobbyists are more sensitive to the locations of power within the local council or schoolboard. Also, the city council or board's responsibility to provide efficient, high-quality services and the desirability of maintaining harmonious relations with the city or school employees can add weight to the union's arguments.[13] Local lobbying efforts could involve a great variety of issues, including wages, benefits, working hours, residency requirements, taxation, work rules, and so on.

Lobbying is done more indirectly through letters, telephone calls, and telegrams to legislators from union members. Marches on city hall and the state capitol are another form of indirect lobbying. Also, police and firefighters, for example, might pack council rooms when issues important to them are being discussed by the city council. If these lobbying efforts prove unsuccessful, the public union may seek to bypass the legislature by using petition and referendum procedures. For example, teachers' unions have been greatly involved in referendum elections on tax increases for financing the schools.

The Legal Environment of Public-Sector Collective Bargaining

Before 1962, the right of public employees to join or form a union was severely limited. Courts accepted the privilege doctrine, which stated that public employment was a privilege. (See chapter 12 for a discussion of the privilege doctrine.) If a public employee was dismissed for exercising his or her civil right to join a union (freedom of association), no constitutional question was involved because a privilege (the employee's job) had been abrogated, not a right. Today, however, the courts reject the privilege doctrine and hold that public employees have a constitutional right to join unions. The courts have never said, however, that public employers are constitutionally obliged to bargain collectively with public unions. The extent of this collective bargaining is determined by numerous federal and state laws.

Several executive orders control collective bargaining in the federal government. President Kennedy's 1962 Executive Order 10988 gave most federal civilian employees the right to form and join unions and bargain collectively. The order excluded the CIA, the FBI, and other agencies that are involved in security functions. Subsequent executive orders expanded and refined the collective bargaining rights of federal employees. The 1978 Civil Service Reform Act (CSRA) incorporates provisions of the earlier executive orders and provides statutory protection of federal employees' right to join unions and to bargain collectively on personnel policies, practices, and other matters that affect working conditions. The 1978 act does not permit negotiations on wages, fringe benefits, prohibited political activities, and position classification.

The CSRA places most federal labor-relations activities under the control of the Federal Labor Relations Authority (FLRA)—a three-member bipartisan board appointed by the president with the advice and consent of the Senate. The FLRA has authority over unit determination, supervision of union elections, resolution of unfair labor practice charges, and decisions concerning which issues are bargainable. Postal workers are not included under the 1978 act, because the Postal Reorganization Act of 1970 provided full collective bargaining rights to postal employees, with the single exception of the right to strike. Postal workers are under the jurisdiction of the National Labor Relations Board.

More than a hundred state laws govern collective bargaining at the state and local levels, and these laws are supplemented by numerous local ordinances, court decisions, and attorney general opinions. Although there are many variations in the state laws governing collective bargaining, the trend has been to provide a comprehensive law to cover all state and local employees. Twenty-six states provide such coverage.[14] An additional fourteen states provide collective bargaining for one to four occupations. In these fourteen states, teachers and firefighters are the most common occupations covered.[15]

Several major provisions are common to the labor–management relations legislation in the states that have comprehensive collective bargaining legislation. Most of these states grant employees the right to join and form a union and to bargain collectively. Typically, management retains the right to determine the mission of the agency and to decide what work is to be done and how it is to be performed. Furthermore, management keeps control over hiring, promotions. and dismissals.[16]

Most states have established some type of centralized administrative agency to administer public-sector labor relations. In some cases, this agency is an existing Department of Labor or Civil Service Commission; in most instances, however, it is a newly created Public Employee Relations Board (PERB).[17] This administrative agency resolves disputes about recognition of unions, hears complaints of unfair labor practices, and supervises implementation of the collective bargaining law.

In most states, the PERB or other central agency determines the appropriate bargaining unit, which consists of one or more public workers who are represented by one union. The most commonly used criteria for determining the bargaining unit are the history of employee representation and the "community of interest" among the employees. (These and other criteria for unit determination will be discussed in a later section.)

After the unit is determined, several unions may compete for the right to represent the unit in collective bargaining. All states with comprehensive statutes provide for exclusive recognition whereby one union has the right to speak for all employees within a particular unit.[18] Exclusive recognition is decided by a majority vote of the employees within a bargaining unit.

Although all states prohibit a closed shop (in which every employee must be a union member prior to employment), five states allow a union shop (in which every employee must join the union after employment), and six states allow an agency shop (in which employees are not required to join the union but must pay dues to the union). Most states allow use of the dues checkoff, whereby the employer deducts union dues from the paychecks of employees and turns the money over to the union. The dues checkoff helps solve the "free rider" problem—nonunion employees sharing the benefits from the union's bargaining efforts without supporting the union. Twenty states that have right-to-work laws prohibit union and agency shops and the compulsory dues checkoff.[19]

One issue concerning the dues checkoff is whether nonunion employees should be forced to pay for a union's political activities that are unrelated to collective bargaining. In *Abood v. Detroit Board of Education*, the Supreme Court said that an agency shop was constitutional so long as union members were not forced to pay for the union's political activities.[20] According to the Court, such forced support violates the employee's right to freedom of speech and association. (See chapter 12 for additional discussion of this issue.)

Every state with a comprehensive collective bargaining law provides at least one of the three primary methods for resolving disputes between management and the unions: mediation, fact-finding, and arbitration. (These will be discussed in a later section.) Mediation is used by thirty-five states, fact-finding by 32, and arbitration by 27.[21]

Determining the Bargaining Unit

Before any union can represent public employees, the appropriate bargaining unit must be determined. A bargaining unit consists of one or more public employees who are represented by one union and are eligible to be represented by that union.[22] Unit determination is important for several reasons. First, if bargaining units are not designed to accommodate governmental structure and authority, the bargaining relationship may be unstable.[23] One student of unit determination has noted that both small and large bargaining units have problems in discovering what issues can be negotiated and in finding someone in government who can say yes or no.[24] Second, unit determination is important because incremental recognition of many small units without concern for the cumulative impact of the individual decisions can result in a balkanization of union representation, which can have adverse consequences.

Heisel has noted that the largest possible unit has several advantages for management.[25] First, the larger the union, the more responsibility it must assume for maintaining a reasonable salary structure among the various classifications in the organization. Most employees are very concerned about how their salaries relate to those of others in the organization, and they are often jealous of what other employees in the organization receive. (See the discussion of equity theory in chapter 5.) If a union represents only one classification or level of employees within an organization, it will attempt to maximize the compensation of that one group, without regard to how its actions might affect other groups in the organization. If the union represents employees in all classifications, however, it must advocate pay relationships that satisfy most major groups in the organization. As a result, both unions and management seek a more rational, unified, and acceptable compensation structure.

A large bargaining unit also reduces whipsawing, a form of one-upmanship in which one union attempts to gain more than another union received in recent negotiations. This problem is exacerbated by the existence of many unions in an organization.

A large unit also promotes a more professional union. Large unions can hire professional business agents and negotiators, who are more objective than employees who act as their own agents can be. Because professionals have more expertise, they recognize impossible demands by employees and waste less negotiating time on futile issues.

Finally, a large unit saves considerable management time and money. Since negotiations require extensive preparation by management, having multiple contracts with many small bargaining units significantly increases labor-relations costs.

Because of the problems associated with having many small bargaining units, there has been a recent trend toward consolidation of existing units. For example, Executive Order 11491 and the Civil Service Reform Act of 1978 encouraged a 32 percent reduction in the number of bargaining units in the federal government between 1975 and 1981.[26] Florida, Iowa, Hawaii, New York, and other states have also reduced the number of units in their jurisdictions, and New York City has collapsed more than 400 units into fewer than 100 over a ten-year period.

Determination of a large bargaining unit will not be opposed by a union if the union has control of the unit. The first concern of a union is recognition, however, so the union will probably seek the largest bargaining unit within which it can achieve recognition.

The criteria for unit determination include history of representation, locus of employer authority, avoidance of fragmentation, and community of interest. If there has been a history of separate representation by a particular union, either for a group of employees or for a particular craft, the case for a separate unit is strong.[27] Despite the merit of other criteria, imposing a new organizational representation scheme on a group of employees who have experienced other traditional groupings is difficult, if not futile. Second, the unit must not be too small to correspond or negotiate effectively with a government body that has sufficient authority over conditions of employment to make bargaining realistic. Third, for reasons noted earlier, management generally seeks a larger unit, particularly for employees in departments or agencies that are directly responsible to the executive branch. However, if a government body has relative funtional autonomy and is not in the direct chain of command in the executive branch (police and fire departments, hospitals, schools), the case for a separate unit is stronger.

The fourth criterion for unit determination is the community of interest among a group of employees. *Community of interest* can be understood in many ways, but the term is used here in three senses:[28] when a group of employees is under the same compensation structure (a single pension fund or the same salary classification ladder); when they are employed according to the same procedures for hiring, firing, or handling grievances, or when their positions have common education, training, and experience requirements. Under these circumstances, a strong case can be made for a single bargaining unit.

Certain employees are generally excluded from a bargaining unit of other regular employees. For example, confidential employees, such as personnel and labor-relations specialists who have access to confidential information of benefit to the union negotiating committee, are generally excluded from the unit. Similarly, administrative and professional employees are not in the same unit with regular employees.

Supervisors are also excluded from most regular rank-and-file bargaining units, although this exclusion has generated considerable controversy. There is little dispute that bona fide supervisors should be excluded from regular bargaining units. It is argued in the public sector, however, that supervisors often have no actual supervisory functions,[29] since titles in the public sector often overstate the responsibilities and discretion that go with the jobs.[30] A good example of this phenomenon occurs among firefighters, and firefighter locals often support inclusion of supervisors, for several reasons.[31] First, and most important, supervisors and regular firefighters work together, eat together, and play together in the familylike atmosphere of the stationhouse. When they are actually fighting fires, they depend on each other for their safety. Given this interdependent relationship, most fire supervisors identify with their subordinates. Second, it is not always easy to specify how the supervisors' duties and activities are significantly different from those of the rank-and-file firefighters. Hoyt Wheeler's survey of more than 450 officers in fire departments found that although most officers did perform some of the activities of supervisors, they also had a considerable number of rank-and-file duties, particularly at the scene of a fire.[32] Third, firefighters' unions, as well as other unions, oppose the exclusion of supervisors because they know it will reduce the power of the union, particularly during a strike, when supervisors are likely to be called upon to provide a skeleton force.

Although unions oppose exclusion of supervisors, management generally seeks to keep supervisors out of the bargaining unit of the rank-and-file, not only because it will enhance management's bargaining position and capacity to survive a strike but also because the heart of a viable labor-relations structure is effective contract administration. If supervisors were in the rank-and-file bargaining unit, any supervisory decision could lead to problems, such as whether a subordinate can file a grievance against a fellow union member or whether a foreman can fairly decide a grievance involving a fellow union member. Because such problems weaken the first line of management–labor communication and cooperation, management generally seeks to exclude supervisors from their subordinates' union.[33]

Several states, including Wisconsin, Connecticut, and Oregon, allow less than bona fide supervisors to join rank-and-file bargaining units but exclude bona fide supervisors from the units. A bona fide supervisor has considerable independent control over hiring, firing, promoting, and disciplining employees, and his or her pay and duties differ significantly from those of the rank-and-file employees. Although the trend in the public sector is to exclude real supervisors from their subordinates' units and to permit only the less than bona fide supervisors to join them, some states, including Hawaii, Massachusetts, Michigan, Minnesota, and New York, allow real supervisors to form their own, autonomous bargaining units.[34] In the federal sector, however, supervisors are excluded from all bargaining units.

The Certification Election

Before a union can represent employees within a bargaining unit, a certification election must be conducted to determine (1) whether the employees want to be represented by a bargaining agent and (2) which agent they prefer. Generally, at least 30 percent of the employees in a unit must indicate that they are interested in being represented before a certification election is held. If any union receives at least 50 percent of the votes in a certification election, it generally receives exclusive recognition, allowing that union to be the sole bargaining agent for all employees in a unit. Most state and federal collective bargaining laws prohibit any attempt by management to use force, threats, or promise of benefits to influence the outcome of the certification election.

The Negotiating Process

Negotiating a contract is the heart of collective bargaining. This section describes the major actors in the process, how they prepare for negotiations, the scope of negotiations, and the actors' strategies during negotiations.

Major Actors in the Negotiating Process

The major actors in the negotiating process are the union leaders and management. Most union leaders have a demanding, multifaceted role. They must be effective in negotiating and in public relations, and they must not appear to be too friendly with management. Also, it is crucial that a union leader maintain close contact with the rank-and-file members and be able to communicate effectively with them.

Because of the fragmentation of management in the public sector, it is difficult to define who is management in the negotiating process. There are several reasons for such fragmentation. One reason is the constitutional system of checks and balances, which distributes authority for policymaking and policy implementation among the legislative, executive, and judicial branches. Even executive responsibilities may be legally shared among separately elected executive officers, and legislatures may delegate rule-making authority to other agencies, such as a civil service commission or a schoolboard. For example, although both budgetary and personnel functions are generally performed within the executive branch, they are rarely coordinated—yet most negotiations concerning personnel have budgetary implications.

The problem of coordinating personnel and budgetary functions is compounded by the intergovernmental nature of government revenues. Many jurisdictions do not generate all of their funds from their own sources. City governments, for example, may receive funds from local taxes, from user charges, and from state and federal grants, and some of these grants may require specific personnel policies that cannot be changed in negotiations with unions.

This fragmentation of management may lead to several results. One consequence is that unions may attempt to bypass management negotiators at the bargaining table and bargain directly with the legislature, city council, or schoolboard. This is known as an end run. As noted earlier, unions are often powerful political forces in city politics and in schoolboard elections; thus, they may have "friends"—candidates they helped to elect—on the local councils and schoolboards. Unions that encounter tough resistance from management negotiators are sometimes tempted to contact their friends on the council or board. Research reveals that when unions can successfully drive a wedge between some council or board members and the management negotiators, they can expect better outcomes from their bargaining. Also, if the unions have friends on the councils or boards, the union negotiators might receive inside information about management's real bargaining position. Because of these potential adverse consequences of fragmentation, many jurisdictions attempt to specify clearly—in law or through administrative guidelines—who has management responsibility for collective bargaining.

The Scope of Negotiations

The scope of negotiations, or the scope of bargaining, refers to the subjects that can be negotiated at the bargaining table. Most state and federal collective bargaining laws specify subjects that are *voluntary* (topics that may be negotiated if both parties agree), *mandatory* (topics that must be negotiated), and *forbidden* (topics that cannot be negotiated). Forbidden topics at the federal level include compensation, agency mission, budget organization, number of employees, selection, dismissals, retirement, position classification, and political activities. State laws generally do not allow management to negotiate the mission of the agency, or how the work is to be done, or the tools to do the work. Additional forbidden topics often include the organizational structure of the agency or the funds allocated to it, the criteria for selecting new employees, and the method of selecting supervisors. Mandatory topics in states with collective bargaining laws generally include wages and compensation. Voluntary topics at the state level often include working conditions, safety, grievance procedures, and union security.

Although most jurisdictions attempt to define the scope of bargaining, conflicts inevitably occur concerning what is bargainable. Therefore, most governments have agencies that decide whether questionable areas are negotiable. The FLRA has this authority at the federal level, and most states use the PERBs to make such decisions.

Conflicts over the scope of bargaining often occur in agencies that employ a large number of professional workers, such as physicians, nurses, teachers, social workers, police, and firefighters. These employees are often as interested in working conditions as they are in pay and fringe benefits. However, many subjects viewed by professionals as included in working conditions may be viewed by management as part of the mission of the agency and therefore as nonnegotiable. For example, teachers consider that class size is directly related to their workloads, whereas management, however, may view class size as a pedagogical issue concerning the proper way to educate students. Similarly, police view two-officer patrol cars as a safety issue and therefore as negotiable, whereas management may believe that the issue is within the general area of "how to structure the work" which is a managerial prerogative. The same types of debates occur regarding the number of cases per social worker and the number of patients per nurse.

There are legitimate reasons for excluding some topics from negotiations. For example, if unions were able to determine the criteria for the selection of employees, much of the merit system could be subverted. Similarly, if unions were able to decide agency missions, the control of public administration by elected officials would be compromised. Conversely, a very narrow scope of bargaining may also create problems. If unions are unable to bargain for an outcome at the negotiating table, they may attempt to obtain it by lobbying the legislature or whatever government agency controls the issue. As a result, the fragmentation problem, noted earlier, is exacerbated. For example, teachers may negotiate wages with a local schoolboard, but they may lobby in the state legislature for an increase in retirement benefits (a nonnegotiable subject). One could argue, however, that retirement benefits are part of compensation and should be included within a total compensation package. Therefore, some believe that a wide scope of bargaining is preferable to assure that management has a comprehensive and integrated approach to bargaining.

Preparation for Negotiations

The success of management and unions at the bargaining table depends heavily on their preparation before the negotiations commence. The first step in this preparation is the selection of a bargaining team. Management selects a chief spokesperson—often the director of labor relations in a jurisdiction. A budget or finance officer is generally on the management team to "cost out" union demands and counteroffers, and a labor attorney is often on the team to provide counsel concerning the wording of agreements. If someone from the personnel department is not the chief negotiator, then someone from the department is generally on the team. Finally, representatives of the relevant departments are included to provide information about the operational impact of union demands. The union team should include individuals with expertise in negotiations and those who understand the impact of management's demands and offers on the workplace and on the morale of union members.

Legislators generally are not at the bargaining table, because they may not be knowledgeable about the bargaining situation and because their presence could undermine management's attempt to present a united front. The legislative body can establish the parameters for negotiation or the ultimate financial limits of the jurisdiction within which the negotiating team must bargain, but noneconomic considerations that are administrative in nature should probably be left in the hands of the chief negotiator.

Generally, neither the chief executive nor the chief administrator is on the bargaining team, because he or she may have to play the role of peacemaker at a later time. By not participating, he or she has the opportunity to review what is going on at the bargaining table without being committed in advance. Also, the bargaining process is very time-consuming, and a busy chief executive might have to come and go, which would be disruptive to the process. In addition, if the chief executive tried to negotiate one contract, he or she would be expected to negotiate other contracts or would be charged with favoritism.

As part of their preparation, both teams analyze the history and experience of the existing contract. Both sides study grievance records to identify problem areas and to better understand the views and likely strategies of the other side. In addition, the management team may consult with department heads and supervisors for suggestions concerning issues that management should take to the bargaining table.

The crucial step in preparation for negotiations is the collection and analysis of data that are necessary for sound judgments at the bargaining table. Management must have complete information concerning the number of employees and their positions, seniority, sex, race, marital status, and skills. Moreover, management must collect extensive information on the use of benefits, such as holidays, sick leave, vacation time, overtime, and health benefits, and, if available, on the relationship of employee characteristics (age, sex, marital status) to the use and costs of benefits. This information can help them project future costs of benefit packages. Wage and benefit data from other comparable jurisdictions must also be collected, and recent contract settlements in similar jurisdictions should be studied. In addition, management needs budget and revenue projections.

Finally, the management team should seek as much information as possible about internal union politics: What kind of leadership does the union have? Are the union leaders in control? Is there a militant minority in the union? The management negotiating team should also be familiar with the skills, abilities, and personalities of the union negotiators or representatives.

Negotiations

Spero and Capozzola note that many labor–management negotiations, particularly those in local governments, follow a common path.[35] The union starts the negotiations with a long list of demands. Then management claims that the union's demands will bankrupt the government. The union then attempts to portray management as tight-fisted and as endangering the health and safety of citizens, and management sometimes responds by depicting the union members as greedy and lazy. Most experts agree, however, that management's interest is better served by maintaining an image of a consistent, controlled keeper of the public trust and purse. Moreover, extreme statements from management only serve to unite the union.

Negotiations often concern disagreements over comparisons with other occupations, comparisons of the same occupation in other jurisdictions, or comparisons with ideal standards. Comparisons are crucial in the union world, because they demonstrate to the union members whether the bargaining team is doing its job and whether their union dues are buying anything.[36] When making comparisons, management generally insists on total-package comparisons (wages, fringe benefits, retirement, and so on), not just comparisons of items selected by the union.

Although negotiations may involve a great deal of posturing and game playing on both sides, good contracts and harmonious labor relations demand that both groups be able to leave the negotiations as winners. If only the union appears to win, the public may demand that the legislature reject the contract. Conversely, a decisive management victory may cause the union members to reject the agreement; thus, the union leaders would be humiliated and the stability of the union would be undermined. Although some posturing in public may be understandable, the negotiators' private discussions should avoid personal attacks and should be factual and directly related to the issues.

Impasse Resolution

According to Wesley: "A bargaining impasse exists whenever one of the two parties is in a fixed (frozen) position on the remaining issues before them, and when after sincere effort, there seems no chance of accommodation, compromise or movement by either side on any of the issues."[37] This definition emphasizes that negotiators should not give up too readily and call in a third party, since third-party involvement often consumes additional time and expense and may intensify acrimony. If an impasse does occur, however, a variety of impasse resolutions are available, including mediation, fact-finding, and arbitration.

Mediation

Mediation is the participation of a third party—usually a representative of the Federal Mediation and Conciliation Service or of a state agency with similar responsibilities in dispute negotiations—to help the parties resolve their dispute.[38] The mediator's principal strategy is to keep the parties communicating; he or she may suggest compromises and may advise each side about realistic expectations. In general, mediation will be most productive (that is, lead to a settlement) when (1) the negotiations have reached a point where both sides feel great pressure to settle; (2) the mediator is trusted by both parties; (3) the number of remaining issues is relatively small; and (4) the impasse results from a breakdown in negotiations, rather than from a sharp disagreement over economic or political issues.[39]

Fact-finding

Fact-finding is a more formal, sometimes quasi-judicial proceeding in which neutral fact-finders hear the presentations of both sides, analyze the facts, and develop nonbinding recommendations, which are usually presented in writing to both parties. In general, these recommendations become public by agreement of the parties, through public or media pressure, or because the ordinance or statute that provides for fact-finding requires publication.[40] The goal of fact-finding is to frame recommendations that the parties will accept or use as the basis for negotiating an agreement. Thus, fact-finding could be viewed as little more than mediation with written recommendations.[41] Although most states that have comprehensive bargaining laws include fact-finding as part of their impasse procedures, considerable evidence indicates that it is not particularly effective in avoiding strikes or in achieving settlements.[42] Fact-finding continues to be used in states that provide for arbitration, however, and arbitrators give considerable attention to the recommendations that come out of the fact-finding process.[43]

Arbitration

Arbitration, which is binding on both parties, can be divided into three categories: (1) voluntary arbitration, which occurs when both parties agree to call in an arbitrator and to abide by his or her decision; (2) compulsory arbitration, which happens when parties are required by law to submit a dispute to an arbitrator, whose decision is binding on both parties; and (3) final-offer arbitration, voluntary or compulsory, which provides for each party to submit a final offer to the arbitrator, who selects one of the proposals. There are some variations of final-offer arbitration, including entire-package and issue-by-issue final-offer arbitration.

In recent years, compulsory arbitration has attracted considerable attention and has generated extensive controversy. By 1979, twenty states had adopted compulsory arbitration for their public safety employees, and eight of the twenty extended the coverage to nonsafety employees. Supporters of compulsory arbitration argue that if public employees are not allowed to strike, they must have access to arbitration; and if arbitration is not provided, damaging strikes by police, firefighters, and other public employees are possible. Therefore, the primary defense for compulsory arbitration is its capacity to prevent strikes, and the available evidence does suggest that far fewer strikes occur where arbitration is required.[44]

Opponents of compulsory arbitration acknowledge that it might reduce strikes but assert that labor peace may not always be the overriding public interest. These opponents argue that some outcomes are more problematic and dangerous than a strike—such as an arbitrated settlement that goes beyond the government's long-term economic capacity. Peter Feiulle, a leading expert on compulsory arbitration in the public sector, notes that there is very little empirical evidence to show that public employee strikes—including even police and firefighter strikes—have caused any major, permanent harm to the public interest.[45] If government can successfully overcome many public-sector strikes, opponents of compulsory arbitration ask why should it take the risk of having excessive arbitral awards imposed on it? Supporters of compulsory arbitration are quick to note, however, that in most jurisdictions that have compulsory arbitration, the arbitrated awards are not significantly different from the bargained agreements.[46]

Opponents of compulsory arbitration say that is is inimical to representative government because important policy and legislative decisions are left to an arbitrator who probably is not a citizen of the community, who may know little about local economic conditions and public finance, and who may not give due consideration to the impact of the immediate dispute on contracts with other bargaining units in the jurisdiction—yet this individual will be able to affect indirectly a community's tax rates and its allocation of resources. Supporters of compulsory arbitration respond that legislatures can structure the arbitration procedures in such a way as to preserve the democratic process. For example, legislatures may restrict the scope of arbitrable subjects, limit the coverage of arbitration legislation, and specify very tight decision criteria and other restrictions.[47]

Another primary objection to compulsory arbitration is that it has a chilling effect on bargaining, because negotiators, particularly union negotiators, may look past bargaining to arbitration as the ground for maximizing each side's interest. This may occur because one or both sides believe that a more favorable award can be obtained through arbitration and because one or both sides believe that arbitration relieves political pressure on them from their respective constituencies. The considerable research on the impact of compulsory arbitration on bargaining reveals, however, that in nearly all jurisdictions that have compulsory arbitration, a majority of agreements are negotiated.[48]

Final-offer arbitration is a procedure that is intended to minimize the chilling effect of compulsory arbitration. Final-offer arbitration limits the arbitrator to choosing between the last and best offer of one of the parties on an entire-package or an issue-by-issue basis. Since the arbitrator must decide between the last, best offers of each side and not compromise between them, there is an incentive to bargain in earnest before the arbitrator is required. The major criticism of final-offer arbitration is that parties may make unreasonable demands, and since only one proposal can be accepted, the arbitrator might therefore have to accept a package that is extreme and not in the public interest. Despite the mixed results of final-offer arbitration, however, many experts believe that it may prove to be the most satisfactory alternative to strikes in the public sector.[49]

Strikes

The number of public-employee strikes increased sharply in the United States in the 1960s. Before 1966, the average number of work stoppages was 29 per year,[50] but it rose to more than 400 per year by the 1970s. Public-employee strikes are not uniformly distributed among all services, occupations, or levels of government. Nearly all public-sector strikes are at the local level, and half of these are in education. Despite the increase in the number of strikes in the public sector in recent years, however, strikes occur in government far less often than in industry.[51] When considering public-sector strikes, one must keep the magnitude of the problem in perspective and remember that only a very small percentage of all public-sector bargaining ends in a strike.

The primary cause of public-sector strikes is disagreement over wages and benefits, which leads to more than twice as many strikes than any other single cause.[52] Next in line are union recognition and union security, followed by administrative matters, such as safety, supervision, shift work, overtime, discipline, discharge, caseloads, and so on.

There is considerable debate concerning the legalization of strikes in the public sector. An old argument against providing the right to strike to government employees is that the sovereignty of the state would be compromised under such grants. A related argument is that legal strikes might constitute an unconstitutional delegation of legislative authority. In states that have permitted public employees to strike, the courts have not invalidated the laws on the basis of the sovereignty argument or the delegation argument. When the government voluntarily provides the right to strike, violation of state sovereignty is not applicable. A state also allows itself to be sued in civil proceedings, which does not violate the sovereignty of the state. Also, so long as the delegation of authority is accompanied by appropriate guidelines and standards, the courts have sustained rather broad grants of authority from the legislative branch to other entities. In any case, a strike (legal or illegal) does not force a government employer to do anything. Government continues to have the final word, even where strikes are legal.

A second argument against the right to strike is that public unions already have considerable political power, which they can use to obtain benefits from legislative bodies. If the strike is added to their political arsenal, they could have a disproportionate impact on public allocation decisions. Of course, the same could be said of unions in the private sector, yet they can strike. Also it is difficult to define a "disproportionate" share of power in the political system, particularly if one assumes that those who have higher stakes in the outcome of a decision should have a greater voice in the making of the decision (for example, public employees' interest in public wage policies).

A third opposition argument is that because public employees enjoy civil service protection and job tenure, they should be willing to forgo the strike. Private employees, who can strike, do not have the assured jobs that most public employees have.

A fourth point in opposition to legalizing public-sector strikes relates to the supply and demand differences between the public-sector and private-sector markets. Public-sector unions often have a monopoly of particular services. If public employees strike, there is no alternative supplier. If private employees strike, the customer may purchase the goods or services from another supplier or simply do without them. The ability of the private-sector purchaser to move to another supplier or go without the product or service acts as a restraint on private-sector employees who are considering a strike. No such restraint exists in the public sector. The differences between the two sectors may not be so distinct, however. Some private-sector unions do control monopolistic services (utility employees). Also, it may not be easy for customers to do without some private-sector products or services. A long coal miners' strike or truckers' strike could cripple the nation. In contrast, the public could survive without the services of some public employees for a considerable time. For example, a teachers' strike, although it entails loss of a monopoly service for many families, does not cause any serious harm in the short run. Similarly, a strike of recreation employees in a city would not be nearly so problematic as a strike of telephone operators.

A related argument against legal strikes in the public sector is that some government services, particularly police protection and firefighting, are so essential that any strike would so seriously endanger the health and safety of the public that strikes should not be permitted. Some communities have been able to survive strikes by the police and firefighters, however; some private-sector services are just as essential, yet the private unions can strike. This arbitrary dichotomy between public and private employees alienates public employees and may contribute to their demand for the right to strike.

A sixth argument against public-sector strikes is that they are not needed for viable collective bargaining. The overwhelming majority of public and private negotiations do not end in a strike; therefore, one could conclude that strikes are not necessary for productive collective bargaining. Public unions argue, however, that the threat of a strike occurs much more often than a strike occurs, and that the threat is necessary to assure that government employers engage in serious bargaining.

Advocates of legalizing public-sector strikes offer what may be the significant point in the controversy: strikes occur whether they are legal or not, and government will be in a better position to plan for and cope with them under a law that allows for their occurrence but provides impasse procedures to avoid them. There is no conclusive evidence that antistrike laws have any affect on the number of strikes, nor is there consistent empirical evidence that legalization of strikes increases their incidence.[53]

The Union Impact on Public Personnel Management

There has been considerable debate on the impact of public unions and collective bargaining on public personnel management. Because public services are notably labor-intensive, and because labor costs are the single largest component of government budgets, the impact of public unions on wages, fringe benefits, employee productivity, and other personnel functions must be reviewed.

Other variables besides the union also affect compensation in the public sector, including the rate of inflation, a community's ability and willingness to pay, the size and density of the jurisdiction, the form of government, and intergovernmental revenue transfers.[54] Therefore, given the numerous independent variables that can affect compensation, it is difficult to isolate the true economic impact of public unions. Most research on the issue of the economic impact of public-sector unions has focused on the uniformed services (police, firefighters, and transit workers).[55] Also, most research has involved the impact of unions on wages, with comparatively little attention given to the impact on fringe benefits and work rules and processes.[56] Most studies show that union wages, as compared with nonunion wages, have improved only marginally for all public-sector occupational groups, but the level of improvement has varied considerably among different groups. Unionized firefighters have gained the largest increases, ranging from 2 percent to 28 percent, but the magnitude of these hourly wage increases is partly attributable to decreases in average duty hours.[57] Transit employees are probably a close second, with an estimated 9 to 12 percent wage differential between unionized and nonunionized organizations.[58] General municipal employees (for example, highways, sanitation, parks and recreation, and library workers) have not achieved significant wage gains from unionization.[59]

As noted earlier, few studies have investigated the impact of unionization on fringe benefits. Four studies that have examined this impact concluded that employees achieved significant gains in fringe benefits through either unionization or collective bargaining.[60] Since fringe benefits comprise a larger proportion of total personnel expenditures in the public sector than in the private sector, the ability of unions to increase fringe benefits is significant. There is also some support for the proposition that as unions become more established, they change their relative priority from wages to fringe benefits.[61]

Collective bargaining may also affect other areas of personnel management, including selection, promotion, dismissal, transfer, grievances, discipline, position classification, and workloads. In an effort to restrict union influence in these areas, federal and state governments often include managment-rights clauses in contracts, which place certain items outside the scope of bargaining. Most of those clauses assert that management retains the right to direct the work of employees; to hire, promote, transfer, and retain employees; to suspend or discharge employees for proper cause; to lay employees off for financial or other appropriate reasons; and to determine the proper methods for implementing the mission of the agency.

The primary goal of management-rights clauses is to protect the merit system and management's control of selection. Unions have attempted to substitute the rule of one (the applicant with highest score must be selected) for the more common rule of three (management can choose one of the top three applicants). The goal of the rule of one is to reduce management's discretion. Similarly, unions favor shorter probation periods to reduce management's discretion in hiring.[62] In general, however, management has retained control over selection.

Unions have also been interested in promotions. Generally, unions seek promotion from within—not only within the organization but also within the unit in which the vacancy is located. Moreover, they favor the use of seniority rather than supervisor's ratings for determining who is promoted. These union objectives do not necessarily conflict with managerial objectives and practice, since most promotions are from within and many are based in large part on seniority.

Because of recent bad economic conditions and the need to reduce government expenditures, unions have revealed much more interest in reductions in force (RIF), generally demanding that seniority be used as the criterion for determining layoffs. As noted in chapter 9, however, seniority may not be the most rational method for accomplishing reduction. In any case, the tendency to use seniority as the chief criterion for RIF is great with or without union pressure.

Greater use of seniority for RIF can adversely affect affirmative action, since women and minority employees are often the last hired and therefore the first fired during RIF. In general, unions have not been strong supporters of affirmative action. They have opposed many special programs aimed at selecting more women and minorities, and they have opposed some training programs designed to accelerate promotions for women and minorities. The AFSCME, however, has been a leader in the fight for equitable salaries for women in the comparable-worth dispute.

Another area in which unions have sought influence is position classification. Unions often assert that position classification is not an objective, scientific process but that it involves value judgments and subjective decisions. Therefore, the unions believe that classification should be a subject for negotiation. Unions may be concerned, for example, about employees who are given responsibilities that are not in their job discriptions; therefore the unions demand additional pay for "out-of-title" work.[63] Unions may also demand that some jobs be assigned to higher pay grades. In most disputes over classification, however, management has been the victor.[64]

One area in which unions have had considerable influence is the discipline and grievance process. In general, unions have sought to formalize the process and to place the burden of proof on government.[65] Of course, the unions' most significant influence on discipline and grievances may be seen not in the contract but in the behavior of supervisors, who know that the unions may protest any disciplinary actions believed to be arbitrary. Therefore, supervisors exercise caution when they are disciplining employees.

Conclusion: Public Unions, Democracy, and the Public Interest

Critics of public employee unions contend that unionization in the public sector undermines democracy and the public interest, because decisions of the unions to withhold their labor, combined with their political activities, give too much power to one special-interest group. Critics also contend that private market forces (the ability of the consumer to use a substitute product or reduce demand) do not exist in the public sector. Therefore, elected officials may be too eager to please the unions to avoid interruption of vital services, which could adversely affect the political future of elected officals. If the public cannot trace the relationship between today's labor settlements and future tax rates, the elected officials may take the politically safe course and attempt to reach a quick settlement, which could have adverse long-run fiscal implications.

The impact of public-sector unions, as noted earlier in this chapter, is not so well defined as some critics of unions contend. Although unions may have been able to gain significant increases in the wages of some public employees (firefighters and transit workers), unionization has not produced such benefits for other public employees.[66] In fact, the impact of the unions on wages appears to be smaller in the public sector than in the private sector—where the unions presumably do not enjoy the great power of public unions.[67]

Similarly, the strike has not proved to be a very potent threat to the public interest and democracy. As more and more government managers and elected officials have acquired experience in labor relations and negotiations, they have become more sure of their ability to manage and survive a strike—even a public safety strike. In addition, after the Proposition 13 drives in a number of states and the development of antitax militancy among taxpayers, elected public officials are finding it in their political interest to oppose union demands.

Perhaps the major threat to the public interest from public employee unions is not the strike but the limited information received by the public about negotiations and the limited influence of the public on the outcome of negotiations. Reforms such as disclosure, open negotiations, and public referendums on final settlements have been suggested to provide more public influence in negotiations. Under disclosure procedures, both sides would submit their original proposals and demands to the legislative body. Before negotiations begin, interested third parties could submit to the legislature their views about the original demands and their recommendations concerning settlement. One objection to disclosure is that both sides are likely to engage in posturing. Posturing is usually done to impress one's own constituency, however, and, as Schick and Courturier note: "In public sector bargaining, attempts to influence public opinion require the appearance of 'moderation' because the public involved is so much larger than the constituencies of either the public employee unions or of the key legislators or management officials who may be involved in bargaining."[68]

Open negotiations have also been tried in several jurisdictions, with mixed results. Opponents of open negotiations contend that such arrangements tend to polarize positions and that participants become less flexible once they have taken a public stance. Critics also say that negotiations require give and take, which is difficult in the "goldfish bowl" atmosphere of open negotiations. Supporters of open negotiations respond that bargaining does occur in open negotiations and that "sunshine" bargaining moderates extreme positions and gives the public much more information than they would have received under a closed-session system.

Another proposed method to give the public greater influence over bargaining is the referendum on collective bargaining settlements, which has been used as a device to settle impasses in Englewood, Colorado, and San Francisco, California. Although the referendum might be a viable alternative for impasse resolution, final voter approval for every agreement would interject too much instability into the bargaining process. Also, it is very unlikely that the public would have sufficient information about every dispute to make educated decisions.

In conclusion, the development of public management's bargaining skills, combined with the political necessity to minimize tax increases, may produce public employers who will have both the ability and the incentive to resist extreme union demands. This balancing of union and employer power should prove beneficial to the public interest.

Notes

1. Some works of general relevance to this chapter are A. Lawrence Chickering, ed., *Public Employee Unions: A Study of the Crisis in Public Sector Labor Relations* (San Francisco: Institute for Contemporary Studies, 1979); Benjamin Aaron, Joseph R. Grodin, and James L. Stern, eds., *Public Sector Bargaining* (Washington, D.C.: Bureau of National Affairs, 1979); Muriel K. Gibbons, Robert D. Helsby, Jerome Lefkowitz, and Barbara Z. Tener, eds., *Portrait of a Process—Collective Negotiations in Public Employment* (Fort Washington, Pa.: Labor Relations Press, 1979); Charles S. Phyne and Robert H. Drummer, *The Law of Municipal Labor Relations*, 2d ed. (Washington, D.C.: National Institute of Municipal Law offices, 1979); Harry T. Edwards, R.T. Clark, and Charles B. Craver, *Labor Relations Law in the Public Sector: Cases and Materials* (Indianapolis: Bobbs-Merrill, 1979); Alan E. Bent and T. Zane Reeves, *Collective Bargaining in the Public Sector* (Menlo Park, Calif.: Benjamin/Cummings, 1979); Richard P. Schick and Jean J. Courturier, *The Public Interest in Government Labor Relations* (Cambridge, Mass.: Ballinger, 1977), Murray B. Nesbitt, *Labor Relations in the Federal Government Service* (Washington, D.C.: Bureau of National Affairs, 1976); Mollie H. Bowers, *Contract Administration in the Public Sector* (Chicago: International Personnel Management Association, 1976); Jack Steiber, *Public Employee Unionism: Structure, Growth and Policy* (Washington, D.C.: Brookings, 1973); W. Donald Heisel, *New Questions and Answers on Public Employee Negotiation* (Chicago: International Personnel Management Association, 1973); Sam Zagoria, ed., *Public Workers and Public Unions* (Englewood Cliffs, N.J.: Prentice-Hall, 1972); David T. Stanley, *Managing Local Government Under Union Pressure* (Washington, D.C.: Brookings, 1972); Harry H. Wellington and Ralph K. Winter, Jr., *The Unions and the Cities* (Washington, D.C.: Brookings, 1971).

2. For an examination of early unionization in the postal service, see Sterling D. Spero, *The Labor Movement in a Government Industry: A Study of Employee Organization in the Postal Service* (New York: Macmillan, 1927).

3. John Burton, "The Extent of Collective Bargaining in the Public Sector," in Aaron, Grodin, and Stern, *Public Sector Bargaining*, p. 2.

4. Bureau of the Census, *Labor Management Relations in State and Local Government* (Washington, D.C.: U.S. Government Printing Office, 1981).

5. Ibid.

6. This is a conclusion of Burton's review of research accounting for union growth in the public sector. See Burton, "Extent of Collective Bargaining in the Public Sector," p. 16.

7. For a discussion of why public employees join unions, see L.V. Imaundo, "Why Federal Government Employees Join Unions: A Study of AFGE Local 916," *Public Personnel Management* 2 (January–February 1973): 23–28; Kenneth S. Warner, Rupert F. Chisholm, and Robert F. Munzenrider, "Motives for Unionization Among State Social Service Employees" *Public Personnel Management* 7 (May–June 1978): 181–191; Russell L. Smith and Anne H. Hopkins, "Public Employee Attitudes Toward Unions," *Industrial and Labor Relations Review* 32 (July 1979): 484–495.

8. David Shapiro, "Relative Wage Effects of Unions in the Public and Private Sectors," *Industrial and Labor Relations Review* 31 (January 1978): 195.

9. Orley Ashenfelter and Ronald G. Ehrenberg, "The Demand for Labor in the Public Sector," in Daniel S. Hamermesh, ed., *Labor in the Public and Nonprofit Sector*

(Princeton, N.J.: Princeton University Press, 1975), pp. 55–78.

10. Bent and Reeves, *Collective Bargaining in the Public Sector,* 163.

11. Martin J. Bill, "The Public Employee as Lobbyist" in *The Role of Politics in Local Labor Relations* (Washington, D.C.: Labor–Management Relations Service, 1973), p. 6.

12. Ibid.

13. Ibid.

14. Richard C. Kearney, *Labor Relations in the Public Sector* (New York: Marcel Dekker, 1984), p. 63.

15. Ibid., p. 62.

16. Ibid., p. 66.

17. Ibid.

18. Ibid., p. 67.

19. Ibid., p. 69.

20. *Abood v. Detroit Board of Education,* U.S. 209, 975 Ct. 1792 (1977).

21. Kearney, *Labor Relations in the Public Sector,* p. 27.

22. Heisel, *New Questions and Answers on Public Employee Negotiation,* p. 13.

23. Wellington and Winter, *Unions and the Cities,* p. 99.

24. H. Lohne, "Bargaining Units in the Federal Service," *Monthly Labor Review* 91 (December 1968): 38–39.

25. Heisel, *New Questions and Answers on Public Employee Negotiation,* p. 16.

26. Kearney, *Labor Relations in the Public Sector,* p. 27.

27. Wellington and Winter, *Unions and the Cities,* p. 104.

28. Ibid., p. 110.

29. For a defense of including supervisors in bargaining units, see Bruce S. Cooper, "Federal Actions and Bargaining for Public Supervisors: Basis for an Argument," *Public Personnel Management* 6 (September–October 1977): 341–351.

30. Wellington and Winter, *Unions and the Cities,* p. 113.

31. Perry Moore, "Lessons from the Dayton Firefighters' Strike," *Public Personnel Management* 8 (January–February 1979): 34.

32. Hoyt N. Wheeler, "Officers in Municipal Fire Departments," *Labor Law Journal* 28 (November 1977): 733.

33. Steven L. Hayford and Anthony V. Sinicropi, "Bargaining Rights Status of Public Sector Supervisors," *Industrial Relations* 15 (February 1976): 61.

34. Kearney, *Labor Relations in the Public Sector,* p. 87.

35. Sterling Spero and John M. Capozzola, *The Urban Community and Unionized Bureaucracies* (New York: Dunellen, 1973), pp. 109–110.

36. Bent and Reeves, *Collective Bargaining in the Public Sector,* p. 84.

37. Roy Wesley, *Impasse Resolution* (Washington, D.C.: Labor-Management Relations Service, 1976), p. 3.

38. Steven B. Rynecki and Thomas Gausden, "Current Trends in Public Sector Impasse Resolution," *State Government* 49 (Autumn 1976): 273.

39. Thomas A. Kochan, "Dynamics of Dispute Resolution in the Public Sector," in Aaron, Grodin, and Stern, *Public Sector Bargaining,* pp. 178–179.

40. Wesley, *Impasse Resolution,* p. 7.

41. Kochan, "Dynamics of Dispute Resolution," p. 183.

42. Ibid., p. 183.

43. Ibid., p. 184.

44. Hoyt N. Wheeler, "An Analysis of Firefighter Strikes," *Labor Law Journal* 26 (January 1975): 17–20; Peter Feuille, *Final Offer Arbitration* (Chicago: International Personnel Management Association, 1975), pp. 10–11; J. Joseph Loewenberg, Kenneth F. Walker, H.J. Glasbeek, Bob Hepple, and Walter J. Gershenfeld, *Compulsory Arbitration: An International Comparison* (Lexington, Mass.: Lexington Books, D.C. Heath, 1976), p. 165; James L. Stern, Charles M. Rehmus, J. Joseph Loewenberg, Hirschel Kasper, and Barbara Dennis, *Final-Offer Arbitration: The Effects on Public Safety Employee Bargaining* (Lexington, Mass.: Lexington Books, D.C. Heath, 1975), p. 189.

45. Peter Feuille, "Selected Benefits and Costs of Compulsory Arbitration," *Industrial and Labor Relations Review* 33 (October 1979): 67.

46. Hoyt N. Wheeler, "Is Compromise the Rule in Firefighter Arbitration?" *Arbitration Journal* 29 (1974): 176–183; Stern et al., *Final-Offer Arbitration*, p. 187.

47. Feiulle, "Selected Benefits and Costs of Compulsory Arbitration," p. 72.

48. Ibid., p. 74.

49. Bent and Reeves, *Collective Bargaining in the Public Sector*, p. 251.

50. David Lewin, "Collective Bargaining and the Right to Strike," in Chickering, *Public Employee Unions*, p. 148.

51. Ibid., p. 150.

52. Samuel M. Sharkey, *Public Employee Strikes: Causes and Effects* (Washington, D.C.: Labor Management Relations Service, 1970), p. 5.

53. Bent and Reeves, *Collective Bargaining in the Public Sector*, p. 233.

54. For a concise discussion of various factors affecting public-sector compensation, see David Lewin, Raymond Horton, and James Kuhn, *Collective Bargaining and Manpower Utilization in City Governments* (Montclair, N.J.: Allanheld, Osmun, 1979), chapter 4.

55. David T. Methe and James L. Perry, "The Impacts of Collective Bargaining on Local Government Services: A Review of Research," *Public Administration Review* 40 (July–August 1980): 360.

56. Ibid.

57. Ibid., p. 366. Also see Russell L. Smith and William Lyons, "The Impact of Firefighter Unionization on Wages and Working Hours in American Cities," *Public Administration Review* 40 (November–December 1980): 568–584.

58. Ibid.

59. Ibid.

60. See Melvin Lurie, "The Effect of Unionization on Wages in the Transit Industry," *Journal of Political Economy* 69 (December 1961): 558–572; Thomas A. Kochan and Hoyt N. Wheeler, "Municipal Collective Bargaining: A Model and Analysis of Bargaining Outcomes," *Industrial and Labor Relations Review* 29 (October 1975): 46–66; Paul F. Gerhart, "Determinants of Bargaining Outcomes in Local Government Labor Negotiations," *Industrial and Labor Relations Review* 30 (April 1976): 331–351; James L. Perry and Charles T. Levine, "An Interorganizational Analysis of Power, Conflict and Settlements in Public Sector Collective Bargaining," *American Political Science Review* 70 (December 1976): 1185–1201.

61. Lurie, "Effect of Unionization on Wages in the Transit Industry," pp. 448–472; Smith and Lyons, "Impact of Firefighter Unionization on Wages and Working Hours in American Cities," pp. 568–584.

62. Kearney, *Labor Relations in the Public Sector,* p. 185.

63. Ibid., p. 192.

64. Ibid., p. 194.

65. Ibid., p. 189.

66. Methe and Perry, "Impacts of Collective Bargaining on Local Government Services," p. 366.

67. Sharon P. Smith, *Equal Pay in the Public Sector: Fact or Fantasy* (Princeton, N.J.: Princeton University, Industrial Relations Section, 1977), pp. 120–129.

68. Schick and Courturier, *Public Interest in Government Labor Relations,* p. 204.

11
Representative Bureaucracy and Affirmative Action

Key Words

Representative bureaucracy

Equality of opportunity

Affirmative action

Passive representation

1964 Civil Rights Act

Title VII of the 1964 Civil Rights Act

Age Discrimination in Employment Act

Griggs v. Duke Power Company

Albemarle Paper Company v. Moody

Goals versus quotas

Reverse discrimination

Affirmative action plan (AAP)

Introduction

The United States has valued a representative bureaucracy since the early days of the Republic. The Jacksonian spoils movement reflected desires by excluded economic groups to obtain a larger voice in government. Therefore, it is not surprising that minorities and women also desire a larger role in public bureaucracies. Today, these groups pressure not only for equality of opportunity but also for affirmative action or positive steps to employ more minorities and women. Critics of affirmative action claim, however, that it often produces reverse discrimination against "innocent" white males and that it subverts the merit principle. As a result, few issues in public personnel management have engendered more controversy than affirmative action.

Much of the philosophical basis for affirmative action rests on the theory of representative bureaucracy. Therefore, the assumptions of this theory and criticisms of it are examined in this chapter. Although there is great support for representative bureaucracy as a goal, there is much disagreement concerning the proper method of achieving it. The least controversial route is equal employment opportunity, or nondiscrimination, because it is assumed that if minorities and women have an equal opportunity to obtain employment, the effects of past discrimination will gradually disappear. A much more controversial route to representative bureaucracy is affirmative action, which suggests that public employers must take active, positive steps to hire more minorities and women if the evil effects of past discrimination are to be eliminated in a reasonable time period.

This chapter examines the development of these two roads to representative bureaucracy. A brief history of the employment of minorities and women in the public service is presented. Next, the trend toward equality of opportunity and its impact on various personnel management functions are examined. This examination is followed by an analysis of the number and the power of women and minorities in federal, state, and local governments. This analysis suggests that affirmative action must continue if representative bureaucracy is to be attained. The controversial issue of affirmative action goals and quotas is also examined, along with Supreme Court decisions on this issue. The chapter concludes with a description of the primary elements of affirmative action plans.

The Theory of Representative Bureaucracy

Most public personnel management functions are affected by the moral and legal requirement to provide equality of opportunity to minorities and women, and much of the philosophical support for affirmative action rests on the theory of representative bureaucracy. This theory holds that as more minorities and women are employed in public organizations, bureaucratic policies are more likely to reflect the needs and desires of minorities and women. Although the concept of representative bureaucracy is not new in the literature of public administration, there is considerable confusion concerning how it operates. Although the idea of a representative bureaucracy can be found as early as the Jeffersonian and Jacksonian periods of United States history (see chapter 2), the first comprehensive proposal for representative bureaucracy was presented by J. Donald Kingsley in his analysis of the British civil service.[1] Kingsley argued that if administration is to be responsive to changes in political climate, it must represent the dominant class in society. Kingsley also assumed that traditional controls by the elected branches of government are insufficient to affect the bureaucracy.

Norton Long was the first to present a comprehensive exposition of representative bureaucracy in the United States.[2] Long argued that the federal bureaucracy is more representative of the people than Congress is because of the more diverse demographic background of the bureaucracy and because of the wider expertise and diverse values that bureaucrats bring to government. Long thought that bureaucrats represent interests that are underrepresented in Congress. He claimed that the U.S. federal bureaucracy is basically representative of the people, and asserted that such representation is beneficial, but he provided no data to support his assertions. Later, Paul Van Riper specified that a representative bureaucracy must consist of a reasonable cross section of society in terms of occupation, class, and geography and that is must be in tune generally with the ethos and attitudes of society.[3]

In 1968, Frederick Mosher expanded on Van Riper's argument by stating that administrative decisions are influenced by administrators' orientations and values, which, in turn, are influenced by the bureaucrats' backgrounds, training, education, and current associations.[4] Mosher also made a distinction between passive, or sociological, representation and active, or functional, representation:

> The passive (or sociological) meaning of representativeness concerns the sources of origin of individuals and the degree to which, collectively, they mirror the total society. It may be statistically measured in terms, for example, of locality of origin and its nature (rural, urban, suburban, etc.), previous occupation, father's occupation, education, family income, family social class, race and religion. A public service which is broadly representative of all categories of the population in these respects, may be thought of as satisfying Lincoln's prescription of government "by the people" in the limited sense.[5]

Mosher did note, however, that little was known about the relationship between an individual's background and pre-employment socialization and his behavior in office.

The theory of representative bureaucracy has several components. First, it suggests that bureaucrats are engaged in the making of policy—that they propose much of the legislation that legislators pass. Also, politicians may pass vague laws that give considerable discretion to the bureaucrats who implement them. Since the bureaucrats are often the experts, the legislators may defer to them. This deference contributes to the bureaucrats' power. Bureaucrats may also be involved in resolving disputes between competing groups that want favors from the bureaucracy.

Second, the theory of representative bureaucracy holds that the traditional external controls on bureaucracy are ineffective, since numerous restraints may circumscribe executive control, legislative oversight, and judicial review of bureaucrats. Third, since the external controls are weak, the theory of representative bureaucracy suggests that they must be supplemented by internal controls.

The basic element of internal control is congruence of values between administrators and the public at large. If bureaucrats make policy, and if the bureaucrats have the same values as the American people, then the decisions made by the bureaucracy will be similar to the decision that would be made if the entire American public voted or acted on the issues.[6] This contention is based on the assumption that when values are similar, rational decisions made to maximize these values will also be similar.

A representative bureaucracy is responsible because it represents the public's values. Measuring values is very difficult, however, and selecting bureaucrats who share the values of the general public is even more difficult. The theory of representative bureaucracy holds that one's values are formed by one's social environment. Socialization, particularly before adulthood, is believed to form values. Thus, since values differ among racial and social groups, a representative bureaucracy actually mirrors the social characteristics—race, occupation, social status, and so on—of the American public. Figure 11–1 provides a model of the linkages in the theory of representative bureaucracy.

Criticisms of the Theory of Representative Bureaucracy

There are several criticisms of the logic that supports the theory of representative bureaucracy. First, the theory assumes that the traditional external controls of bureaucracy are inadequate, but this assertion may not be correct. Indeed, although one can point to the many limitations of the executive, legislative, and judicial controls of bureaucracy, effective internal controls may be equally difficult to put in place in the absence of external control. Furthermore, the knowledge that external controls could be used serves to restrict bureaucratic behavior.

A second criticism of representative bureaucracy concerns the theory's linkage of socioeconomic characteristics, values, and policy. The theory substitutes secondary measures (socioeconomic characteristics) for the desired primary measures (values), although little is known about the relationship between the two.

Proponents of representative bureaucracy contend that the acquisition of values occurs primarily in childhood; otherwise, they would not be concerned about the socioeconomic backgrounds of the bureaucrats' fathers. Critics point out, however, that value acquisition is a process that continues throughout the life of the bureaucrat.[7] Indeed, the most telling criticism of the theory of representative bureaucracy is the realization that the agency itself socializes individuals in a common set of bureaucratic values. The bureaucrat who wishes to move to the top levels of an agency must reflect the norms and values of that agency. Gates are opened only when the gatekeepers are assured that the bureaucrat has the proper values. Thus, values—particularly those that are relevant to the bureaucrat's job—are shaped not only by childhood experiences but also by a continuing socialization process in the bureaucracy. Bureaucrats have very similar

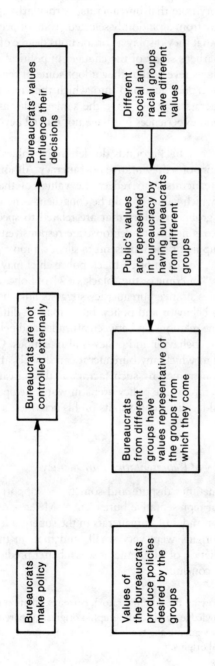

Figure 11–1. Model of the Linkages in the Theory of Representative Bureaucracy

262 • *Public Personnel Management—A Contingency Approach*

values, irrespective of their origin or race. Bureaucracy is a great socializer.[8]

Critics of the theory note that bureaucrats, particularly upper-level bureaucrats, differ significantly from a randomly selected group of people with the same family backgrounds—that they display a conspicuous degree of upward mobility. Furthermore, James Barber's study of the changes in political values among upwardly mobile individuals reveals that they adopt some of the attitudes and values of the higher socioeconomic group into which they move.[9] Therefore, upwardly mobile bureaucrats may not have the same values as individuals who shared similar childhood experiences but have not moved beyond their early socioeconomic group.

Even if socioeconomic backgrounds do determine values, additional problems exist with the theory of representative bureaucracy. Although the goal of the theory is to have bureaucrats who reflect the values of their socioeconomic groups, it is not clear which values should be congruent—the values that are felt most strongly by the group or values that are related to specific policy issues. How much congruence is needed to demonstrate responsiveness? A bureaucrat may find that the group he or she represents is silent on most issues or espouses many conflicting views. For example, a black police chief may find it difficult to discern the "black view" of crime or the "black view" of police administration.

The theory of representative bureaucracy suggests links between values and behavior and between behavior and policy, but it may be difficult to prove that these linkages exist. The relationship between attitudes and behavior is not clear, and the linkage between behavior and policy is also tenuous. One critic has concluded that the extent to which any bureaucrat can directly affect policies of interest to a group is constrained by such factors as the bureaucrat's position in "the organizational hierarchy, the policy arena in which he operates, his conception of his role, formal-legalistic constraints on his activities, and a host of other variables."[10]

Research on the Theory of Representative Bureaucracy

Research findings sometimes dispute and sometimes support the linkages suggested by the theory of representative bureaucracy. Meier and Nigro found that correlations between attitudes of bureaucrats in the supergrades (GS 16–18) and their socioeconomic origins were very small, and that, in most attitude categories, the agency affiliation of a bureaucrat was a better predictor of the bureaucrat's attitudes.[11] They concluded:

> On most issues, knowing the administrator's current affiliation is far more important than a knowledge of his demographic origins. Apparently, agency socialization tends to overcome any tendency for the supergrades to hold attitudes rooted in their social origins.[12]

Other research, however, provides some support for the linkages suggested in the theory. One study of black and white police officers in fifteen cities found that black officers were more likely than white officers to view ghetto residents as honest, industrious, respectable, and religious.[13] Also, black teachers tend to view black parents and pupils more favorably than their white counterparts do.[14] Other studies have discovered that white therapists and professional counselors find it difficult to empathize with the problems of nonwhite clients.[15]

The mixed research results relating to the theory of representative bureaucracy prompted Frank Thompson to conclude that the question is less whether the linkages in the theory exist than under what circumstances they exist.[16] Thompson suggests that the linkages are more likely to exist under the following circumstances:

1. Institutions and groups in society provide an ideology of minority pride and seek the advancement of minority interests. The existence of such groups would mitigate the influence of organizational socialization and peer pressure on minority bureaucrats.
2. Minority officials are concerned with issues that have direct impact on the advancement of their race. Issues that directly conflict with agency norms or work group pressures are especially likely to trigger the linkage.
3. Minority employees associate in an agency. Such associations can provide a peer group, which encourages and reinforces any inclination to help the bureaucrat's racial community.
4. Minorities occupy discretionary jobs, especially jobs in the lower levels of an agency. Minority bureaucrats at the lower levels are more likely to have been in the organization for shorter periods of time and thus have received less exposure to work socialization and the pressure to become "organization" men or women.
5. Members of a minority group work in close proximity to one another. Interaction among minority bureaucrats can suggest distinct racial perspectives on questions of agency policy.

Although there is little empirical support for the linkages assumed by the theory of representative bureaucracy, there are good reasons for continuing to seek a bureaucracy that is broadly representative of minorities and women. A more representative bureaucracy is a symbolic affirmation that the government is committed to equality of opportunity.[17] Without significant numbers of minorities and women in bueaucracy, government's pronouncements about equal opportunity will be considered hollow and meaningless. In addition, more government job opportunities for minorities and women help improve the economic status of these disadvantaged groups. Moreover, minorities and women in the bureaucracy can serve as role models for those who otherwise might not consider

government careers possible. For example, if girls do not see female police officers and firefighters, they might never think of these occupations as possible career options. Finally, minorities and women are more likely to view a bureaucracy as legitimate when their numbers within it increase. For example, a police
force is more likely to be accepted in black neighborhoods as the number of black
officers increases.

Minorities and Women in the Public Sector

Racial, religious, ethnic, and sexual discrimination have always been widespread
in the public service.[18] Since blacks and women have been subject to the most
pervasive discrimination, equal employment opportunity efforts have been directed at these groups. The concept that the public service should be limited to
whites was taken for granted at the founding of the nation[19] and was formally
enacted into law in 1810, when Congress passed an act providing that "no other
than a free white person shall be employed in conveying the mail."[20] Although
this law applied only to the postal service, there were no blacks anywhere in the
federal civil service until 1867.

There were very few blacks in the public service following the Civil War, and
there were only 620 blacks in the federal service when the 1883 Civil Service Act
was passed.[21] The merit system created by the 1883 act tended to increase black
representation in the federal service, because it made open discrimination difficult, and by 1892, there were 2,393 blacks in the federal service.[22] Whatever its
other effects, however, the merit system did not prevent blacks from being discriminated against through removals, nor did it prevent segregation and other
inequalities within federal service.[23]

The most important setbacks for blacks after the establishment of the merit
system occurred in the Taft and Wilson administrations. Since Taft did not believe that blacks should serve in areas where whites disliked their presence, he
reduced the appointments of blacks in the South. The Wilson administration had
the worst record of discrimination against blacks in the history of the merit system.[24] Segregation was introduced into the Postal and Treasury Department offices, shops, restrooms, and lunchrooms, and black clerks were reduced in rank.
The Wilson administration not only condoned discrimination, it openly encouraged it. The Civil Service Commission required a photograph on job application
forms, and the Navy required that black clerks work behind screens.[25]

In general, the three Republican administrations after Wilson continued the
policy of discrimination. Some progress was made, however, and the percentage
of blacks in the federal service rose to 9.6 percent by 1928.[26] Perhaps the outstanding achievement of this period was the desegregation of the Census Bureau
in the 1920s by Secretary of Commerce Herbert Hoover.[27]

During the 1940s and the 1950s, several developments helped open the federal service to blacks. In 1940, the Ramspeck Act formally outlawed discrimination in both employment and promotion policies.[28] In 1941, President Roosevelt issued Executive Order 8802, which prohibited discrimination in defense industries and in the government.[29] This order also established the Fair Employment Practice Committee (FEPC), which was to receive and investigate complaints of discrimination and make recommendations for redress of grievances.[30] Since the FEPC lacked enforcement powers, however, government officials ignored its recommendations, and acts of discrimination and segregation continued to occur.

In 1946, the FEPC was discontinued, and the Civil Service Commission (CSC) assumed responsibility for preventing discrimination in federal employment. Like the FEPC, the CSC lacked adequate enforcement power, but in 1948, President Truman created the Federal Employment Board (FEB) within the CSC to investigate complaints of discrimination and to enforce compliance.[31] Although the FEB operated until 1955, it proved ineffective for several reasons, not the least of which was the paranoia of the McCarthy era, during which conservative officials often equated equal employment opportunity for blacks with communism.[32] In 1955, President Eisenhower established the President's Committee on Government Employment Policy (PCGEP), whose mission was to take whatever steps were deemed necessary to overcome discrimination in government employment.[33] Although the PCGEP made more advances than its predecessors, significant progress toward equal opportunity did not occur until the 1960s.

From Roosevelt to Eisenhower, presidential efforts to deal with the problem of discrimination in the federal service suffered from several serious deficiencies.[34] First, more emphasis was placed on government-contracted jobs than on government itself. Second, the boards or committees that were established to enforce the executive orders had little or no enforcement powers. Finally, there was little congressional support for presidential attempts to eliminate discrimination; Congress was apathetic, and much of its leadership was hostile.

Although women have been employed in the public service since the founding of the nation, they have not been treated as equals, and there have been periods when there were no female federal employees. As in the case of blacks, discrimination against women was formally sanctioned by law.[35] An 1870 statute was interpreted to hold that appointing officers could exclude women for reasons unrelated to their qualifications, and until 1919, women were excluded from about 60 percent of all civil service examinations.[36] The law also provided for unequal compensation, and not until 1923 did the Classification Act prohibit such treatment based on sex. Moreover, veterans preference, which has existed in various forms since the origins of the federal service, continued to obstruct the employment of women. Although women made some progress during World War II, it was not until the 1960s that important progress began to be made.

Equal Employment Opportunity

In the early 1960s, the civil rights movement became a dominant national issue and had a major impact on federal personnel administration. In 1961, President Kennedy issued Executive Order 10925, which established the President's Committee on Equal Employment Opportunity (PCEEO) and directed it to scrutinize and study employment practices of the government of the United States and to consider and recommend additional steps that should be taken by executive departments and agencies to realize more fully the national policy of nondiscrimination within the executive branch of the government.[37] The PCEEO took many more vigorous steps than previous committees had. It encouraged the adoption of special measures, such as recruitment drives at primarily minority high schools to increase the number of blacks in the federal service, and it took an annual census of minority employment to make monitoring and evaluation of progress possible.

The Kennedy program was continued by President Johnson, who gave management of the government's equal employment opportunity efforts to the Civil Service Commission. Johnson also signed into law the 1964 Civil Rights Act.[38] This act, which is broad in scope, prohibits discrimination in housing, in public accommodations, and in other areas. Title VII of the act prohibits employment discrimination based on race, national origin, sex, or religion. Title VII also created the Equal Employment Opportunity Commission (EEOC) to investigate charges of employment discrimination and to enforce the provisions of Title VII. The prohibitions of Title VII were extended to public employers by the 1972 Equal Employment Opportunity Act.[39] In 1965, President Johnson issued Executive Order 11246, which required government contractors to take affirmative action to hire more minorities. President Johnson also brought women into the overall federal EEO program in 1967 with Executive Order 11375. The Age Discrimination in Employment Act was also passed in 1967.[40] This act, as amended in 1978 prohibits employers from discriminating against employees aged 40 to 70. (Table 11–1 outlines the legal framework for equal employment opportunity.)

The Supreme Court, like the Congress and the president, has made decisions that advance equality of opportunity. One such decision is the 1971 case *Griggs v. Duke Power Company*.[41] (See chapter 4 for a description of this case.) In *Griggs*, the Court declared that a supposedly neutral selection criterion (the requirement of a high school diploma) was constitutionally unacceptable, because it excluded many minorities and was not related to job performance. For the first time, the Court said that intent to discriminate need not be shown to invalidate a selection criterion. If a selection device (test, education or experience requirement, and the like) tends to exclude minorities and women disproportionately (adverse impact), and if the device is not related to job performance, it cannot be used. (See chapter 4 for an extended definition of adverse impact.) Moreover, in

Table 11–1
The Legal Framework for Equal Employment Opportunity

Fourteenth Amendment: This amendment prohibits state and local governments from depriving any person of the equal protection of the law and due process of law.

Equal Pay Act of 1963: This amendment to the Fair Labor Standards Act requires that all employers provide equal pay for equal work for both men and women, unless the differences are the result of a bona fide merit system, seniority system, or some factor other than sex.

Title VII of the Civil Rights Act of 1964, as amended by the Equal Opportunity Act of 1972: These laws prohibit discrimination in compensation and conditions and privileges of employment on the basis of race, color, religion, sex, or national origin. The 1972 amendment extended coverage to public employers with fifteen or more employees.

Age Discrimination Act of 1967, as amended in 1978: This amendment to the Fair Labor Standards Act prohibits employers with 20 or more employees from discriminating against persons aged 40 to 70 in any privileges, terms, and conditions of employment because of their age.

Rehabilitation Act of 1973: This law prohibits any federally assisted program from discriminating against a handicapped person, who is defined as an individual with a physical or mental impairment that substantially limits one or more major life activities.

Federal guidelines: Guidelines and regulations have been established by numerous federal agencies to provide information and directives for compliance with federal law. The Equal Employment Commission developed the original guidelines (EEOC "Guidelines") in 1970. In 1978, the EEOC, the U.S. Civil Service Commission, and the Departments of Labor and Justice adopted the *Uniform Guidelines*.

the 1975 case *Albemarle Paper Company v. Moody,* the Court said that subjective supervisory ratings could not be used to show that a particular selection instrument was job-related.[42] In other words, the Court said that a selection device could not be validated as performance-related by the use of subjective supervisory ratings that are subject to bias and that may also be unrelated to job performance.

The *Griggs* and *Albemarle* decisions stress that selection devices should be related to job performance. In most cases, however, it is not easy for an employer to show that a selection device is related to performance. Before the 1982 case *Connecticut v. Teal,* an employer could avoid this requirement by hiring sufficient minorities and women to prevent a finding of adverse impact.[43] Thus, the crucial factor—the "bottom line"—was how many minorities were hired, not how legitimate and valid each step in the selection process was. In the *Teal* decision, however, the Court said that it is necessary to validate every step in a selection process, even if the entire process has no adverse impact on minorities or women. The Court's rejection of the "bottom-line" approach could be far-reaching. Every step of the employment process could be challenged as discriminatory, even when sufficient numbers of minorities and women are hired to avoid a finding of adverse impact. (See chapter 4 for further discussion of the *Teal* decision.)

Equal Employment Opportunity and the Elements of Personnel Management

The personnel manager must be concerned with preventing discrimination in selection, performance appraisal, promotion, compensation and benefits, and dismissal.

Selection

Discrimination in hiring on the basis of unchangeable characteristics that are inherent in race and/or sex is unlawful. Employers must adhere to selection requirements and tests that do not cause an adverse impact and, if it does exist, the employers must be prepared to demonstrate a relationship between the suspect selection procedures and job performance.

The Age Discrimination Act prohibits discrimination in the selection of persons aged 40 to 70. The only exception is when age is related to job performance. For example, maximum hiring ages for bus drivers were upheld by the courts as a measure related to the safety of bus passengers. More recent decisions, however, indicate that the courts will require more substantial evidence that age is directly and substantially related to job performance before they will accept a maximum hiring age.

Physical restrictions that might have an adverse impact on employment opportunities for minorities or women may be found to be discriminatory if they cannot be demonstrated to be directly related to job performance. For example, arbitrary weight and height requirements exclude most women, Hispanics, and Orientals from public safety jobs. The Court states that such requirements must be validated.[44] Also, physical agility tests that have an adverse impact on females must be demonstrated to be job-relevant.

Entrance requirements, such as special training or education, that have an adverse impact on minorities or women must be related to job performance. Also, arrest records cannot be used if they have an adverse impact on the hiring of minorities, unless, with such records, an employer can demonstrate a reasonable connection between the conviction and job performance. For example, arson convictions would be relevant to a job seeker's predicted successful performance as a firefighter.

The Supreme Court has given mixed opinions on citizenship as a condition of employment. In 1973, the Court found New York's blanket prohibition of aliens from permanent jobs to be in violation of the equal protection clause of the Fourteenth Amendment.[45] In 1978, however, the Court held that New York could require that all police officers be citizens.[46]

Sexual preference is not specifically mentioned in Title VII as an unlawful basis for discrimination, and the Court and the EEOC hold that adverse action against homosexuals with respect to employment is not within the scope of Title

VII. In general, an employer cannot discriminate against a person whose homosexuality has not adversely affected his or her work. An employer may be able to take adverse action against a person, however, if the employer can demonstrate that the employee's homosexuality obstructs effective job performance. This obstruction could be demonstrated by the employee's inability to get a security clearance. Another relevant consideration would be certain actions of the employee—such as public flaunting of homosexuality.[47]

Performance Appraisal

Since the performance appraisal may be used for rewarding, promoting, or retaining employees, it may become a crucial component in determining discrimination. A review of recent court decisions suggests that performance appraisals should have several characteristics if they are to pass judicial examination.[48] The appraisals should be based on formal job analyses and should be as formal and objective as possible. Also, evaluators should have written instructions and training in the use of appraisal techniques, and they should have substantial daily contact with those whom they are evaluating.

Compensation and Benefits

The Equal Pay Act prohibits wage differentials between men and women for substantially equal work that requires equal skill, effort, and responsibility under similar working conditions. The courts will not accept artificial job classifications that result in wage differentials between men and women when the job requires equal skill, effort, and responsibility.

Title VII also prohibits all employment discrimination based on sex. Some interpret Title VII to outlaw salary differentials between men and women, even when they perform dissimilar jobs that require equal skill, effort, and responsibility (that is, jobs of comparable worth). The courts have historically rejected this interpretation as contrary to the intent of the Equal Pay Act, which limits liability to disparities in substantially equal jobs. However, the Supreme Court, in *County of Washington v. Gunther,* did say that jobs need not be equal before a claim of sex discrimination in pay can be brought to court.[49] Moreover, in 1983, a federal district judge ruled that the state of Washington must give pay increases to nearly 15,000 female employees because they had the same level of skills as more highly paid men in dissimilar jobs.[50] This decision could eventually cost the state of Washington $500 million. The case is being appealed, however, and the Supreme Court has yet to make a definitive decision on this issue. (See Chapter 7 for an extended discussion of comparable worth.)

The EEOC has defined fringe benefits broadly to include medical, hospital, accident, and life insurance; retirement benefits; profit-sharing and bonus plans; leaves; and other terms, conditions, and privileges of employment.[51] Before Title

VII, some insurance plans excluded the husband and children of female employees but not the wife and children of male employees; such actions are prohibited by Title VII. Moreover, the Supreme Court's prohibition of sex-based pension plans probably indicates that it is unlawful for any other employer-provided benefit program—such as group health, life, and disability benefit plans—to use sex as a determinant of benefits.

A 1978 amendment to Title VII prohibits all employment discrimination based on pregnancy, and it applies to all females, regardless of marital status.[52] A pregnant employee must receive the same sick leave and disability benefits granted to employees with other disabilities, and accrued benefits and seniority must be applied on the same basis for pregnant women as for employees who are off the job because of disabilities.[53]

Discrimination has also occurred in retirement benefits. According to the EEOC, Title VII prohibits a retirement plan that differentiates between men and women. Since women tend to live longer than men, some employers either required women to pay more to the retirement system or provided reduced retirement benefits to them. These policies were declared illegal by the Supreme Court in the *Norris* decision of July 1983. The decision will probably require unisex pension plans in the future.

Termination

The Age Discrimination Act of 1967, as amended in 1978, prohibits compulsory retirement before age 70. This extended upper limit necessitates a sound performance appraisal system. Before the extension of the limit, employers may have overlooked poor performance of employees who were nearing age 65. Now, employers must be prepared to document poor performance if they wish to discharge workers between 65 and 70. If a worker charges age discrimination, the burden of proof that the employee is a poor performer rests with the employer.

A seniority system that provides a last-hired, first-fired approach to layoffs may undermine attempts to include more minorities and women in the workforce. The problem becomes particularly acute when economic conditions necessitate numerous reductions in force. The Supreme Court has held that a bona fide seniority system (one that is applied uniformly to all employees and is not a subterfuge to allow discrimination) is permissible even when the system tends to perpetuate discrimination that occurred before passage of the Equal Employment Act of 1972.[54] If minorities or women wish to fight dismissals produced by a nondiscriminatory seniority system, they must prove that they attempted to obtain positions with the organization before the 1972 law was passed and that they were rejected because of discrimination. In this way, they can claim that they would have had additional seniority but for the earlier discrimination.[55]

Although it appears that government has made significant progress in eliminating employment discrimination within its agencies, the true test of progress is the actual number of minorities and women in government. In other words, how representative are federal, state, and local bureaucracies today?

The Number of Minorities and Women in the Public Service

As noted earlier, Mosher described passive representation as the degree to which a bureaucracy mirrors the demographic composition of the population. Although much of the debate about the theory of representative bureaucracy concerns the link between passive representation and active or functional representation, there is also disagreement about the measurement or definition of passive representation. From a macro perspective, the entire public service is representative if each demographic group's percentage of the general population equals that group's percentage of the total public service employment. Educational and career opportunities, however, vary among different racial and social groups. Therefore, it may be impossible for the bureaucracy to mirror the social and demographic makeup of the general population perfectly. For example, women comprise over 50 percent of the population, yet they make up a much smaller proportion of lawyers, doctors, and engineers. Some contend that it would be unrealistic, therefore, to expect 50 percent of all government employees in these professions to be women.

Another possible standard or baseline for measuring progress toward a representative bureaucracy is the percentage of minorities and women in the employer's workforce. In this case, the percentage of minorities and women within a particular employment category in a bureaucracy is compared to the percentage of minorities and women in the workforce. If the local workforce contains significantly fewer minorities and women than the national workforce does, the local bureaucracy may be allowed to use the local percentage.

A third possible standard for measuring progress toward a representative bureaucracy is the percentage of qualified and available minorities and women in the relevant workforce. Of course, this standard appeals to those who are concerned that equal opportunity may subvert merit, since only *qualified* minorities and women are employed under this standard. This standard provides little incentive, however, to increase the number of qualified minorities and women in society and bureaucracies. Acceptance of this standard indicates a rather complacent attitude about the underrepresentation of women and minorities in many occupations. Furthermore, there is considerable disagreement over how to define *qualified* and *available*. The EEOC guidelines refer to *qualifiable* applicants. Thus, the EEOC may use the percentage of both *qualified* and *qualifiable* minorities and women in the workforce when determining the appropriate percentage of such groups in a bureaucracy. In other words, the EEOC expects public employers to provide training and other assistance that can make minorities and women qualified for positions, and deciding who is *trainable* is much more difficult and controversial than deciding who is qualified.

Even if a bureaucracy perfectly reflects the social and demographic composition of the population, it can contain segregated departments. For example, one department might contain a majority of blacks and women, while another department contains almost no minorities or women. Therefore, the distribution of minorities and women among departments and units must be considered. Moreover, the number of minorities and women at particular levels within the bureaucracy must be analyzed, since the percentages of minorities and women in the total bureaucracy may mask huge differences in the number of minorities and women at different levels in the bureaucracy. Such discrepancies are particularly significant in view of the hypothesized linkage between passive and active representation in the theory of representative bureaucracy. Passive representation will produce policies that assist minorities and women only if such representation occurs at the higher, policymaking levels of the bureaucracy.

Employment of Minorities and Women in the Federal Service

Table 11–2 presents the number of women and minorities in the various pay systems in the federal government and the distribution of women and minorities among grade levels in the largest employment group, the general schedule. Women are underrepresented, comprising only 32.8 percent of the total workforce, and they are concentrated in the lower levels. For example, only 6.2 percent of the Senior Executive Service employees are women. These figures indicate that very few women are in the more sensitive, policymaking positions in the federal bureaucracy.

Women are also severely underrepresented in the traditionally male, blue-collar jobs, such as plumbers, welders, mechanics, carpenters, and the like. Women have only 8.6 percent of all blue-collar positions in the federal government. Few women are in these occupations because there are strong social and work group norms that men should perform these jobs. Historically, few female role models have been found in these occupations, and opposition by men and unions in these areas have discouraged female applicants.

The small number of women in the higher-paid blue-collar occupations contrasts sharply with the large number of women in the lower-paid clerical and secretarial positions. This discrepancy contributes to the comparable worth controversy. Although the Equal Pay Act of 1963 prevents wage discrimination among similar jobs, it does not prevent unequal pay for jobs of comparable worth. Many women claim, with considerable justification, that they are paid considerably less than men who are doing jobs of comparable worth to the organization. (See chapter 7 for an extended discussion of the comparable worth issue.)

Minorities tend to be overrepresented in the federal bureaucracy, but this

Table 11–2
Number and Percentage of Full-Time Federal Employees, by Pay System, General Schedule and Equivalent Grade Grouping, Sex, and Minority/ Nonminority, November 1980

Pay System/Grade	Total Number of Employees	Sex (%) Men	Women	Minority (%)
All pay systems	2,438,906	67.1	32.8	23.5
General schedule	1,455,528	54.6	45.4	20.8
GS 1–4	273,939	22.8	77.1	32.9
GS 5–8	444,991	34.9	65.0	26.2
GS 9–11	353,587	66.7	33.2	16.4
GS 12–13	284,545	87.5	12.5	10.4
GS 14–15	98,466	93.3	6.7	7.7
Executives	8,419	93.8	6.2	7.0
Wage systems	440,881	91.4	8.6	29.7
Nonsupervisory	362,720	81.6	8.4	36.1
Leader	11,466	93.1	6.9	32.0
Supervisory	38,140	96.5	3.5	23.0
Other wage systems	64,555	92.0	8.0	20.2
Postal pay systems	512,636	81.8	18.2	26.6
Other pay systems	21,442	54.1	45.9	14.7

Source: Adapted from U.S. Office of Personnel Management, *Federal Civilian Work Force Statistics: Equal Employment Opportunity Statistics, 1980* (Washington, D.C.: U.S. Government Printing Office, 1982), p. xiv.

overrepresentation is a result of the large concentration of minorities at the lower levels. For example, almost one-third of all GS 1–4 positions are held by minorities, whereas only about 7 percent of all positions in GS 14–15 and the Senior Executive Service are held by minorities. Thus, minorities continue to be severely underrepresented at the higher levels, and they have few of the most sensitive policymaking positions in the federal bureaucracy.

Employment of Minorities and Women in State and Local Governments

As table 11–3 reveals, women make up 41 percent of all state and local government positions. Women are not only underrepresented in state and local bureaucracies, they are also concentrated at the lower levels. In 1980, the median salary of white females was only 74 percent of the white males' median salary. The great number of women employed at lower levels and the fact that these women receive less pay for the same job account for the salary differential.

Since the passage of the 1972 Equal Employment Opportunity Act, the

Table 11–3
Composition of State and Local Employment, by Function, 1973 and 1980

Function	1973 (N = 3,808,508)		1980 (N = 3,987,431)	
	% Minority	% Female	% Minority	% Female
Financial administration	11.4	52.8	16.9 (+5.5)	57.0 (+4.2)
Streets and highways	11.8	7.1	15.4 (+3.6)	10.1 (+3.0)
Public welfare	23.6	71.8	25.1 (+1.5)	75.8 (+4.0)
Police protection	9.3	12.0	11.8 (+2.5)	18.6 (+6.6)
Fire protection	5.0	1.3	9.1 (+4.1)	2.6 (+1.3)
Natural resources	15.9	18.7	19.1 (+3.2)	23.4 (+4.7)
Hospitals and sanitariums	30.4	71.0	27.7 (−2.7)	73.8 (+2.8)
Health	17.8	60.6	24.2 (+6.4)	66.7 (+6.1)
Housing	34.6	27.3	38.2 (+3.6)	32.0 (+4.7)
Community development	15.1	32.3	18.4 (+3.3)	38.5 (+6.2)
Corrections	18.7	26.9	23.8 (+5.1)	29.3 (+2.4)
Utilities and transportation	22.7	11.3	29.5 (+6.5)	16.0 (+4.7)
Sanitation and sewage	38.8	2.7	38.9 (+0.1)	5.8 (+3.1)
Employment security	18.7	54.8	24.6 (+5.9)	61.1 (+6.3)
Other	18.9	40.9	19.5 (+0.6)	49.8 (+8.9)
Total	18.2	34.7	21.1 (+2.9)	41.1 (+6.4)

Source: Adapted from EEOC, *Minorities and Women in State and Local Government, 1973* (Washington, D.C.: U.S. Government Printing Office, 1974); and EEOC, *Minorities and Women in State and Local Governments, 1980* (Washington, D.C.: U.S. Government Printing Office, 1982).

number of positions held by women has increased by 24 percent. However, women continue to be underrepresented in eight functional categories—streets and highways, police protection, fire protection, natural resources, housing, corrections, utilities and transportation, and sanitation and sewage. Most of those fields involve heavy manual labor, danger, or both, and they traditionally have been viewed as occupations in which only men should work. Women are most overrepresented in public welfare, hospitals and sanitariums, health, and employment security. These fields contain jobs that traditionally have been viewed as women's occupations (social workers, nurses, aides, secretaries, and clerical workers).

Minorities occupied approximately 21 percent of all positions in state and local government in 1980—a figure roughly equal to their proportion of the general population. Most minorities were concentrated in the lower levels, however, which is made evident by a comparison of the median salaries of minorities and white males. The gap in salaries between white and black males actually increased between 1973 and 1980.

Minorities tend to be most overrepresented in the lowest-paid fields, such as public welfare, housing, hospitals and sanitariums, utilities and transportation, sanitation and sewage, and employment security. These categories contain either a large number of unskilled laborers or a large number of clerical workers. Both groups tend to receive low pay and have little status and influence in organizations. Minorities continue to be underrepresented in police and fire protection. Employee organizations are most vocal in these two fields, and insistence on entrance exams and credentials may be most intense in these fields. Moreover, turnover may be lower in them. In addition, minorities may feel considerable antagonism from close-knit, white police and fire work groups, who may discourage recruitment and retention of minorities.

These employment figures for federal, state, and local governments lead to several conclusions. First, women are underrepresented at all levels and tend to be least represented at the higher levels. Moreover, they are particularly underrepresented in occupations that have been historically viewed as men's jobs. Second, although minorities are well represented in government employment, they are concentrated in the lower levels of bureaucracy. Third, the absence of discrimination (equal employment opportunity) may not be sufficient for moving large numbers of women and minorities into the higher levels of bureaucracy or into professions and occupations that traditionally have excluded them. More positive, instrumental affirmative actions may be required to produce a truly representative bureaucracy.

Affirmative Action: More Than Nondiscrimination

Although equal employment opportunity and affirmative action are closely related, they are not identical. Equal employment opportunity is an essentially passive approach to achieving representative bureaucracy, in that applicants and employees are not treated differently because of their race, color, sex, age, handicap, or national origin. Affirmative action is more active, and it includes specific positive steps to employ more individuals of a particular race, sex, or disadvantaged group. One principle behind affirmative action is that nondiscrimination alone may not be able to undo the damage done by past discrimination. More instrumental, positive actions may be needed to correct past abuses and to employ more minorities and women. Whereas nondiscrimination is a long-term, slow approach to correcting past damages, affirmative action seeks more rapid movement toward a representative bureaucracy.

An employer may take voluntary affirmative action in a spirit of social responsibility or to avoid possible charges and litigation regarding past discriminatory employment practices. The first employers required to implement affirmative action plans were federal contractors. President Johnson's 1965 Executive Order 11246 required contractors to take affirmative actions to employ more minorities. Similarly, President Nixon's 1969 Executive Order 11748 required federal agencies to pursue affirmative action in employment. Although the 1964 Civil Rights Act does not require affirmative action plans, the EEOC's 1979 guidelines require each person subject to Title VII to take "voluntary action to correct the effects of past discrimination without awaiting litigation."[56] Numerous court decisions have also required affirmative actions to correct past discrimination.

Goals and Quotas

The most controversial aspect of affirmative action is its reliance on goals to achieve a more representative bureaucracy, because critics contend that affirmative action goals often become quotas. In theory, at least, there are differences between goals and quotas. A quota imposes a fixed number of employees or a percentage of the workforce that must be from a disadvantaged group. In implementing a quota system, employers might establish separate eligibility lists for white males and for women and/or minorities. Candidates are then selected from the separate lists until the desired quotas are achieved.

In contrast, a goal is a numerical objective, not a fixed quota. It is realistically based on the expected number of vacancies and the number of available and qualified women and minorities in the relevant labor market. Affirmative action goals do not necessarily conflict with the merit principle. An employer need not hire individuals who are not qualified to perform the job successfully. Furthermore, employers need not hire a less qualified person in preference to a better qualified person, provided that the required qualifications realistically measure the individual's ability to do the job.

Although these differences between quotas and goals exist in theory, some critics of affirmative action suggest that, in practice, goals become quotas. Critics note that when recruiters are attempting to meet affirmative action targets, they may choose women or minorities they otherwise would not have chosen. Because much of the recruitment and selection process continues to be based on subjective considerations and evaluations, employers may rate some women or minorities as qualified or as more qualified than white males when they really are not. Of course, this argument is an admission that selection criteria are subjective and may not be related to job performance. If such is the case, one cannot say that one individual is more qualified than another. Furthermore, supporters of affirmative action note that merit has already been compromised in various ways. Veterans preference is not a merit criterion, yet it is responsible for many employment decisions in the public sector. Similarly, seniority is based on longevity, not on merit, yet many crucial personnel decisions are made on the basis of seniority.

Many white males believe that, because of affirmative action, they are the victims of reverse discrimination—that they are denied employment opportunities solely because of their race or sex. Supporters of affirmative action respond that it is rare to find actual cases in which a white male has been denied a position that is filled by an unqualified or less qualified female or minority applicant. Moreover, supporters also note that white males have benefited from advantages of past discrimination against women and minorities. According to affirmative action defenders, any present preference for women and minorities is necessary to balance past advantages for white males. Opponents respond, however, that many of today's white males are innocent third parties. The perpetrators of discrimination are often firmly entrenched in established bureaucracies and cannot be removed because of their seniority. Moreover, the victims most wronged by discrimination often receive the fewest benefits from affirmative action programs. Employers generally try to hire the most talented women and minorities, yet these individuals are likely to be the women and minorities who have suffered least from discrimination.

Affirmative Action and the Supreme Court

The Supreme Court has given mixed, if not conflicting, opinions on whether the Constitution permits affirmative action quotas. In 1978, the Court dealt with the quota issue in *University of California Regents v. Bakke.*[57] Allan Bakke, a white male, was an applicant to the University of California at Davis Medical School. The school has a two-track admissions system in which a certain percentage of admissions were reserved for minority candidates. As a result, Bakke was denied admission, even though several minority students were admitted who had lower test scores and grade-point averages. The Court ruled that Bakke had been subject to racial discrimination in violation of the equal protection provisions of the Fourteenth Amendment to the Constitution. The Court seemed most concerned about the exclusiveness of the minority admissions quota. Whites could not compete for these special seats, although minorities could compete for both the general and the special admissions.

The Court appeared to have a different view in the case *Weber v. Kaiser Aluminum and Steel Corporation and United Steelworkers of America.*[58] Kaiser Aluminum and the United Steelworkers sponsored a training program for skilled craft jobs. Admission into this program was based on a fifty–fifty, black–white racial quota, and Brian Weber, a white technician, was denied admission, even though he had more seniority than some blacks who were admitted. The Court upheld the plan. Although this decision seems to conflict with the *Bakke* opinion, there are differences in the cases. First, the employer in *Weber* was a private organization, and the Fourteenth Amendment only prohibits government actions that deny equal protection of the law. Second, the quota-based training program did not deny promotional opportunities to whites. Moreover, the program did not guarantee promotions, and whites continued to have various options to attain a promotion.

The Court has applied the *Weber* decision in the public sector. In *Fullilove v. Klutznick,* the Court accepted a quota system for allocating a certain percentage of government contracts to minority contractors.[59] Similarly, the Supreme Court chose not to review an appeals court decision to permit a quota system in the Detroit Police Department. The City of Detroit had voluntarily adopted an affirmative action plan in 1974 that mandated the use of two separate promotional lists—one for white sergeants and another for black sergeants.[60] Promotions to lieutenant were made alternately from the two lists and the department intended to use the two lists until 50 percent of the lieutenants were black. White sergeants brought suit, however, claiming that the separate lists violated both Title VII of the 1964 Civil Rights Act and the Fourteenth Amendment to the Constitution. The Sixth Circuit Court disagreed and said the two-list system was reasonably related to the goal of eliminating past discrimination. The Court also noted that the plan was temporary and would extend only as long as necessary to accomplish the 50 percent goal. These more recent decisions indicate that the distinction between goals and quotas may be greater in theory than in practice. The Supreme Court may allow voluntary quota systems that permit qualified minorities to attain positions in preference to better-qualified white applicants, but it will probably not mandate quotas, except as remedies for findings of past employer discrimination.

Affirmative Action Plans

If a public agency is serious about attaining a representative bureaucracy and is committed to affirmative action in the employment of women and minorities, it should have an affirmative action plan (AAP). Although Title VII of the 1964 Civil Rights Act does not require an AAP, Executive Orders 11246 and 11375 do require that federal contractors establish plans to assure equal employment opportunity. The courts may impose AAPs on employers that have discriminated against women and minorities.

There are several reasons why public organizations should develop voluntary AAPs. First, the development of such plans may allow public agencies to detect discriminatory practices that can be corrected by remedial action. Thus, the organizations will be able to avoid legal suits and bad publicity. Second, good AAPs, like good human resource plans, can promote better use of personnel. Third, an organization may need a written AAP for federal grant requests.

The first step in the development of an AAP is to appoint a top official to prepare and implement the plan. This official must have the authority, status, and power necessary to obtain compliance to the AAP. Moreover, the affirmative action officer should be accountable to the organization's chief executive. Appointment of a top official will demonstrate the organization's commitment to affirmative action.

The second step is to perform workforce analysis, which will reveal the percentage of employees by sex and racial groups in each department and occupational category (for example, administrators, professionals, technicians, clerical workers, and so on).

The third step is to determine estimates of the availability of qualified women and minorities in the occupational categories in the relevant labor market. Although the recruiting area may vary for different occupations, it is often the standard metropolitan area, the county, or the state. Sources of such data are the U.S. Bureau of Labor Statistics, the U.S. Census Bureau, and state employment offices.

The fourth step is to compare the percentage of available and qualified women and minorities in each occupational category in the labor market with the percentage of women and minorities in the same occupational categories in the organization. This comparison will show the degree of underrepresentation and suggest affirmative action goals and timetables, which, of course, depend on the number of vacancies and new positions that occur in an organization. If an agency has little turnover and expansion, affirmative action is much more difficult.

After goals and timetables are established, the organization should audit all major personnel functions to ensure that the AAP is being implemented. The audit should include a review of recruitment, job qualifications, selection, performance evaluations, compensation, layoffs, demotions, seniority provisions, training, and recreational programs. Pertinent questions concerning each of these areas are given in appendix 11A, at the end of this chapter.

Conclusion

Americans want their public organizations to be both representative and effective. Those who view affirmative action as a threat to merit should remember that merit is only one of several values that have shaped U.S. public administration. As early as Jefferson and Jackson, Americans were willing to compromise some efficiency for a more representative bureaucracy. Major economic and geographic groups were thus represented in the bureaucracy. Moreover, the public service has traditionally acted as a special employer of veterans, who often were not the best qualified applicants. Also, most salary increases within public bureaucracies have been decided by seniority, yet seniority may have little relation to merit and performance.

Critics of affirmative action should also remember that merit is not necessarily subverted by affirmative action. It does not require that the unqualified be hired, nor does it demand that strict quotas be rigidly imposed. Affirmative action requires only that public employers take positive steps to hire more women and minorities. It assumes that nondiscrimination alone cannot eliminate the harm of past discrimination. Furthermore, it may be the only way in which we can achieve a representative bureaucracy within reasonable time.

Notes

1. J. Donald Kingsley, *Representative Bureaucracy: An Interpretation of the British Civil Service* (Yellow Springs, Ohio: Antioch Press, 1944).

2. Norton Long, "Bureaucracy and Constitutionalism," *American Political Science Review* 46 (September 1952): 808–818.

3. Paul P. Van Riper, *History of the United States Civil Service: 1789–1957* (Evanston, Ill.: Row, Peterson, 1958).

4. Frederick C. Mosher,*Democracy and the Public Service* (New York: Oxford University Press, 1968).

5. Ibid., pp. 12, 13.

6. Kenneth John Meier, "Representative Bureaucracy: An Empirical Analysis," *American Political Science Review* 69 (June 1975): 526–543.

7. Ibid.

8. For studies that indicate that organizations are powerful socializers, see Herbert Kaufman, *The Forest Ranger* (Baltimore: Johns Hopkins Press, 1960); and Morris Janowitz, *The Professional Soldier* (New York: Free Press of Glencoe, 1960).

9. James A. Barber, *Social Mobility and Voting Behavior* (Chicago: Rand McNally, 1970).

10. Grace Hall Saltzestein, "Representative Bureaucracy and Bureaucratic Responsibility: Problem and Prospects," *Administration and Society* 11 (February 1979): 470.

11. Kenneth J. Meier and Lloyd G. Nigro, "Representative Bureaucracy and Policy Preferences: A Study in the Attitudes of Federal Executives," *Public Administration Review* 36 (July–August 1976): 458–469.

12. Ibid., p. 467.

13. P.H. Rossi, R.A. Berk, and B.K. Edison, *The Roots of Urban Discontent* (New York: Wiley, 1974), pp. 168–169.

14. Ibid., pp. 346–353.

15. E. Mizio, "Puerto Rican Social Workers and Racism," *Social Casework* 54 (May 1973): 267–272; P.L. Winger and S. Dobie, "The Attitudes of the Psychiatraist About His Patient" *Comprehensive Psychiatry* 9 (1968): 627–632.

16. Frank J. Thompson, "Minority Groups in Public Bureaucracies: Passive and Active Representation Linked?" *Administration and Society* 8 (August 1976): 201–226.

17. Meier and Nigro, "Representative Bureaucracy and Policy Preferences," 467.

18. David H. Rosenbloom, *Federal Equal Employment Opportunity in Politics and Public Personnel Administration* (New York: Praeger, 1977), p. 51.

19. Samuel Krislov, *The Negro in Federal Employment: The Quest for Equal Opportunity* (Minneapolis: University of Minnesota Press, 1967), p. 7.

20. Rosenbloom, *Federal Equal Employment Opportunity*, p. 52.

21. Van Riper, *History of the United States Civil Service*, p. 242.

22. Lawrence Hayes, *The Negro Federal Government Worker* (Washington, D.C.: Howard University Press, 1941), p. 21.

23. Rosenbloom, *Federal Equal Employment Opportunity*, p. 53.

24. Ibid.

25. Krislov, *The Negro in Federal Employment*, pp. 20–21.

26. Ibid., pp. 22–23.

27. Ibid.

28. Rosenbloom, *Federal Equal Employment Opportunity*, p. 60.

29. Ibid., p. 61.

30. Ibid.

31. Ibid., p. 63.

32. Ibid., p. 65.

33. Ibid.

34. Winfred Rose and Tiang Ping Chia, "The Impact of the Equal Employment Opportunity Act of 1972 on Black Employment in the Federal Service: A Preliminary Analysis," *Public Administration Review* 38 (May–June 1978): 246.

35. Rosenbloom, *Federal Equal Employment Opportunity*, p. 56.

36. Van Riper, *History of the United States Civil Service*, p. 261.

37. John F. Kennedy, "Executive Order 10925, Establishing the President's Committee on Equal Employment Opportunity," in *Code of the Federal Register*, Title 3 (Washington, D.C.: The President, 1961).

38. *The Civil Rights Act of 1964*, P.L. 88–352, 78 Stat. 241, 28 U.S.C. Section 1447 (1976).

39. *Equal Employment Opportunity Act of 1972*, P.L. 93–380, 88 Stat. 514, 20 U.S.C. Section 1228 (1976).

40. *The Age Discrimination in Employment Act of 1967*, P.L. 90–202, 81 Stat. 602, 29 U.S.C. Sections 621–634 (1976).

41. *Griggs v. Duke Power Company*, 401 U.S. 424 (1971).

42. *Albemarle Paper Co. v. Moody*, 422 U.S. 405 (1975).

43. *Connecticut v. Teal*, USLW 4716 (1982).

44. *Dothard v. Rawlinson*, 433 U.S. 321 (1977).

45. *Sugarman v. Dougall*, 413 U.S. 634 (1973).

46. *Foley v. Connelie*, 98 S.Ct. 1067 (1978).

47. Karen Ann Olsen, *Equal Employment Opportunity and Affirmative Action* (Washington, D.C.: Labor–Management Relations Service, 1979), p. 12.

48. Dwane Thompson, "Performance Appraisal and the Civil Service Reform Act," *Public Personnel Management* 10 (Fall 1981): 281–288.

49. *Gunther v. County of Washington*, 452 U.S. 161 (1981).

50. *American Federation of State, County and Municipal Employees v. State of Washington*, Civil Action No. C82–465T (W.D. Wash., 1983).

51. Olsen, *Equal Employment Opportunity and Affirmative Action*, p. 12.

52. Ibid.

53. *Nashville Gas Company v. Satty*, 434 U.S. 136 (1977).

54. Robert Roberts, "Last-Hired, First-Fired and Public Employee Layoffs: The Equal Opportunity Dilemma," *Review of Public Personnel Administration* 2 (Fall 1981): 29–48.

55. Hindy L. Schachter, "Retroactive Seniority and Agency Retrenchment," *Public Administration Review* 43 (January–February 1983): 77–81.

56. Equal Employment Opportunity Commission, "Affirmative Action Guidelines," *Federal Register,* January 19, 1979, p. 4426.

57. *University of California Regents v. Bakke,* 46 U.S. Law Week, 4896 (1978).

58. *Weber v. Kaiser Aluminum and Steel Corp. and United Steelworkers of America,* 440 U.S. 954 (1979).

59. *Fullilove v. Klutznick,* 49 U.S. Law Week (1980); William Kelso "From Bakke to Fullilove: Has the Supreme Court Finally Settled the Affirmative Action Controversy?" *Review of Public Personnel Administration* 1 (Fall 1980): 69.

60. *Hansen Bratton et al. v. City of Detroit et al.,* Docket No. 83–551, *cert. denied* January 10, 1984.

Appendix 11A: Audit Requirements

1. Recruitment
   a. Has an applicant flow record been established so that persons can be identified as protected class members? (This is necessary so that the organization's recruitment procedures can be evaluated as to their effectiveness in attracting member of protected classes as job applicants.)
   b. Is recruitment conducted primarily by "walk-in" or "word-of-mouth?" (This could result in a small number of protected class job applicants, depending on the organization's location and the make-up of the current work force.)
   c. Is an affirmative action file maintained to include protected class applicants who have not been hired but are qualified candidates for future openings?
   d. Are protected class members utilized in the recruitment process?
   e. Have community resource organizations and citizen action groups which may serve as recruitment sources for protected class members been informed of the employer's policy and job openings?
   f. Do advertisement of job openings indicate the employer's policy of equal employment opportunity?
   g. Are media resources with a high percentage of readership or audience composition of protected classes used for advertising job openings?
2. Minimal Job Qualifications
   a. Are qualifications job-relevant and based on up-to-date job descriptions?
   b. Has the "minimal" level of qualification been established based on a careful job analysis?
   c. Have job qualifications been analyzed to determine whether they have an adverse impact on members of protected classes?
   d. Have the job qualifications of current employees been surveyed by job

From Karen Ann Olsen, *Equal Employment Opportunity and Affirmative Action*. (Washington, D.C.: Labor–Management Relations Service of the United States Conference of Mayors, 1979), pp. 18–22. Reprinted with permission.

classification to identify whether current qualifications, particularly those for education and previous experience, are realistic?

3. Selection Procedures

a. Do application forms require information regarding protected class status (race, color, creed, religion, sex, national origin or age) or other areas of inquiry which could be used to illegally discriminate against applicants? (If such information is collected on the application form, an employer may be required, in case of charges of discrimination, to prove that such information has not been used to illegally discriminate against the applicant—a difficult case to prove.)

b. Are protected class members utilized to screen applications and interview applicants?

c. Where previous job-relevant experience and education of applicants are rated, have specific written standards been established for such evaluations

d. Are all examinations, including written, oral and performance tests, job-relevant?

e. Are examinations scheduled and conducted consistent with principles of equal opportunity and open competition?

f. What is the strategy for determining passing scores?

g. What are the criteria for selection of oral examination panels?

h. Does the oral examination panel receive training to increase the objectivity and reliability of evaluations and to understand the organization's commitment to examination procedures consistent with principles of equal employment opportunity?

i. Do all examinees receive equal treatment?

j. Have examination results been analyzed to determine whether there is an adverse impact on members of protected classes?

k. Do performance tests, if used, include measurement of job-relevant skills based on careful job analysis?

l. Are pre-employment interview questions relevant to job performance?

m. Have areas of interview inquiry been reviewed and questions eliminated which could be used to illegally discriminate against applicants based on race, color, creed, sex, religion, national origin or age? (For example, questions which relate to child care plans asked of women but not of men are considered to be discriminatory on the basis of sex.)

n. Do previous employer reference checks include personal information which is not relevant to job performance?

o. Are applicants informed that previous employers will be contacted to obtain job-relevant information which may have an effect on their opportunities for employment with the organization?

p. Have employees and supervisors been informed that protected class employees are eligible for promotion to any job for which they qualify, regardless of whether such jobs have in the past been filled by member of the protected classes?

q. Are supervisors required to submit a written justification for passing over qualified protected class employees for promotions?

r. What is the employer's policy regarding promotion from within versus appointment from outside the organization? Does this policy have an adverse impact on protected class members?

s. What procedures have been established to identify employees interested in and qualified?

t. Is selection for promotion based on job-relevant criteria?

u. Does the certification and appointment procedure ensure the consideration of best qualified candidates?

v. Does the system provide job-relevant criteria for consideration by the appointing authority in selecting the best-qualified candidates for appointment?

w. What policy is applicable to those certified candidates who are repeatedly passed over?

x. Do appointing officials receive training in interviewing and selection consistent with equal employment opportunity principles?

y. Are appointing officials required to interview all candidates certified to them; if not, are they encouraged to do so?

4. Performance Evaluations

a. Have specific performance standards been developed for evaluation? ("Global" or "overall" ratings are particularly vulnerable to bias based on factors other than performance—which may include race, sex, national origin, etc.)

b. Have performance standards been communicated adequately to employees and supervisors?

c. Does the performance evaluation procedure provide for an interview between supervisor and employee in which the employee's performance evaluation is reviewed, and in which the employee is given an opportunity to add written comments?

d. Are written performance evaluations considered in making training and job assignments, transfers and promotions?

5. Wages and Benefits

a. Where there is a salary range for hiring or promotion, are females and/or minorities offered lower starting pay than males?

b. Have similar jobs been compared with respect to skill, effort, responsibility and working conditions to determine whether there is equal pay for equal work?

c. If pay differentials do exist for jobs that are substantially equal given skill, effort, responsibility and working conditions, what is the basis for such pay differentials? (Pay differentials may legally exist based on bona fide seniority, merit or incentive programs or on piecework systems, but are illegal if based on sex, race, etc. of job incumbents.)

d. Have all supervisory and managerial personnel who participate in compensation decisions been briefed on the requirements of the Equal Pay Act?

e. Have jobs in the same "family" (for example, clerical jobs) been compared to determine if they are properly graded? (For example, if women in lower salary grades perform duties of jobs classified into higher salary grades, this may constitute a violiation of the Equal Pay Act.)

f. What factors are salary increases based on—performance, seniority, automatic step increases, "cost-of-living" adjustments or collective bargaining provisions? Are these factors equitably applied in granting individual salary increases?

g. Are some benefits available only to "principal wage earner" or "head of household?" (Such a practice is discriminatory against female employees.)

h. Are benefits provided for wives and families of male empoyees also available to husbands and families of female employees?

i. Are benefits provided for wives of male employees also available to female employees?

j. Are pregnancy, miscarriage, childbirth and recovery dealt with on the same basis as other temporary disabilities?

k. Are males and females eligible for retirement on the same basis, including equal retirement age and equal benefits?

6. Layoff and Recall

a. Have affirmative action records been established to monitor layoff and recall, and to see if current practices have a disparate effect on protected class members?

b. Are layoff and recall conducted on an organization-wide seniority basis, in cases where protected class members previously could not enter certain job classifications and therefore acquire job or departmental seniority?

7. Demotions, Disciplinary Action and Discharge

a. Have affirmative action records been established to monitor demotions, disciplinary action and discharge, in order to see if there current practices have a disparate effect on protected class members?

b. Does a personnel or equal employment opportunity officer formally monitor disciplinary actions so that discrimination can be identified and promptly rectified?

c. As a matter of good personnel policy, and to provide a defense against discrimination charges, are written records maintained on disciplinary action and rule infractions (even when no disciplinary action was taken)? Does the organization maintain job performance records that document poor performance when it occurs?

d. Are supervisors and managers provided with training in progressive discipline for just cause, and consistent application of discipline?

e. Are supervisors and managers provided with written discipline standards that provide specific, objective guidelines for administering disciplinary action?

f. Are appeal procedures equally available to all employees?

g. Have termination records been reviewed to determine whether any of the following forbidden criteria were the basis for terminations: termination of female for marrying or becoming pregnant (sex discrimination); termination after employee was placed in job where failure was inevitable; termination for complaining about discrimination or filing charges of discrimination against the employer; and termination based on employee's failure to get along with co-workers who practice discriminatory harassment?

8. Seniority and Transfer Provisions

a. Are seniority lists segregated by race, color, religion, sex or national origin? (Segregated seniority lists on the bases of these factors are illegal under Title VII.)

b. Are seniority lists segregated for "heavy" and "light" job classifications? (It is unlawful discrimination based on sex if there are dual seniority lists for "heavy" jobs held by men and "light" jobs held by women.)

c. Does current seniority system penalize minorities and women as a result of past discrimination? (For example, a departmental seniority system that makes it difficult for minorities and females to transfer out of lower-paying departments, into which they've been locked by previous discrimination, may be illegal unless it can meet the "bona fide" seniority system exception.)

d. If layoffs are pending, has every practical possibility been explored for avoiding a disparate impact on minorities and females who may have less seniority, due to past discrimnation, than white males?

9. Training and Career Development

a. Are affirmative action records maintained regarding the participation of women and minorities in training programs and career development opportunities?

b. Have these records been analyzed to determine whether women and minorities are underrepresented, in relation to their percentage of the work force, in training programs and career development opportunities?

c. What are the criteria for selecting employees for training? (Such selection decisions should not be based on race, color, age, sex, national origin or religion.)

d. Are all employees informed of training and educational opportunities (tuition refund, for example) made available by the organization?

    e.   Among the persons who administer the training and career development programs, are there any minorities and women?

    f.   Have training programs been developed to provide supervisors and managers with information on equal employment opportunity?

10. Social and Recreational Programs and other Employment Conditions

    a.   If social and recreational programs are provided for workers, are they made equally available to all employees?

    b.   Is the working environment monitored periodically to ensure that it is free of intimidation and other types of harassment based on race, color, creed, age, disability, sex, religion or national origin?

    c.   Are supervisors and managers aware of their responsibilities to take action, including discipline as necessary, to stop such harassment if it occurs?

    d.   Have work rules been reviewed to determine that they are not discriminatory? (Examples of discriminatory rules: longer rest periods for women than for men; prohibiting employees from speaking foreign languages on the premises; and "protective" rules such as prohibiting women from lifting object in excess of a certain weight limit.)

    e.   Have work rules been consistently enforced?

    f.   Are work assignments made on a nondiscriminatory basis?

12
Rights and Duties of Public Employees

Key Words

Privilege doctrine

Board of Regents v. Roth

Arnett v. Kennedy

Deconstitutionalization

Pickering v. Board of Education

Whistle-blowing

Hatch Act

United States Civil Service Commission v. National Association of Letter Carriers

Elrod v. Burns

Branti v. Finkel

Sovereign and official immunity

Section 1983 of the 1871 Civil Rights Act

Monroe v. Pape

Wood v. Stuckland

Butz v. Economou

Maine v. Thiboutot

Ethics in Government Act of 1978

Codes of ethics

Financial disclosure laws

Appeals mechanisms

Subjective versus objective responsibility

Introduction

Citizens, elected officials, and the courts expect public employees to exhibit a high standard of ethics. Since public employees represent the state in the everyday lives of citizens, they are expected to be above reproach. Citizens are particularly displeased when governmental power or tax revenues are abused through questionable bureaucractic behavior. Therefore, the personal and professional conduct of public employees has historically been guided by legal and ethical standards that are not generally applied to average citizens. Legislatures have drafted laws and the courts have made decisions that have constricted public employees' freedom of speech and association and that have significantly curtailed their political activities.

This chapter examines the development of law concerning the constitutional rights of public employees. Although the Supreme Court in the last twenty-five years has reduced the number of restrictions on public employees' behavior, significant controls remain. One that has attracted considerable attention in recent years is the personal liability of public employees for damages committed by them in the exercise of their official duties. In recent years, the Supreme Court has reduced the immunity of public employees to damage suits by citizens, and the course and impact of this development are also reviewed in this chapter.

During the 1970s, a number of well-publicized scandals prompted both the Congress and state legislatures to pass codes of ethics for public employees. The content and effects of these codes are analyzed in this chapter. Despite ethical codes, however, public employees sometimes engage in misconduct that demands discipline. The types of discipline commonly used in public organizations are described here, as are some general guidelines or principles for the correct application of discipline. When employees believe that discipline has been inappropriately applied, they generally have a right to enter their complaints or grievances in the appeals systems that exist in most public organizations. The final section of the chapter describes these appeals systems and notes the major criticisms of them.

Rights of Public Employees

Legislatures and courts have established restrictions on the behavior of public employees both during and outside working hours. These restrictions have involved public employees' due process rights, their freedom of speech and association, and their political activities. The Supreme Court has attempted to balance public employees' individual liberties against the requirements for effective administration of government services. During most of U.S. history, this balance tended to lean toward effective government administration. In the last twenty-five years, however, the Supreme Court has shifted the balance in the direction of more liberty for public employees. Nevertheless, public employees' right to engage in political activities continues to be significantly restricted.

Due Process Rights of Public Employees

The Fifth and Fourteenth Amendments of the Constitution protect citizens against government denial of their "life, liberty or property without due process of law." Although due process is an elusive concept that is difficult to define, it generally involves notice of a proposed government action and the reasons for it and an opportunity to respond. Questions concerning the appropriate due process requirements in the dismissal of public employees have been a continuing issue in U.S. constitutional law.

During most of U.S. history, the Supreme Court held that the government could require public employees to forgo some of their civil and political rights as a condition of employment. The legal doctrine supporting this curtailment was the doctrine of privilege.[1] According to this doctrine, public employees did not have a constitutional right to public employment; instead, public employment was viewed as a privilege. Therefore, if a public employee was dismissed for having exercised a political or civil right, no constitutional question was involved, because a privilege (the employee's job) had been abrogated, not a right. In 1892, Justice Holmes stated the doctrine rather succinctly: "The petitioner may have a constitutional right to talk politics, but he has no constitutional right to be a policeman"[2] According to this view, when a citizen accepts public employment, he or she must accept the restrictions that accompany the job. Thus, these restrictions do not violate the employee's rights, because they are voluntarily accepted.

The Supreme Court began to modify the privilege doctrine during the 1960s and early 1970s. The doctrine eroded for two primary reasons. First, abuses of the loyalty-security program during the 1950s suggested to the Supreme Court that dismissal of a public employee could have a permanent negative effect on an individual's reputation.[3] Therefore, in *Cafeteria Workers v. McElroy,* the Court acknowledged that there are some constitutional restraints upon state and federal governments in dealing with their employees.[4]

A second reason for the change in the privilege doctrine concerned the possible extension of the doctrine to many recipients of government largesse programs. If government employment could be viewed as a privilege, could not welfare benefits, licenses, and government contracts also be viewed as privileges? If so, then the recipients' political and civil rights could be curtailed as those of public employees were. The Supreme Court was unwilling, however, to extend the privilege doctrine to all government largesse recipients. In *Goldberg v. Kelly,* the Court stated that "the extent to which procedural due process must be afforded to the recipient is influenced by the extent to which he may be condemned to suffer grievous loss . . and depends upon whether the recipient's interest in avoiding that loss outweighs the governmental interest in summary adjudication."[5] This decision indicates that where an adverse action against a public employee results in a "grievous loss," the employee has a right to procedural due process. The decision did not indicate, however, what constitutes a "grievous loss."

In *Board of Regents v. Roth,* the Supreme Court attempted to delineate the circumstances under which the dismissal of a public employee might trigger a right to procedural due process:[6] when a public employee has a "property interest" in the job, such as tenure or a contract; when the dismissal harms the employee's reputation and/or adversely affects his or her future employability; or when the dismissal is in retaliation for the exercise of constitutional rights, such as freedom of speech or association.[7] Although the Court enunciated these guidelines, it has found it difficult to apply them in specific circumstances. In fact, in the process of applying them, it has dramatically limited the applicability of procedural due process to public personnel management.[8]

The Court's difficulty in applying the guidelines was apparent in *Arnett v. Kennedy.*[9] Kennedy was a nonprobationary federal employee who was dismissed for accusing his supervisor (Arnett) of bribing a third party to make false accusations against him. Kennedy claimed that he had a constitutional right to a trial-type hearing before an impartial hearing officer prior to his dismissal and that, therefore, he should be reinstated. Although the justices agreed five to four that Kennedy should not be reinstated, they could not agree on a majority opinion. The authors of the *Roth* decision (Justices Rehnquist, Burger, and Stewart) thought that Kennedy had no constitutional rights to procedural due process. They believed that Kennedy had no property right in his position, because the controlling statue, the Lloyd–Lafollette Act of 1912, allowed dismissal for such cause as would promote the "efficiency" of the service. They reasoned that although Kennedy did have a statutory expectation or right that he could be removed only for the purpose of promoting the efficiency of the service, this right was qualified by the statute itself (the Lloyd–LaFollette Act), which does not require hearings.

Justices Powell, Blackmun, and White agreed that although the legislature may elect not to give a property interest to employees (that is, job tenure), once it is given, the government cannot withdraw it without appropriate procedural safeguards. The three justices agreed, however, that only very minimal safeguards were required. Thus, the *Arnett v. Kennedy* decision is significant because three justices—Rehnquist, Burger, and Stewart—agreed that most dismissals do not require constitutional procedural safeguards, and three other justices—Powell, Blackmun, and White, believed that only minimal constitutional requirements were necessary. David Rosenbloom, a leading authority in this field, believes this decision was the beginning of deconstitutionalization of the relationship between government and its employees.[10]

The deconstitutionalization approach was articulated by the Supreme Court in *Bishop v. Wood*.[11] The city of Marion, North Carolina, had dismissed Bishop, a policeman, without giving him a hearing. Bishop, who was classified as a "permanent employee," claimed that he had a property interest in his job and a constitutional right to a pretermination hearing. The city ordinance that provided the permanent employee status and that also covered dismissals required that employees be given written notification of dismissals and the reasons for them, but it did not require a hearing. Although the Supreme Court concluded that Bishop's discharge might have been a mistake based on incorrect information, it nevertheless held that his constitutional right to due process was not violated. The Court stated:

> The federal court is not the appropriate forum in which to review the multitude of personnel decisions that are made daily by public agencies. We must accept the harsh fact that numerous individual mistakes are inevitable in the day-to-day administration of our affairs. The United States Constitution cannot feasibly be construed to require judicial review for every such error. In the absence of any claim that the public employer was motivated by a desire to curtail or to penalize the exercise of an employee's constitutionally-protected rights, we must presume that official action was regular and, if erroneous, can best be corrected in other ways. The Due Process clause of the Fourteenth Amendment is not a guarantee against incorrect or ill-advised personnel decisions.[12]

The Court was thus saying that judicial involvement in the procedural aspects of public personnel management must be curtailed. As a result, public personnel managers obtained greater freedom to dismiss employees without fear of violating the employees' constitutional right to due process.

Freedom of Speech

In general, public employees can exercise their freedom of speech with few restraints. The leading Supreme Court decision concerning the free speech rights of public employees is *Pickering v. Board of Education*.[13] Pickering, a schoolteacher in Illinois, was dismissed by the local schoolboard for writing a letter that was critical of the board to a local newspaper. Pickering criticized the way the board was presenting a series of bond issue proposals. He was also critical of the amount of money spent by the board on the athletic program. The Court recognized that the public employer did have interests as an "employer in regulating the speech of its employees that differ significantly from those it possesses in connection with regulation of speech of the citizenry in general." The Court believed, however, that the schoolboard had gone too far and had violated Pickering's First

Amendment rights. The Court said that the test for regulation of public employees' speech is whether the government's interest in limiting their speech is greater than its interest in limiting similar speech by any member of the general public.

When a public employee is dismissed for publicly criticizing an employer about an issue of general public importance, the Court probably will not uphold the dismissal. When the employee's speech involves matters that are not of public concern, however, and when such speech clearly undermines the harmony and proper performance of the work group, the government's ability to limit it may increase. Also, the Court will uphold the dismissal of an employee who releases classified information that is vital to national security.

Public employees' freedom of speech is related to the issue of whistle-blowing.[14] A whistle-blower is a public employee who releases information concerning waste, fraud, or abuse of power by his or her agency. If the information released is not vital to national security and if it concerns a matter of general public interest, the speech is probably protected. The 1978 Civil Service Reform Act also protects employees who release information concerning inefficiency, fraud, or abuse in their agencies. The law does not protect release of classified information or of data that protect rights to privacy for individual citizens. Although there are considerable legislative and judicial protections against dismissals of whistle-blowers, public organizations continue to have considerable power to discourage whistle-blowing. For example, whistle-blowers may receive few promotions, or they may be transferred to unpleasant assignments or locations. Furthermore, whistle-blowers can be socially ostracized by fellow employees. One should be careful, however, in encouraging even more protection for whistle-blowers. They may not have all the facts, and they are too often motivated more by personal anger than by the public interest. In addition, whistle-blowing can undermine mutual trust in an organization.

Political Activity

Although public employees enjoy freedom of speech, that freedom does not extend to giving partisan speeches or to engaging in partisan political activity. According to the merit concept, if employees are appointed because of their merit, and if they are to be permanent employees in both Republican and Democratic administrations, then they must remain politically neutral. Otherwise, so the reasoning goes, public employees would cease to be neutral tools for carrying out the goals of the elected political leaders. The concept of neutral civil servants has been around for a long time in the United States. In 1802, President Thomas Jefferson issued a circular that suggested political neutrality for federal employees. The Pendleton Act of 1883 established procedures for restricting political activities. In 1907, President Theodore Roosevelt issued Executive Order 642, which restricted the political activities of classified federal employees. From 1907 to 1939, the Civil Service Commission issued more than 3,000 rulings that detailed the forms of political activity that were curtailed by Roosevelt's guidelines.

In 1939, the Political Activities Act, popularly known as the Hatch Act, was passed. This act adopted as statutory law the 3,000 rulings of the Civil Service Commission and also defined the prohibited political activities. The act applied to all classified federal employees. In 1940, the prohibitions of the Hatch Act were extended to all state and local employees who were substantially funded by federal funds. The Hatch Act prohibits active involvement in political campaigns by federal employees. It also prohibits any pressure by employers to obtain contributions, votes or political support from employees. Penalties for violation of the Hatch Act range from a minimum of thirty days' suspension to dismissal.

It has been difficult to define precisely the prohibitions of the Hatch Act; in general, however, it prohibits a federal employee from the following activities:

1. Being a candidate in a partisan election.
2. Soliciting campaign contributions.
3. Being a delegate to a political convention.
4. Speaking at a partisan political rally or meeting.
5. Engaging in electioneering (that is, handing out campaign literature, driving voters to the polls, and so on).
6. Participating in voter registration drives for only one party.
7. Circulating a partisan nominating petition.
8. Holding office in a political club.

The Hatch Act does not prohibit all political activity by federal employees, however; for example, the following are not prohibited:

1. Expressing personal views on political subjects and candidates.
2. Participating in nonpartisan elections, such as elections of local schoolboards.
3. Being candidates in local nonpartisan elections.
4. Placing political stickers on their own cars.
5. Being actively involved in local nonpartisan issues, such as tax referendums, constitutional amendments, civil rights, and so forth.
6. Signing partisan nominating petitions.
7. Making voluntary contributions to partisan political campaigns.
8. Attending political conventions (not as a delegate).

Although the Election Campaign Act of 1974 reduced federal restrictions on the political activities of state and local employees, most states maintain so-called Little Hatch Acts, which contain many provisions similar to those of the national legislation.

The Hatch Act and the Little Hatch Acts have been challenged as unconstitutional limits on First Amendment rights and as insufficiently clear, but the Supreme Court has rejected both challenges. In 1947, a five-to-four decision of the Supreme Court upheld the constitutionality of the Hatch Act restrictions in *United Public Workers of America v. Mitchell.*[15] Since the *Mitchell* case was a five-to-four decision, public employee organizations maintained the hope that the Court would eventually reverse itself and declare the Hatch Act an unconstitutional infringement on public employees' First Amendment rights. Public employees contended that because the Hatch Act was so vague, they could not know what was or was not prohibited. Such vagueness, they argued, was unacceptable when it was balanced against the possibility of overbreadth in the sensitive area of free speech and expression. In other words, when public employees are not able to know what is or is not prohibited, they may be overly cautious in the exercise of their First Amendment rights.

The Supreme Court did not agree with this view, however; in 1973, it reaffirmed the *Mitchell* decision in *United States Civil Service Commission v. National Association of Letter Carriers.*[16] Six justices agreed that the prohibitions in the Hatch Act "are set out in terms that the ordinary person exercising ordinary common sense can sufficiently understand and comply with, without sacrifice to the public interest."

Although the Court has upheld the constitutionality of legislation limiting public employees' political activity, the Congress could draft new, more liberal legislation. Therefore, public employees turned their attention to Congress after losing in the courts, and in 1976, Congress passed the Federal Employees Political Activities Act, which considerably liberalized the restrictions in the Hatch Act. President Ford vetoed the act, however, stating that it endangered "the entire concept of employee independence and freedom from coercion."[17] The Democrats are usually more supportive of public employees' desire to liberalize the Hatch Act. After President Carter was elected, he encouraged Congress to change the law. In 1977, the House of Representatives did pass a bill that would have removed many of the restrictions on public employees, but the Senate failed to take action on it. Given that the Democrats controlled both the White House and the Congress and yet no change was possible, one can safely assume that the Hatch Act prohibitions will continue into the foreseeable future. In any event, much of the argument over the restrictions may be academic. Various surveys of public employees reveal that most would not become more actively involved in politics if the restrictions were removed.[18] Therefore, the Hatch Act restrictions may have little real impact on the political activity of public employees.

Freedom of Association

Various Supreme Court decisions have upheld the right of public employees to join organizations voluntarily, including political parties and labor unions.[19] In recent years, however, the major issue has not been whether public employees can voluntarily join organizations but whether they can be *forced* to join or support organizations. This issue has involved both patronage and forced employee contributions to unions.

For most of U.S. history, patronage dismissals have been common. The winning party had the right to appoint its loyal supporters to office and to remove those who were loyal to or appointed by the opposing party. Patronage was reduced only as legislatures provided merit systems that prohibited patronage appointments and dismissals. In the case of *Elrod v. Burns,* however, the Supreme Court held that the dismissal of nonpolicymaking public employees was an unconstitutional violation of their freedom of association.[20] Justices Brennan, White, and Marshal reasoned that denial of freedom of association can be allowed only when there is a government interest of vital importance. Brennan asserted that the traditional defenses of patronage were insufficient to curtail freedom of association. He believed that patronage promotes inefficiency when it leads to wholesale replacement of large numbers of public employees. Brennan also disagreed that patronage is necessary to maintain political loyalty and to ensure that the electorate's wishes are carried out. He noted that limiting patronage dismissals to policymaking positions is sufficient to achieve the goal of responsiveness. Finally, Brennan was not convinced that patronage is necessary to preserve the political parties. He concluded:

> In summary, patronage dismissals severely restrict political belief and association. Though there is a vital need for government efficiency and effectiveness, such dismissals are on balance not the least restrictive means for fostering that end. There is also a need to insure that policies which the electorate has sanctioned are effectively implemented. That interest can be fully satisfied by limiting patronage dismissals to policy-making positions. Finally, patronage dismissals cannot be justified by contribution to the proper functioning of our democratic process through their assistance to partisan politics since political parties are nurtured by other less intrusive and equally effective methods. More fundamentally, however, any contribution of patronage dismissals to the democratic process does not suffice to override their severe encroachment on First Amendment freedoms. We hold, therefore, that the practice of patronage dismissals is unconstitutional under the First and Fourteenth Amendments.[21]

Although a majority of the Court agreed in *Elrod* that the patronage dismissals were unconstitutional, they failed to agree on exactly why they were unconstitutional. The Court provided additional clarification in *Branti v. Finkel,*[22] a case that involved the patronage dismissal of two assistant public defenders by a newly appointed public defender of the opposition party. Some might assume that assistant public defenders are involved in policymaking and therefore are subject to patronage dismissals per the *Elrod* decision. The Court disagreed, however, saying that the critical question in the permissibility of patronage dismissals is not the label of "policymaker" but rather whether the government can show that party affiliation is necessary for effective performance.[23] If party affiliation is not necessary for effective performance, the need for patronage dismissals is insufficient to justify infringement of public employees' freedom of association.

As a result of *Elrod v. Burns* and *Branti v. Finkel,* public employees cannot be forced to join a political party to keep their jobs. In *Abood v. Detroit Board of Education,* the Supreme Court determined, however, that public employees may be forced to support some of the activities of labor unions.[24] In this case, nonunion teachers in Detroit objected to the use of part of their mandatory union dues for support of the political activities of the union. They claimed that they were forced to pay for political activities of the union with which they disagreed and in which they had no voice. The teachers concluded that such forced contributions violated their freedom of association. The Court disagreed, however, and upheld the constitutionality of the agency shop arrangement, whereby an employee who is not a union member must pay a service fee to the union that is recognized by the employer.

Although a majority of the justices believed that the agency shop constitutes a small infringement on public employees' First Amendment rights, they concluded that it is justified by the legislature's assessment that an agency shop is essential to the maintenance of good labor relations. The Court agreed with the teacher, however, that mandatory contributions to the political activities of the union, as opposed to the union's collective bargaining activities, did constitute an unacceptable infringement on the employees' First Amendment rights. Therefore, the Court said that nonunion public employees can be forced to pay for only the portion of union dues that is required for collective bargaining activities; they cannot be forced to pay for the union's political and social activities. Of course, it is difficult to define which union activities are political and which are not. Also, unions find it troublesome to develop proper accounting procedures for political versus collective bargaining expenses.

Public Employees' Morals and Dress

When the privilege doctrine was in effect, the government regulated many of the personal affairs of public employees; everything from church attendance to appropriate sexual behavior was prescribed. With the demise of the privilege doctrine, however, the courts have demanded that public employers demonstrate that proscribed activities are detrimental to the government's efficiency and performance. For example, the Supreme Court overturned the dismissal of an employee alleged by his public employer to be a homosexual.[25] The Court noted that the employee had a good work record and that there was no security risk involved in his job. Also, the Court noted that the employee had not flaunted his sexual preferences, nor was there any evidence that his sexual preference had any effect on his performance. However, the Court did uphold the dismissal of a homosexual whose behavior was much more open and notorious and thereby sufficient to produce a rational connection between the homosexual behavior and the efficiency of the state. Moreover, the Court is more likely to uphold restrictions on sexual activities when the employee's job involves the national security; the danger in such cases is blackmail by foreign powers. Thus, the crucial issue is the effect of the proscribed activity on the employee's job performance.

The same logic also applies to employees' styles of dress and personal appearance. The Court has generally upheld dress codes and personal appearance codes (for example, length of hair, beards, and so on) when they apply to employees in uniformed organizations, such as police and fire departments. The Court defends such codes as necessary to help the people identify who is a public safety officer. Also, the Court has reasoned that such codes are necessary to prevent internal disruptions in the organizations. The Court is less likely to uphold appearance codes in nonuniformed agencies unless the employer can show that the employee's dress affected operations adversely.

The Supreme Court has upheld city residency requirements that restrict where employees may live,[26] concluding that the requirements are reasonably related to the effectiveness and efficiency of city operations. Such requirements ensure that employees live sufficiently close to be available during an emergency. Also, the requirements theoretically ensure that city employees will be more concerned about their city because they live in it. Moreover, when city employees live in the city, they can help support it by their taxes and purchases from local business. Finally, given the flight of many whites to the suburbs, residency requirements help assure a racially balanced workforce.

Personal Liability of Public Employees

One method by which citizens can control the behavior of public employees is to sue them for tort damages that they cause in the exercise of their official duties. In law, a *tort* is a civil injury or wrong against an individual's constitutional, statutory, or common law rights.[27] The injured individual may sue to recover compensation for the damage to his or her rights. Because public employees must administer thousands of laws, they can be exposed to many tort actions by citizens who believe that they have been injured. If the public employee is held personally liable for a wrong committed in the administration of his or her official duties, he or she must pay for the damages.

For most of U.S. history, public employees enjoyed almost total immunity from personal liability. The two concepts of sovereign immunity and official immunity protected public employees from tort damages.[28] Sovereign immunity is a doctrine that prohibits citizens from bringing suit against a sovereign government unless the government gives it permission. The doctrine, which originated in English common law, is based on the assumption that citizens cannot sue the sovereign that protects their rights. Perhaps it is also based on the desire of courts to avoid excessive judicial intervention in governmental affairs. In any case, it is an ancient concept in common law that has served to protect public employees from tort suits. Official immunity extends to the public employee. Under this immunity, public officials can perform acts that, if done as private citizens, would expose them to tort damage claims.

Over the years, the U.S. government reduced its sovereign immunity. By 1855, the federal government established the Court of Claims and waived its immunity when contracts were in dispute.[29] In 1946, the Court of Claims Act and the Federal Tort Claims Act provided a process whereby citizens could obtain compensation for tort damages. Although the federal government reduced much of its immunity, however, public employees continued to enjoy immunity. In *Barr v. Mateo*, the Supreme Court defended broad official immunity as necessary to assure that public officials are not burdened by a fear of civil suits.[30] The Court believed that such suits would "consume time and energies which would otherwise be devoted to governmental service and the threat of which might appreciably inhibit the fearless, vigorous and effective administration of policies of government."[31]

In *Monroe v. Pape*, the Supreme Court did acknowledge that there may be some limits to official immunity.[32] This case revolved around Section 1983 of the Civil Rights Act of 1871.[33] This act, which was passed after the Civil War, was designed to protect the newly freed slaves against abuses by state governments. Section 1983 reads:

1961

> Every person who, under color of any statute, ordinance, regulation, custom, usage, of any State or Territory, subjects or causes to be subjected, any citizen of the United States or other person within the jurisdiction thereof to the deprivation of any rights, privileges, or immunities secured by the Constitution and laws, shall be liable to the party injured in an action at law, suit in equity or other proceeding for redress.[34]

In *Monroe v. Pape*, the Court employed the seldom-used Civil War statute to hold that the Chicago police had violated constitutional rights protected by Section 1983 and that they could be held liable in a civil suit. The *Monroe* case and Section 1983, on which it is based, applied only to state and local governments and employees. In 1971, however, in *Bivens v. Six Unknown Named Agents of the Federal Bureau of Investigation,* the Supreme Court extended the same level of liability to federal employees.[35] Although the Court acknowledged in both *Monroe* and *Bivens* that public employees are subject to some liability, it failed to define the limits of the liability. In general, the Court continued to provide immunity when the official acted in good faith, without any malicious intent to harm.[36] Thus, public employees generally were liable only when they acted in a brutal, harsh, and arbitrary manner.

In 1975, however, in *Wood v. Strickland,* the Supreme Court seemed to extend the limits of employee liability.[37] The Court stated that a public employee is not immune from liability for damages under Section 1983:

1. if he knew or reasonably should have known that the action he took within his sphere of official responsibility would violate the constitutional rights of the (individuals) affected, or
2. if he took the action with the malicious intention to cause a deprivation of constitutional rights or injury to the (individual).[38]

In *Wood*, the Court seemed to say that good faith, or absence of malicious intent, is not sufficient to protect public employees from liability. The employees must show that they did not know and should not reasonably have known they were violating the constitutional rights of an injured party.[39] Some claim that *Wood* changes good faith from a subjective question of what the official believed at the time to an objective question of what he or she should have known at the time. The same logic and test of *Wood* was extended to federal officials in *Butz v. Economou*.[40] The impact of these decisions has been to expand the personal liability of public employees, because it is easier for an injured party to show their culpability.

The Supreme Court has not only made it considerably easier for citizens to show that public employees are liable for their actions, it has also expanded dramatically the scope of their liability in *Maine v. Thiboutot*.[41] The Court ruled that the phrase "and law" contained within Section 1983 referred not only to laws concerning equal or civil rights but to all federal statutes. Prior to this case, Section 1983 was used to protect only civil rights and equal protection rights. After *Thiboutot*, citizens could use Section 1983 to press damage claims against any state and local employee who violated *any federal statute*, not just constitutional requirements. In addition, the Supreme Court also held in *Maher v. Gagne* that attorney's fees can be awarded to successful litigants in all cases brought under Section 1983. This decision will also encourage an even greater number of liability suits against public employees.[42]

The increased exposure of public employees to personal liability suits for performance of their official duties can have significant consequences. Some believe these Court decisions were necessary to allow citizens protection against unnecessary bureaucratic power.[43] They claim that these decisions may force public employees to take greater care to protect citizens' procedural and substantive rights during the adminstration of official duties. Others, worry, however, that the public employees' increased exposure to liability suits will encourage them to play it safe by doing very little. Public employees may avoid difficult but necessary decisions for fear of being sued, and public administrators may develop various protective measures (such as extensive review processes or many levels of decision) that are designed more to diminish their liability than to respond to the needs of citizens. Thus, procedures may be developed to respond to the exceptional or occasional situation, rather than to the usual and normal circumstance.[44]

Codes of Ethics for Public Employees

In recent years, both state and federal governments have adopted formal codes of ethics and conflict-of-interest laws in response to the Watergate scandals and other well-publicized cases of corruption. Whereas only four states had formal ethics codes before 1960, a majority of the states adopted such codes after 1973.[45] Today, forty-five states have some form of ethics code. Although the federal government adopted the "Code of Ethics for Government Services" in 1958, the most comprehensive attempt by the federal government to establish a code of ethical behavior is found in the Ethics in Government Act of 1978.[46]

The 1978 act provides for financial disclosure by public officials. Moreover, the act also attempts to control what have been referred to as "incestuous" relationships between bureaucrats and the industries that they regulate or from which they buy goods and services. Before the Ethics Act, it was not unusual for a bureaucrat to leave government employment and become an employee of a corporation that had been regulated by his or her former agency. The 1978 Ethics Act attempts to reduce such associations by prohibiting contacts between former top government officials and the agencies in which they once worked. In addition, the law forbids various attempts by former bureaucrats to influence policy over which they once had decision-making authority.

According to Hays and Gleissner, most state ethics codes are little more than conflict-of-interest statutes or financial disclosure laws.[47] Hays and Gleissner found that many state ethics codes contain language that prohibits public employees from accepting any gift given for the purpose of affecting the employees' conduct of their official duties.[48] Furthermore, employees are directed not to use their official positions or state time, equipment, or facilities for private purposes. In addition, public employees are prohibited from selling goods or services to any organization in which they hold a personal financial interest. Finally, employees are not to accept any compensation or employment that might affect their official decisions.[49]

The major criticism of ethics codes is that they are not adequately enforced. Hays and Gleissner found that although most states have ethics commissions to enforce their ethical codes, these commissions are generally understaffed and meet infrequently.[50] There is little evidence that commissions actually investigate violations of state ethics laws. In the Hays and Gleissner survey, only six states reported that they had disciplined workers for ethics code violations in the previous five years.[51] Similarly, there appears to be little enforcement of ethical codes at the federal level. Indeed, it is very likely that a majority of federal employees are not even aware that there is an employee code of conduct.[52] A 1979 effort to have the federal code posted in government offices failed, in part, because only eleven copies were available in the entire federal establishment.[53]

One reason ethics codes may not be enforced is that they are primarily designed as symbolic or political statements to persuade citizens that the government is concerned about the ethics of bureaucrats. Because there are so many professions in government, and because so many different decision-making situations occur, any single, universal code is often so general as to be useless. Ethics codes state general, transcendent values of what ought to be, but they say little about what actually is.[54] Public employees, like most people, might agree to the general principles, but they need guidelines to deal with operational decisions that contain ambiguous ethical dimensions.[55]

Another major criticism of ethics codes is that they generally contain only negative statements about what public employees should not do. By concentrating on sins to be avoided, the codes imply that public employees' propensity to do wrong is greater than their potential to do good. Critics suggest that codes should contain more positive statements concerning what public employees should do as well as what they should avoid.

Financial disclosure laws, like ethics codes, have received considerable criticism. John Rohr notes that many financial disclosure laws are ritualistic in nature because the purpose of disclosure has little relationship to anything except the appearance of having disclosed. Most disclosures do not involve wrongdoing; they concern only the *potential* for wrongdoing. Since it is difficult for public employees to know which of their specific financial assets may be construed to be related to some future decision, they disclose all their assets. For this reason, some people criticize many financial disclosure laws as invasions of public employees' privacy. In addition, some critics believe that such laws discourage many talented individuals from entering public service.

Although ethics codes have received considerable criticism, they do have their defenders. The symbolic nature of most ethics codes has been criticized by some, but others claim that this symbolism is important, because it assures the public that the bureaucracy is governed by legal and ethical norms.[56] Others argue that formal codes of ethics emphasize that the community, not the individual, is the "arbiter of what is ethical."[57]

Discipline

Despite the existence of ethics codes and the possibility of damage suits, public employees sometimes engage in misconduct that demands discipline by public managers. Because disciplining an employee is traumatic for both the supervisor and the employee, it should be done only as a last resort. Management can avoid having to discipline employees in several ways. First, it should assure that the number of rules is minimal and that they are job-related. Second, management should attempt to convince employees that rules are necessary and reasonable. If employees accept the rules as legitimate and appropriate, most discipline will be inner-directed self-discipline. Third, managers should assure that the demands of positions and the skills and abilities of employees are complementary. If they are not, the manager should seek additional training or transfers for misplaced employees. Finally, managers must be sure to explain any rules and to communicate clearly what is expected.

Although managers may attempt to avoid disciplining employees, at times it is unavoidable. If an employee has received clear instructions about what is to be done, and if the supervisor has provided ample counsel concerning how to improve undesirable behavior, discipline is the next logical step if the employee continues substandard performance.

Types of Discipline

The different types of discipline can be organized according to a hierarchy, with increasingly severe levels of discipline being administered until an infraction ceases. The severity of the discipline depends on numerous factors. First, the nature of the offense dictates the necessary level of discipline. Some offenses, such as theft or assault on fellow employees, may require the most severe discipline— summary dismissal—whereas others may require other forms of corrective discipline. Second, the employee's previous work history and length of service in the organization affects the level of discipline. An employee with little seniority who has already committed numerous offenses invites more severe discipline than an employee who has a long, unblemished work record. Third, if an employee has not received proper training for the job expected of him or her, violations may not really be the employee's fault; therefore, discipline may be minimal. Fourth, what has been done in similar cases suggests an appropriate level of discipline.

The various types of discipline can be arranged in a progressive sequence according to their severity. The first type is an oral warning than an employee's actions are unacceptable. The supervisor's interpersonal skills are critical for this type of discipline. Indeed, the supervisor is a crucial component in all forms of discipline. Furthermore, the supervisor must keep good records of employees' performance to provide legal support for possible disciplinary actions. Also, the supervisor must be knowledgeable about appeals and grievance procedures to assure due process for employees. The supervisor must do all these things and still maintain a friendly, supportive relationship with employees—a difficult task.

The second type of discipline is a written warning from the supervisor that the employee's performance has not improved. This is the first step in the formal process of discipline. The written warning is sent to the employee and is also placed in his or her record. It may be used later as documentary evidence in a legal proceeding.

The third level of discipline is a short suspension of several days to one month. This is not very effective, however. If there is no replacement for the employee, the workloads of other employees increase because of the suspension. Moreover, the employee may return to work with a worse attitude than when he or she left. Also, a suspension of even one or two weeks without pay can be a severe financial blow to many employees. The main reason for a short suspension is to provide an immediate solution to a pressing problem. For example, a short suspension may be appropriate for an employee whose constant arguments with fellow workers are disrupting the workplace. A short suspension may also be used to provide time to investigate a serious charge against an employee.

The fourth level of discipline is demotion. Demotion is not a satisfactory method of discipline, however, because it carries a constant stigma that continues to humiliate the demoted employee, who then has little incentive to improve. Since organizations should seek to use the highest skills of individuals, demotion makes sense only when the new assignment makes better use of the employee's skills and abilities.

The most severe form of punishment is discharge. There are numerous reasons for avoiding discharge. First, if an employee appeals the decision and is reinstated, the workplace environment may be considerably worse than the condition that precipitated the dismissal in the first place. Firing also wastes the recruiting and training cost invested in the employee. Moreover, firing can have a traumatic impact on the employee and his family. On the other hand, firing an employee may be the best long-term solution. Some employees may be so disruptive to the environment and morale of the workplace that nothing short of dismissal will suffice. Also, firing a poor performer may create a job opening for a more deserving and better prepared employee. Furthermore, the dismissed employee may find a position that better utilizes his or her skills and interests. Because of the extreme reluctance of most managers to fire an employee, the number of dismissals averages from less than 1 percent to 1.5 percent of public jurisdictions' workforces.

Guidelines for Constructive Discipline

If discipline is to be effective, supervisors and managers should adhere to some commonly accepted guidelines concerning the proper method for administering it.

Clear Rules and Regulations. Management must make certain that employees know what the rules are. New employees should receive written notice of important rules during their orientation, and each employee should have a handbook that describes the rules. When there are changes in the rules or when new ones are issued, management should be sure to communicate them to the employees. Although posting rules and regulations on bulletin boards may meet formal notification requirements, management should also use more informal interpersonal channels to communicate rules to employees. The better job management does in explaining the rules and why they are necessary, the easier it will be to enforce them.

Immediate Discipline. A manager should initiate the disciplinary process as soon as possible after he or she notices the infraction. When the discipline closely follows the violation, the employee is more likely to associate it with the offense, rather than with the supervisor who is imposing the discipline. Immediate discipline does not mean that an employee should be judged hastily or on the basis of incomplete facts. When all the facts are not available, yet immediate action appears mandatory, the employee can be suspended pending investigation and resolution of the problem. The Supreme Court has held that a federal employee can be suspended without pay pending appeal unless "irreparable injury" can be shown by the employee. Loss of pay is not considered an irreparable injury, because the Back Pay Act provides for lost compensation if the employee wins the appeal.[58]

Consistent Discipline. The legitimacy of rules is undermined quickly when management disciplines some employees for a particular offense but fails to discipline others for the same offense. If adequate warning is given by communication of rules, and if discipline is consistent, employees should not be surprised when they are disciplined for violating rules. However, when there is uncertainty regarding whether an offense is to be punished and regarding the degree of punishment, the offender will feel that the supervisor is making arbitrary decisions and will blame the supervisor, rather than the offense, for the discipline.[59] If a rule cannot be enforced or can be enforced against only a small percentage of all offenders, the rule should be dropped.

Due Process. Before initiating any disciplinary action, a manager should have all the relevant facts concerning the alleged offense. The employee should have an opportunity to provide his or her version of the facts. Supervisors and managers should also be aware of the procedural requirements for discipline contained in civil service regulations and in union contracts.

Impersonal Discipline. A manager should always criticize the behavior, not the individual. Whenever an employee is disciplined, he or she is likely to become defensive. This defensiveness is aggravated, however, when the supervisor criticizes the person, rather than the person's behavior. For example, a manager should not discipline an employee for absenteeism by making general references to the employee's laziness or lack or responsibility. Instead, the manager should focus attention on the behavior—that is, the absences. Focusing on behavior allows the manager to counsel the employee about how to change his or her offending behavior. One can change one's behavior more easily than one can change one's personality.

Appeals Procedures

Most public organizations provide several appeals mechanisms that can be used by employees who have grievances. A grievance occurs when employees believe that they have been improperly disciplined or when they think that they have not been treated fairly in the distribution of organizational rewards, such as pay, promotion, and so forth. Indeed, many public organizations provide multiple appeals mechanisms. First, many have established internal appeals procedures, most of which provide for eventual appeal to an appellate group or officer outside the agency. For example, an employee might appeal an agency decision to a civil service board or commission or to the personnel director of a jurisdiction. Second, public organizations that have collective bargaining contracts with unions also have grievance procedures specified in the contract. In addition to these agency and collective bargaining appeal mechanisms, separate appeals systems can exist for equal rights issues, for unemployment compensation, for workers' compensation, and for health and safety regulations.

This maze of appeal systems often creates problems, because employees may not know which system is appropriate for their cases. Since many cases involve more than one issue, several appeals systems can be involved, and overlapping jurisdictions can cause considerable confusion and delay. Both employees and organizations have an interest in the most simple, most efficient, and fastest appeal system possible. Justice delayed is justice denied, and as a case lingers in one or more appeals systems, it tends to disrupt agency operations. Reforms at the federal and state levels in the 1970s tended to reduce the number of separate appeals systems, thereby reducing some of the confusion.

Agency Appeals Procedures

Although there are numerous variations of agency appeals mechanisms, most contain several common steps. Since most organizations place great emphasis on the supervisor's responsibility for resolving grievances at the lowest level possible, the first step requires that the aggrieved employee confer with his or her supervisor about the grievance. In most cases, problems are resolved at this informal first level by means of supervisory counseling. In equal opportunity cases, the employee may discuss his or her case informally with the affirmative action officer before talking informally to the supervisor.

If the supervisor is unable to resolve the problem through informal counseling, the employee may file a formal written grievance. The major reason for this procedure is to document that a formal appeal has been initiated.

The third step is appeal to the head of the agency. This appeal promotes consistency among agency actions. The agency director can assure that different supervisors are processing similar cases in a similar manner and that a uniform agency policy is established.

The fourth step is a formal written appeal to an appellate group or officer outside the agency. Often, this appellate group is the civil service board or commission for the jurisdiction. If the employee is dissatisfied with the decision at this stage, he or she may appeal to the courts.

Negotiated Grievance and Appeals Procedures

Almost all negotiated agreements in government contain grievance procedures with three basic steps.[60] In the first phase, the employee discusses his or her complaint with the supervisor. If the problem cannot be resolved through informal discussions, the employee informs the union grievance committee. If the union decides to appeal the grievance, a written complaint is forwarded to the next management level.

During the second phase in the grievance procedure, the grievance may be appealed to any number of subsequent managerial levels. In large cities, the agency head may make the final pre-arbitration decision. In smaller cities, the city manager or mayor may give the final decision before arbitration. State governments often use agency and department heads and a state grievance committee to make their final decisions before arbitration.

In more than 80 percent of negotiated grievance procedures in the public sector, the last stage is final binding arbitration by a neutral third party.[61] Grievance arbitration may be conducted by a single arbitrator or by a panel of neutral parties. Most jurisdictions do not use panels, however, because of the additional expense. Both management and the union must agree to the selection of an arbitrator. Most arbitrators are chosen from lists provided by the American Arbitration Association (AAA) or the Federal Mediation and Conciliation Service (FMCS). Some jurisdictions hire a permanent arbitrator, who is retained for the length of the contract. The major advantage of a permanent arbitrator is reduction of the selection and scheduling process. Also, a permanent arbitrator is more familiar with the particular contract. Despite these advantages, however, most jurisdictions seek a different arbitrator for each grievance.

Excessive time delays are a major problem in grievance arbitration. Months may pass after a grievance is filed before it reaches arbitration, and another year may go by before the arbitrator gives a decision. Perhaps one reason for the excessive delay is the overjudicialization of the arbitration process, which results from the fact that an overwhelming number of arbitrators are lawyers.

Federal Appeals Procedure

A federal employee can appeal a disciplinary action if it involves suspension for more than fourteen days, reduction in grade or pay, or dismissal. The agency must give thirty days' written notice before the action is imposed. During this time, the supervisor and employee should attempt to resolve the problem. If the problem is not resolved, the employee may respond both orally and in writing to the agency head. Agencies may provide formal hearings, but they are not required to do so. The employee may be represented by an attorney during the oral session with the agency head.

If the employee is dissatisfied with the agency's decision, he or she may appeal to the Merit Systems Protection Board (MSPB) The board generally assigns the case to an administrative law judge or another MSPB employee, who schedules a formal hearing and then makes a decision. The full MSPB may review, reverse, or overturn this decision, and the employee may appeal the decision of the MSPB to the courts.

Conclusion: Control of Public Employee Behavior in Organic and Mechanistic Organizations

Organic organizations exist in unstable environments and administer complex and ambiguous tasks. As a result, these organizations find it difficult to issue rules and regulations that can govern the multitude of issues that develop in the course of administering policy. Furthermore, the existence of too many rules can impair the flexibility needed by organic organizations to respond to their changing environments. Moreover, a higher proportion of the employees in organic organizations are in the administrative, professional, and technical (APT) category, and APT employees tend to find that many rules undermine their professional expertise and autonomy. Since APT employees often seek to fulfill their higher-order needs of autonomy and self-actualization in the workplace, the existence of many rules may thwart their fulfillment of these needs.

Because of the foregoing constraints, organic organizations tend to place more emphasis on what Frederick Mosher describes as "subjective responsibility."[62] This type of responsibility places less emphasis on to whom and for what one *is* responsible and more on to whom and for what one *feels* responsible. Thus, conscience is emphasized, rather than accountability and answerability. Mosher notes that subjective responsibility hinges more on the backgrounds and socialization processes of public employees. In organic organizations, therefore, the backgrounds and professional training of employees become more crucial to the assurance of ethical behavior.

In contrast, mechanistic organizations can rely more on rules to govern the behavior of employees. Because tasks are much simpler in mechanistic organizations, rules can be drafted to cover most problem areas. Moreover, since the environments of mechanistic organizations are more stable, they need not worry about the loss of flexibility caused by the generation of rules. Finally, employees in mechanistic organizations tend to have less education and may value autonomy and discretion less than the employees of organic organizations do. Therefore, they may feel less frustrated by the existence of numerous rules. Thus, mechanistic organizations tend to rely more on what Mosher refers to as "objective responsibility," which connotes the responsibility of a person to "someone else, outside of self, for some thing or some kind of performance."[63]

The tension between objective and subjective responsibility reflects attempts by legislatures and courts to balance the rights of employees and the government's need for efficiency and effectiveness. Although many constraints on public employees' rights have been removed, considerable controls remain. As the percentage of APT employees continues to increase in the public workforce, more employes may resist external controls that they view as discriminatory, arbitrary, and unrelated to their performance. If public organizations become more organic in the future, controls that are essentially negative—describing what should not be done rather than what should be accomplished—may become more anachronistic. As more APT employees enter government service, the primary assurance that administrators will do good as well as avoid wrongdoing will be the government's success in recruiting professionals whose commitment to the public interest exceeds their need for self-aggrandizement.

Notes

1. A. Dotson, "The Emerging Doctrine of Privilege in Public Employment," *Public Adminstration Review* 15 (Spring 1955): 77–88.

2. *McAuliffe v. Mayor of New Bedford*, 155 Mass. 216, 26 N.E. 517 (1892).

3. Deborah Goldman, "Due Process and Public Personnel Management," *Review of Public Personnel Administration* 2 (Fall 1981): 19–27.

4. *Cafeteria Workers v. McElroy*, 36 U.S. 886 (1961).

5. *Goldberg v. Kelly*, 397 U.S. 254 (1970).

6. *Board of Regents v. Roth*, 408 U.S. 564 (1972).

7. Ibid.

8. Goldman, "Due Process and Public Personnel Management," p. 21.

9. *Arnett v. Kennedy*, 416 U.S. 134 (1974).

10. David H. Rosenbloom, "The Employees in Court: Implications for Urban Government," in Charles H. Levine, ed., *Managing Human Resources: A Challenge to Urban Governments* (Beverly Hills, Calif.: Sage, 1977), p. 67.

11. *Bishop v. Wood*, 426 U.S. 341 (1976).

12. Ibid.

13. *Pickering v. Board of Education*, 391 U.S. 563 (1968).

14. James S. Bowman, "Whistle Blowing in the Public Service: An Overview of the Issues," *Review of Public Personnel Administration* 1 (Fall 1980): 15–27.

15. *United Public Workers of America v. Mitchell*, 330 U.S. 75 (1947).

16. *United States Civil Service Commission v. National Association of Letter Carriers*, 413 U.S. 548, (1973).

17. Gerald R. Ford, *Veto of Hatch Act Repeal: Message From the President of the United States* (Washington, D.C.: U.S. Government Printing Office, 1976).

18. Jeffrey C. Rinehart and Lee Brenick, "Political Attitudes and Behavior Patterns of Civil Servants," *Public Administration Review* 35 (November–December 1975): 603–

611. Also see William Pearson, "The Effect of State Hatch Acts on State Executives Political Activities," *Southern Review of Public Administration* 2 (September 1978): 221–238.

19. *Shelton v. Tucker,* 364 U.S. 479 (1960).

20. *Elrod v. Burns,* L.Ed. 2d. 547 (1976).

21. Ibid.

22. *Branti v. Finkel,* 445 U.S. 507 (1980).

23. Neil D. McFeeley, "Patronage: The Public Service and the Courts," *Public Personnel Management* 10 (Fall 1981): 343–351.

24. *Abood v. Detroit Board of Education,* 52 L.Ed. 2d 261 (1977).

25. *Singer v. U.S. Civil Service Commission,* 9th Cir. No. 74–2073 (January 14, 1976).

26. *McCarthy v. Philadelphia CSC,* 47 L.Ed. 2d 366 (1976).

27. Howard Ball, "Toward a Constitutional Law of Torts: The Burger Court and Official Liability." *Southern Review of Public Administration* 6 (Spring 1982): 7–25.

28. Ibid., p. 9.

29. David Rosenbloom, "Public Administrators' Official Immunity and the Supreme Court: Development During the 1970s," *Public Administration Review* 40 (March–April 1980): 166–173.

30. *Barr v. Mateo,* 360 U.S. 564 (1959).

31. Ibid., p. 571.

32. *Monroe v. Pape,* 365 U.S. 167 (1961).

33. *Civil Rights Act of 1871,* U.S.C. Section 1983.

34. Ibid.

35. *Bivens v. Six Unknown Named Agents of the Federal Bureau of Narcotics,* 403 U.S. 388 (1971).

36. Ball, "Toward a Constitutional Law of Torts," p. 15.

37. *Wood v. Strickland,* 420 U.S. 308 (1975).

38. Ibid., p. 322.

39. Paul T. Hardy and J. Devereux Weeks, *Personal Liability of Public Officials Under Federal Law* (Athens, Ga.: University of Georgia, Institute of Government, 1980).

40. *Butz v. Economou,* 438 U.S. 478 (1978).

41. *Maine v. Thiboutot,* 100 S.Ct. 2502 (1980).

42. *Maher v. Gagne,* 100 S.Ct. 2574 (1980).

43. Rosenbloom, "Public Administrators' Official Immunity and the Supreme Court," p. 171.

44. Walter Groszyk and Thomas Madden, "Managing Without Immunity: The Challenge for State and Local Government Officials in the 1980s," *Public Administration Review* 41 (March–April 1981): 272.

45. Steven Hays and Richard Gleissner, "Codes of Ethics in State Government: A Nationwide Survey," *Public Personnel Management* 10 (1981): 48–68.

46. For an analysis of this act, see J. Jackson Walter, "The Ethics in Government Act, Conflict of Interest Laws and Presidential Recruiting," *Public Administration Review* 41 (November–December 1981): 659–666.

47. Hays and Gleissner, "Codes of Ethics in State Government," p. 53.

48. Ibid., p. 54.

49. Ibid., p. 54.

50. Ibid., p. 52.

51. Ibid.

52. James S. Bowman, "The Management of Ethics: Codes of Conduct in Organizations," *Public Personnel Management* 10 (1981): 59–66.

53. Ibid.

54. Gerald Caiden, "Ethics in the Public Service: Codification Misses the Real Target," *Public Personnel Management* 10 (1981): 146–152.

55. Ibid.

56. Kenneth Kernaghan, "Codes of Ethics and Administrative Responsibility," *Canadian Public Administration* 17 (Winter 1974): 527–541.

57. Ralph Chandler, "The Problems of Moral Reasoning in American Public Administration: The Case for a Code of Ethics," *Public Administration Review* 43 (January–February 1983): 34.

58. *Sampson v. Murray*, 415 U.S. 61 (1974).

59. George Strauss and Leonard Sayles, *Personnel*, 4th ed. (Englewood Cliffs, N.J.: Prentice-Hall, 1980), p. 224.

60. Richard Kearnery, *Labor Relations in the Public Sector* (New York: Marcel Dekker, 1984), p. 289.

61. Ibid., p. 290.

62. Frederick Mosher, *Democracy and the Public Service* (London: Oxford University Press, 1968), p. 8.

63. Ibid., p. 7.

13
Conclusion

S everal trends indicate that public organizations will tend to be more organic in the future. First, more and more public employees have higher levels of education. Over 40 percent of public-sector jobs are high-level professional and managerial positions, compared to only 25 percent of those in the private sector.[1] Furthermore, government spending accounted for 42 percent of all professional and managerial jobs in the U.S. economy in 1980 but for only 26 percent of all lower-level positions.[2] In addition, more than one-third of all college graduates were employed by the public sector in 1980. Occupations such as social work, law enforcement, city management, education administration, health administration, and human services administration are increasingly dominated by individuals with professional training and degrees.

Jay Shafritz has noted that as the number of professionals in public organizations increases, there is less need for the traditional, mechanistic organizational structure.[3] Professionals expect to have considerable discretion in how they do their jobs. They reject close supervision and demand to help in deciding how the work is to be done. They also resist proliferating rules that govern their behavior. Furthermore, they want to be involved in establishing performance goals for themselves and in evaluating their progress toward these goals. Finally, they are more likely to seek intrinsic rewards from the work itself.

A second trend indicating the tendency toward organic organizations is the demand for greater productivity in the public sector. When governments' revenues are insufficient to provide the services demanded of them, they must turn to productivity improvement as one solution to this imbalance in demands and revenues. Since the products of governments are often services, productivity improvement in the public sector generally involves increasing the amount and quality of services with the same number of employees. Since over 95 percent of all public workers are employed in service delivery, while only 5 percent are producing goods,[4] improvement in employee motivation is the key to improvement in the delivery of public services.

Future public employees are likely to have college educations and to consider themselves professionals. Such employees are motivated by recognition for successful completion of challenging and worthwhile tasks. Most of the productivity improvement techniques discussed in this book (job enrichment, quality control circles, flexitime, and labor–management committees) imply a movement away from the centralized, hierarchical managerial style that is typical of most mechanistic organizations. Moreover, a primary ingredient in the success of the Japanese style of management is greater employee participation in the operation of the workplace, a characteristic of organic organizations. In chapter 9 of their bestselling book *In Search of Excellence*—entitled "Productivity Through People"— Peters and Waterman note that the best-run American companies realize that their employees are their most important asset.[5] The fundamental lesson from the top companies is, "Treat people as adults. Treat them as partners; treat them with dignity; treat them with respect."[6] The companies described by Peters and Waterman seem to be more organic than mechanistic organizations.

A third trend that indicates the need for organic organizations in government is the growing emphasis on employee rights. As noted in earlier chapters, various laws protect public employees against arbitrary removals. The courts also provide ample protection for the due process rights of public employeers. John Naisbitt, in his bestselling book about the future, *Megatrends,* notes that even in the private sector, the employer's traditional common law right to dismiss employees is being undermined.[7] More and more courts are ruling that private employees have been "wrongfully discharged" and therefore are entitled to sue for damages. These trends indicate that public managers can no longer pursue the directive, authoritarian style of leadership that is common to mechanistic organizations. Public managers must be salesmen, rather than generals; they must persuade as well as direct.

Chapter 5 noted that if leaders have little power to punish or reward, they must depend more on referent power—the power that resides in the leader's charisma and personal attraction. This power is more likely to exist and develop in the employee-oriented leadership style of organic organizations. Peters and Waterman found that outstanding companies had leaders who embodied the chief values of their companies and who were able to communicate these values to their employees, including the lowest-level workers.[8] These findings indicate that the interpersonal style and ability of managers will be crucial in future organic organizations.

A fourth trend indicating the need for a more organic structure is the movement of the baby boom generation through public organizations. The huge number of public employees in the 25-to-40 age group produces terrific competition for comparatively few leadership positions. If these numerous employees are not to be constantly frustrated by the lack of promotion opportunities, they must be able to express themselves and participate in work teams and groups. Moreover, they must receive more intrinsic satisfaction from their work.

A fifth trend indicating a need for organic structures is the decline in the size of the labor force. During the last fifteen years, the entry of the baby boom generation and huge numbers of women into the labor force provided the additional employees needed for economic expansion. For example, women accounted for 60 percent of the growth of the entire U.S. labor force from 1970 to 1980.[9] Even though increased female participation in the workforce will continue in the 1980s, the increase will not be nearly so dramatic as it has been over the past fifteen years. Also, the baby boom is over. Thus, all statistics point to a decrease in the labor force in the next few decades. For example, the number of 14- to 19-year-olds entering the workforce between 1980 and 1990 is expected to decline by 25 percent.[10] Therefore, public organizations will find it more difficult to attract and keep the highly educated, competent employees they will need. Thus, they will increasingly turn to organic structures to provide more attractive work environments.

In conclusion, I would like to return to two of the cultural values discussed in the first chapter—effectiveness (efficiency, productivity) and liberalism (due process, employee rights)—which have significantly affected public personnel management in the past. Generally, when effectiveness was emphasized, employee rights became secondary. There was a tension and conflict between these values. Therefore, it is both surprising and encouraging that the two values may merge in the future to form a common movement toward more organic public organizations.

Notes

1. "Government Spending Generates Jobs," *Public Administration Times*, October 15, 1983, p. 12.
2. Ibid.
3. Jay M. Shafritz, *Position Classification: A Behavioral Analysis for the Public Service* (New York: Praeger, 1973), p. 78.
4. Dianne Layden, "Productivity and Productivity Bargaining," *Public Personnel Management* 9 (1980): 246.
5. Thomas J. Peters and Robert H. Waterman, Jr., *In Search of Excellence: Lessions from America's Best-Run Companies* (New York: Warner Books, 1984).
6. Ibid.
7. John Naisbitt, *Megatrends* (New York: Warner Books, 1982), pp. 186–188.
8. Peters and Waterman, *In Search of Excellence*, pp. 81–86.
9. Joan Lindroth, "How to Beat the Coming Labor Shortage," *Personnel Journal* 61 (April 1982): 268.
10. Ibid.

Index

Abood v. Detroit Board of Education, 235–236, 298

Absenteeism, 115, 185; and dismissal, 172; and flexitime, 212; and illness, 172; and job enrichment, 73, 211; and job satisfaction, 120; and pay, 156, 158, 177; policy, 172; and training and development programs, 195

Achievement-oriented leadership, 124

Achievement tests, 85, 86, 90

Across-the-board cuts, 204

Active representation, 259, 272

Actuarial funding, 176

Adams, John Quincy, 30, 32

Administrative, professional and technical category. *See* APT category

Adverse impact, 87–88, 266–267

Advertising of positions, 14, 57, 83

Affirmative action, 3, 9, 42, 275–280; audit, 279, 283–288; and courts, 276, 277–278; goals and quotas, 276–278; and pay, 285; and performance appraisal, 285; plans, 278–279; and politics, 12; and promotion, 224–225, 278; and recruitment, 283; and retrenchment, 10, 223–225, 249–250; and selection, 284–285; and training and development, 182, 249–250, 277–278, 287–288; and unions, 249–250

Age: and discrimination, 42, 266, 268, 270; and interviews, 93; and performance appraisal, 137, 138

Age Discrimination in Employment Act, 266, 268, 270

Agency shop, 235, 298

Air Force, 213

Albemarle Paper Co. v. Moody, 87, 267

Alternative ranking, 143

American Arbitration Association (AAA), 308

American Federation of Government Employees, 231

American Federation of State, County and Municipal Employees (AFSCME), 169, 231, 250

American Federation of Teachers (AFT), 229, 230, 231

American Tobacco v. Patterson, 205

Appeals, 46–47, 63, 305, 307–309; *see also* Grievance procedures

Application forms, 88–90

Appraisal interview. *See* Interview, appraisal

APT category, 73–74, 101, 102; and productivity improvement, 217–218; and public employee behavior, 309, 310; *see also* Professionals

Aptitude tests, 85, 86, 90–91

Arbitration, 236, 244–246, 308

Argyris, C., 116

Army, 213

Arnett v. Kennedy, 292

Aronson, Sidney, 32

Arrest records and selection, 268

Arthur, Chester, 36

Assessment centers, 83, 93–95, 98, 102

AT&T, 94

Atlanta, 89

Authority, diffusion of, 4

Avoidance, 116

Back Pay Act, 306

Bakke, Allan, 277

Barber, James, 262
Bargaining impasse, 243–246
Bargaining unit, 236–239
Barr v. Mateo, 300
Behavior modification, 115–118, 189; *see also* Reinforcement theory
Behaviorally anchored rating scales (BARS), 139, 142–143
Bell, C., 191
Benefits. *See* Fringe benefits
Biographical data, 81, 83, 89–90, 100
Bishop v. Wood, 293
Bivens v. Six Unknown Named Agents of the Federal Bureau of Investigation, 300
Blackmun, Justice, 292
Blacks. *See* Minorities
Blake, Robert, 194
Blue Cross/Blue Shield, 173
Board of Regents v. Roth, 292
Bonuses, 48, 165, 166, 217
Boston, 89
Bounday-spanning subsystem, 5, 6, 17
Bowers, David, 194
Branti v. Finkel, 297–298
Brennan, Justice, 297
Brownlow Committee, 38–39
Buchanan, James, 32
Budget: and cities, 240; competition in, 15; and human resource planning, 82; and job evaluation, 58, 72; line-item, 207–208; personnel costs, 1–2, 4; and productivity, 207–208; and union negotiations, 240, 242; *see also* Retrenchment
Bumping rights, 205
Burger, Justice, 292
Burns, Tom, 16–18
Butz v. Economou, 301
Buy-out, 216

Cafeteria Workers v. McElroy, 291
Capozzola, John M., 243
Career planning, 14; and job evaluation, 58; and promotion, 98, 100, 101, 102; *see also* Training and development
Carter, Jimmy, 46, 161, 166, 296
Cascio, Wayne, 66
Case studies, 187, 189, 196, 197–198

Central tendency and performance appraisal, 138, 140, 152
Certification election, 239
Chicago, 89
CIA, 234
Cities: and budget, 240; and grievance procedures, 308; and merit system, 28, 40, 50; and minorities, 8; and pensions, 174, 175; and performance appraisal, 142, 143, 144, 145; and productivity measures, 208–209; residency requirements, 89–90, 299; and unions, 240; *see also* Local governments
City managers, 9, 50
Citizenship and employment, 268
Civil Rights Act (1891), Section 1983, 300–301
Civil Rights Act (1964), Title VII, 42, 56, 86, 88, 169, 205, 266, 268–269, 269–270, 276, 278
Civil Service Act (1883), 264
Civil Service Commission, 33, 35–36, 39; and Civil Service Reform Act, 46–47; and equal employment opportunity, 266; and minorities, 264; and political activities of public employees, 294–295; and position classification, 66; and selection, 87
Civil service commissions, 4, 44, 50, 275; *see also* Civil Service Commission
Civil Service Reform Act (1970), 4, 28, 40, 46–50; and Civil Service Commission, 46–47; and job evaluation, 71; and pay-for-performance, 164–166; and performance appraisal, 46, 47, 49, 57, 132, 148–149, 151, 165–166; and position classification, 46, 47; and recruitment, 46, 47; and unions, 234, 237; and whistle-blowing, 294
Claims audit, 173
Classification Act (1923), 38, 66, 265
Classification Act (1949), 39, 66
Cleveland, Grover, 36–37
Clientele of public organizations, 15
Closed career systems, 36
Closed shop, 235
"Code of Ethics for Government Service," 302

Colby, P.W., 165
Collective bargaining, 15, 41, 58, 70–71, 137; *see also* Unions
Communication and performance appraisal, 133
Community of interest, 237
Comparable worth, 42, 57, 168–170, 269, 272; *see also* Women, and pay
Compensation of personnel, 3, 7, 10, 24, 41; *see also* Fringe benefits; Pay
Competitors of public organizations, 15–16
Compulsory arbitration, 228, 244–246
Compulsory retirement, 270
Computer innovation, 12, 182, 217
Concurrent validity, 84–85
Conflict-of-interest laws, 5, 302–303
Connecticut, 238
Connecticut v. Teal, 88, 267
Consideration and leadership, 121–122
Construct validity, 91
Content theories of motivation, 108, 109–112, 115, 118, 126
Content validity, 85
Contingency analysis of personnel management, 16–21, 23–26, 125–126, 150, 177
Contractors, federal, 276, 278
Contrast effect and performance appraisal, 138
Control group designs, 195–196
Coordination of benefits (COB), 173
Cost-of-living adjustments, 175–176
Counseling; and performance appraisal, 131, 146, 186; and promotion, 100–101
County governments, 43, 158, 161; *see also* Local governments
County of Washington v. Gunther, 169, 269
Court of Claims, 300
Court of Claims Act, 300
Courts: and affirmative action, 276, 277–278; and dismissal, 314; and minorities, 42; and pay discrimination, 169–170; and performance appraisal, 149–150; and residency requirements, 89; and selection, 57, 86–88, 89–90; and seniority, 205–206; and strikes, 246–

27; and unions, 234–236; *see also* U.S. Supreme Court
Courturier, Jean J., 251
Criterion-related validity, 84–85
Curtis, George William, 33

Daley, Richard, 45
Damage suits against public employees. *See* Liability of public employees
Dan River Steam Station, 86
Decision of 1789, 30
Deconstitutionalization, 292–293
Decotiis, T.A., 143
De Marco, John, 196–197
Democratic party, 12, 32, 296
Demographic conditions, 7–8, 314–315; and human resource planning, 82; and productivity, 209; and representative bureaucracy, 259
Demotion, 133, 286–287, 305
Design of organization, 18–19
Desk audit, 60–61, 67
Dessler, Gary, 108
Detroit, 89, 278
Development. *See* Training and development
Directive leadership, 124
Disability insurance, 161, 170
Discharge. *See* Dismissal
Discipline, 290, 303–306; *see also* Demotion; Dismissal; Suspension
Discrimination. *See* Affirmative action; Courts; Equal employment opportunity; Minorities
Dismissal, 3–4, 305; and absenteeism, 172; appeals, 305; and due process, 3, 44, 290–293, 306, 314; and merit system, 30; number of, 43; and patronage, 297–298; and performance appraisal, 133; and probation period, 98; protection from, 43–44; and unions, 240, 249
Distinguished Executive Award, 48
Doherty, Mary H., 168
Dress codes, 299
Drucker, Peter, 144
Due process rights, 3, 44, 290–293, 306, 314
Dues checkoff, 235–236
Duke Power Co., 86

Early retirement, 174–175, 176
Eaton, Dorman, 33
Economic conditions, 4, 10; and performance appraisal, 10; and recruitment, 80–81, 83
Effectiveness, 9–10, 51, 315; and productivity, 207, 218; and recruitment, 80; and training and development, 182, 192
Efficiency, 206–207
Effort-to-performance expectancy, 113–114
Eisenhower, Dwight D., 39, 265
Election Campaign Act, 295–296
Eligibility lists, 95–97
Elitism and public service, 29, 31, 51
Elrod v. Burns, 297–298
Employee-centered leadership, 122, 138
Employee participation, 117
End run, 240
Engineers, 41, 67
Englewood, Colorado, 251
Environment of organization, 5–18
Equal employment opportunity, 42, 266–271; *see also* Equal Employment Opportunity Commission
Equal Employment Opportunity Act, 42, 273–274
Equal Employment Opportunity Commission, 56; guidelines, 271–272, 276; and selection, 87, 89, 266, 268–269
Equality of opportunity, 257–258, 263, 264–265
Equity theory, 114–115, 118, 125
Essay and performance appraisal, 139, 144
Esteem needs, 109, 110–111
Ethics codes, 5, 26, 290, 302–303
Ethics in Government Act (1978), 302
Evaluation of personnel, 2
Examination boards, 34
Examinations. *See* Tests
Executive Order 642, 294–295
Executive Order 8802, 265
Executive Order 10988, 41, 230, 234
Executive Order 11246, 266, 276, 278
Executive Order 11375, 278
Executive Order 11491, 237
Executive Order 11748, 276
Exit interview, 14

Expectancy theory of motivation, 112–114, 118, 146; and pay, 164; and performance appraisal, 146; and training and development, 184
Extinction, 116
Extrinsic rewards, 120, 124

Fact-finding, 236, 244
Factionalism and public employees, 43, 44–45
Factor ranking, 56, 64, 68–70, 71–72
Fair Employment Practices Committee (FEPC), 265
FBI, 234
Federal Aviation Administration, 213
Federal Employees Activities Act, 296
Federal Executive Institute seminar, 165
Federal Labor Relations Authority (FLRA), 234, 241
Federal Mediation and Conciliation Service, 244, 308
Federal Pay Comparability Act (1970), 158
Federal Salary Reform Act (1962), 158
Federal Tort Claims Act, 300
Federalist party, 30–31, 51
Feiulle, Peter, 245
Fillmore, Millard, 32
Final-offer arbitration, 244–245, 246, 308
Financial disclosure laws, 302–303
Fire departments, 6, 99; dress codes, 299; and early retirement, 175; and job enlargement, 209, 210, and minorities, 275; and pensions, 174; and strikes, 245, 247; and unions, 228, 229, 231, 233–234, 235, 238, 241, 248, 250; and women, 264
Firefighters Local 1784 v. Stotts, 205–206, 223–225
Firing. *See* Dismissal
Flexitime, 12, 125, 209, 212–213, 218, 314
Florida, 237
Forbidden topics of negotiation, 240, 241
Forced-choice checklists, 144
Forced distribution, 144
Ford, 94
Ford, Gerald, 161, 296
Foreign Service, 70, 99
Forest Service, 99

Freedom of association, 290, 292, 296–298
Freedom of speech, 290, 292, 293–294
French, W., 191
Fried, Robert, 8–10
Fringe benefits, 13–14, 161, 170–176, 177–178; and affirmative action, 285–286; and equal employment opportunity, 269–270; and motivation, 124–125; and organizational effectiveness, 156–157; and salary surveys, 161; and unions, 171, 228, 248–249
Fullilove v. Klutznick, 278
Functional representation. *See* Active representation

Ganschinietz, Bill, 63–64, 72
Garfield, James A., 33, 34, 35
General Accounting Office, 48
General Electric, 94
Gleissner, Richard, 302–303
Goldberg v. Kelly, 291–292
Golembiewski, R.T., 197–198, 212
Goodsell, Charles, 11–12
Grade inflation, 4, 43, 45–46, 59
Graft and corruption, 37
Grant, Ulysses S., 33, 34
Graphic rating scale, 139–142, 144, 152
Great Britain, civil service, 28, 33, 36, 258
Greiner, John M., 210, 215–216
Greiner, Wendy M., 167
Grid organization development, 125, 183, 194–195
Grievance procedures, 9, 14, 26, 290, 307–309; and job evaluation, 58; and states, 308; and unions, 241, 249, 250, 307
Griggs v. Duke Power Company, 42, 86, 266–267
Guiteau, Charles, 35

Hackman, J. Richard, 113
Halo effect, 138, 140, 152
Handicapped, discrimination against, 42
Harriman, Ann, 168
Hatch Acts, 44, 295–296
Hawaii, 237, 239
Hayes, Rutherford B., 33, 34
Hays, Stephen, 302–303

Health insurance, 161, 170, 171, 172–173
Health maintenance organizations (HMOs), 173
Heisel, W. Donald, 236
Helfand, Gary, 214
Heneman, H.G., 143
Herzberg, Frederick, 109, 111–112, 118, 125, 210
Hiring freezes, 204
Holidays, 161, 170, 171, 172
Holmes, Oliver Wendell, 291
Homosexuals, 268–269, 298–299
Hoover, Herbert, 264
Hoover Commission, 38, 39, 40
Horton, Raymond, 216
Hospitals, 6, 14, 15–16, 157
House, Robert, 122–123
Human resource planning, 81–83; and budget, 82; and performance appraisal, 133; and promotion, 100; and retrenchment, 202
Huse, Edgar F., 190

IBM, 94
Image of government, 82–83
Immunity of public employees, 290, 299–302
Impasse resolution. *See* Bargaining impasse
In-basket test, 94, 189
In Search of Excellence (Peters and Waterman), 314
Incident processes, 187, 190, 197–198
Inducement-contribution calculation, 13–14
Inelastic demand for public service, 232
Ingraham, P.W., 165
Initiating structure and leadership, 121–122
Instrumentality, 113
Insurance, 161, 170, 171, 172–173
Intelligence tests, 90–91
Intergroup interventions, 125, 193
International Association of Firefighters, 231
International City Management Association, 208–209
Interpersonal bias, 142
Interview: appraisal, 146–148, 150, 152; and job analysis, 60; and minorities,

93; and performance appraisal, 146–148, 150, 152; and promotion, 98; and recruitment, 81, 83; and selection, 91, 92–93; and women, 93
Intrinsic rewards, 120, 136
Iowa, 237

Jackson, Andrew, 31–33, 257, 279
Jacobs, Rich, 143
Japan, productivity improvement, 213–214, 218–219
J.C. Penney, 94
Jefferson, Thomas, 30, 32, 258, 279, 294
Job analysis, 38, 55, 60–61, 62; and interview, 60; and pay, 163; and performance appraisal, 150; and selection, 92, 94; and training and development, 183
Job classification. *See* Position classification
Job description, 61–62; customizing, 43, 45; inflation of, 45–46; and job evaluation, 57; and job satisfaction, 121
Job design, 6, 13, 14, 100
Job enlargement, 209–210
Job enrichment, 314; and local governments, 73, 210; and motivation, 112, 117, 125; and position classification, 210; and productivity, 209, 210–212, 217–218; and state governments, 73, 210; and turnover, 73, 211; and unions, 210, 211–212
Job evaluation, 13, 14, 55–74; and budget, 58, 72; and career development, 58; and Civil Service Reform Act, 71; and collective bargaining, 58, 70–71; and contingency approach, 23; location of, 59; and mechanistic organizations, 72–74; methods, 63–70; and organic organizations, 72–74; and pay, 56–57, 63, 69, 71, 72, 163, 169; and performance appraisal, 56, 57–58, 72; and recruitment, 56, 57, 67, 84, 86; and selection, 56, 57, 67; and state governments, 64; and training and development, 56, 58, 67; and unions, 58, 70–71; and women, 168–169, 170

Job Evaluation and Pay Review Task Force, 67
Job Evaluation Policy Act (1970), 66–67
Job rotation, 187, 188, 197
Johnson, Andrew, 33, 34
Johnson, Lyndon, 266, 276
Jones, M.R., 108
Jump, Bernard, 176

Kafry, Ditsa, 143
Kahn, Robert, 156–157
Kaiser Aluminum, 277–278
Katz, Daniel, 156–157
Katzell, R., 206
Keeley, Michael, 146
Kelly, Joe, 108
Kennedy, John F., 41, 42, 230, 234, 266
Kingsley, J. Donald, 258
Klingner, Donald, 62

Labor costs, 3–4, 15
Labor-management committees, 121, 209, 215–216, 218, 314
Lacho, Kenneth J., 134, 143, 144, 147
Last hired, first fired, 205, 223, 270
Lateral entry, 36, 74, 80, 98–99
Lawler, Edward E., 73, 110, 113, 114, 120, 157–158
Layoffs: and affirmative action, 286; and equal opportunity, 205–206, 270; and performance appraisal, 133; and seniority, 133, 203, 204–205, 249, 270; and unions, 223–225
Leaderless group discussion (LGD), 94
Leadership, 314; and motivation, 108, 121–122, 125–126; situational factors, 122–124; testing, 102
Learning, 184, 195
Lectures, 187, 188–189, 196, 197
Legal issues. *See* Courts
Leniency and performance appraisal, 140, 144, 152
Lewin, Kurt, 112
Liability of public employees, 290, 299–302
Liberalism, 8–9, 315; and productivity, 218; and recruitment, 80
Life insurance, 161, 170
Lincoln, Abraham, 33
Line managers, 59–60, 94
Little Hatch Acts, 295–296

Lloyd–LaFollette Act, 43–44, 292
Local governments: and job enrichment, 73, 210; and merit system, 37–38, 43, 45–50; and minorities, 274–275; and pay, 158, 161, 164, 166–167, 273, 275; and pensions, 174, 175; and political activities of public employees, 295–296; and position classification, 64; and promotion, 101; and quality circles, 213; and retrenchment, 201–202; and training and development, 196; and unions, 41, 101, 229, 233–235; and women, 273; *see also* Cities; Counties
Long, Norton, 259

McConomy, Steven, 63–64, 72
McGehee, William, 185
McKinley, William, 37
Madison, James, 30
Maher v. Gagne, 301
Maine v. Thiboutout, 301
Maintenance subsystem, 5, 7, 10, 19
Management by objective, 10, 12; and performance appraisal, 139, 144–146; and productivity, 209
Management-rights clauses, 249
Managerial subsystem, 5, 7
Mandatory topics of negotiation, 240
Marion, North Carolina, 293
Markham, Steve, 172
Marshall, Thurgood, 297
Maslow, Abraham H., 109; *see also* Needs, theory of
Massachusetts, 239
Mechanistic organizations, 16–21, 23–26; and job evaluation, 72–74; and motivation, 125–126; and pay, 177; and performance appraisal, 150; and productivity improvement, 217–218; and promotion, 102–103; and public employee behavior, 309–310; and selection, 101–102; and training and development, 197; and unions, 230
Mediation, 236, 244
Megatrends (Naisbitt), 314
Meier, Kenneth J., 262
Merit pay, 10, 46, 50, 164, 168, 209
Merit system: and cities, 25, 40, 50; development, 27–42; and local government, 37–38, 43, 45–50; and

minorities, 264; problems, 43–46; and selection, 96; and state governments, 43, 49–50; and union development, 229
Merit Systems Protection Board (MSPB), 46, 47, 309
Meritorious Executive Awards, 48
Miami, 89
Michigan, 239
Minimum qualifications, 88–90
Minnesota, 239
Minorities, 28, 42, 257–288; and assessment centers, 94; and cities, 8; and interviews, 93; and local governments, 274–275; numbers in public service, 271–275; and pay, 56–57; and performance appraisal, 137, 138, 269; and position classification, 67; and promotion, 101, recruitment, 8, 83; and retrenchment, 205–206, 223–225, 249–250, 270; and selection, 86–88, 93, 94, 268–269; and seniority, 205–206; and state governments, 274–275; training and development, 182; *see also* Affirmative action; Equal employment opportunity
Model Public Personnel Administration Law, 50
Monroe, James, 30
Monroe v. Pape, 300
Moore, Perry, 145, 146
Morale: and flexitime, 212; and fringe benefits, 171; and job enrichment, 73; and quality circles, 215; and residency requirements, 89–90; and retrenchment, 203–204, 206
Morals of public employees, 298–299
Mosher, Frederick, 28, 37, 38, 74, 259, 309–310
Motivation, 2, 7; definition, 108; and job enrichment, 112, 117, 125; and leadership, 108, 121–122, 125–126; and learning, 184; and mechanistic organizations, 125–126; model of, 118–120; and organic organizations, 125–126; and pay, 115, 124–125, 164; and performance appraisal, 107–108, 124; and personnel functions, 124–125; and productivity, 125, 313; and retrenchment, 203–204; theories

of, 109–118; and training and development, 125
Motivation-hygiene theory. *See* Two-factor theory of motivation
Mouton, Jane, 194

Naisbitt, John, 314
Nalbandian, John, 139, 151
NASA, 166
National Civil Service League, 50
National Civil Service Reform League, 34
National Education Association, 229, 230, 231
National Federation of Federal Employees, 231
National Labor Relations Board, 234
National Park Service, 99
National Treasury Employees Union, 231
Navy, 213, 264
Needs, theory of, 109–111, 118
Netherworld of public personnel management, 45–46
Neuse, Stephen M., 170
New Deal, 12
New York City: bargaining units, 237; police, 205, 268
New York City Customs House, 33
New York Civil Service Reform Association, 34
New York state, 237, 239
Nigro, Lloyd, 196–197, 262
Nixon, Richard M., 276
Norris decision, 270

Objective performance evaluation, 10
Office of Personnel Management, 47, 48, 149
Office of Special Counsel, 47
Office of Strategic Services, 93–94
Official immunity, 299–300
Ohio State University, 121–122
On-the-job training, 187, 196, 197
Open-systems view of management environment, 5–7, 23
Operations analysis, 185–186
Oral tests, 91–92
Oral warnings to employees, 304
Oregon, 238

Organic organizations, 16–21, 23–26, 313–315; and job evaluations, 72–74; and motivation, 125–126; and pay, 177; and performance appraisal, 150; and productivity improvement, 217–218; and promotion, 101–103; and public employee behavior, 309–310; and selection, 101–102; and training and development, 197–198
Organization development (OD), 183, 191–195, 196–197, 198
Organizational analysis, 185
Orientation programs, 97–98
Overprotection of public employees, 43–44

Paired-comparison ranking, 143
Participative leadership, 124
Passive representation, 259, 272
PATCO, 231
Path-goal theory of leadership, 123–124, 126; and performance appraisal, 147
Patronage, 5, 31–34, 50, 80, 297
Pay: and affirmative action, 285; caps, 48, 49, 149, 166; and Civil Service Reform Act, 164–166; and equal employment opportunity, 268; equity, 56–57, 157–158, 162–163, 177; and external pay analysis, 63, 69; importance to employees, 157, 164–165; and job evaluation, 56–57, 63, 69, 71, 72, 163, 169; and local governments, 158, 161, 164, 166–167, 273, 275; and mechanistic organizations, 177; merit, 10, 46, 50, 164–168, 209; and minorities, 56–57; and motivation, 115, 124–125, 164; and organic organizations, 177; and organizational effectiveness, 156–157; and performance appraisal, 131, 132, 133, 137, 146, 149, 163–168, 186; plans, 162–163; and position classification, 63, 69–71, 162; and productivity, 209; schedules, 162–163; and seniority, 137, 163, 279; and state governments, 158, 161, 164, 167–168, 273, 275; and strikes, 246, 247, 248; and suspension, 306; and turnover, 156, 158, 177; and unions,

228, 236, 240; and women, 8, 42, 269, 272; *see also* Comparable worth; Courts, and pay discrimination

Pearce, Jane L., 149, 164–165, 166

Peer evaluation, 134–136, 150

Pendleton Act of 1883, 34, 35–36, 43, 51, 294

Pensions, 161, 170, 173–176; and states, 174, 175; and unions, 228; and women, 270

Performance appraisal, 7, 14, 39, 131–152; and affirmative action, 285; and age, 137, 138; and cities, 142, 143, 144, 145; and Civil Service Reform Act, 46, 47, 49, 57, 132, 148–149, 151, 165–166; and counseling, 131, 146, 186; and courts, 149–150; and dismissal, 133; and economic conditions, 10; and equal employment opportunity, 269; evaluator, 134–139, 151–152, 259; and interview, 146–148, 150, 152; and job analysis, 150; and job evaluation, 56, 57–58, 72; and law, 149–150; and layoffs, 133; and management by objective, 139, 144–146; and mechanistic organizations, 150; methods, 139–146; and minorities, 137, 138, 269; and motivation, 107–108, 124; and organic organizations, 150; and pay, 131, 132, 133, 137, 146, 149, 163–168, 188; process, 134–146; and promotion, 98, 100–101, 131, 132, 133, 146; purposes, 132–133; and retirement, 270; and states, 133, 142, 143, 144, 145–146; and training and development, 131, 132, 133, 146, 183, 186; and women, 137, 138

Performance tests, 91

Performance-to-outcome expectancy, 113–114

Perrow, Charles, 207

Perry, James L., 149, 164–165, 166

Person analysis, 186

Personality tests, 90–91, 102

Peters, Thomas J., 314

Physical agility tests, 268

Physical restrictions and selection, 268

Physiological needs, 109, 110–111

Pickering v. Board of Education, 293–294

Pierce, Franklin, 32

Pittsburgh, 89

Police: dress codes, 299; and effectiveness measure, 208, 209; and minorities, 275; and pensions, 174, 175; and productivity measures, 210; and strikes, 245, 247; training, 14; and unions, 228, 229, 231, 241, 248; and women, 205, 264

Political Activities Act, 295

Political activities of public employees, 294–296

Politics, 10–12; and affirmative action, 12; and pay, 167; and productivity improvement, 207; and Senior Executive Service, 48–49; and unions, 12, 230–234, 235–236, 240

Polk, James K., 32

Porter, Lyman, 113, 120

Position classification, 9, 13, 38, 39, 56; appeals, 63; defined, 63; and Civil Service Reform Act, 46, 47; and factor ranking, 71–72; history of, 66–67; and job enrichment, 210; and minorities, 67; and pay, 63, 69–71, 162; process of, 67–68; and recruitment, 57; rigidity, 43; and training and development, 2, 183; and unions, 240, 249, 250

Position description. *See* Job description

Position ranking, 64

Positive reinforcement, 116

Postal Reorganization Act (1970), 234

Powell, Justice, 292

Practice of Management, The (Drucker), 144

Predictive validity, 85

Pregnancy, and discrimination, 270

President's Committee on Equal Employment Opportunity (PCEEO), 266

President's Committee on Government Employment Policy (PCGEP), 265

Private sector, 2–5; and assessment centers, 94; and pay, 157, 168–169; and unions, 229, 231–233, 250

Privilege doctrine, 234, 291–292

Probationary periods, 98, 249
Problem-solving ability, development of, 192, 198
Process theory of motivation, 108, 112–115, 118, 126
Production-centered leadership, 122, 138
Production subsystem, 5, 6, 10, 12
Productivity, 4, 10, 185, 202, 313–314; and bonuses, 217; improvement measures, 209–217; and job enrichment, 209, 210–212, 217–218; meaning of, 206–207; and mechanistic organization, 217–218; and motivation, 125, 313; obstacles to improvement, 207–208; and organic organizations, 217–218; and pay, 209; and retrenchment, 204, 206–219; and sick leave, 172
Productivity bargaining, 12, 209, 216–217
Proehl, C.W., 197–198, 212
Professionals, 18, 28, 40, 313–315; numbers employed in public service, 1, 40; recruitment, 41, 82–83; and unions, 241; *see also* APT category
Programmed instruction, 187, 189, 196, 197
Promotion, 39; and affirmative action, 224–225, 278; and assessment centers, 94; and career planning, 98, 100, 101, 102; and counseling, 100–101; and interviews, 98; and mechanistic organizations, 102–103; and minorities, 101; and organic organizations, 101–103; and performance appraisal, 98, 100–101, 131, 132, 133, 146; and personnel functions, 100–101; and seniority, 86, 98, 99, 100, 101, 102–103, 224–225; and training and development, 101; and unions, 98, 99, 101, 249; from within, 98–100; and women, 101
Property rights in federal jobs, 292–293
Proposition 13, 251
Public Employee Relations Board (PERB), 235, 241
Pullman-Standard v. Swint, 205
Punishment, 116

Quality circles, 12, 125, 209, 213–215, 218, 314

Questionnaires: and job analysis, 61, 67; and job description, 121; and survey feedback, 193–194

Ramspeck Act, 265
Rank-in-person, 36, 40, 41, 47; and job evaluation, 64, 70, 73–74; and promotion, 99, 100
Rank-in-position, 36, 47; and promotion, 99, 100
Ranking scales in performance analysis, 139
Rating scales. *See* Behaviorally anchored rating scales (BARS)
Rawls, J.R., 157
Reagan, Ronald, 166, 230–231
Recency, and performance appraisal, 138
Recruitment, 2, 6, 14, 79–103; and affirmative action, 283; and Civil Service Reform Act, 46, 47; and competition, 16; interviews, 81, 83; and job evaluation, 56, 57, 67, 84, 86; literature, 57; and minorities, 8, 83; and position classification, 57; and professionalism, 41, 82–83; and training and development, 182–183
Reduction in force (RIF), 249–250, 270; *see also* Retrenchment, 249–250, 270
References and recruitment, 81, 83, 90
Referendums and union settlements, 234, 251
Rehnquist, William, 292
Reinforcement theory, 108, 115–118, 126, 164, 184; *see also* Behavior modification
Replacement rates, 174–175
Representative bureaucracy, 9, 25, 257–264, 279
Republican party, 12, 35, 264
Residency requirement, 89–90, 299
Responsiveness of bureaucracy, 9, 80
Retirement benefits, 174–175, 270; *see also* Pensions
Retrenchment, 4, 10, 201–206; and affirmative action, 10, 223–225, 249–250; analytical skills, 203; and minorities, 205–206, 223–225, 249–250, 270; and motivation, 203–204; and productivity, 204, 206–219; and seniority, 10, 203, 205–206; and states, 201–202; and unions, 204,

249–250; and women, 205–206, 249–250, 270; *see also* Layoffs; Reduction in force (RIF)
Reverse discrimination, 42, 257–258, 277–278
Right-to-work laws, 235
Rohr, John, 303
Role analysis technique (RAT), 192–193
Role playing, 187, 190, 191, 196, 197–198
Roll, J. and D., 213
Roosevelt, Franklin D., 39, 265
Roosevelt, Theodore, 37, 294–295
Rosenbloom, David, 292–293
Rule of one, 249
Rule of three, 96–97, 249

Safety needs, 109, 110–111
St. Paul, 89
Salaries. *See* Pay
Salary surveys, 13, 16, 56, 158–161, 169
San Francisco, 251
Sanitation workers, 6, 217, 229
Satisfaction with job, 120–121, 158, 161
Schick, Richard P., 251
Schoolboards, 240, 241, 293–294
Schwab, D.P., 143
Scientific management, 27, 28, 37–38, 72
Scott, Dow, 172
Sears, 94
Security clearance, 269, 291, 299
Selection of personnel, 6, 8, 79–103; and affirmative action, 284–285; and courts, 57, 86–88, 89–90; and equal employment opportunity, 266–267, 268–269; instruments, 83–86, 95–97, 101–103, 133; interviews, 91, 92–93; and job analysis, 92, 94; and job evaluation, 56, 57, 67; and mechanistic organizations, 101–102; and minorities, 86–88, 93, 94, 268–269; and organic organizations, 101–102; and unions, 240, 249; and women, 86, 96, 268
Self-actualization needs, 109, 110–111
Self-evaluation, 134, 136, 150
Senior civil service, 39–40, 46; *see also* Senior Executive Service
Senior Executive Service, 40, 47–49, 70; and bonuses, 48, 165, 166, 217; and minorities, 273; and pay, 165; and

performance appraisal, 148–149; and women, 272
Seniority, 3; and affirmative action, 287; and courts, 205–206; and layoffs, 133, 203, 204–205, 249, 270; and minorities, 205–206; and pay, 137, 163, 279; and promotion, 86, 98, 99, 100, 101, 102–103, 224–225; and retrenchment, 10, 203, 205–206; and unions, 204, 223–225; and women, 205–206
Sensitivity training groups, 187, 190–191, 192–193, 196
Service Employees International Union (SEIU), 231
Services, classification of, 38
Sexual harassment, 8
Sexual preference. *See* Homosexuals
Shafritz, Jay, 43, 45, 72, 73, 313
Sick leave, 161, 170, 171–172
Sink, D., 197–198
Skills inventory, 82
Skinner, B.F., 115
Social needs, 109, 110–114
Social and recreational programs, 288
Social Security, 43, 149, 174–175
Socialization of bureaucrats, 260–262
Socioeconomic background of bureaucrats, 260–262
Sociological representation. *See* Active representation
Sovereign immunity, 299
Spero, Sterling, 243
Spoils system, 28, 31–34, 51, 257
Stalker, G.M., 16–18
State governments: ethics codes, 302–303; and grievance procedures, 308; and job enrichment, 73, 210; and job evaluation, 64; and merit system, 43, 49–50; and minorities, 274–275; number of public employees, 1–2, 4; and pay, 158, 161, 164, 167–168, 273, 275; and pensions, 174, 175; and performance appraisal, 133, 142, 143, 144, 145–146; and political activities of public employees, 295–296; and promotion, 101; and quality circles, 213; quotas in hiring, 5; and retrenchment, 201–202; and unions, 4, 101, 229, 230, 231, 233–236, 237,

238–239, 240–241; and vacations and holidays, 171; and women, 273
Staton, Ted, 145, 146
Stearns, G. Kent, 134, 143, 144, 147
Stewart, Justice, 292
Stotts, Carl, 223
Strikes, 15, 228, 229, 245, 246–248, 250; and courts, 246–247
Supervisors: and discipline, 304; and unions, 238–239, 250
Supervisory coaching, 187, 188, 196, 197
Supportive leadership, 124, 125–126
Survey feedback, 193–194
Suskin, Harold, 70
Suspension of employees, 304–305, 306
Suttle, J.L., 110, 114
Systems awards. *See* Fringe benefits

T-groups, 190–191, 192, 197–198
Taft, William Howard, 264
Tardiness, 212
Targeted cuts, 204
Task analysis, 185
Taylor, Frederick, 38
Taylor, Zachary, 32
Teachers: strikes, 246; unions, 229, 230, 231, 233–234, 235, 241
Team building, 125, 192–193
Teamsters Union, 231
Technological conditions, 12, 13, 18, 23
Temporary appointments, 43, 45
Tests: administration, 95–97; and leadership, 102; and promotion, 98; validity, 84–86, 90–92; and recruitment, 81, 83–86; and selection, 95–97, 102
Thayer, Fred, 48
Thompson, Duane, 149–150
Thompson, Frank, 263
Time-series evaluation, 196
Tolman, Edward C., 112
Torts, 299
Training and development, 2, 7, 14, 38, 181–198; and affirmative action, 112, 249–250, 277–278, 287–288; costs, 186–189, 196; evaluation of, 195–196; and job analysis, 183; and job evaluation, 56, 58, 67; and job satisfaction, 121; and learning, 184, 195; and mechanistic organizations,

197; methods, 187–191, 196–197; and minorities, 182; and motivation, 125; and needs, assessment of, 185–187; and organic development, 197–198; and performance appraisal, 131, 132, 133, 146, 183, 186; and position classification, 2, 183; and professionals, 40; and promotion, 101; and recruitment, 182–183; and turnover, 185, 195; and unions, 182; and women, 182
Transfers, 287
Transit workers, 248, 250
Truman, Harry S., 265
Turnover, 14; and equity, 115; and human resource planning, 82; and job enrichment, 73, 211; and job satisfaction, 120; and pay, 156, 158, 177; of police officers and firefighters, 175
Two-factor theory of motivation, 111–112, 125, 210
Tyer, Charlie B., 134, 142, 143, 144, 145, 147

Unemployment and government hiring. *See* Economic conditions
Uniform Guidelines on Employee Selection Procedures, 87
Unions, 15, 28, 40, 41, 228–251; and affirmative action, 249–250; bargaining units, 236–239; and budget, 240, 242; certification elections, 239; and Civil Service Reform Act, 234, 237; contributions to, 297–298; and courts, 234–236; development and growth, 228–231; and discipline, 250; and dismissals, 240, 249; and flexitime, 213; and fringe benefits, 171, 228, 248–249; and grievance procedures, 241, 249–250, 307; impact on management, 248–250; and impasse resolution, 243–246; and job enrichment, 210, 211–212; and job evaluation, 58, 70–71; and labor-management committees, 215; and layoffs, 223–225; legal issues, 232; and lobbying, 233–234, 241; and mechanistic organization, 230; negotiations with,

239–243; and pay, 228, 236, 240; and politics, 12, 230–234, 235–236, 240; and position classification, 240, 249, 250; and professionals, 241; and promotion, 98, 99, 101, 249; and quality circles, 214; and residency requirements, 89; and retrenchment, 204, 249–250; and selection, 240, 249; and seniority, 204, 223–225; and state governments, 4, 101, 229, 230, 231, 233–236, 237, 238–239, 240–241; and training and development programs, 182; and women, 168–169
Union shop, 235
United Public Workers of America v. Mitchell, 296
U.S. Bureau of Labor Statistics, 279
U.S. Census Bureau, 264, 279
United States Civil Service Commission v. National Association of Letter Carriers, 296
U.S. Congress: and civil service reform, 4, 30; and merit system, 29–30, 33; and pensions, 173–174; and position classification, 66–67
U.S. Constitution, 28; First Amendment, 293–294, 295–296, 297, 298; Fifth Amendment, 291; Fourteenth Amendment, 277, 278, 291, 293, 297
U.S. Department of Education, 41
U.S. Department of Justice, 87
U.S. Department of Labor, 86, 87
U.S. Department of State, 70
U.S. Postal Service, 71, 228, 234, 264
U.S. Supreme Court, 42, 223–225; and affirmative action, 277–278; and equal employment opportunity, 266–267, 268–269, 270; and job evaluation, 56; and pay discrimination, 169–170; and personal liability of public employees, 300; and rights of public employees, 291–299; and selection, 86–88, 96; and seniority, 205, 223–225; and suspension, 306; and unions, 235; *see also* Courts
United Steelworkers, 277–278
United Steelworkers v. Weber, 224–225
University of California v. Bakke, 277
University of Michigan, 122

Universities, 10, 16, 136
Urban Institute, 208–209

Vacancies, announcement of, 99–100
Vacation days, 161, 170, 171, 172
Valence, 113
Validity of selection instruments, 84–86, 94–95
Van Buren, Martin, 32
Van Riper, Paul P., 28, 259
Veterans: dismissal, 44; preference in selection, 3, 5, 44, 95–96, 276; and recruitment, 81
Veterans Preference Act, 44
Villere, Maurice F., 134, 143, 144, 147
Voluntary arbitration, 244–245
Voluntary topics of negotiation, 240–241
Vroom, Victor, 113

Wages. *See* Pay
Warren, Malcolm W., 182
Washington, George, 29–30
Washington state, pay discrimination, 169, 269
Waterman, Robert H., Jr., 314
Watson, Charles, 196–197
Weber v. Kaiser Aluminum and Steel Corporation and United Steelworkers of America, 277–278
Weight and height requirements, 268
Wesley, Roy, 243–244
Wheeler, Hoyt, 238
Whig party, 32
Whipsawing, 237
Whistle-blowing, 46, 47, 48, 294
White, Justice, 292, 297
Whyte, W.F., 117
Wilson, Woodrow, 264
Wisconsin, 238
Women, 8, 42, 257–288; and assessment centers, 94; and fringe benefits, 269–270; and interviews, 93; and job evaluation, 168–169, 170; and labor force, 315; and local government, 273; numbers in public service, 271–275; and pay, 8, 42, 269, 272, *see also* Comparable worth; and performance appraisal, 137, 138; and promotion, 101; and retrenchment, 205–206, 249–250, 270; and selection, 86, 96,

268; and seniority, 205–206; and training and development, 182; and veterans preference, 96, 265
Wood v. Strickland, 300–301
Word processors, 182, 217
Work groups, 192–193
Working conditions, 241

Workloads, 246, 249
Written warnings to employees, 304

Yankelovich, D., 206

Zero-base budgeting, 10
Zedeck, Sheldon, 143

About the Author

Perry Moore is dean of the College of Liberal Arts and professor of political science at Wright State University, Dayton, Ohio. He has published numerous articles on public personnel management and public budgeting.